This retreat, which is so well fitted into the busy life of the layperson, nonetheless includes all the essential parts of a genuine retreat of the *Spiritual Exercises*. Although focused on the Divine Mercy, it also includes the insights of St. Ignatius Loyola and St. Louis de Montfort. It is also influenced by the Venerable Father Lanteri, who brings his own intensity and devotion into the retreat. All of this should make a devout person at home and yet push the person on to higher levels of devotion and spirituality.

— FR. BENEDICT J. GROESCHEL, CFR
Author, lecturer, retreat master, and TV host

Consoling the Heart of Jesus is a beautiful work, and yet another path to the Heart of Jesus, one especially suited to men and women of our day who are living busy, demanding lives. It is a solution for the person who can find neither the time nor the money to travel to a retreat house for a weekend or longer. It is also an appealing method of retreat that can be adopted by a prayer group, parish group, or sodality. With the help of this book, may many more souls find and rest in the Heart of Jesus.

— MOTHER AGNES MARY DONOVAN, SV
Superior General of the Sisters of Life

For those wishing to know something about the Ignatian *Spiritual Exercises* and for those who think they already understand them, this book will prove invaluable. Confidently written in an informal, easy-to-read style, broadly theorized with the aid of Saints Faustina, Louis de Montfort, and Thérèse of Lisieux, and thoroughly researched as the References and Notes indicate, it gives a refreshing approach to making a retreat on one's own.

— FR. CORNELIUS MICHAEL BUCKLEY, SJ
Ignatian Retreat Master

Remarkable. Beautiful. Simple. May the Lord fill the hearts of all who make this inspired retreat.

— BR. JAMES CURRAN, LBSF
Founder of the Little Brothers of Saint Francis

Michael Gaitley, MIC, drawing on the rich Catholic tradition, has given us in this book, a weekend "immersion course" to help us respond to our call to holiness. For those who don't have the time or money to get away for a traditional retreat, this book is a godsend.

— RALPH MARTIN
President of Renewal Ministries and host
of the long running Catholic TV program,
"The Choices We Face."

Through *Consoling the Heart of Jesus*, I came to realize that the Man who walked in Nazareth and died on Calvary, the same Man who appeared to Saints Faustina and Margaret Mary, walks with me each day throughout life's pilgrimage. Jesus is my constant companion, and he desires to be yours as well. I strongly encourage anyone who yearns to encounter Love Incarnate on a daily basis to read this retreat.

— ANNE-MARIE FUNK
Graduate Student, Theology

Michael Gaitley, MIC, is to be highly commended for his beautiful book, *Consoling the Heart of Jesus*. In our busy, hectic, modern world, his approach, based on the time-tested principles of the great St. Ignatius of Loyola, as understood by Fr. Lanteri, will draw the faithful retreatant ever more deeply into the mystery of the Heart of Christ. By seeking to console the Heart of Jesus, "bruised for our iniquities," we in return receive an abundance of graces to overcome our own weaknesses and grow in holiness by laying a sure foundation on the Rock, our Lord and Savior Jesus Christ.

— DR. TIMOTHY O'DONNELL, STD
Author of *Heart of the Redeemer*

Consoling the Heart of Jesus

A Do-It-Yourself Retreat
Inspired by the Spiritual Exercises of St. Ignatius

Michael E. Gaitley, MIC

MARIAN PRESS
STOCKBRIDGE MA 01263
PRO CHRISTO ET ECCLESIA

2010

Available from:
Marian Helpers Center
Stockbridge, MA 01263

Prayerline: 1-800-804-3823
Orderline: 1-800-462-7426
Website: www.marian.org

Imprimi Potest:
Very Rev. Daniel Cambra, MIC
Provincial Superior
The Blessed Virgin Mary, Mother of Mercy Province
January 27, 2010

Library of Congress Catalog Number: 2010920254
ISBN: 978-1-59614-222-0

First edition (3rd printing): 2010

Cover Art: All reasonable efforts have been made to find the copyright holder.

Cover Design: Br. Angelo Casimiro, MIC, and Kathy Szpak
Page Design: Kathy Szpak

Editing and Proofreading: David Came, Dan Valenti,
Mary Flannery, and Andrew Leeco

For texts from the English Edition of *Diary of St. Maria Faustina Kowalska*

Nihil Obstat:
George H. Pearce, SM
Former Archbishop of Suva, Fiji

Imprimatur:
Joseph F. Maguire
Bishop of Springfield, MA
April 9, 1984

Printed in the United States of America

In loving memory,

Janeise Cowan
Grace and Maryn Gaitley
Fr. Mark Garrow, MIC

O God, one in the Holy Trinity, I want to love You as no human soul has ever loved You before; and although I am utterly miserable and small, I have, nevertheless, cast the anchor of my trust deep down into the abyss of Your mercy. ... In spite of my great misery I fear nothing, but hope to sing You a hymn of glory forever. Let no soul, even the most miserable, fall prey to doubt; for, as long as one is alive, each one can become a great saint, so great is the power of God's grace. It remains only for us not to oppose God's action.

— *Saint Faustina*

Contents

In Gratitude

Consoling the Heart of Jesus is my response to a request from parishioners at my home parish, St. Peter Chanel Catholic Church, in Hawaiian Gardens, California. In August of 2001, at the invitation of the Pastor, Fr. Lawrence Darnell, I gave the parish a one-day preached retreat. Afterward, several people asked me to write down for them the talks I'd given. So, in my spare time during the first semester of my seminary theological studies (which began shortly after the retreat), I wrote a rough draft of *Consoling*.

At the end of the semester, I wasn't pleased with what I'd written and thought about giving up the project. Around that same time, one of the associate priests of St. Peter Chanel Parish, Fr. Gregory Staab, came to visit the seminary where I was living. One day during his visit, he asked to read my rough draft. After reading it, he encouraged me to finish it and then send him a copy, which I eventually did.

With my permission, Fr. Greg made photocopies of my completed manuscript and distributed them to many of the parishioners at St. Peter Chanel. After a while, photocopies of the photocopies were made, and the retreat spread. Several of the people who read it were persistent in asking me to have it published. It's largely because of their pressure that finally, years later, *Consoling the Heart of Jesus* is now in print. It's also because of such people that I decided not to change the original manuscript's conversational tone. I say that because whenever I would promise to revise the manuscript and look into having it published, I invariably heard something like, "Good, but when you revise it, don't dare change the tone!" The force and frequency of such comments convinced me that I'd better obey, so I scrapped my plans for making major stylistic changes. For the most part, the retreat remains as it was, with some additional material.

Having given a brief history of how *Consoling the Heart of Jesus* came to be, it should be clear why I gratefully acknowledge Fr. Lawrence Darnell, OMV; Fr. Gregory Staab, OMV; and parishioners from St. Peter Chanel Parish. My gratitude also goes out to the many people whose prayers and encouragement helped me to see this project to its conclusion, especially to Mary and St. Joseph, Janeise Cowan, David Deaton, Jonathan Ghaly, Heather McGrath, Linda Gaitley, William and Blanche Grego, Alex Fotinakes, Nicholas Sully, Tony Sully, Maggie Devine, John and Juanita Montana, Dr. Daniel and Maria Valentini, Dr. Robert Stackpole, STD, Rebecca Urban, Luke Condit, Carol McGinness, Sr. Teresa Condit, OSIH, Br. Gerald Joaquin, OMV, Fr. Seraphim Michalenko, MIC, Fr. Mark Garrow, MIC, Fr. Kazimierz Chwalek, MIC, Fr. Daniel Cambra, MIC, Fr. Andrew Davy, MIC, Deacon James McCormack, MIC, Br. Angelo Casimiro, MIC, Br. Richard Dolan, MIC, Br. Roman Pupiec, MIC, Br. Stanislaw Bednarz, MIC, Fr. Denis Gang, TOR, Fr. Brian Smith, Sr. Maria of Abba Miravalle, OSIH, Br. Christopher Coyne, SOLT, Sr. Mary John Paul Asemota, O.Praem., Sr. Marie Guadalupe Robles, OLM, Br. Anthony Joseph Dsuza, LBSF, David Darois, Alicja Skupny, Vinny Flynn, Maggie Pelkey, Matthew and Katie Hartfiel, Suzann Clark, Jason Lewis, Irene Dutra, Sr. Brigid Prosser, SSCJ, Sr. Maeve Nativitas O'Doherty, SV, Erin Dunne, Anne-Marie Funk, Joan Solomon, Nathan Doerr, Dr. Kenneth Dargis, Martha McNeill, Elizabeth Simon, Gerri Edmonds, Gerry Schuetz, Anastasia DuPuis, Pawel and Marzena Porebscy, Cezary Ruta, Anna Tarnowska-Waszak, Felix Carroll, Sarah Chichester, and last but certainly not least, Sr. Bernadette Marie Allain-Dupré, FM. Special thanks to David Came, Dan Valenti, Mary Flannery, Dr. Kenneth Dargis, and Deacon James McCormack, MIC, for their extensive comments on the manuscript and to Br. Angelo Casimiro, MIC, and Kathy Szpak for their patient and persevering help designing the cover. For the opportunity to work on and publish this retreat, I'm grateful to my religious family, the Congregation of Marian Fathers of the Immaculate Conception. Finally, my deepest gratitude goes to God, for his infinite mercy.

Michael E. Gaitley, MIC, STL
National Shrine of The Divine Mercy
Stockbridge, Massachusetts
February 2, 2010
Feast of the Presentation

Acknowledgments

Permission is gratefully acknowledged to cite from the following works:

Excerpts from *Eschatology: Death and Eternal Life* by Josef Ratzinger. Translated by Michael Waldstein. Edited by Aidan Nichols, OP. Copyright © 1988. Used with permission: The Catholic University of America Press, Washington, DC. www.cuapress.cua.edu.

Excerpts from *Story of a Soul* by St. Thérèse of Lisieux. Translated by John Clarke, OCD. Copyright © 1975, 1976, 1996 by Washington Province of Discalced Carmelites, ICS Publications, 213 Lincoln Road, NE, Washington, DC 20002-1199 U.S.A. www.icspublications.org.

Excerpts from *The Spiritual Exercises of St. Ignatius of Loyola*. Translated by Louis J. Puhl, S.J. (Newman Press 1951). Reprinted with permission of Loyola Press. To order copies of this book call 1-800-621-1008 or go to www.loyolapress.com.

Excerpts from *True Devotion to Mary* by St. Louis de Montfort. Translated by Frederick W. Faber. Copyright © 1941 by TAN Books, Charlotte, North Carolina. www.tanbooks.com.

Special thanks to Michael Collopy for permission to reproduce the image of Christ crucified on the inside front cover.

On References, Notes, Pronouns, and Boldface Type

Because a do-it-yourself retreat shouldn't have the feel of a scholarly work, I decided not to use footnotes. I moved material normally found in footnotes to the end of the book under the section titled "References and Notes" and organized it according to page number. Those who are interested can easily find source material (references) and additional information on certain topics treated in the text (notes) by consulting that section. The only exception to my "no footnotes" rule is Appendix One, which isn't exactly part of the retreat.

Some readers, especially those used to the style of other Marian Press publications, may be surprised that I don't capitalize personal pronouns that refer to Jesus. This is not meant in any way as a lack of respect or reverence for our Lord. I decided not to capitalize such pronouns for two main reasons. First, because I refer to Jesus so often in the text, the sheer number of capitalized pronouns might have become distracting to some readers. Second and most importantly, while the theology of the retreat clearly rests on the divinity of Christ, its theme centers on the idea that his human nature longs for human consolation. This is the theme of the upper room, where Jesus said to his disciples, "I no longer call you servants ... but friends" (Jn 15:15), and where one of his best friends, the Beloved Disciple, rested his head on the Lord's breast (see Jn 13:23). The style that uses lowercase pronouns, a style also adopted by contemporary Church documents and translations of the Bible, seems to me more appropriate to the intimacy of this theme.

Finally, the reader will probably notice that sometimes Jesus' words appear in boldface type while at other times they do not. This is intentional. The boldface words come exclusively as citations from the *Diary of St. Faustina*, which is one of the major sources for the retreat. Because Jesus' words in publications of the *Diary* always appear in boldface type, I follow that convention. By the way, if the idea seems strange to you that Jesus' words might be found in something other than the Bible, now would be a good time to try out the References and Notes section. (See the first entry.)

INTRODUCTION
A Retreat That's Easy to Make

Few things help one to grow in holiness more quickly than the *Spiritual Exercises of St. Ignatius.* Unfortunately, Ignatius's famous retreat isn't so easy to make. I say that because the full experience of what he intended requires 30 days of silence and prayer — but who's got 30 days? While there's a shortened, eight-day version of his retreat, many people don't even have that much time to spare. Still, those who do have the time don't always have the money. (Ignatian retreats can be expensive.) Moreover, even when time and money are no problem, finding a retreat director often is.

I wrote *Consoling the Heart of Jesus* to help those who are serious about growing in holiness but who have neither the time nor the resources for making the *Spiritual Exercises.* Unlike the *Exercises,* my retreat is easy to make: It doesn't require a director, doesn't cost much, and best of all, it only takes one weekend. Of course, such a short retreat can't possibly give the full experience of the 30-day version — but it's a great alternative. Why? Because it communicates the most essential principles of the *Spiritual Exercises,* the very principles that have made Ignatius's retreat such a powerful instrument of conversion for nearly 500 years.

I said my do-it-yourself retreat takes one weekend. That's true. However, it would certainly need to be a *full* weekend dedicated to the prayerful reading of the text. The time it takes to make the retreat equals the time it takes to read it, and most people can do so in a weekend. Still, this doesn't prevent those who like to read more slowly from making it, nor does it exclude those who can't get away for a whole weekend. For my retreat can also be prayerfully read over the course of several weeks or even months. In fact, I know many people who have profitably gone through it by reading it during a weekly Holy Hour over a few months. Then again, I know even more people for whom a weekly Holy Hour seems like an impossible luxury yet they, too, have managed to make the retreat, even while keeping a hectic schedule. Obviously, that's not the weekend ideal, but even under such stressed circumstances, the retreat still seems to yield spiritual fruit.

So, *Consoling the Heart of Jesus* is a retreat almost anyone can make no matter how busy he is. In fact, that was one of my main goals in writing it. I specifically wanted to make the most effective principles of the most powerful retreat, the *Spiritual Exercises of St. Ignatius*, easily available to the busy people of today.

A Retreat with a Bold Claim

Yet, if people are so busy, why would they want to spend their precious time reading *this* retreat, especially when there are so many other books they could profitably use for spiritual reading? For instance, why not simply spend time with Scripture or the life of some saint? Of course, Scripture and spiritual books can be of great profit to our souls. However, my do-it-yourself retreat is just that: *a retreat* — but not just any retreat. As I mentioned, it's inspired by the *Spiritual Exercises*, and like the *Exercises*, it contains a built-in order that can help us grow in holiness in a short period of time. Ordered meditation and prayer, a hallmark of Ignatian spirituality, greatly assists the process of conversion. Scripture alone and most spiritual books don't provide such ordered material for meditation.

Although *Consoling the Heart of Jesus* doesn't offer the full array of meditations found in the *Exercises*, it does claim to help bring about the same abundant spiritual fruit. In other words, like Ignatius's famous retreat, it claims to give us everything we need to become great saints and in a short period of time. Does this sound impossible? Too good to be true? To help us understand how a brief, undirected retreat can make such a bold claim, we need to get to know Fr. Lanteri.

Venerable Fr. Pio Bruno Lanteri (1759-1826) was a man on fire with the desire to become a saint. At first, he tried to attain his goal by joining the most rigorous religious congregation in the Church, the Carthusians. After just eight days, however, the silence, prayer vigils, and fasting became too much for him, and he had to leave. Though deeply disappointed, Lanteri didn't give up his goal. Because of his weakness, however, he figured he'd have to find a particularly powerful way to the heights of holiness. Sometime later, he went on an Ignatian retreat for the first time. To his great joy, he found exactly what he'd been looking for: an extraordinarily powerful way by which even someone like him could become a saint.

Lanteri was so overjoyed at discovering the *Spiritual Exercises* retreat that he dedicated his life to sharing it with others. With ardent zeal and enthusiasm, he invited people to make his version of it, telling them it provides everything a person needs to become "a saint, a great saint, and quickly." He also made the bold claim that one could get all he needed to become such a saint not in 30 days (the "long" retreat) but in just eight. He had such confidence in the power of his Ignatian retreats because he gave them with a particular emphasis, what one might call his "secret weapons." What were Lanteri's secret weapons? The very same things that later saints would emphasize in their "quick" and extraordinarily effective ways to holiness, namely, Divine Mercy and Mary.

This retreat is written in the spirit of Fr. Lanteri today. Since his death more than 180 years ago, there's been more insight into the inestimable treasures of Divine Mercy and Marian devotion. I'm thinking in particular of the writings of holy men and women such as Sts. Thérèse of Lisieux (1873-1897), Faustina Kowalska (1905-1938), Maximilian Kolbe (1894-1941), Blessed Mother Teresa of Calcutta (1910-1997), and the Venerable Servant of God Pope John Paul II (1920-2005). I'm convinced that with the insights of such experts behind us, we now have even greater spiritual ammunition for Lanteri's secret weapons, thus making his manner of giving the *Exercises* even more effective. Divine Mercy and Marian devotion today are truly powerful means for all to grow in holiness.

Having looked at Fr. Lanteri's threefold strategy for attaining great sanctity — Divine Mercy and Marian devotion within the context of the *Spiritual Exercises* — and having further seen that now there's even deeper insight into his secret weapons, at this point, I can repeat my earlier claim without it sounding impossible or too good to be true. In this do-it-yourself retreat, you can find everything you need to become "a saint, a great saint, and quickly" not just in Ignatius's 30 days, nor even in Lanteri's eight, but in one *Consoling* weekend.

A Retreat for Little Souls

I mentioned earlier that in his zeal to become a saint, Fr. Lanteri tried to join the Carthusians but then had to leave because he was too weak. Now I'd like to focus on the idea of "weakness" and how it relates to the bold claim I just made, namely, that this weekend retreat can give us everything we need to become great saints. To bring all this into focus, it'll be helpful to reflect on two considerations. The first has to do with St. Louis de Montfort (1673-1716).

Like Lanteri, de Montfort had a burning desire to become a saint. Also like Lanteri, he saw himself as a weak soul who needed to find an extraordinarily powerful way to sanctity. He believed he found such a way in a new form of Marian spirituality he famously describes in his classic work, *True Devotion to Mary*. De Montfort predicted a couple of interesting things about his book. First, he said that after his death, angry demons would come to hide the unpublished manuscript so no one could ever read it — and, in fact, the manuscript was lost for over a century after his death. He went on to say that it would eventually be discovered and published and that its Marian spirituality would help form some of the greatest saints in the history of the Church.

The last part of de Montfort's prediction — that his book would form some of the greatest saints — contains the heart of what I'd like us to consider. Obviously, it's a rather bold prediction, especially when we think about the great saints who lived before *True Devotion* was published. Still, if we take his prediction seriously, we might begin to think: "Well, Mother Teresa and Pope John Paul II were pretty holy. Perhaps they're the saints de Montfort was talking about."

This makes sense, especially if we consider not only that both of them intensely lived the Marian spirituality of de Montfort's book but also that they were deeply formed by Lanteri's other secret weapon, Divine Mercy.

Yet there's a problem. De Montfort's prediction wasn't just about a few people. In fact, he had in mind a whole army of the greatest saints. Perhaps this gets us thinking, "Wonderful. So where are they?" I suggest that we are supposed to be those saints, that we are the ones meant to fill the ranks of that army, and that we truly can be those saints. When I put it like this, it probably sounds ridiculous, especially when our weakness and littleness come to mind.

Well, if it does sound ridiculous — good. It means we're ready for the second consideration. Before we get to it, I should first say something about what I mean by our "weakness" and "littleness."

What's our weakness and littleness? Let me put it this way: Does the idea that you can become a great saint seem more like a joke than a real possibility? If it seems like a joke, is that because you think of yourself as being too (take your pick) selfish, sinful, prideful, lazy, busy, greedy, rich, poor, mean, jaded, cold, indifferent, fun loving, lustful, gossipy, angry, uninterested, bored, confused, distracted, envious, smart, stupid, sophisticated, stylish, unfaithful, uncaring, wounded, brokenhearted, rebellious, rational, addicted, worldly, wimpy, normal, scared, aggressive, superficial, modern, old fashioned, good looking, ugly, plain, twisted, loud, quiet, famous, unknown, violent, vindictive, passive, depressed, crazy, imbalanced, inconsistent, insincere, young, or old to be a saint? If so, if you think you're too *something* to be a saint (let alone one of the great saints de Montfort mentioned), then, like me, you're probably a "little soul." If this sounds depressing, don't worry. It's not. In fact, it's good news. We'll see why as St. Thérèse of Lisieux gives us the second consideration.

According to St. Thérèse, it's precisely the little souls who will become the kind of great saints de Montfort foresaw. For Thérèse taught that Jesus wants to work some of his most mar-

velous miracles of mercy in our day, miracles in which he takes
the littlest of souls and forms them into the greatest of saints.
Thérèse could teach that because she understood three things
exceedingly well: our modern times, God's amazing mercy, and
the teaching of St. Paul.

According to St. Paul, where evil and sin seem to prevail,
God sends his grace in ever greater abundance (see Rom 5:20).
This Pauline principle applies especially to our day that, in many
ways, is marked by unprecedented evil. Because of such unprecedented evil, God graciously offers unprecedented mercy. Thus,
our time truly can be called a "time of mercy," a time when God
especially wants to demonstrate that his "power finds perfection
in weakness" (2 Cor 12:9), a time when it's easier than ever
before to become a saint. We'll hear more on this topic from St.
Thérèse later. Until then, I'd like to offer for our further consideration one nun's prayer:

> I will not profit from exercises designed for strong
> souls. O my God, show me the exercises designed for
> feeble souls. Would the saints have forgotten or
> disdained them? Yet even if the saints did not think of
> these poor souls, who are nevertheless most numer-
> ous, you, Lord, my mercy, have not abandoned them.
> You yourself, Good Master, have burdened yourself
> with them. I know that better than anyone. I am one
> of those souls and I bless you for having revealed to
> the weak and the little ones what you do not always
> accord to the valiant and the strong.

Bless the Lord, for we're about to begin spiritual exercises
designed for "feeble," "poor," and "little" souls. Relying on the
little giants of the spiritual life (Fr. Lanteri, St. Louis, St. Thérèse,
and company), I'm proposing a short way for such souls to
become great saints. If you think you might be one of these
little ones, if you want to become a saint, and if you have neither
the time nor the resources to make the *Spiritual Exercises*, then
enjoy a retreat made just for you.

A Retreat with a Schedule?

Before we begin the retreat, I have some advice for those who plan on making it over the course of a weekend. If this describes you, then please continue reading. If, however, you plan on making the retreat over a longer period of time, then feel free to skip this section and begin Part One ... but before you go, I have one practical suggestion. (Don't worry weekenders, this will be short.)

Some people find talking things out to be a helpful way of absorbing spiritual insights. If you're one of those people, you might want to consider making this retreat with others — a group retreat. This can be done when everyone in the group reads the same sections of the retreat and then gets together regularly to discuss what they've read. (If the group becomes larger than, say, 12 people, then you might want to think about dividing up into smaller groups.) People who've made this retreat in a group tell me they found it to be very fruitful. (Okay, all those who aren't making this retreat in a weekend can go now.)

So, you want to make this retreat in a weekend. Well, then you're probably interested in hearing some suggestions as to how you might schedule your time. That's what I'll be offering in this section. As you read my suggestions, please keep in mind they're simply that, suggestions. They're not set in stone. Still, if you've only got a weekend, following them will help you to finish the retreat in that amount of time. Speaking of time, I don't recommend dipping deeply into the "References and Notes" section if you want to finish in a weekend.

Before presenting my suggestions for scheduling a *Consoling* weekend, I should make one general recommendation: Try to keep distractions to a minimum. People who make a *Consoling* weekend are often surprised at how many distractions suddenly come out of nowhere. Don't be discouraged by this. Distractions will happen. Having said that, there's a lot you can do to prevent a good number of them. For instance, you might want to schedule your weekend at a retreat house. Or, if you make the retreat at home, you might want to prepare a relatively quiet place where you won't be distracted by the phone and where those you live with will know not to disturb you.

*F*RIDAY EVENING. I suggest you begin the retreat on Friday evening and *read Part One*. Give yourself about two hours. You can probably read it more quickly than that, but two hours will allow you to take short breaks and ponder the text. For example, if you begin reading before supper, then you can think about what you've read while you eat. (This advice goes for all the meals during the retreat.) If, however, you start well after suppertime and begin to become tired, don't worry about trying to push on through with the reading. Take a long break by going to bed. You can make up the time on Saturday or Sunday.

Before going to bed, whether you've finished Part One or not, try to keep your mind on what you've read as you fall asleep. Maybe there was one idea that particularly touched your heart. Well then, let that idea be like background music as you enter into dreamland. If you begin to hear other music as you get ready for bed — problems at work, troubles at home — gently turn the volume down by prayerfully handing everything over to the Lord. Then, turn your attention back to the sounds of what you've read.

*S*ATURDAY. On Saturday, when you wake up, begin to listen again to the music of the retreat. Listen to it as you get ready for the day (for instance, as you shower). You might even want to sing along to the music by speaking to the Lord about what you read the night before.

If you can read at least a little of the retreat before having breakfast and coffee, then do so — that way breakfast and coffee time become break-from-the-reading time. (Strategic breaks are key.) However, if you're especially hungry or if you can't function without coffee, then by all means, eat and drink before you begin reading. Speaking of eating and drinking, I don't recommend fasting during the retreat. Setting aside a weekend for the Lord and putting out the effort to do so much spiritual reading is a sufficient offering. Plus, you'll need your energy. If there's Mass on Saturday morning and you'd like to go, no problem. Simply schedule your reading around it. *The goal for Saturday morning is to finish the first three obstacles of Part Two.* If you can't get through all three, don't worry. You can make up for it after lunch.

If you're tired in the afternoon, feel free to take a nap. Doing so much spiritual reading will probably make you tired. Just don't sleep the whole afternoon away, because then you probably won't finish the retreat during the weekend. *The goal for Saturday afternoon is to read through obstacles four and five.* As a longer break during the afternoon, you might think about getting some exercise. Speaking of breaks, I recommend taking five-to-ten minute breaks as you need them. I find it helpful to take one after every half hour to an hour of reading. During such breaks, you might simply rest your eyes, take a little walk, eat a snack, or go to the chapel.

The goal for Saturday evening is to read the conclusion. Because the conclusion is more practical than other sections of the retreat, you might want to take some brief notes. In fact, you should feel free to take notes any time during the retreat, if it helps. Just try not to spend so much time on them that you don't finish your reading goals. Having said all that, I should mention that I've included review questions at the end of Part One, a thorough review after Part Two (the Conclusion), and a Consoler "Cheat Sheet" at the very end of the book. You might find that these three aids to review make taking notes unnecessary.

My suggestions for Saturday night are the same as for Friday night: Let your earlier reading be like background music as you're going to sleep. I also recommend that you spend around 10 minutes reflecting on the main graces from the day, shortly before going to bed. For example, you might ask yourself: "Which section of the retreat moved me the most? Which sections challenged me?" Listen to the answers to such questions as your bedtime music.

*S*UNDAY. Rejoice, for it's the Lord's Day. It's also a kind of buffer-day. In other words, it's a day when you can finish reading what you didn't have time for on Saturday. More important, *it's a day for deepening what you've read.* As time allows before or after Mass (or both), I recommend that you review your notes and consult the aids to review I mentioned earlier, repeat some of the more fruitful meditations, and maybe even dip into Appendix Two. This appendix, as I'll explain in more detail later, is meant to help retreatants deepen their experience of specific themes of the retreat after it's over. (It's not actually part of the retreat.) This doesn't mean you can't start reading on Sunday those themes in this appendix that particularly resonated with you during your earlier reading. You can. Thus, you might look at Appendix Two as a kind of bonus reading for Sunday, if you have the time and desire for it.

As for Appendix One, I suggest saving that reading for another time. The material it contains seems most helpful to people after they've had at least a week or so of trying to live out the spirituality of the retreat. Because people seem to find Appendix One especially helpful, I highly recommend getting to it eventually.

At the end of the retreat, if you begin to worry that you haven't absorbed everything you've read, don't. You can always refer back to the retreat in your free time (especially to the aids to review and Appendix Two), and you can schedule another *Consoling* weekend. Since I finished writing the first draft of this retreat (eight years ago), I've re-read it, on average, about once a year. With each new reading, the old themes seem to enter my heart more deeply, and I'm brought back to my spiritual foundation.

PART ONE

Laying
the Foundation

Beginning with Desire

THE DESIRE FOR HOLINESS. To make a good Ignatian retreat, it's important to begin with an ardent desire for sanctity. So, I'd like to start right off by asking, *Do you want to be a saint?* In other words, *Do you desire to be on fire with love for God and neighbor?* If you can answer such questions with a full and enthusiastic "Yes!" that's great. I suspect, though, that many of us just might find that our true response to such questions may not be so full and enthusiastic. In fact, our true response might be closer to something like, "Well, I used to want to be a saint, but now I'm not so sure." This section is written especially for those whose yes to wanting to become a saint might not be completely full.

There was probably a time in each of our lives when we heard or read about the life of a saint, our hearts burned within us, and we said to ourselves, "I want to love God like that!" After a while, however, especially as we became more conscious of our selfishness and sin, the flames of desire died down and maybe even went out. I'm sure more than a few of us have experienced times when even the suggestion that we might become saints evoked shock: "Me? A saint?! Come on, get real. I know who I am. I just hope I can sneak into purgatory."

Burning desire grows cold when what we desire seems to become unattainable. For instance, when I was a kid, I used to dream of playing basketball like Michael Jordan. As I got older, I noticed that other guys were taller and had more skill on the court. Therefore, my desire to "be like Mike" quickly died. I think something similar happens with the dream of becoming a saint. At first, hearing or reading about the lives of saints captivates us and generates the desire to want to be like them. Then, we begin to realize others are more virtuous and better than we are. That's when discouragement begins to kick in, and the flame of desire for holiness peters out. That's when we start to settle for mediocrity and the bare minimum, "I just hope I can sneak into purgatory."

*S*T. *THÉRÈSE REMOVES OBSTACLES TO DESIRE.* Saint Thérèse of Lisieux is one of the most popular saints in the Catholic Church today because of her amazing ability to stir into flame the smoldering embers of our desires for sanctity. She brings back hope, dispels cynicism and mediocrity, convinces us ordinary people that we really can become saints, and does all this not with empty rhetoric but with the weighty voice of a Doctor of the Church. Unfortunately, because we're only on a weekend retreat, we don't have time now to read St. Thérèse's classic work, *Story of a Soul.* Still, we can quickly get to the heart of her wisdom by reading two paragraphs from her book that give a summary of her famous teaching, "the Little Way." Let's read these paragraphs slowly and prayerfully, so Thérèse's spirit might fan into flame our desires for holiness.

In the first paragraph, Thérèse sets up for us her explanation of the Little Way by describing what inspired it:

> Alas! I have always noticed that when I compared myself to the saints, there is between them and me the same difference that exists between a mountain whose summit is lost in the clouds and the obscure grain of sand trampled underfoot by passers-by. Instead of becoming discouraged, I said to myself: God cannot inspire unrealizable desires. I can, then, in spite of my littleness, aspire to holiness. It is impossible for me to grow up, and so I must bear with myself such as I am with all my imperfections. But I want to seek out a means of going to heaven by a little way, a way that is very straight, very short, and totally new.

Notice a few things here. First, Thérèse is like most of us in that she, too, feels little compared to the saints. How easy it is to relate to her comparison of the grain of sand and the mountain when we compare ourselves to the saints. Yet, amazingly, she doesn't get discouraged by this disparity. Most of us, when we see the huge difference between ourselves and the saints, easily begin to lose hope. Where we get discouraged, however, Thérèse finds courage. With her characteristic boldness, she searches out a "totally new" way to holiness, trusting that God "cannot inspire unrealizable desires." The second paragraph of her text describes this remarkable, new way:

> We are living now in an age of inventions [19th century], and we no longer have to take the trouble of climbing stairs, for, in the homes of the rich, an elevator has replaced these very successfully. I wanted to find an elevator which would raise me to Jesus, for I am too small to climb the rough stairway of perfection. I searched, then, in the Scriptures for some sign of this elevator, the object of my desires, and I read these words coming from the mouth of Eternal Wisdom: "*Whoever is a LITTLE ONE, let him come to me.*" And so I succeeded. I felt I had found what I was looking for. But wanting to know, O my God, what You would do to *the very little one* who answered your call, I continued my search and this is what I discovered: "*As one whom a mother caresses, so will I comfort you; you shall be carried at the breasts, and upon the knees they shall caress you.*" Ah! never did words more tender and more melodious come to give joy to my soul. The elevator which must raise me to heaven is Your arms, O Jesus! And for this I had no need to grow up, but rather I had to remain *little* and become this more and more (emphasis in original).

This citation summarizes well St. Thérèse's Little Way, the spiritual elevator in which we'll travel during this retreat. I introduce it here to help us remove the obstacle that often prevents our desires for holiness from growing, namely, the recognition of our weakness. I hope that after having reflected on Thérèse's words, this obstacle is being removed, that we'll trust Jesus to take us into his arms and carry us to holiness, and that the flame of desire for sanctity will now begin to grow within us. With that hope, let's do a meditation.

*D*ESIRE *MEDITATION.* Behold Jesus in front of you, hanging on the Cross. See his gentle, sorrowful face. His Heart aches because so many for whom he's dying have rejected his goodness and love. Will you reject him, too? Before you answer, listen to his words from the Cross, "I thirst." He's speaking to you. He thirsts for you. Do you thirst for him? He thirsts that you might thirst for him. Tell him that you thirst for him. Ask him to help you thirst for him more. Beg him for this grace.

Jesus thirsts for your love, and he wants your help. Will you help him? Before you answer, look at how much he has given you. He created you in love, washed away yours sins in his blood, clothed you with his divine life, and prepares a place in his Father's house for you to dwell with him in joy for all eternity — and there's more. Jesus wants to share with you his mission. He wants your help in bringing everyone back home to his Father. That, too, is his gift to you. Will you accept it? Will you help him? He's counting on your help. He needs you.

Many let Jesus down. They not only refuse his love, but they refuse the gift of the mission he wants to give them. Will you also let him down? Don't worry if you've said no to him in the past. He makes all things new, and his mercy can bring good out of evil. Again, he wants to share with you his mission. Maybe your sharing in it looks different than before; maybe it's exactly the same. No matter. He offers it, and he leads you to it, step by step, with his gentle hand. All you need to do is say yes. See how much he loves you, and say yes. Say yes to his love. Believe in his love, and say yes to his will for your life, even if you don't know the details. Remember the gentleness of his face and the sorrow.

If you're having difficulty saying yes to Jesus, turn to Mary. She knows how to say yes to God, and she'll help you. Ask her: "Mary, my mother, please lend me your yes. Please be with me during this retreat. Help me not to let Jesus down. Help me to have courage and to believe in his love for me." Ask the angels and your favorite saints to pray for you. Beg the Father and the Holy Spirit to give you a thirst for Jesus, to give you a burning love for the one who burns with love for you.

Now listen to some great news. After having been rejected by so many in our day, Jesus makes it easier than ever before to become a saint. He offers unprecedented graces. In fact, he himself will take charge and make you holy. All you have to do is let him. It won't be too difficult. Trust him. He speaks to you words such as these: "I see your weakness, but be not afraid. Just trust me. I will do it. Let me do it. If only you will trust me and let me do it, I will make you into a saint." Such words remind us of what he said to St. Faustina: **"Be not afraid of your Savior, O sinful soul. I make the first move to come to you, for I know by yourself you are unable to lift your- self to Me."** Such words also remind us of what St. Margaret Mary understood so well when she wrote: "His Sacred Heart will do everything for me if I let him. He shall will, he shall love, he shall desire for me and make up for all my faults."

Look again at Jesus, hanging on the Cross. See his gentle, sorrowful face. Hear him say to you, "I thirst." Now earnestly pray: "Jesus, I thirst for you. Help me to thirst for you more. Use me, Jesus. Form me into a saint. Make up for all my faults. I trust in you. With Mary's help, I give you my yes."

CONCLUSION. Having said yes to Jesus, we've got one important step to take before turning our full attention to the beautiful and simple means by which he'll form us into great saints (Divine Mercy and a true devotion to Mary). This step has to do with learning a bit more about the *Spiritual Exercises of St. Ignatius.* As we take this step, we'll discover, as did Fr. Lanteri, that some principles of the *Exercises* can help us continue to say yes to Jesus and allow him to carry us to sanctity. He needs us. We need him. So, with the help of St. Ignatius, let's let him do it.

The Great Principle
of the *Spiritual Exercises*

St. Ignatius of Loyola was a genius. He had the amazing ability to hone in on, organize, and communicate to others the essential principles of the spiritual life. A group of the most important of these principles he called his "First Principle and Foundation."

In this section, we're going to look more closely at certain aspects of Ignatius's First Principle and Foundation. Let's begin by reading it:

> Man is created to praise, reverence, and serve God our Lord, and by this means to save his soul.
>
> The other things on the face of the earth are created for man to help him in attaining the end for which he is created.
>
> Hence, man is to make use of them in as far as they help him in the attainment of his end, and he must rid himself of them in as far as they prove a hindrance to him.
>
> Therefore, we must make ourselves indifferent to all created things, as far as we are allowed free choice and are not under any prohibition. Consequently, as far as we are concerned, we should not prefer health to sickness, riches to poverty, honor to dishonor, a long life to a short life. The same holds for all other things.
>
> Our one desire and choice should be what is more conducive to the end for which we are created.

If this famous foundation doesn't seem so special now, don't worry. We'll come to appreciate it more after we've learned something about the early history of the congregation Ignatius founded: the Jesuits.

*T*HE EARLY JESUITS. When reading about that difficult period of Church history known as the Reformation, one can't help but think that God had to do something drastic to prevent the "gates of hell" from prevailing (see Mt 16:18). God's drastic move was to inspire Ignatius of Loyola to begin the Society of Jesus (Jesuits), a group of men with a corporate zeal rarely seen in the history of the world. With astonishing energy and tenacious determination, they spearheaded the Counter Reformation that saved the Church. This incredible accomplishment, and many others that followed, has evoked the awe and respect of countless people, even of unbelievers. For example, the fiery founder of Russian Communism, Vladimir Lenin, on hearing of the Jesuits' famous fervor and astounding triumphs, reportedly was moved to exclaim, "Give me ten men like those Jesuits, and I'll conquer the world!"

Our own awe and respect for the early Jesuits grows when we consider that they did their incredible deeds without the same protection and support that other religious enjoyed. For example, in other religious congregations of the time, the walls of their monasteries kept the dangers of the world out while life in community served to strengthen each member's faith. A missionary Jesuit such as St. Francis Xavier left all that behind as he ventured into the unfamiliar, un-Christianized lands of Asia ... *alone*. One would think that leaving behind the traditional supports of religious life for a hostile pagan world would have conquered poor Francis. On the contrary, Francis, like so many other early Jesuits, conquered the world. He single-handedly baptized more than 100,000 people and was eventually declared Patron of the Missions for the universal Church. He and other Jesuit missionaries set the world ablaze for Jesus Christ — a fire the likes of which hadn't been seen since St. Paul.

So, at this point, we're probably beginning to ask ourselves, "How did they do it? What was their secret?"

*T*HE SECRET OF THE EARLY JESUITS: THE FIRST PRINCIPLE AND FOUNDATION. The secret of the early Jesuits' zeal was the First Principle and Foundation, which we read earlier. Its five simple paragraphs present one's origin, mission, and destiny. Put differently, they summarize the goal of life and the means of attaining it. Of course, if one reads the First Principle and Foundation without having been formed in the spirituality of the Jesuits, it may seem dry and uninspiring. Yet, if one approaches it as one of the initiated, as one who, for instance, has made the 30-day Ignatian retreat, then it leaps off the page and sets the heart pulsing with adrenaline — at least that was the case for someone like St. Francis Xavier. What got him so excited about five simple paragraphs?

To understand the great enthusiasm certain people have for the First Principle and Foundation, we need to look at two things: the 30-day retreat and the notion I call "first things first."

THE 30-DAY RETREAT. A 30-day Ignatian retreat is an intense period of prayer during which one literally experiences the First Principle and Foundation as it unfolds and is expressed in the life of our Lord and Savior, Jesus Christ. During the course of such a retreat, one meditates for several hours each day, striving and begging for the grace "to know the Lord more intimately, love him more deeply, and desire to follow him more closely." If the retreat is made well, this petition is granted, and one tastes the sweetness and beholds the goodness and glory of the Lord. Thus, one of the main effects of the retreat is that it makes the goal of one's life amazingly vivid and clear.

It might be helpful to imagine the First Principle and Foundation as a photo a soldier carries with him as he marches into battle, a photo of his wife and children. When the soldier looks at it, he's reminded of where he comes from, what he's fighting for, and the importance of his mission. The photo may not mean much to others, but to him, it says everything, and from its word he draws his strength.

The great Jesuit missionaries like St. Francis Xavier drew their strength from the five simple paragraphs of the First Principle and Foundation. As they took on seemingly endless toils for the sake of God's greater glory, the familiar words of the First Principle and Foundation had the same effect as a soldier's family photo. Recalling those words somehow renewed the life-changing experience of their 30-day retreats and poured gasoline on the flames of love that already burned in their hearts.

The amazing ability of the First Principle and Foundation to give vision and energy (after it's brought to life by a 30-day retreat) led one of the early secretaries of the Jesuits, Jerome Nadal, to summarize their whole spirituality as "a clarity that grips us and leads us on." Together, the First Principle and Foundation and 30-day retreat make the goal of life so vividly clear that it truly does grip a person and lead him on.

"*FIRST THINGS FIRST.*" I've been saying that the First Principle and Foundation, which comes alive during a 30-day retreat, makes the goal of life clear and desirable. Well, the principle "first things first" basically means that when one keeps his eyes on such a vivid goal, the "first thing," then all else falls into place. It can also imply that when one goes after a "second thing" first, he loses not only the second thing but the first as well. Jesus taught this principle during his most important sermon, "Seek first the kingdom of God and all these things will be given you as well" (Mt 6:33).

The First Principle and Foundation teaches that we're made to live the "first thing" (a life of praise, reverence, and service to God) by using "second things" (the other things on the face of the earth) only insofar as they help us to live the first thing. Not only that, it teaches that if a second thing becomes an obstacle to living out the first thing, then we should rid ourselves of it. To find the right balance between this "using" and "ridding," Ignatius says, "We must make ourselves indifferent to all created things." Perhaps this line particularly struck you when you first read the First Principle and Foundation. For most people, it jumps off the page. Why? Because, at least for many of us, having an attitude of indifference before such good things as chocolate, race cars, and fireworks already seems unrealistic.

Still, there may be among us those hard-core types who roll up their sleeves and say to themselves, "Well, if this attitude of indifference (detachment) is the means for getting to heaven, I'd better get to work." Thus, such people begin a grand project of trying to detach themselves from their attachments in order to attain indifference. This, however, is the wrong way of going about it. Yes, we need to be detached, but focusing on our attachments means putting second things first — and that spells trouble. An example may help us understand better why this is the wrong way.

Let's say we've decided to be hard-core. Let's say we're determined to detach ourselves from one of our pesky attachments. Specifically, let's say we've zeroed in on our attachment to doughnuts. Now then, because we want to have Ignatian indifference, we force ourselves to let go of them ... there, we're free. This "freedom," however, only lasts a brief time. The hand that once held the doughnut begins to shake and suddenly shoots for something else: ice cream! Or, as we begin to relax, the doughnuts come back with a vengeance as they somehow jump up into our mouths and down to our bellies. No, this isn't the way to become indifferent.

In striving for indifference, sheer acts of the will won't work — at least not for long. But don't worry, there's hope. There's a secret Ignatius wants to teach us. It's the principle I've already mentioned, "first things first," the principle of keeping our eyes fixed on the goal, the first thing. It's the principle St. Peter discovered the hard way when he began to sink into the sea after taking his eyes off Jesus (see Mt 14:24-31). It's the principle we might call "the primacy of contemplation," the primacy of keeping the eyes of our hearts lovingly on the Lord.

The principle works like this: If we stay fixed on the beauty and glory of the Lord Jesus, if we taste *his* wonderful sweetness, then we'll discover he's much better than any doughnut. If we truly behold his glory, then we'll say with St. Paul that all else is dung! (see Phil 3:8). If we keep our eyes on the first thing, then like the early Jesuits, we'll exclaim, "All for the greater glory of God!" And we'll charge to our goal past dozens of doughnuts with ease.

"Uh, that's great," someone might say, "but getting such a vivid goal and clear insight into the First Principle and Foundation supposedly takes a whole 30-day retreat. But who's got 30 days to spend on retreat?" To such a person, I respond, "*Relax*, have a doughnut, and realize that the Lord will help us with this situation."

The Lord Jesus wants to help us more than we want to be helped. He sees much more clearly than we do that the culture of death in which we live cruelly grinds up so many lives. Think for a moment of all the babies who are killed each day through abortion and then of the sad state of their parents. Briefly ponder the countless people who ache from that familial suicide known as divorce. Imagine for a minute the silent despair of those millions who are trapped in addiction to such things as pornography or drugs. We think of these tragic realities from time to time, and it makes us sorrowful. But Jesus sees humanity's pain constantly — in every detail — and it shatters his Heart. Thus, Jesus desperately longs to reach out with his saving, healing, and consoling touch. Whether or not he can depends in large part on us.

After his ascension into heaven, Jesus reaches out to the world primarily through his disciples, and the more his disciples allow him to live in and through them, the more fully Jesus is able to continue his work of love and mercy. Saints are those disciples through whom he can save, heal, and console most fully. Thus, Jesus longs for saints, and he's more than willing to help those who aspire to sanctity.

Now, here's a divine dilemma: God wants us to become saints, yet one of the best saint-making tools, the 30-day Ignatian retreat, is hardly an option. That's a tough one for us ... but not for God. He's infinite Wisdom and Power. He can make things happen. He's already made it possible for us little ones to get a clear and vivid principle and foundation quickly and easily without having to make a whole 30-day retreat. Sound good? Read on.

A 30-Day-Retreat-Sized Principle and Foundation (in one shot)

It seems too good to be true, but it is true. God has given us a 30-day-retreat-sized principle and foundation in one shot. In other words, he can quickly make the goal of our lives vivid and clear, which, if we keep our eyes on it, will make being detached from things relatively easy. Although God can give it in one shot, it's not so easy to grasp in one shot. Therefore, we'll need one more history lesson. (Don't worry, it'll be brief.)

*T*HE JANSENIST HERESY. Anyone who knows the history of heresy has heard of Jansenism. Jansenism is the heresy that hurts the Lord's Heart more than any other, and sadly, it has also been one of the most influential. Remember Fr. Lanteri from the introduction and how he loved to promote the *Spiritual Exercises* retreat? Well, part of the reason he loved to promote it was that it so successfully combated the hurtful ideas of Jansenism, which he hated. Nobody likes Jansenism: not Jesus, not Fr. Lanteri, and I think even the Jansenists themselves don't like it. For, though they mistakenly think it's true, deep down in their hearts they wish it weren't. The devil is about the only one who likes Jansenism — after all, it hurts the Lord immensely.

To get a good look at Jansenism without going through its whole history, let's travel to the time and place when and where it was thriving most: 17th century France.

In France during this period, few Catholics go to receive Holy Communion. The preachers of Jansenism teach everyone that they have to be perfect to approach God. Since nobody's perfect, few people go to Jesus. In fact, the situation has gotten so bad that a bishop who accepts Jansenist ideas recently boasted that for a whole year not one person in his diocese received communion unworthily. How did he know that? Because he hasn't allowed anyone to receive Holy Communion! No wonder this hurts the Lord so much. He comes in the Eucharist, the Sacrament of Love, so people will lovingly receive him, but nobody does. Let's go into one of the churches to see exactly what's going on.

As we enter this particular church, we genuflect before the Lord Jesus in the Blessed Sacrament. Now look around. Everything seems normal. No, wait. What's that in front of the tabernacle? Somebody has placed a big painting there. What's that image on it? Let's move in for a closer look.

There, now we can make it out. The painting depicts the frightening face of some bearded guy who looks angry and just about ready to smack us. Hey, that's supposed to be Jesus! It looks like those Jansenists have been at it again. They go around putting these ugly paintings in front of the tabernacles in churches. In other words, they give people the idea that Jesus is just out to ruin all their fun, punish them, and make them unhappy. Look at how even the few people who enter the church cower and seem afraid of the Lord. This must be tearing his Heart apart as he looks on from the tabernacle. How can he bear it? He can't.

JESUS "SNAPS." In 17th century France, while Jansenism was scaring everyone away from the Eucharist and poisoning peoples' image of Jesus, there came a time when even Jesus — capable of bearing seemingly infinite suffering — couldn't take it anymore. He was overwhelmed.

Have you ever seen someone snap? For instance, have you ever seen a neglected mother snap? Imagine a mother who generously gives of herself to her children but whose children never show her gratitude. After a time, even the best of mothers might snap in such a situation. In other words, she might begin to cry and complain about the ingratitude of her children. Well, Jesus, who had been so neglected by the ones for whom he gave up his life, like a forgotten mother, snapped. Yes, overwhelmed with sorrow, in his meek, humble, and gentle way, the Lord snapped. Here's how.

From his sorrow at being so misunderstood and abandoned, Jesus looked for someone who would take pity on his aching Heart. From the tabernacle, he cast his gaze out on all of France, searching for a true friend on whom he could unburden some of his heartache and through whom he might finally convince people to believe in his tender love and mercy. Eventually, he found such a friend: a little nun named Sr. Margaret Mary. To this blessed soul, Jesus released an ocean of anguish as he disclosed his divine Heart. Appearing on the Cross, he said to her in a voice full of sadness and grief:

There it is, that Heart so deeply in love with men, it spared no means of proof — wearing itself out until it was utterly spent! This meets with scant appreciation from most of them; all I get back is ingratitude — witness their irreverence, their sacrileges, their coldness and contempt for me in this Sacrament of Love.

On another occasion, the Lord appeared in front of the exposed Blessed Sacrament with a similar message. Margaret Mary describes the experience:

Jesus Christ, my kind Master, appeared to me. He was a blaze of glory — his five wounds shining like five suns, flames issuing from all parts of his human form, especially from his divine breast which was like a furnace, and which he opened to disclose his utterly affectionate and loveable Heart, the living source of all those flames. It was at this moment that he revealed to me the indescribable wonders of his pure love for mankind: the extravagance to which he'd been led for those who had nothing for him but ingratitude and indifference. "This hurts me more," he told me, "than everything I suffered in my passion. Even a little love from them in return — and I should regard all that I have done for them as next to nothing, and look for a way of doing still more. But no; all my eager efforts for their welfare meet with nothing but coldness and dislike. Do me the kindness, then — you, at least — of making up for all their ingratitude, as far as you can."

Here it is. In these revelations to St. Margaret Mary, the Lord Jesus gives us a power-packed principle and foundation in one shot: his Sacred Heart. He says to us: "Behold this Heart which loves so much yet is so little loved. Do me the kindness, you at least, of making up for all their ingratitude, as far as you can." Yes, he says this to us, to you and to me. Let's see how this can be the principle and foundation of our lives, so that we, like the early Jesuits, might be set ablaze with love.

According to the Church, the center of our lives ought to be the Eucharistic Heart of Jesus, "the source and summit of the Christian life." She also teaches that this Sacred and Eucharistic Heart contains all the mysteries of the faith in summary and adds that devotion to the Sacred Heart is not optional but mandatory for all Catholics. When we realize that the Sacred Heart and the Eucharist are one and the same, it then becomes clear why the Sacred and Eucharistic Heart of Jesus is for us a fitting principle and foundation, indeed. Yet, if we want it to be a true principle and foundation, one in which we discover who we are, where we've come from, and what our mission is, then we need to see the Eucharistic Heart as it truly is. Because seeing the Eucharist with indifference or in the way the Jansenists portray it is so common today, it might be helpful to reflect on this point further.

*J*ESUS AS HE TRULY IS IN THE BLESSED SACRAMENT. Remember the secret of the early Jesuits? That's right, they always kept their eyes fixed on the First Principle and Foundation as the vivid goal that gripped them and drove them forward. Well, if we look at the Eucharistic Heart of Jesus not as the Jansenists portray it (the painting of the mean, bearded guy) but as it truly is, then we'll be filled with zeal like those Jesuits who set the world on fire. Simply a glance at Jesus' Heart can release in us a rushing torrent of love and strength, *if* we see him as he truly is. It's not a piece of bread there, and it's not some mean ogre. It's the Lord. Yes, it's the Lord making a plea for help, a plea for love. Let's now try to understand how the Eucharistic Heart of Jesus can unleash a torrent of love in us.

Imagine your best friend is sitting in a chair in front of you. Picture him there, overcome with grief. He's so distressed he sways back and forth and looks like he's about to fall to the floor. What's your response? Do you say, "Oops, sorry to interrupt. I'll come back when you feel better, so you don't bring me down with you"? No, I hope none of us would have such cold hearts. Instead, we probably wouldn't even have to think about what to do. We would automatically run to the aid of our friend and try to console him. Something clicks in us during such situations — it becomes not a matter of what we should do but of what we must do. When we see a true friend in such a state, our immediate response is to support and console him.

Well, if this is the response we would make to our best earthly friend, what response ought we to give to our greatest friend, to the one who loves us more than any other, to the one whose Heart right now suffers the most painful sorrow of all? What's our response when we hear him say to us, "Behold this Heart which loves so much yet is so little loved"? Once again, if we truly see the situation — our friend overwhelmed with sorrow — then our response should be automatic, "Jesus, I must help you." That's a great response, especially when we're in our Lord's Eucharistic presence.

Now, with the help of St. Thérèse of Lisieux, let's make a little meditation to help us understand better Jesus' Eucharistic Heart as it truly is.

We just stepped inside a big, Gothic cathedral. The lights are all out, except for one that brightly shines on the main altar. There, in the center of the altar, sending splintering rays in a thousand directions, stands a brilliantly golden monstrance with Jesus in the Eucharist enthroned at its center. Behold him there as he waits for his friends to come to him. Now look. See that people do come and go. Many ask for something, "Jesus, give me this, help that person, remove this cross ..." and then they leave. The Lord Jesus, who is so kind and good, readily gives to them. Now look. Saint Thérèse has just arrived. Observe her prayer as she looks deeply into the Heart of Jesus, truly present there in the Blessed Sacrament. What's her attitude toward him? Interesting. Her face is full of compassion. It's as if she sees that this good Lord who gives and gives is tired, sorrowful, and himself in need of help and consolation. Now listen to what she says.

Did you catch that? She's not asking Jesus to give to *her*, rather, she's asking what she can give to *him*. What an amazing turn!

As St. Thérèse gazes on the Eucharistic Heart of Jesus, she doesn't see him as if he were a machine into which one puts a coin and then automatically gets graces. Instead, she sees him as living and real. In fact, she sees that he has a human heart. She sees a man who has feelings, a man who is hurt when people are cold, ungrateful, and afraid of him. So, Thérèse decides she wants to console his aching Heart, which is so neglected. Like her, why don't we who have been given so much by this good and gentle Savior allow our gaze to penetrate more deeply into his Sacred and Eucharistic Heart.

OUR VISIT TO JESUS IN THE BLESSED SACRAMENT. Behold Jesus in the Monstrance again. See him as he truly is. See him as he reveals himself with the words, "Behold this Heart which loves so much ... ." See the first movement of these words — look how much Jesus has loved you. See how he has created you, saved you from the pits of hell, and given you your faith, family, friends, and every good thing. Look at your life and see how much he has lovingly given you, "Behold this Heart which loves *you* so much." What a tremendous friend!

Now feel the second movement of his words. Let him whisper to you, "Behold this Heart which loves so much *yet is so little loved.*" See the pain of the Lord's Sacred Heart. See how so few go to him, love him, and want to be his true friends. Do you see the Lord? Do you see how utterly simple he is?

A person is complex and complicated when he has all kinds of different desires. A person is simple if he has but one desire. Jesus is simple because he has only one desire, a desire that's best described as a *thirst*. He thirsts that all humanity be brought into his communion of love with the Father and the Holy Spirit (Jn 17:24). For us to share in this communion, though, we have to come to love him. Thus, Jesus thirsts for our love. But because this one desire of the Lord is not satisfied, because his love is rejected, a second aspect of Jesus is easy to understand: He's a man of sorrow. Yes, Jesus is both simple and sorrowful. The words of the Psalmist apply to him: "Reproach has broken my heart and I am cast down. I looked for one who would grieve together with me, but there was none: and for one who would comfort me, and I found none" (Ps 69:21).

Who are we if we don't have compassion on such a sorrowful friend who looks to us for comfort? He says to us: "Behold this Heart which loves so much yet is so little loved. Is there anyone who will console this Heart? Is there anyone who will be my friend?"

What's our response to this? What do we say when we see the Lord's sorrow and hear his plea for friends who will console him? Yes, let's be his friends. Let's decide right now that we'll console him. Let's tell him, "Yes, I will console you, Lord. I will be your friend." Let's decide it. Tell him your answer, "Jesus, I choose to be your friend, to console you."

Is this your decision? Do you decide that you will be Jesus' friend, that you will console him? If so, then your principle and foundation has become to look at Jesus' sorrowful Heart and say, "Here I am, Lord. I come to console you." In other words, *your principle and foundation is to console the Heart of Jesus, which is so sorrowful.* If this is our decision, to console Jesus, to be his friends, then we're ready to begin Part Two of this retreat — but maybe all of us aren't so ready. Maybe some of us have difficulties with the idea of consoling the Heart of Jesus. Before we proceed to Part Two, I'd like to address a difficulty that may be coming up in some of our minds.

One Difficulty: How Can We Console Jesus if He is Happy in Heaven?

You may not need to read this section of the retreat. You may be one of those people for whom the testimony of St. Margaret Mary (and other mystics of the Church) is enough. You may be one of those people who say, "I believe that Jesus revealed the deep and ongoing sorrow of his Sacred Heart through St. Margaret Mary, and I want to console him." If this describes you, then feel free to skip ahead to Part Two. If, however, you're one of those people for whom the very idea that we can console Jesus raises difficulties, then this section is written primarily for you.

To begin this section, I should issue a warning: What you're about to read is more theological than the other sections of the retreat. In fact, it's more of a theology lesson than spiritual reading. Now, if you're not a theologian, don't worry. After all, you're probably not a historian either, and those history lessons we covered earlier weren't so bad, right? I don't think this theology lesson will be that bad either, and even if it does take some extra attention, it'll be worth the effort. For, if your principle and foundation is now to console Jesus, then you probably want to know everything you can about it, right?

THE DIFFICULTY. The main difficulty people sometimes have with a spirituality of consoling Jesus, as I've been describing it, usually goes something like this:

> Jesus is in heaven. People in heaven are happy — they don't suffer. Therefore, Jesus is happy, and he doesn't need anyone to console him, because only people who are suffering need to be consoled.

The response to such a difficulty, in my experience, tends to follow this line of reasoning:

> Yes, it's true that Jesus is happy in heaven and that, therefore, he no longer suffers. So, to speak of giving consolation to Jesus actually applies only to giving consolation *to the members of his body.* In other words, we console Jesus by consoling one another, for we're all members of the Mystical Body of Christ (see 1 Cor 12:12-27). For example, we console Jesus when we alleviate the suffering of the poor, the sick, and the lonely, for they truly are Christ to us. The Lord Jesus himself tells us this in Sacred Scripture, "Whatsoever you do to the least of my people, that you do unto me" (Mt 20:25).

There's a lot of truth to this response. It describes well one of the ways we can console Jesus, namely, by consoling *the members* of his Mystical Body. In fact, a whole section of Part Two of this retreat (Obstacle No. 5) focuses on this way of consoling Jesus. Yet the core of our principle and foundation, as described earlier, is *first* to focus on giving consolation to Jesus Christ, the *Head* of the Mystical Body. So how can we give consolation to Jesus Christ the Head if he's happy in heaven?

In his encyclical letter dedicated to devotion to the Sacred Heart, *Miserentissimus Redemptor*, Pope Pius XI raised this same question. His initial answer to it is concise. He simply cites the words of St. Augustine, "Give me one who loves, and he will understand what I say." Okay, great. That may work for some people. But there are others out there who love (or who are at least trying to love) yet still don't understand. For those of us who fit this description, thankfully, Pope Pius XI offers further explanation. I'm going to summarize two ways by which he explains how we can console Jesus Christ, the Head of the Mystical Body. The first way has to do with the idea that we can give Jesus "retroactive consolation." The second way has to do with the idea that, in a sense, Jesus can be disturbed even while he's happy in heaven.

*R*ETROACTIVE CONSOLATION. The idea of giving retroactive consolation to Christ has something to do with consoling him now for his suffering *in the past*. Although he doesn't use the word "retroactive," Pope Pius XI seems to endorse such an idea in his encyclical letter on the Sacred Heart, *Haurietis Aquas:*

> Now if, because of our sins also which were as yet in the future, but were *foreseen*, the soul of Christ became sorrowful unto death, it cannot be doubted that then, too, already He derived somewhat of solace from our reparation, which was *likewise foreseen*, when "there appeared to him an angel from heaven" (Lk 22:13), in order that His Heart, oppressed with weariness and anguish, might find consolation. And

so even now, in a wondrous yet true manner, *we can and ought to console that Most Sacred Heart which is continually wounded by the sins of thankless men,* since — as we also read in the sacred liturgy — Christ Himself, by the mouth of the Psalmist complains that He is forsaken by His friends: "My Heart hath expected reproach and misery, and I looked for one that would grieve together with me, but there was none: and for one that would comfort me, and I found none" (Ps 68:21) (emphasis added).

From these words of Pope Pius XI, we can begin to understand how we retroactively console Christ "now" as he suffered his Passion way back "then." The key to this understanding is the teaching that Jesus Christ, because he was (and is) truly God, was able to know ("foresee") all people of all times, a teaching that was reiterated more recently in the *Catechism of the Catholic Church:*

Jesus knew and loved us each and all during his life, his agony, and his Passion and gave himself up for each one of us: "The Son of God ... loved me and gave himself for me" (Gal 2:20).

With this teaching in mind, we can easily conclude with Pope Pius XI not only that Jesus' knowledge of our sins that were "as yet in the future" caused him great sorrow but also that Jesus' knowledge of our acts of love, which were also "as yet in the future," brought him great consolation.

One theologian of the Sacred Heart, Timothy O'Donnell, STD, while commenting on the words of Pope Pius XI cited above, explains the idea that Jesus really did see us and that although he was sorrowful because of our sins, he found consolation in our acts of love:

Just as [Jesus] allowed himself to be saddened by the vision of the sins of mankind, so did he also allow himself to be consoled by all the human acts of compassionate consolation throughout history until the end of time. So, despite the fact that the future consolers of our Lord were not *personally* present during the passion, the reparatory value of their foreknown actions did in fact console Christ. This loving consolation was received by our Lord not in an ever-growing sequence, but instantaneously in his *nunc stans* — everlasting now. This is the great truth which many artists have sought to communicate down through the ages by painting various saints from different time periods standing at the foot of the cross. Although separated by time, their great love for Christ did in fact console him in his agony, since our Lord foresaw all their acts of loving consolation (emphasis in original).

So, even if Christ the Head of the Mystical Body is "happy in heaven," we can still console him (according to the idea of retroactive consolation), because the same Jesus Christ, throughout his earthly life and especially during his suffering and agony, could see us and know how much we love him.

For instance, during his Passion, Jesus could see all the times we would love and adore him in his sacred presence in the Most Blessed Sacrament, and this consoled him. Of course, exactly how the Lord would have experienced such a consoling vision of we who live nearly 2,000 years after his Passion remains a mystery. After all, none of us possess such supernatural sight. Nevertheless, people do get something of the idea. For example, it's not so hard to imagine Jesus full of sorrow in the Garden of Gethsemane, because he could somehow foresee the rejection, betrayal, and apostasy of future generations. At the same time, it's not so hard to imagine Jesus, during that same agony in the garden, being consoled by his awareness of the many people in the future who would love and follow him. Perhaps we can't explain all this theologically, but we surely can imagine it. It makes sense to us, and it made sense to Christians who went before us. Indeed, for centuries, popular and beloved books of Christian piety have described Christ's agony in the garden precisely in this way. Generations of the faithful who read such books had a kind of spiritual instinct that allowed them to affirm, "Yes, it was like that."

The teaching that Jesus foresaw our acts of love, especially during his Passion, is confirmed not only by the spiritual sense of countless Christians but also in a special way by the testimony of many mystics, particularly by St. Faustina Kowalska. Take, for example, the Novena to Divine Mercy that our Lord dictated to her. This novena stands as a great testimony to what I've been referring to as "retroactive consolation." No less than six of the nine days of the novena speak directly to the mystery that we can somehow console Jesus now when he suffered then. Thus, we read:

[Second Day] **Today bring to Me the souls of priests and religious, and immerse them in My unfathomable mercy.** *It was they who gave me strength to endure My bitter Passion.* ...

[Third Day] **Today bring to Me all devout and faithful souls and immerse them in the ocean of My mercy.** *These souls brought Me consolation on the Way of the Cross. They were that drop of consolation in the midst of an ocean of bitterness.* ...

[Fourth Day] **Today bring to Me those who do not believe in God and those who do not yet know Me.** *I was thinking of them during my bitter Passion, and their future zeal comforted My Heart.* ...

[Fifth Day] **Today bring to Me the souls of those who have separated themselves from My Church, and immerse them in the ocean of My mercy.** *During My bitter Passion* **they tore at My Body and Heart, that is, My Church. As they return to unity with the Church My wounds heal and in this way** *they alleviate My Passion.* ...

[Sixth Day] **Today bring to Me the meek and humble souls and the souls of little children, and immerse them in my mercy.** ... *They strengthened*

Me during My bitter agony. I saw them as earthly Angels, who will keep vigil at my altars. …
[Ninth Day] **Today bring to Me souls who have become lukewarm, and immerse them in the abyss of My mercy. These souls wound My Heart most painfully.** *My soul suffered the most dreadful loathing in the Garden of Olives because of lukewarm souls. They were the reason I cried out: "Father, take this cup away from Me, if it be Your will"* (emphasis added).

Having heard from the pope, the sense of the Christian faithful, and one of the great mystics of the Church, we can safely conclude that retroactive consolation is a theologically solid way of explaining how it is that we can console Jesus, the Head of the Mystical Body, even if now he's "happy in heaven."

*H*APPY IN HEAVEN? There's another way of explaining how we can console Jesus, the Head of the Mystical Body, even if he's happy in heaven, and it doesn't go against the idea of retroactive consolation. In fact, this second way of explaining the mystery complements the idea of retroactive consolation. Moreover, it goes with the idea I described earlier about consoling Jesus in the members of his body, and it shows how such consolation can also console the Head of the Body. This second explanation begins by asking: Is Jesus "happy in heaven"? The fascinating answer to this question might challenge the way many of us understand Jesus to be in heaven, but it's a good challenge.

Pope Pius XI writes in his encyclical letter on the Sacred Heart, "[W]hen persecutions are stirred up against the Church, the Divine Head of the Church is Himself attacked and troubled." In other words, not only are Christians attacked and troubled when they're persecuted (obviously) but so is Christ himself. Here, the Pope is commenting on a passage from the Acts of the Apostles, chapter nine. Let's look more closely at what's going on in this passage.

Acts chapter nine contains the remarkable account of Jesus' sudden appearance to Saul, who was persecuting the Lord's disciples. During that blinding apparition, Jesus asks Saul not "Why are you persecuting my disciples?" but rather, "Why are you persecuting *me*?" (9:4). In other words, he identifies his disciples with himself. As Saul, who becomes St. Paul, would later write, Christ's disciples are the very members of his body (see 1 Cor 12:12-27).

Clearly, the members of the Church, Christ's body, become attacked and troubled during persecutions, but how can we understand that "the Divine Head of the Church," who is Christ in heaven, is also "Himself attacked and troubled"? Sure, he's united to his Church, but if he suffers when the Church suffers, doesn't this take away from the idea that heaven is a place of joy? Furthermore, wouldn't all this go against the teaching of Pope Pius XII when he wrote that the Sacred Heart of Jesus in heavenly glory "is no longer subject to the varying emotions of this mortal life"? What are we to make of all this? Does Christ in heaven suffer when his disciples suffer or not? Is he simply happy in heaven while we're weeping in this valley of tears?

One expert in Christology, Fr. Thomas Weinandy, OFM, Cap., offers something of a solution to this problem without trying to explain away the mystery. He says that while Christ in heaven does not have the varying emotions of this mortal life, he does have varying emotions of a glorified life. Having made this crucial distinction, Fr. Weinandy goes on to write:

When I say that the risen Christ "suffers," I do not mean that he physically and emotionally suffers as we do who are not risen. As a risen and glorious man, the Son of God can no longer suffer physically and emotionally in the same sense as we do. However, as risen and glorious, Christ is still a man, and thus still possesses human emotional states, though now in a risen manner. He still possesses the human emotions of joy, compassion and love. He continues to find sin and evil, and the suffering they cause, repugnant. Being in communion with the members of his body, who are not risen, their experiences are his experiences. The manner in which he, as risen, experiences these "un-risen" experiences of his earthly body, I do not know. Thus, I am stating something that I believe has to be the case, but I do not understand the manner or the mode in which it is the case.

So, Christ's suffering in heaven, like his experience of knowing future generations, is something of a mystery to us. We can't fully grasp how Christ in heaven is "attacked and troubled" when the Church on earth suffers, but somehow, according to the pope and Fr. Weinandy, he is so disturbed.

Okay, so let's say we accept that Christ is somehow disturbed in heaven. There's still a problem. For how are we to understand that Christ somehow suffers even while he enjoys the glorious and heavenly bliss of communion in the Trinity? Isn't it impossible to experience both bliss and suffering at the same time? Saint Thérèse of Lisieux helps us understand this paradox when she writes the following about her own experience of bliss and pain:

> In the Garden of Olives our Lord was blessed with all the joys of the Trinity, yet his dying was no less harsh. It is a mystery, but I assure you that, on the basis of what I myself am feeling, I can understand something of it.

Hearing this testimony evokes wonder at the mystery. Perhaps Christ in heaven really does experience a mixture of bliss and a kind of sorrow until the suffering of the human family comes to an end.

The topic of the resurrected Christ's communion with suffering humanity is one on which Pope Benedict XVI has long pondered. In a book he wrote before becoming pope, he cites a passage in the writings of one of the early Church

Fathers, Origen of Alexandria (185-254), that helped explain for him some of the mystery of how Christ in heaven is somehow affectively linked with the ongoing sufferings of the human race. Calling it an "unspeakable mystery," Origen attempts something of an explanation:

> My Saviour grieves even now about my sins. My Saviour cannot rejoice as long as I remain in perversion. Why cannot he do this? Because he himself is "an intercessor for our sins with the Father." … How can he, who is an intercessor for my sins, drink the "wine" of joy, when I grieve him with my sins? How can he, who "approaches the altar" in order to atone for me a sinner, be joyful when the sadness of sin rises up to him ceaselessly? "With you," he says, "I will drink in the Kingdom of my Father." As long as we do not act in such a way that we can mount up to the Kingdom, he cannot drink alone that wine which he promised to drink with us. … Thus it is that he waits until we should be converted, in order that we may follow in his footsteps and he rejoice "with us" and "drink wine with us in the Kingdom of his Father." … We are the ones who delay his joy by our negligence toward our lives.
>
> … [But] the apostles too have not yet received their joy: they likewise are waiting for me to participate in their joy. So it is that the saints who depart from here do not immediately receive the full reward of their merits, but wait for us, even if we delay, even if we remain sluggish. They cannot know perfect joy as long as they grieve over our transgressions and weep for our sins.
>
> … You will have joy when you depart from this life if you are a saint. But your joy will be complete only when no member of your body is lacking to you. For you too will wait, just as you are awaited. But if you, who are a member, do not have perfect

joy as long as a member is missing, how much more must our Lord and Saviour, who is the head and origin of this body, consider it an incomplete joy if he is still lacking certain of his members? ... Thus he does not want to receive his perfect glory without you: that means, not without his people which is "his body" and "his members."

Although the future Pope Benedict thought there were some problems with the mythological expression of this passage, he still gave his opinion that it best captures an important truth about the relation between human life, history, and love. Developing this truth in the same book in which he cites the passage from Origen, he writes that love is such that it's always *for* someone. He then applies this idea to the love the saints in heaven have for those who are still suffering on earth:

Love cannot, then, close itself against others or be without them so long as time, and with it suffering, is real. No one has formulated this insight more finely than Thérèse of Lisieux with her idea of heaven as the showering down of love towards all. But even in ordinary human terms we can say, "How could a mother be completely and unreservedly happy so long as one of her children is suffering?"

That last line gets to the heart of the mystery. How could Jesus Christ, who loves us with an even greater love than that of a mother, be completely happy in heaven while the members of his body are suffering? It seems he can't be. This side of eternity, we can't fully understand exactly how it is that he suffers with us, but according to the mystics, he does suffer, and furthermore, he desires that we console him.

Because the idea of motherly love has come up, I should at least mention that Jesus' mother, Mary, whom we know is bodily in heaven, must also suffer with her Son on account of us. For how could she be completely and unreservedly happy when one of us, her children, is still suffering on earth? It seems she can't be. As if to confirm this point, in several Church-approved Marian apparitions (for instance, at Fatima, Portugal), Mary revealed the deep sorrow her Immaculate Heart feels at seeing the suffering of her children on earth. The visionaries who saw such apparitions often reported that Mary's face looked deeply sorrowful and that she even wept. So, if Christ suffers in heaven when he sees human suffering on earth, surely his mother (our mother) must also suffer with him and with us. Once again, remarkable testimony from St. Faustina proves particularly illuminating:

> During the night, the Mother of God visited me, holding the Infant Jesus in Her arms. My soul was filled with joy and I said, "Mary, my Mother, do You know how terribly I suffer?" And the Mother of God answered me, *I know how much you suffer, but do not be afraid. I share with you your suffering, and I shall always do so.* She smiled warmly and disappeared (italics in original).

CONCLUSION: CLEARING UP LINGERING DIFFICULTIES. Exactly how it is that Jesus Christ, the Head of the Mystical Body, suffers and, therefore, desires our consoling love is a great mystery. Following the lead of Pope Pius XI, I've explained at least two ways by which we can understand this mystery better: first, by treating the notion of retroactive consolation and, second, by explaining how Christ can, in a sense, be said to still suffer even as he's "happy in heaven." However we explain it, the point is clear: Christ somehow still suffers and longs for us to console him — but make no mistake about it. His longing is not a sign of weakness. He's not emotionally needy or self-pitying as if he were some immature man. We can better grasp this idea when we realize that Christ chose to put into his Heart such a burning longing for our love and that he did so because he loves us. Let's conclude on this point.

Sound theology teaches us that God, because he's God, doesn't need us, his creatures. Further, we know that when the Word became flesh, God chose to exist as a man with both a divine and human heart. In fact, he chose for his own the most sensitive, compassionate, and loving human heart of all. By choosing such a heart for himself, he accepted that he would suffer the most burning desire for love — for every human being longs to be loved. Indeed, God loves us so much that, in Christ, he made himself vulnerable: He made himself "need" our love! According to Pope John Paul II, this is one of God's great mercies to us, namely, that in Christ Jesus, he allows himself to be in need of mercy from us. When teaching this, perhaps John Paul had in mind a conclusion he had come to earlier in his life, before he became pope:

> After many experiences and a lot of thinking, I am convinced that *the objective starting point of love is the realization that I am needed by another.* The person who objectively needs me most is also, for me, *objectively,* the person I most need. This is a fragment of life's deep logic (emphasis in original).

Clearly, the words of this passage apply to human love — and that's precisely why they're appropriate here. In Christ Jesus, God no longer calls us slaves but friends (see Jn 15:14-15). Now, as Aristotle pointed out long ago, true friendship requires a kind of equality and mutuality — it can't be one sided. Thus, Christ humbled himself and accepted to feel a burning thirst ("need") for our love, so we might enter into genuine friendship with him. God knows we need him, but how could we be his true friends unless in some sense he also needed us?

Of course, there's a big difference between Jesus' "need" for us and our need for him. His need for our love comes from his own great love for us, a love that can't stand to see us perish, which is what will happen if we don't love him. For, when we turn our backs on the friendship and love that God in Christ Jesus offers us, we die — eternally. Yet Jesus came that we might have life and have it abundantly (see Jn 10:10). Moreover, the burning desire for us that he chose to have in his Heart is that we go to him and love him and thus receive his life and love and spread it to others. It's in *this* sense that we ought to understand Christ's need for our love. In sum: Jesus' need for our love is because he knows how desperately we need his love — he knows that, for us, it's a matter of life and death.

I hope all the difficulties we might have had with the idea of consoling the Heart of Jesus have now been resolved — except one. There's one last difficulty I didn't treat here because Part Two will resolve it. That difficulty has to do with the misunderstanding that the spirituality being taught here is just about pain and sorrow with no place for joy. As we'll see, joy, praise, and thanks have a crucially important role in the living out of our principle and foundation of consoling the Heart of Jesus.

Review Questions for Part One
(Don't worry. You won't be graded on your answers.)

I. REGARDING: "BEGINNING WITH DESIRE"

1. Do I want to be a saint?
2. Do I believe I can become a saint? (If not, reread St. Thérèse's words about the Little Way.)
3. Have I decided to "let Jesus do it"? That is, have I decided to let him form me into a saint? (If you haven't, I invite you to do so now, remembering St. Thérèse's "elevator" and St. Margaret Mary's words: "His Sacred Heart will do everything for me if I let him. He shall will, he shall love, he shall desire for me and make up for all my faults.")

II. REGARDING: "THE GREAT PRINCIPLE OF THE *SPIRITUAL EXERCISES*"

1. What is meant by the idea "first things first"?
2. How does "first things first" relate to developing an attitude of indifference?
3. How did the 30-day retreat help the early Jesuits live "first things first"?
4. How can I live "first things first" without having to make a 30-day retreat? (Hint: See the next point.)

III. REGARDING: "A 30-DAY-RETREAT-SIZED PRINCIPLE AND FOUNDATION (IN ONE SHOT)"

1. Why would God give a 30-day-retreat-sized principle and foundation in one shot? (Hint: Think "divine dilemma.")
2. Why did Jesus snap?
3. What's the principle and foundation of this retreat?
4. Why does focusing on this principle and foundation have the power to release so much love in us?

IV. REGARDING: "ONE DIFFICULTY: HOW CAN WE CONSOLE JESUS IF HE IS HAPPY IN HEAVEN?"

1. What is retroactive consolation?
2. Might Jesus be disturbed even while in heaven? If so, how might we explain it? (Hint: Re-read the citations from Fr. Weinandy and Pope Benedict XVI when he was Cardinal Ratzinger.)
3. How does St. Faustina's testimony help us understand the idea of giving consolation to Jesus? (See both block citations from her *Diary*.)

PART TWO

Overcoming
Obstacles to Living
the Foundation

So, living our principle and foundation begins when we focus on the Heart of Jesus and hear him say to us: "Behold this Heart which loves so much yet is so little loved. Is there anyone who will console me?" Our automatic response is, "I will console you, Jesus." That's our response, right? Right. Okay, so we tell Jesus we want to console him, and then he says to us, "Oh, thank you. Then that means you will perform acts of *reparation*."

Right there is usually where the brakes go on. For many of us, the word "reparation" is a like a big, red stop sign that puts an end to our drawing close to the Lord's Heart. In fact, I wouldn't be surprised if some of us, on hearing this word, might respond to the Lord by saying: "Well, Lord, I do want to help you and be your friend and all, but I don't know about this reparation stuff. It sounds like there's a lot of suffering and sacrifices involved and, well, as you remember from the beginning of the retreat, I'm one of the little ones." Perhaps this is what part of us is saying. Thus, we come to the first obstacle to living our principle and foundation: fear of suffering. But don't worry, for the Lord says to us: "Be not afraid. Listen. I am meek and gentle of heart."

To get past this first obstacle, we need to become convinced of the Lord's gentleness. He knows we're little. He knows we easily get scared and put on the brakes. He knows we need to be led by a gentle hand. Yet it often takes time for us to realize he knows. He knows that, too — and he's very patient. Now, if we're willing, he'd like to begin teaching us to trust him. Shall we begin? Good. Then let's start the first lesson in the Lord's "school of trust." Let's begin to deal with our fear of suffering by coming to realize the Lord's great gentleness.

First Obstacle: Fear of Suffering

*J*OE'S STORY. To help us understand better the Lord's gentleness, I'd like to recount a young man's experience during his 30-day retreat. I'll call him "Joe." (Yes, Joe is a real person, and what I'm about to describe really happened.) Joe started his 30 days of prayer with a great desire to become a saint, which, as we've seen earlier, is an important disposition for beginning an Ignatian retreat. Yet Joe lacked another important disposition for making such a retreat well: trust.

Joe was like those people who, as we heard about earlier, read the First Principle and Foundation and focused entirely on gaining an attitude of indifference. He put his eyes not on the goal (first thing) but on the means (second thing), and then he tried to attain that means (indifference before all created things) by his own willpower. Now, remember what I said before: Striving to become indifferent by simply making sheer acts of the will won't work — at least not for long. Joe had to learn this lesson the hard way.

Before his retreat, Joe had read stories of ordinary people who had made the 30-day retreat, experienced deep conversion, and then had gone on to become great saints. He was particularly moved by the stories of certain Jesuit saints who had begun their retreats by doing severe penances. Joe said to himself: "I want to become a saint, and this retreat is my opportunity. But to do it, I've got to imitate those Jesuits who were so generous with God by giving him great penances." So, Joe began his retreat by doing a lot of penance: He hardly ate any food, didn't turn the heat on in his room (during a bitterly cold November), only took cold showers, and so on. After about two weeks of that, he hit "the wall." It happened as he was about to take a shower. After undressing and as he was about to step under the stream of ice-cold shower spray, his body cried out, "No more!" He couldn't do it. He couldn't take another cold shower. So, feeling deeply discouraged, Joe took a nice warm shower, got dressed, and then went straight to the chapel.

Once in the chapel, Joe slumped into a big chair for his morning meditation. (It was the first meditation of the retreat he made while sitting rather than kneeling.) As he sat there in the big, comfy chair, he felt like a big, comfy failure. He didn't even raise his eyes to the tabernacle. In fact, he didn't even make an effort to meditate. He just sat there, stewing in his discouragement. After a few minutes of that, Joe suddenly heard a soft, gentle voice speaking to his heart: "Little lamb, little lamb, don't run ahead of me and don't lag behind. Just walk *with* me." A deep peace came with those words, and Joe kept them in his heart. He eased up on his penances and began to focus trustingly on the Lord. That's when the retreat began to work its wonders. For then Joe began to taste the sweetness of the Lord Jesus, and his goal became vivid and clear.

Unfortunately, the sweetness didn't last. On the final day of the retreat (and one time earlier), Joe began to slip back into the same fears that had tortured him during the difficult first few weeks. Imagine the scene. Joe had just spent 29 days in silence and prayer. It had been such a beautiful time with the Lord when he trusted, yet so difficult when he didn't. As he came to what was supposed to be the culminating, climactic moment of the retreat, "The Contemplation to Attain Divine Love," he began to pull away from the Lord.

The last meditation of the *Spiritual Exercises*, the "Contemplation to Attain Divine Love," begins with two considerations. Saint Ignatius describes them as follows:

> The first [consideration] is that love ought to man-
> ifest itself in deeds rather than in words. The second
> is that love consists in a mutual sharing of goods,
> for example, the lover gives and shares with the
> beloved what he possesses. ... Thus, one always
> gives to the other.

After reflecting on these considerations, Joe began to feel a little uneasy. Nonetheless, he continued on to the first few points of the contemplation. One of those points gives the following instruction:

> This is to ask for what I desire. Here it will be to ask
> for an intimate knowledge of the many blessings
> received, that filled with gratitude for all, I may in all
> things love and serve the Divine Majesty.

After reading this instruction, Joe put on the brakes. What do you think might have caused his hesitation?

As Joe read the preliminary point, "Ask for an intimate knowledge of the many blessings received," the many and tremendous blessings God had given him throughout his life flooded into his mind. Normally, such knowledge would have filled Joe with peace and joy. This time, however, the thought of so many blessings began to terrify him as he asked himself, "What will God want in return for all that he's given me?" He reflected again on the two considerations that began the meditation: Love is through *deeds*, the lover *gives*. Suddenly, those frightful words from Sacred Scripture came to his mind, "Everyone to whom much is given, much will be required" (Lk 12:48). It seemed to Joe that the rest of his life would have to be one big crucifixion in order to make a return to God for all the good God had done for him. So Joe stopped. Paralyzed by the fear of what God might ask of him, he couldn't continue. Precisely at that point, the Lord directly intervened.

As you read what I'm about to recount from Joe's experience, understand this: If anyone gives God 30 days of intense prayer and spiritual exercise, God *will* speak. Surely, he had already spoken to Joe earlier in the retreat, but it was during this last contemplation that the Lord Jesus spoke to Joe more clearly than ever before.

Jesus had patiently suffered through Joe's hesitation and lack of trust, but now it seemed he could take it no longer. So, just as in the case of Jansenism in 17th century France, Jesus snapped. He spoke to Joe who was still stuck and full of distress. In sad but gentle and loving words, he spoke to Joe's heart:

> "Joseph, Joseph, why are you hesitating? Why do you fear?"

> Joe responded, "Lord, if I look at all you've given me, I'm terrified of what you might want in return."

> The Lord continued: "Joseph, haven't I shown you how gentle I am with you? Haven't I shown you only kindness? Why do you fear? Look at your life. Have I ever allowed anything you couldn't bear?"

Joe had to admit, "No, Lord, all you've shown me is mercy and love, and the tough times came when I went off on my own."

Then, the Lord began, "Joseph, all I want ..."

He had all of Joe's (nervous) attention, "Yes, Lord?"

"All I want is for you to be my friend. All I want is for you not to be afraid of me and to come to me."

"That's all, Lord?"

"That's all."

After this conversation, Joe's heart overflowed with peace. Perhaps peace is beginning to fill our hearts as well. For the Lord's words to Joe are addressed to all little souls: "All I want is for you to be my friend. All I want is for you not to be afraid of me and to come to me. That's all." Can you hear the Lord speaking these words to you? He does. Listen with your heart. You don't have to make a 30-day retreat to hear them. Here they are, right now, for you. Take them to heart, and realize how simple it is to please the Lord.

With the Lord's words to us in mind, let's renew our decision to be his friends. There's no reason to be afraid. Reflect on his questions to Joe and to us: "Haven't I shown you how gentle I am with you? Have I ever allowed anything you couldn't bear?" When we haven't fled from the Lord's love, when we've given him a chance to show it, haven't we always found his embrace to be gentle? Maybe we've never given him the chance to show us. Let's give him the chance now by taking to heart his words to Joe and to us, and in the warmth of that embrace, let's get to know the Lord as he truly is. Furthermore, let's listen to his loving invitation from the Gospel: "Take my yoke upon you, and learn from me; for I am gentle and humble of heart, and you will find rest for your souls. For my yoke is easy, and my burden is light" (Mt 11:29). Truly, it's so simple and relatively easy to follow the Lord and to be his true friends. There's nothing to fear — and yet we still fear.

Before we take on the second obstacle that prevents us from going to the Lord, namely, our weaknesses, sinfulness, and attachments, it might be helpful to look more closely at this first one. Specifically, let's dedicate a fair share of our time to reflecting on what we're often so afraid of: suffering.

*D*EFLATING THE "SECOND THING." Fear of suffering tends to come up a lot for those who strive to console Jesus. After all, those who want to console him commit themselves to making reparation, and reparation often involves suffering. Despite the risk of focusing too much on this "second thing," it's important that we look at it more closely. I say that because the bad spirit often inflates this second thing so much that it becomes larger than life, frightens us, and blocks our view of the "first thing," namely, Jesus. My aim here is to deflate suffering down to its true size, so we'll see it's not so scary. In fact, once it's deflated, we might even begin to find in suffering a source of joy — but let's not get ahead of ourselves. Let's start by dispelling a big misconception about suffering.

People often think they can escape suffering. They can't. Suffering finds us all. Everyone in the world suffers: rich and poor, healthy and sick, young and old. It might not always look like certain people suffer, but suffering comes in various forms, many of which are hidden. Truly, if we look back on our own lives, we find at least some confirmation of the idea that suffering is part of the human condition.

While we may know that suffering is an inevitable aspect of life, there's at least a small part of us that silently rebels against this fact and spends a lot of time and energy trying to find ways to avoid it. Like suffering itself, this part of us is a simple fact of life. That being said, we don't have to let it control our lives. Indeed, we should resist that temptation. For, again, suffering finds us all, no matter how much we strive to avoid it, and those who make such striving the center of their lives often end up being the ones who suffer the most.

The best way to deal with suffering is to accept it, unite it to Christ in his suffering, and begin to find its hidden treasure.

By accepting suffering, I don't mean we should be completely passive such that we don't act to avoid the suffering of poverty, illness, and the like — the part of us that strives to avoid suffering has a legitimate role in our lives. So what do I mean by accepting suffering? To explain this idea, it'll be helpful to contrast it with something else.

It seems to me there are at least two different Christian approaches to suffering. The first approach (the approach of big souls) tends to be very active. It involves actively choosing lots of penances, mortifications, and sacrifices. Such an approach has a long history in the Church and has helped produce a number of saints. It's not what I'll be presenting here. This retreat is for little souls, and the approach to suffering that follows is for them.

I propose a passive approach to suffering that's in keeping with a theme of this retreat: "letting Jesus do it." In other words, I propose that we first ask Jesus to choose for us the suffering that he knows will form us into saints (for he knows best) and then simply accept what he sends. If you're worried that it won't be enough, that he won't really find crosses for you, that he'll forget — don't. I can only say from experience, there's no need to worry. He won't forget. Yet maybe that's not the problem. Maybe you're not worried that Jesus will forget to find crosses for you. Maybe you're worried that he'll remember and that the crosses he'll choose will be too heavy. I will again say from experience, don't worry. Jesus is amazingly gentle. He knows what we can take and what we need. In fact, you might even come to find, as I have, that he's gentler with us than we are with ourselves — but don't just take my word for it. Let's listen to more of Joe's story.

OUR FRIEND JOE AGAIN. During what's called the "Third Week" of the 30-day retreat, Joe was having a tough time. The Third Week is that part of the retreat when one follows the Lord through the suffering of his Passion. Now, in his great zeal, Joe had forgotten that he was simply supposed to follow the Lord during the Passion. Jesus had warned him again as the week approached: "Little lamb, little lamb, don't run ahead of me, and don't lag behind. Just walk *with* me." Because Joe had forgotten that warning, it's not surprising that when the week began, Joe hit the wall again as he realized he couldn't keep up with the Lord's suffering. The Lord saw him hesitating and said to him: "Joseph, you need to make a decision right now. Will you walk with me into the darkness?" Although he was afraid of the darkness of the Passion, which he had already started to feel, Joe had also begun to see the beauty of the Lord, so he mustered the courage to respond, "Yes, Lord, I will walk with you." The Lord replied, "Then take my hand and walk with me, keeping your eyes on me." Joe did as instructed, and as so often happens when we respond to the Lord in faith, something amazing happened. The dreaded "Third Week" became the most beautiful part of the whole retreat.

As Joe walked with Jesus through the Passion, keeping his eyes on his friend, he became amazed at just how much Jesus was suffering. No wonder all the Lord wanted was for someone to hold his hand through such darkness — it would have been too much to bear alone! So there was Joe, comforting Jesus through the bloody scourging, the insults, and the Way of the Cross. All Jesus wanted, as he would remind Joe at the end of the retreat, was a friend and companion through such darkness. He simply wanted someone to hold his hand, love him, and thank him for what he was suffering for us. Joe was happy to endure his own little sufferings (for example, the effort it took to meditate), because he realized that those little things were nothing compared to what Jesus was suffering. Moreover, Joe came to understand that he didn't need to worry about his weakness, for what he himself couldn't give to Jesus in terms of consolation, others could.

In the middle of the night, toward the end of a meditation, Joe was with Jesus, who was suffering in the cold, dark cistern awaiting his trial before Pilate. It was then that Joe believes he heard Jesus telling him to go to bed. But Joe didn't want to because he was afraid Jesus would be left alone in all his suffer-ing. Just then, as he was hesitating and thinking about Jesus' loneliness, Joe saw in his imagination the image of a nun who was going for a Holy Hour somewhere else in the world. Next, he heard these words deep in his heart: "Joseph, you've spent enough time tonight in this school of love. Take your rest, my friend. Look, another one of my friends has come. Thank you for being with me."

After having just read more of Joe's story, it might be helpful to reflect on what it teaches about the gentle way by which the Lord leads little souls. Therefore, I'm going to present some points from it for us to ponder.

First, notice that the Lord helped Joe to shift his focus from his own suffering to that of the Lord. In other words, he helped Joe take his eyes off the "second thing" and put them on the "first thing." When Joe did that, everything changed. Might we also benefit from such a shift of focus? Might things change in our lives if we were to shift our focus from our own suffering to that of the Lord?

Second, notice that the main thing the Lord wanted from Joe was not that Joe suffer but simply that he be with him in his suffering. This reminds us of the Lord's words to Joe at the end of the retreat: "All I want is for you to be my friend. All I want is for you not to be afraid of me and to come to me." When Joe simply followed the Lord, it was enough. In other words, the Lord doesn't necessarily want from us great suffering but great love. Do we see the tremendous value there is to simply being with the Lord?

Third, there is a place for our own personal suffering. Notice that Joe offered to the Lord his own little suffering (the effort it took to meditate). Of course, that's nothing compared to what the Lord went through, but isn't that true of all our sufferings when we compare them to those of the Lord? Yet, amazingly, even our littlest sufferings take on great value when we unite them to Jesus' Passion. Because Joe's story didn't get into this point and because it will help us further deflate the "second thing," let's look at it more closely. Saint Faustina Kowalska's story will help us.

LESSONS FROM FAUSTINA'S STORY. Jesus taught St. Faustina a remarkable prayer, the Chaplet of Divine Mercy. (For full instructions on how to pray it, see "References and Notes.") By that prayer, Faustina learned to unite her own little sufferings to Jesus' infinite sacrifice on the Cross and then to offer it to God the Father, "Eternal Father, I offer You the Body and Blood ... of Your dearly beloved Son ... ." Through the prayer, Faustina also learned to confidently and boldly ask for huge graces, "Have mercy on us and on the *whole world.*" Even when her own sufferings were small, this combination of offering Jesus' sacrifice on the Cross and interceding with bold confidence made Faustina's prayers astonishingly powerful. How powerful? Well, consider Jesus' stunning words to her: **"For your sake I will withhold the hand which punishes; for your sake I bless the earth."**

Remember how at the beginning of this retreat, I said that Jesus would help us? Well, he has. Do you see how the idea of relying with bold confidence on Jesus' suffering is so helpful? Look at it this way. Sometimes we may not be as bold in our prayers as we could be simply because we know that souls are bought only at the price of suffering. Therefore, since our suffering or willingness to sacrifice may be limited, we don't ask for huge graces. Deep down we might be afraid of what such huge graces would cost us, but who are we fooling? How much suffering would we have to do to merit the salvation of even one soul? On our own we can merit nothing. If, however, with confident love, we unite our own little sufferings to Jesus' Passion (through praying the chaplet, for instance), they take on infinite merit! So what are we waiting for? Let's boldly ask for conversions, graces, and all that is truly good, knowing that such prayer brings great delight to the Lord.

In keeping with the goal of this retreat, I have a suggestion for where we might want to begin making our bold petitions. How about by confidently asking Jesus to (gently) make us into great saints? Let's just not forget to rely on *his* merits. That's the secret.

As I was dealing with the obstacle to our having boldness in prayer because of suffering, I wonder if another difficulty might have come up, a difficulty having to do with St. Faustina's suffering. When I described Faustina as someone who offered her little sufferings to Jesus, I bet some people who know her whole story began to think to themselves, "Wait a minute. She didn't just have 'little sufferings.' As a matter of fact, she suffered *a lot*."

Yes, it's true. Saint Faustina suffered terribly. Yet the Lord himself raised her in her littleness to his great strength in keeping with his words, "My power is made perfect in weakness" (2 Cor 12:9). He gave her a particular vocation of suffering that corresponded both to her love *and* to her littleness, and he himself helped her advance as she accepted her little crosses with great love. Eventually, her little crosses weren't so little. Yet it was he who gently led her to graduate in his "school of love." In fact, Faustina would be the first to admit that she always remained little during all the grades through which Jesus carried her.

We who may still be in the first grade of the school of love (a school of the Cross) need not get discouraged when we look at a graduate like St. Faustina. The Lord knows what grade we're in and what we can take. He's a perfect and gentle teacher, and his first advice to his students is to pay attention to the lesson at hand. He says to us, "Don't look ahead in the book!" Yes, the bad spirit may try to discourage us by getting us to look ahead, but we should strive to remain in the present moment. We should keep our eyes on our teacher and do the simple work at hand. Still, if an advanced problem comes up, even if we ourselves bring it on, our teacher himself will help us and maybe even take most of it upon himself. So there's nothing to fear. If we keep our eyes on the Master, he'll have pity on us and carry us along the way. That's how little ones progress.

As we approach the end of this section, let's remember that while suffering is unavoidable, with Jesus, it can become sweet and take on great value. That's because when we offer up our own little sufferings (and they're all little compared to the Lord's), we have the joy of knowing that we're giving consolation to Jesus. Moreover, when we unite our sufferings to those of Jesus, we have the further joy of knowing that grace and mercy is poured out on others. For, when we unite our sufferings to the Lord's, they truly are redemptive. I'd like to close these sections on suffering by briefly treating the topic of redemptive suffering.

REDEMPTIVE SUFFERING. In his great goodness and mercy, Jesus allows us to participate in his redeeming action in the world. In fact, he needs us. In a very real sense, he needs our suffering to be united with his in order to save souls. We can begin to understand this mystery if we reflect on some puzzling words of St. Paul: "I rejoice in my sufferings for your sake, and in my flesh I complete what is lacking in the suffering of Christ for the sake of his body, the Church ..." (Col 1:24). How can St. Paul write that there's something "lacking" in the suffering of Christ? Jesus' suffering is objectively enough to save everyone, and the graces his suffering merits are available to all. In this sense, there's absolutely nothing lacking in his suffering. Yet there's a kind of "lack" in Christ's suffering in the sense that not everyone subjectively accepts his grace and mercy. Moreover, there's also a lack in his suffering when people don't *fully* accept his grace and mercy, that is, when they do so halfheartedly and with reservations and conditions. It's precisely in such situations where people reject or don't fully accept God's grace that our sufferings and bold prayers can come in to "complete what is lacking."

There's a mysterious respect the Lord has for human free will. He will not (and cannot) force us to choose him and love him. Yet, when we use our free will on behalf of others, we somehow can influence the free will of those other people. How this happens, we don't know. Still, because of this influence we can have on one another, Jesus and Mary constantly plead with us to pray and to offer up our sufferings, especially for unrepentant sinners. Think, for instance, of Our Lady of Fatima who was so sad because, as she said to the shepherd children, many souls go to hell because no one prays and offers up suffering for them. Or think of our Lord's sobering words to St.

Faustina, "Be assured that the grace of eternal salvation for certain souls in their final moment depends on your prayer."

Why is our role so important? We don't know, but it is. Our prayers and little sufferings really can have great power to move souls — so let's not waste them. In fact, let's go to Jesus' Eucharistic Heart with great confidence and boldly beg the Father for the grace of conversion for unrepentant sinners as we unite our own little sufferings to the suffering of Christ:

> Father, behold the suffering of your Son, Jesus. I lift him up to you. Although I'm weak and don't have much to offer by myself, dear Father, your Son's merits are infinite. So, behold, to your Son's suffering, I unite my own, and I ask you to save all those poor, unrepentant sinners who have no one else to pray for them. Yes, Father, I believe that your Son's infinite merits can accomplish this.

As we're on our way to church to make this bold prayer, we step inside and, that's right, yet another obstacle rises up before us.

Second Obstacle: Our Weaknesses, Sinfulness, and Attachments

Have you ever had the experience where, when it came time to pray, you found yourself dragging your feet? For instance, have you ever gone to your local parish for Eucharistic Adoration or a Rosary and found that the fliers posted on the bulletin board in the vestibule suddenly became irresistibly interesting? Maybe the announcement "Bingo Thursday Nights" held your attention for the first time. Or perhaps you remember a time when you went into the church itself, knelt down to pray, and your mind raced to other plans and activities, to anything but prayer. Of course, distractions in prayer are common, but have you ever gone through those times when you actually welcomed distractions so as to avoid Jesus? Why do we do that? Why do we sometimes avoid the Lord?

Those times when we're tempted to avoid the Lord seem to come up most often after we've sinned, especially after we've sinned more than usual. At such times, we may be ashamed and reluctant to go to Jesus. We may be afraid of what he might say and that he'll be angry with us. We may be too full of pride to humble ourselves and look at what we've done. Thus, when we're weighed down by sin, we'd rather be distracted than face the Lord in prayer. For those of us who want to console the Lord's Heart, however, this won't do, for avoiding Jesus deeply pierces his Sacred Heart. Hasn't he shown us how gentle he is? What are we afraid of?

Our own darkness can be a major obstacle that prevents us from going to the Lord. Thankfully, in our friend, St. Thérèse of Lisieux, we have a great helper in the task of removing this obstacle. She'll help us find the courage to go to the Lord when we feel the weight of our weaknesses, sinfulness, and attachments.

WEAKNESSES. Our weaknesses can often prevent us from going to Jesus. By "weaknesses," I mean our imperfections and inability to make concrete progress in the spiritual life. For instance, we may desire to be patient, gentle, and kind, but despite our resolutions and efforts, we find that we're often not as loving as we'd like to be.

Our weaknesses can send us into a downward spiral that begins when we notice them. So, for instance, we may come to realize that month after month we tend to confess the same venial sins. As we reflect on these recurring faults, we may begin to think we'll never overcome them. This then leads us to hate our weaknesses as we feel discouraged because of them. Finally, in our discouragement, we hide from the Lord, because we doubt his love for us and maybe even see him as the mean ogre depicted in the Jansenist paintings.

St. Thérèse helps us to avoid this downward spiral into the darkness of discouragement. She teaches us a completely different attitude. Like all of us, she surely had weaknesses. Unlike many of us, though, she didn't hate them and get discouraged. In fact, she accepted her weaknesses and even loved them, and she tells us we ought to love our weaknesses, too. If this sounds like the height of spiritual sloth, don't worry, it's not. Let's see exactly what she means.

Remember how at the beginning of Part One, we learned about St. Thérèse's "totally new" way to holiness and how she described it as a kind of "spiritual elevator"? Well, now she wants to tell us to love our weaknesses, because they're our ticket onto that elevator. In fact, she wants all little souls to know that they've got this ticket and that they just need to step into the elevator. Yet there's a problem. So many little souls don't even know there is such an elevator. They're too busy gaping at the rough stairway of perfection, which they're obviously too little to climb. Staring away at that big stairway, they think to themselves, "It's impossible for me to reach the heights of holiness." That's when holy desires dissipate, along with the energy to persevere. To those discouraged little souls, Thérèse says — no, she cries: "Don't lose hope! Don't give up! There's an elevator right next to you, and you've got a ticket for it!"

Do we hear her? Great. Do we see the elevator? Well, probably not. It's invisible, and before we can step into it, we first need to know a bit more about what it is and what stepping into it means.

The elevator is the Heart of Jesus. Now, those of us with good memories might be saying: "Wait a minute. That's not what Thérèse said earlier. Earlier she said that the elevator is the arms of Jesus." That's right. She did. It's that, too. Here's what I mean. Mercy has two aspects: heart and arms. The heart part always comes first. It's like this: Mercy begins with a movement of the heart, a movement of compassion for someone who suffers. Then, this compassion tends to overflow into a movement of the arms, a movement that reaches out to help alleviate the suffering of the other. These two aspects of mercy, heart and arms, are beautifully depicted in the Image of Divine Mercy, which can be found on the inside back cover of this book. In this image, we see Jesus' pierced Heart and the two rays of mercy that reach out, like two arms, to embrace the one who suffers.

Anyway, the heart part of mercy is what I mean when I say the Heart of Jesus is the elevator. The arm part of mercy is what Thérèse means when she says the arms of Jesus are the elevator. We're just describing different aspects of the same thing: the mercy of Jesus. Let's look more closely at Jesus' twofold mercy — heart and arms — which is our way (elevator) to holiness.

As we just learned, seeing another's suffering starts in our hearts the first movement of mercy (compassion). Some kinds of suffering, however, move our hearts more quickly and deeply than do others. This is true of all hearts, including the Heart of Jesus. Saint Thérèse, who knew the secrets of Jesus' Heart so well, teaches us about one specific kind of suffering that seems to move the Lord's Heart more than any other.

Jesus' Heart is particularly moved with compassion when he sees anguished little souls stuck at the bottom of the rough stairway of perfection. His Heart absolutely breaks when he further sees so many of these souls falling into the pits of discouragement, despondency, and even despair. In fact, this situation has become too much for him. It's caused him to snap, once again. Yet this time when he snaps, look out! For this time he does more than simply reveal his Heart, as he did to St. Margaret Mary. This time the arms of his heartfelt compassion reach down to embrace such little souls and carry them to the heights of holiness, as he taught to St. Thérèse.

How blessed we are to live in such a time of God's mercy! Of course, that God offers us such extraordinary mercy might not seem fair to the big souls who came before us and to those who still make the laborious climb up the steep stairway of perfection — but who can begrudge God's generosity? After all, he's surely generous to all, and he's free to do what he wants with his mercy (see Mt 20:15). The best thing for us is simply to accept his superabundant mercy with gratitude.

Okay, so the elevator is the Heart and arms of Jesus, which are so generously open to us little souls. Now, are we ready to accept? Are we ready to step in? Great. Then here's how we do it: by continually trying to step up. In other words, we step into the elevator of Jesus' arms by trying to climb the stairway of perfection. Yes, even if we can't climb these stairs, the way we step into Jesus' arms is by continuing to *try* to climb, by continuing to *try* to grow in virtue and holiness. Yet this kind of stepping up (stepping in) requires that we make our efforts with a different attitude than before. For, whereas before we may have gotten discouraged by our inability to climb the stairs, now we try not to. We accept that we might never even climb one stair! Nevertheless, we peacefully keep trying, knowing that Jesus comes down, lifts us up, and eventually carries us to the heights. We might not see him doing it, but he does. We might not feel like we're going anywhere, but we are. We might not think anything has changed, but it has.

Yes, the elevator of the Little Way is a bit strange. It's a way of holiness that doesn't seem to work. In other words, little souls who are in the elevator often look no different than other souls. They have vices and struggles and imperfections just like everyone else, but that's actually part of the Lord's strategy as he works in little souls: He likes to keep them little. He knows that if they were to see themselves bounding with great strides up the steep stairway of perfection, they suddenly wouldn't be so little, and so they wouldn't move his Heart as deeply. They'd become big souls who don't feel the need to rely completely on Jesus for everything, and so they wouldn't reach those highest heights in heaven reserved for those who accept the lowest places here on earth. Yes, Jesus likes to keep little souls little, so he can give them the biggest gifts, and though it may seem like they don't make any progress, they actually do. Jesus just hides this fact from them.

Okay, so we're on the elevator. That is, we keep trying to step up, still seem to be making little or no progress, and yet we keep trusting that Jesus is raising us to the heights of holiness. Now, I have to admit, riding this elevator isn't always easy. For it truly isn't easy to keep up hope while remaining down in the darkness of being little, especially when our old friends, the Jansenists, come along to try to steal away our hope.

Remember the Jansenists? They're the ones who can't stand to see sinners going to Jesus. Well, guess what. They especially can't stand it when the sinners going to Jesus are the weakest and littlest of souls. Therefore, they often try to discourage such souls who struggle at the bottom of the stairway. Before the Little Way, the Jansenists succeeded splendidly. They sent droves of little souls into the pits of despair. Yet now they're angry, because they see all these new little souls at the bottom of the stairway who refuse to despair. In fact, seeing this drives them nuts, and in their crazy misery, they rush right up to those faithful little souls and try even harder to push them over the precipice of despair with words such as these:

Hey, you there, trying to climb that stair. Yeah, you. Don't you see this stairway is way too big for you? You'll never make it to the top. What's that? You think the Little Way is going to take you there? Haven't you realized that even the Little Way is too big for someone like you? Look at you. You're pathetic. You can't even point to one virtue in which you're big. And you think you're following St. Thérèse? Ha! Have you ever taken a close look at her? She was full of virtues! She's a Saint with a capital "S." And guess what. The Church doesn't give that title to just anyone. A saint has got to have heroic virtue. Thérèse had it. What about you? Ha! You've got *nothing*. You can't even stand in Thérèse's shadow. Yes, there's no doubt about it. Even the Little Way is too big for someone like you.

The Jansenists may be right. Maybe we don't have a single virtue in which we're big. Or do we? By the grace of God, little souls going the Little Way are big on *trust*. They trust in the mercy of God. They trust in God's promise of mercy, the promise that he'll satisfy their desires for holiness, even if it seems impossible. They trust in the merciful Heart of Jesus that, they know, can't resist their humble confidence. They trust, they trust, they trust. Such humble trust is something the Jansenists don't understand. They just don't get it. Still, maybe the Jansenists do get something. For they make a good point: St. Thérèse sure seemed to have a lot more virtues than humble confidence. In fact, when we look closely at her life, it sometimes seems as if she weren't such a little soul after all. For example, when we see her fervor, self-sacrifice, and suffering, she begins to look very big, indeed. So, maybe her Little Way is really just a big way wrapped in flowery rhetoric. Maybe it's just a sugar-coated version of the rough stairway of perfection. Maybe it's not simply about humble confidence after all.

When Jansenist ideas like these begin to settle in our minds, we start to go from Thérèse's elevator to the Jansenist roller coaster. That roller coaster goes something like this. First, we read or hear about Thérèse's Little Way and are lifted high with hope, "Maybe I really can become a saint!" Then, at other times, we hear people talk about Thérèse's heroic holiness, become awed by her innumerable sacrifices, unwavering kindness, and total detachment from creatures, and then we feel crushed to the dust. As we're eating that dust, we think to ourselves: "I guess Thérèse really wasn't so little after all. There's no way I can be like her. There's no hope that I can become a saint." Thus, the roller coaster goes up, up, up with hope and then rushes down, down, down to discouragement and despair.

If any of us are on this ride, it's time to step off. Yes, it's time to step off the coaster and back into the elevator, and it's time to stay there. How? By reading and taking deeply to heart one of the greatest letters ever written.

Thank God for St. Thérèse's sister, Marie. If it weren't for her, Thérèse would never have written the letter that crushes the Jansenist roller coaster to smithereens and sets souls securely in the little elevator. Here's the background to that glorious letter.

Thérèse had written an earlier letter to her sister Marie in which she illustrated the Little Way with a story about a little bird with broken wings. Marie read the story, but it didn't have the effect Thérèse had intended — it didn't enkindle Marie's hope for holiness. Why didn't it? Because Marie knew better. She knew her holy sister and she knew her miserable self. She knew that Thérèse was a saint and that she wasn't. Thus, poor Marie wrote back to Thérèse, expressing doubt that she could soar with her sister on the heights of love. Thérèse's remarkable response to Marie deserves slow, prayerful reading. For it's not just addressed to Marie. It's written to all little souls. It's meant for you and for me:

> Dear Sister, ... How can you ask me if it is possible for you to love God as I love Him? ...
>
> If you had understood the story of my little bird, you would not have asked me this question. My [_____ (fill in the blank: virtues, talents, many gifts, etc.)] *are nothing*; they are not what give me the unlimited confidence that I feel in my heart. They are, to tell the truth, the spiritual riches that *render one unjust*, when one rests in them with complacence and when one believes they are *something great*. ... Ah! I really feel that it is not this at all that pleases God in my little soul; what pleases Him is that *He sees me loving my littleness and my poverty, the blind hope that I have in His mercy.* ... That is my only treasure. ... [W]hy would this treasure not be yours?
>
> ... Oh, dear Sister, I beg you, understand your little girl, understand that to love Jesus, to be His *victim of love*, the weaker one is, without desires or virtues, the more suited one is for the workings of this consuming and transforming Love. ... [B]ut we must consent to remain always poor and without strength, and this is the difficulty ... . Ah! let us remain then *very far* from all that sparkles, let us love our littleness, let us love to feel nothing, then we shall be poor in spirit, and Jesus will come to look for us [and] He will transform us in flames of love.
>
> ... Oh! how I would like to be able to make you understand what I feel! ... It is confidence and nothing but confidence that must lead us to Love (emphasis in original).

Interesting. The one whom Pope St. Pius X called the "greatest saint of modern times" doesn't say that what makes her so pleasing to God are her virtues, sacrifices, desires, or good works. In fact, to her, all that is *nothing*. No, what makes her so pleasing to God, she says, is that *she loves her littleness and her poverty*. Indeed, her "only treasure" is a "blind hope" in God's mercy. Did we catch that? It's her *only treasure*. Again, it's not her virtues, sacrifices, or anything else. It's simply her blind hope in God's mercy. It's her trust. So when we hear people say, "Oh, that Thérèse wasn't such a little soul. She was quite big!" we can remember that she, a Doctor of the Church, tells us that her only treasure was her humble confidence in God's mercy.

Now, here's a good question for each of us to ask ourselves, "Can I trust Jesus?" When we move on to face the next obstacle (No. 3), we'll look more closely at what trust is and how we can live it. It's enough to say here that trust isn't so difficult or complicated. Little children do it easily. I'd also add that if we trust Jesus — which we *can* do — then Thérèse's treasure of holiness will also be ours. For, again, "It is confidence and nothing but confidence" that will lead us to the heights of holiness. So, can we trust Jesus? Why not? Why can't this treasure be ours?

Remember, our weaknesses and lack of virtue aren't the problem. In fact, according to Thérèse, the weaker we are, having neither virtues nor even desires, the more ready we are to be taken up by the elevator of the Little Way. The problem is our "bigness" and lack of trust. So, we should strive to remain little and trusting. We should strive to see our weaknesses not as so many obstacles, but rather as part of a three-fold ticket to holiness. In other words, (1) if we can accept and even love our weaknesses, (2) if we can say no to temptations to give up our efforts to grow in holiness even after seemingly endless falls, and (3) if we can look up at Jesus' merciful Heart with great confidence, then we can be assured that the arms of his Heart will scoop us up and place us high in the heights of holiness, even right there beside Thérèse herself! But don't just take my word for it. Read again Thérèse's letter to Marie or simply listen in on her heartfelt prayer:

> O Jesus! why can't I tell all *little souls* how unspeakable is Your condescension? I feel that if You found a soul weaker and littler than mine, which is impossible, You would be pleased to grant it still greater favors, provided it abandoned itself with total confidence to Your Infinite Mercy (emphasis in original).

*S*INFULNESS. Okay, I hope we now realize our weaknesses are not obstacles to going to Jesus. Yet, even if we learn to love our weaknesses, there's still a problem. For, when we're talking about imperfections and sins of weakness (those venial sins over which we don't have much control), then St. Thérèse's words make sense. But what about when we're talking about deliberate sin? There's a big difference between unintentionally falling asleep during a time of prayer and actually deciding to take a nap rather than attend Sunday Mass. Such sins are another story, right? How can the very evil that crucified Jesus be a consolation to him? Sure, Thérèse can say, "What pleases him is to see me love my littleness and my poverty," but would she also include her sinfulness as part of that poverty? Perhaps surprisingly, Thérèse teaches that even our deliberate sins and willful attachments can be a means to consoling Jesus.

I once heard a story, attributed to St. Thérèse, that illustrates her Little Way of humble confidence with regard to dealing with one's sinfulness. In the story, two daughters have done something serious to offend their loving father. Later, when they hear their father's approaching footsteps, one of them runs off and hides while the other runs to her father, jumps into his arms, and confesses her offense to him. The father loves both his daughters, but one has broken his heart while the other has consoled it.

St. Thérèse reminds us of the daughter who jumps into her father's arms when we read the lines that gloriously conclude her autobiography:

Even though I had on my conscience all the sins that can be committed, I would go, my heart broken with sorrow, and throw myself into Jesus' arms, for I know how much He loves the prodigal child who returns to Him.

We'll always be stumbling and falling. We've got to accept that fact while striving to avoid sin. Yet, when we do fall, even seriously and voluntarily, we ought to have the attitude of the repentant child who jumps into her father's arms with great confidence in his mercy. We sometimes forget that this is what most pleases the Lord, namely, when we go to him with confidence despite, or rather, *because* of our sins, weaknesses, and attachments.

Still, the extravagance of God's mercy might not be something we simply find hard to remember — we might also find it hard to believe. People sometimes get stuck in a subtle form of pride from which they respond to the Lord's offer of mercy with words such as these: "No, I won't receive it. I've been too bad. I've committed this sin one too many times. Surely, I've already used up my last chance to have his mercy." Such words not only punish the person saying them but also the Lord, whose Heart breaks when he hears them. After all, why was Jesus scourged and crowned with thorns? Why did he suffer and die on the Cross? Why was his Heart pierced with a lance? All of this was so we might receive his mercy. Therefore, when people say, "It's too cheap to just go to confession after what I've done." They're wrong. The grace of forgiveness available in the Sacrament of Confession is not cheap. It cost the Lord dearly. While this painful fact should make us want to flee from sin, it should also remind us that God's mercy is always there for us because of the infinite price that's already been paid. To be sure, in order to receive the Lord's mercy, we need to have the intention not to sin again, but this doesn't mean we won't sin again. We will sin again, in one form or another, but God's mercy is always there for us when we turn away from sin and go back to him.

To help us remember and believe more firmly in the Lord's great mercy, let's meditate on some words of mercy that Jesus spoke to various mystics.

To many mystics — for example, to St. Margaret Mary, Sr. Josefa Menedez, and St. Faustina Kowalska — Jesus shared some of the deepest sorrow of his Sacred Heart. For instance, he often complained to these dear friends of the flames of love that burn his Heart. He explained to them that these flames burn him because he longs to heal and forgive sinners but that very few of them come to him to receive his forgiveness. Thus, his rejected mercy stays in his Heart and burns it, causing him great pain. He said to St. Faustina:

> **The flames of mercy are burning Me. I desire to pour them out upon human souls. Oh, what pain they cause Me when they do not want to accept them!**

With these "burning flames" of the Sacred Heart in mind, we can better appreciate Jesus' words to Sr. Josefa, "It rests Me to forgive." We can also appreciate similar words he spoke to another blessed soul, "When you give me your sins, you give me the joy of being your Savior." What amazing testimony! Our very sins, when we cast them into the flames of the Lord's Heart, actually give him rest and joy! If only we would always believe that he so ardently desires to forgive us. When sin weighs down upon us, may we remember Jesus' love for us and the longing of his Heart to forgive. To help us remember, let's ponder some more of Jesus' words, this time to Sr. Josefa:

> I am Love! My Heart can no longer contain its devouring flames. I love souls so dearly … . My Heart is burning with desire to attract souls to itself in order to forgive them.

We must be convinced that when we place our sins in the furnace of Jesus' Sacred Heart, it makes the flames of his love explode into an ever greater conflagration. These flames, unlike the flames of his rejected mercy, don't burn him and bring him great pain. Instead, they burn up our sins and bring him great consolation. That's why when we empty our sinful hearts before Jesus, it gives him rest, allows him to love us even more, and gives him the joy of being our Savior. He waits and longs for this. May we realize what immense value there is to placing this kindling, which is our sinfulness (weaknesses and attachments, too), into the flames of his Heart. When we produce some of this fuel, rather than get discouraged, let's repent of it and cast it into those burning flames. May we never weary of this, for he never wearies of forgiving. An excerpt from the meditation book, *Come to Me in the Blessed Sacrament*, by Fr. Vincent Martin Lucia, summarizes all this for us, while including a new and remarkable insight:

> Like fire that transforms everything into itself ... Jesus transforms everything to good in the fire of His Divine Love, drawing good out of evil, drawing a greater good out of a greater evil, consuming even our very faults and failures (like straw thrown into a burning furnace) and using them to make us more humble and to bring us even closer to His divine Heart. "In my weakness, I find my strength."

Did you catch Fr. Lucia's new insight? It's the part about how the fire of Jesus' love draws good out of evil, drawing an even greater good out of a greater evil. This is a truly amazing aspect of God's merciful love: From our evil it can bring out not only good but an even greater good! This is precisely what God did with the sin of Adam and Eve. He brought a greater good out of their sin by giving us Jesus Christ, our Savior. Thus, during the *Exultet* at the Easter Vigil Liturgy, the Church sings, "O happy fault ... which gained for us so great a Redeemer!" Such is the greatness of God's mercy. Now, this doesn't mean we should sin so God can bring a greater good out of it. As St. Paul says, it doesn't work like that (see Rom 3:8). Nevertheless, we truly can pray and have confidence that God will grant the heartfelt prayer of repentance that says:

O Jesus, I feel that I've ruined everything by my sin. I'm so sorry for what I've done, and I will do my best not to do it again. Dear Jesus, by the power of your infinite mercy, I trust that somehow you can fix not only the evil I've done but bring an even greater good out of it.

Such humble and bold confidence consoles the Lord's Heart. He hears and answers such sincere prayers. It's up to him when and how he'll answer them, but he truly does answer them. Thus, there's no reason for us to get discouraged or despair because of our sinfulness, and there's every reason to go to Jesus who is so rich in mercy.

*A*TTACHMENTS. Having looked at the importance of having confidence in Jesus when we experience our weakness and having further read that we console him by giving him our sins, we're now ready to turn our attention to a third area that falls under the category "Second Obstacle," namely, attachments.

As we begin focusing on our attachments, it might be helpful to recall something we learned earlier about the First Principle and Foundation and the notion "first things first," something I referred to as the "primacy of contemplation." Basically, the primacy of contemplation means that if we stay fixed on the goodness and glory of the Lord, we'll automatically and with a certain ease let go of our attachments — in other words, we'll begin to have an attitude of indifference without having to force it. Let's keep this idea of the primacy of contemplation at the back of our minds as we now deal specifically with attachments.

It may happen that we don't go to the Lord because we have attachments and are afraid he'll make us get rid of them. For instance, we may still be clinging to our coveted doughnuts, tightly clasping them at our chests. Now, if the Lord sees us doing this, does he say, "Well, you'd better stay away from me until you're ready to let go of those doughnuts"? No, that's the Jansenist Jesus, the one who demands that we be perfect before we go to him. Instead, the real Jesus says — no, he pleads —

"Come to me." One might likely reply, "But, Lord, I'm so attached to this or that." Still, he beckons, "Come to me."

Jesus simply wants us to go to him. When we do go, to our surprise, he often tells us: "No, you're not ready to let go of those doughnuts, but please just come to me, be with me, and console my Heart. Do me the kindness of holding my hand, for my Heart is filled with such sorrow." So there we are, clutching the doughnuts with one hand and holding onto the Lord with the other. No, it's not perfect, but that's the way it often goes with us little ones. This attitude of going to the Lord as we are is a surprisingly effective way to console Jesus and progress in holiness.

Go to Jesus as you are. Open your heart to him as it is (not as you wish it to be). And know that Jesus loves sincerity, that he loves it when we're completely open with him. Why does he love this? Because the more open we are with him, the more deeply he can heal us — and this especially applies to his being able to heal us of our attachments. Let's see how we can be more open with the Lord about our attachments, so he can heal us of them more deeply.

Okay, so let's begin by going back to that scene where we're clutching our doughnuts with one hand and holding onto Jesus with the other. Was the Lord offended? No. Was he indifferent? No. In fact, he was pleased. Jesus is always pleased when we humbly go to him as we are. He's also pleased when we keep in mind who he is. Of course, he's God — but he's also our friend. As our friend, he especially loves it when we keep in mind his gentleness and mercy. Hasn't he shown us how gentle he is with us? He wants us to remember that. He also wants us to remember that he knows we're little. In other words, he knows we're not big enough to climb the rough stairway of perfection. So why are we often so afraid he'll ask us for something beyond our strength? Haven't we already heard how he says to us: "No, you're not ready to let go of that just yet, but come. Don't be afraid. Come and sit here with me"?

The Lord is so gentle and wise in leading us. The steps he'll ask us to take toward holiness will be steps that are appropriate to little souls — "little steps." Yes, he knows just the right step that prepares us for the next and then the next until, before we know it, such little steps have brought us much farther and higher than we ever expected to climb. (Surprise! The elevator is working.) Moreover, he does all this with surprisingly little pain.

One of the ways the Lord makes our progress relatively easy is by beginning to detach our hearts from something well before he asks it of us. He usually does this without us realizing it. One day, there's something we thought we could never live without, something that, on a bad day, we'd be terrified even to mention to him, because we'd be afraid he'd tell us to let go of it. Then, the next day, the day on which he asks us to give it over to him, we find that we hardly want it anymore. This is one of God's great mercies to little souls who trust in him. He gently and imperceptively changes their desires. In case we haven't already given him this degree of power over our lives, let's give it to him now:

> Jesus, behold, I give you my heart. If my desires aren't in harmony with yours, then please change them according to your wisdom and love. Dear Jesus, you know that by myself, I'm too weak to change my desires, but you can do it. Jesus, I trust you to do it. Jesus, I thank you in advance for doing it.

Of course, making this prayer doesn't mean there won't be times in our lives when the Lord asks us to let go of something to which we still cling very tightly. It may seem during such times that the Lord wants from us a big step, indeed. Yet, here again, there's no need to be afraid. The Divine Physician is gentle and can make even this kind of heart surgery easy, if only we'll trust him. So, if it happens that there's some deep attachment we really must get rid of now, we begin to hear the Lord beckoning, "Come to me." We go to him hesitatingly as we clutch the attachment with all our might. With a twinkle in his eye and a smile, he keeps beckoning, "Come. Come. Come closer." We go to him, and we look at him. We look at our attachment. Then, we look at him. Slowly, as we're standing in his gaze, the strings of our attachment begin to break, though we may not even realize it. An analogy may help us understand this better. Have you ever played fetch with a dog? You throw a ball and the dog retrieves it. Sometimes when the dog returns, however, it doesn't drop the ball. "Drop it," you say, but the dog doesn't drop it. You try grabbing the ball from the dog's mouth, but it doesn't let go and maybe even growls. If this happens, what do you do? Here's a suggestion. If the dog won't drop the ball, try getting down there with it. Pet it real nicely and say, "Nice doggie ... that's a *good* dog." As it begins to wag its tail and relax, grasp the ball without the dog noticing, and pull it out with a quick and easy jerk. It works like a charm. Well, that's sometimes how the Lord deals with us. Sound strange? Allow me to explain.

When we go to Jesus, especially to his Real Presence in the Blessed Sacrament, he fills us with his love and peace, and at the same time, in his great mercy, he silently loosens our grip on our attachments. After some time, without us realizing it, he holds what he's just pulled out of our mouths. There it is in his beautiful hands, or rather, there it is as it's burning up in the flames of his merciful Heart: that dirty, old ball covered with spit! The moral, of course, is to trust the Lord, to go to him. He'll help us become detached, and it'll happen with a certain ease.

Yes, trust the Lord. Go to him as you are with all your attachments, and don't worry. With some things he'll say, "No, you're not ready to get rid of that, but please just sit here with me and console my Heart, which hurts so much." At other times, as you're sitting there before him, clinging to something very tightly, he just might begin by saying, "Nice doggie ... ." But again, don't worry. Be completely honest about your deepest attachments. You can even say, "Lord, you *know* I'm not ready to let go of this ... but if you want, you can change my desire for it." That's not a cop out. In fact, Jesus made a similar prayer in the Garden of Gethsemane, "My Father, if it be possible, let this cup pass away from me;

yet not as I will, but as thou wilt" (Mt 26:39). So, trust him. Don't be afraid to stand before his gaze of love. If any surgery is needed, know that with the primacy of contemplation, it's virtually painless. As we've just come to learn, the Divine Physician uses anesthesia.

R*EVIEWING OUR PRINCIPLE AND FOUNDATION.* I hope many of the obstacles that prevent us from going to Jesus and that, therefore, prevent us from consoling his Heart are getting removed. Now that we've spent all this time looking at obstacles, let's take a moment to review our principle and foundation.

What do we do first when we want to remember our principle and foundation? That's right. We look at Jesus' Sacred Heart and hear him say, "Behold this Heart which loves so much yet is so little loved." Then, seeing his sorrow, each of us should respond, "Jesus, I want to console your Heart."

This time, as we're reviewing our principle and foundation, let's reflect on something new. As we look at the Lord's Heart and hear him say to us, "Behold this Heart which loves so much ... ," let's reflect. Has the Lord loved us "so much"? Indeed he has, and in so many ways. Think about this: We're making a retreat. How many people get to make a retreat? Not many. How much the Lord loves us to give us this time of retreat. Now think of this: We have a solid principle and foundation. How many people have a clear and solid principle and foundation? Probably not many. How much the Lord loves us to give us a clear and solid principle and foundation. Yes, the Lord has given us so much. Mindful of this, let's look at his Heart and hear him, again, saying to us, "Behold this Heart which loves so much yet is so little loved." Let's each respond with a strong, "Yes, Jesus, I will console you!" How about it? Is that our response? Great.

Now, how about this: Why don't we be especially generous? After all, the Lord has given us so much. Let's say to him, "Jesus, I want to console you in the greatest possible way." Why not? We've learned how gentle he is. He won't give us more than we can take. So, are you with me? Do you want to console Jesus in the best possible way? Great. Then let's get to it. Yes, let's get started by making some good old reparation.

Reparation. There's that frightening word again. Perhaps we're still putting on the brakes because we're afraid of suffering. Let's deal with this stubborn obstacle once and for all.

Third Obstacle: Fear of Suffering, Again

In an attempt to knock down the obstacle "fear of suffering," I'm going to give it a one-two punch. In other words, I'm going to treat it in two parts. In the first part, we'll see that the best possible way to console Jesus is so simple and easy — there's nothing to fear. In the second part, we'll come to understand just how powerful this best possible way is — there's everything to gain.

1. The Best Way is the Simplest and Easiest

*W*HAT'S THE BEST WAY TO CONSOLE JESUS? If we want to console the Lord's Heart in the best possible way, then we first need to find out what that best way is. To do this, I propose we begin by trying to discover what hurts the Lord's Heart most. For, if we can discover what that is, then we might not be too far from finding out how we can best console his Heart.

So, what hurts the Lord most? Was it the nails that were driven into his wrists and feet? Or was it the sight, through his supernatural vision, of serious sins such as adultery or murder? Surely, seeing such sins would have pierced Jesus' Heart. It may come as a surprise, however, that such sins don't seem to be the ones that hurt him most. So what does hurt him most? Jesus gave an answer to St. Faustina. He told her that what hurts him most is the sin of distrust, that is, when people don't trust in his merciful love, especially when it's those closest to him who don't trust him. That may sound strange, at first. After all, sins involving sex or violence tend to capture our attention the most. Yet it's different with the Lord. The following little meditation from his Passion may help us understand this point better.

It is night. See the Lord Jesus as he's arrested in the Garden of Gethsemane, bound with chains, and then led to the house of the High Priest. The temple guards treat him roughly and lead him into a cold, dimly lit room — the room of his trial. As the priests and elders file in, some of them mock Jesus. Then, growing in boldness, they begin to strike him, pull his beard, and spit in his face. While receiving all this abuse, Jesus prays for them. Above all, he's most hurt by the thought that these men — men for whom he'll give up his life — have decided to reject him.

Briefly, there's a pause in the violence as the priests and elders discuss among themselves how best to condemn Jesus to death. In the flickering light of torches, you see the deep sorrow on the Lord's sullied face. As you contemplate his downcast countenance, his already closed eyelids suddenly tighten and his brow stiffens. A faint groan issues from his mouth, and it looks like he's about to fall over. You ask him with surprise, "What's the matter, Lord? What just happened?" Without looking up, he whispers, "My friend Peter just denied me three times."

This brief meditation may help us to understand better the sensitivity of the Lord's Heart. For what wounds him most is, indeed, when those closest to him reject him and don't trust him. That's why Peter's denials hurt him so much. That's also why (we can imagine) Judas' betrayal of Jesus with a kiss must have ripped the Lord's Heart more than the scourging that would later tear at his back. Of course, the Lord is wounded whenever someone doubts his goodness and love, but when such doubt fills the hearts of his closest friends, the very ones to whom he has revealed so much of his love, it's almost too much for him to bear.

Thankfully, I have some good news. Although it truly is so easy to hurt the Lord in the greatest possible way, it's also so easy to console him in the best way. For, if what hurts Jesus most is a lack of trust, then what do you think consoles him most? That's right, *trust*. However, it's a bit more complicated than this, for what does trust really mean?

Shortly before writing this retreat, I found a surprising answer to this crucial question while speaking with an expert on the message of Divine Mercy, Fr. Seraphim Michalenko, MIC, at the National Shrine of The Divine Mercy in Stockbridge, Massachusetts.

At one point during our conversation, I asked Fr. Michalenko, "Father, it's all about consoling the Heart of Jesus, isn't it?"

He looked pleased with my question and answered with an enthusiastic, "Yes, it is!"

Encouraged by his response, I continued, "And we want to console Jesus in the best possible way, right?"

"Right," he said.

"And the best way to console him is to remove the thorn that hurts his Heart most, the thorn that's lack of trust in his merciful love."

"Right again."

Confidently, I stated my conclusion, "And so the best way to remove that thorn and console him is to trust him."

"Michael, you're absolutely right."

"Great!" I said to myself, "It's all about trusting Jesus in order to console him."

At that point, I thought I was all set. I thought I completely understood. Well, that's when Fr. Seraphim interrupted my contentment: "And how do you *live* trust? What's its concrete expression in your daily living?"

I was stumped, "I don't know."

His answer changed my life: "The way you live trust is by praise and thanksgiving, to praise and thank God in all things. That's what the Lord said to St. Faustina."

As soon as I heard that, I knew it was true, for I remembered how Blessed Mother Teresa of Calcutta had often written about the importance of accepting everything with a smile, with praise and thanksgiving. I also thought to myself: "Yes, this is true. For this is the Little Way of surrender, acceptance, and childlike trust taught by St. Thérèse of Lisieux." I think I had in mind one of my favorite passages from her autobiography:

"Jesus does not demand great actions from us but simply *surrender* and *gratitude*. Has he not said: '… OFFER TO GOD THE SACRIFICES OF PRAISE AND THANKSGIVING'[?]" (Ps 49:14; emphasis in original).

So, the best way to console Jesus' Heart is to give him our trust, and according to the expert, the best way to live trust is with an attitude of praise and thanksgiving, the way of joyful, trustful acceptance of God's will. Because this is the best way to console the Lord's Heart, we'd do well to look more closely at how we might live it. We've already learned something about this way in the section dedicated to overcoming Obstacle No. 1 (when we heard about accepting suffering), but now we'll look at it in greater detail as a spirituality of trustful acceptance.

*H*OW TO LIVE JOYFUL, TRUSTFUL ACCEPTANCE. Living joyful, trustful acceptance isn't complicated. One simply offers himself to God with confidence and then accepts everything with praise and thanksgiving, seeing all as coming from God's loving, fatherly hands. In its concrete details, this way of trustful acceptance means that we strive to let nothing disturb us and, further, that we strive to continually praise and thank God for everything. Thus, when good things come our way (by good things, I mean what makes it easy to give praise and thanks), we strive to praise and thank God for them. For instance, on a given day, we might praise and thank God for a good meal with family and friends, beautiful music, or a wonderful scene of nature. Then, when God sends (or permits) those things that often make it difficult to praise and thank him (crosses), we strive to praise and thank him for them, too. Because it's much harder to offer praise and thanks for the crosses in our lives, let's look more closely at this part of trustful acceptance.

When we live in a spirit of joyful, trustful acceptance, the focus isn't on actively choosing our own crosses. That's more for people living the big way of holiness. Rather, as the name indicates, the focus is on joyful, trustful *acceptance*. We trust God to gently send us crosses that will most benefit us, and then we strive to accept them with a smile.

It's kind of a question of efficiency. Instead of wasting energy trying to choose lots of penances, the spirituality of trustful acceptance focuses on accepting well the crosses God chooses for us. For divinely chosen crosses are just the right ones: not too heavy and not too light. If we keep this in mind, it'll be easier to accept them with praise and thanksgiving. Still, even if we know this, there will surely be those times when it's not so easy to praise and thank God for our crosses. I've got two suggestions for such times.

First, I suggest we try putting ourselves in God's shoes. In other words, I propose we reflect on what it must be like for God to have to see us suffer under the weight of our crosses. To help us do this, I offer the following illustration.

Imagine a father whose child needs a serious surgery. The father knows that without the surgery, his child's illness will only get worse and might even lead to death. He also knows that the surgery will hurt (for example, the shots, the post operation pains, and so on). Although the father doesn't want his child to have to suffer the surgery, he knows it's the only way for him to get better. So, of course, he takes his child to the hospital.

Now, imagine how the father would feel if his child were to kick and scream all the way to the hospital. Worse yet, imagine how he'd feel if his child were to curse him, refuse to believe in his goodness and love, and act as if his father only wanted to hurt him. It's hard enough for the father to have to see his child suffer, but such behavior would surely break his heart. So it is with God and us.

As the father in the story knows his child is sick and in need of surgery, God our Father knows we're spiritually sick and that to get better we need the "surgery" of carrying a cross. (It's a simple fact of the spiritual life that crosses are necessary to help heal us of our selfishness.) It's hard enough for God to have to see us suffer, but when we kick and scream under the weight of our crosses and refuse to believe in God's goodness and love because of them, this breaks his Heart. Reflecting on how such a childish attitude breaks the Lord's Heart might help us to accept crosses in our lives with less complaining and more praise and thanks. For, again, crosses are part of the healing process that's meant to make our souls healthy and loving. While it's surely not easy for God to have to see us suffer, he knows that allowing us to suffer is sometimes the only way of bringing us to spiritual health.

My second suggestion for how we might better accept crosses in our lives is simply to be mindful that living joyful, trustful acceptance is the best way to console Jesus. Amazingly, this way of consoling the Lord is so easy compared to what we might have thought it would have entailed. We might have thought the best form of reparation would have meant our own bloody crucifixions, but it doesn't. Now that we've learned about trustful acceptance, it should be clear that reparation isn't so scary — even this, the best form of it. See how easy Jesus has made it for us to please him? We don't need to be afraid. Still, this might require more convincing, for we may be under the influence of the myth that says the more we make ourselves suffer, the holier we are. An event in the life of St. Faustina, recounted by one of her biographers, shows this to be false:

> Before she was to begin her annual retreat, Sister Faustina went to ask her spiritual director if she could practice certain mortifications during that time. To her disappointment, Fr. Sopocko gave his consent only to some of her requests.
>
> When she returned home, she went to the chapel for a moment and there she heard in her soul: **There is more merit to one hour of meditation on My sorrowful Passion than there is to a whole year of bloody scourging; the contemplation of My painful wounds is of great profit to you, and it brings me great joy.**

These words of Jesus reveal that what gives him greater joy is not when we try to take on more suffering, but simply when we remain with him in his. We obviously can't endure a passion equal to his, but we can be with him (by means of prayer) as he suffers his out of love for us. Jesus himself tells Faustina that being with him in this way is worth more than "a whole year of bloody scourging." In other words, he gives primacy to our prayerfully being with him as he endures the Passion over our putting ourselves through self-made suffering.

At this point, it may be illuminating to ask, "What's the one, concrete, daily practice Jesus asks of us through his revelations to St. Faustina?" Guess. What do you think it might be? (Most people don't get this.) The chaplet? No. Mercy Sunday? No. It's the three o'clock hour devotion. Jesus asked that our lives always be marked by deeds of mercy (like praying the chaplet for others), but he specifically asked for something special during the three o'clock hour, the hour he died on the Cross. Did he ask that during this hour we grab a scourge and whip ourselves? No. Did he ask that we eat glass? No. Jesus didn't ask that we endure a passion but simply that we be with him as he suffers his, especially in his abandonment on the Cross. He simply desires that we keep him company amid his pain and sorrow. This is simple and relatively easy — and it doesn't have to take a long time. Jesus understands we may have other duties during the three o'clock hour. Ideally, he'd like us to make the Stations of the Cross, but even if we can't, he's happy when we at least turn our minds to him, even for a few seconds, during his abandonment on the Cross.

So, what Jesus wants from us as his consolers is simple. He asks that we go to him, be with him in his Passion, and joyfully accept (and offer in union with his Passion) the relatively little crosses he allows us to carry. In sum: He wants our trustful smile as we spiritually sit at the foot of the Cross while accepting our own small sharing in it.

Jesus requested something else of St. Faustina. Along with his request that she be with him in prayer during the three o'clock hour, he asked her to have an image of his mercy painted, the Image of Divine Mercy. That image can be found on the inside back cover of this book. (For more information about it, see Appendix Two under the section "Image of Divine Mercy.")

The Image of Divine Mercy depicts Jesus in a way that's radically different from the Jansenist paintings we heard about before. In the Image of Divine Mercy, Jesus steps toward us as rays of love and mercy issue from his Heart. At the bottom of the image is a simple prayer the Lord directed Faustina to include, "Jesus, I trust in you." Can you guess why Jesus would have directed her to include this particular prayer? (Here's a hint: He'd already been deeply wounded by people's lack of trust in him.) Jesus asked for this prayer because our trust is what gives his Heart the most relief.

One might say the Image of Divine Mercy is Jesus' heart medication. It's like this: Jesus suffers from a terribly painful heart condition, so he's written for himself a prescription for medication that will relieve him of his agony. What's the medication? It's when we receive the rays of his love and mercy and say the prayer, "Jesus, I trust in you" — for this truly consoles his Heart. So, how about it? Will we have mercy on Jesus and fill his prescription? Will we give him our trust, our praise and thanksgiving, and a smile in all circumstances? "Jesus, I trust in you." This is what consoles him best in his suffering. This is what relieves the agony of his Heart.

Because this is meant to be a retreat and not a theological treatise, let's make a meditation in order to take to heart what we've been learning in this section.

A MEDITATION FOR CONSOLING JESUS IN THE BEST WAY. We're at the bottom of the hill of Calvary, also known as Golgotha. Look up the hill. See Jesus at the top, hanging on the Cross. He doesn't see us because he's surrounded by a huge crowd of people.

The people who surround the Cross laugh at Jesus. They mock him and insult him right to his face. They aren't afraid to go to him. No, they go right up to him, laughing and even spitting at him. The Lord loves them, but his Heart is broken because of their rejection, which means their own death if they don't change, for he is Life.

Many dark shadows go in and out of the crowd. They're

demons. They enjoy stirring up the crowd to mock and torture Jesus more. Seeing us at the bottom of the hill, two of them approach. The first one stands about seven feet tall, and his face is a featureless void. He stops directly in front of you. As he towers over you, he says in a terrible, hissing voice, "You jussst ssstay right where you are and everything will be jussst fine." Meanwhile, the other demon, a ghost-like little creature no bigger than a sparrow, settles on your shoulder and whispers in your ear:

> You don't belong here. Don't you have other things to do? You don't need to be here. This is much too painful for you to see. After all, aren't you the reason for that man's torture? Don't you have some important business to take care of? Isn't that television show you like so much going to start soon? Go ahead. Go take your mind off this. There's nothing you can do. Look at the huge crowd. What difference is your being here going to make?

These words are tempting. Thoughts come into your mind: "Yes, what am I among so many? Jesus won't notice if I go home. He'll never even know I was here. Besides, it's cold, and he'll probably be dead soon anyway."

So there you are at the bottom of the hill. The crowd is overwhelming. These demons are frightening. You're a sinner aren't you? Perhaps you've lost your right to be here since you've sinned so much, and really, what can one person do amid such a multitude of people? Standing here, hesitating, you're stuck at the bottom of the hill. Meanwhile, Jesus suffers alone.

What was that? Did you hear it? What's such a beautiful sound doing amid so much blasphemy and raucous laughter? It's a woman's voice. Sweetly, it begins to fill your soul, bringing it light and peace:

> Listen and put it into your heart, my dear little child. The thing that frightens you, the thing that afflicts you, is nothing. Do not let it disturb you. Am I not

here who am your Mother? Are you not under my care and protection? Am I not the source of your joy? Are you not in the hollow of my mantle, in the crossing of my arms. Do you need something more? Let nothing else worry you or disturb you.

Mary is with us. Let's go with confidence to the foot of the Cross. Let's run there. Nothing can harm us. Mary is with us! She'll teach us what to do. Let's go console Jesus with Mary.

Filled with courage, we run up the hill. Demons scream in horror as they're cast aside by some invisible force. One cries out, "No! Don't let them! Everything will be ruined!" The ugly mob parts like the Red Sea, and some are struck dumb. We arrive at the foot of the Cross. Look up. Behold that Heart which loves so much yet is so little loved. Unfortunately, Jesus still doesn't see us. His sorrowful gaze is on the crowd.

Turn now to Mary. Speak to her from your helplessness: "Mary, what can I do? I'm so weak, and I, too, have hurt Jesus and caused this."

Smiling, despite her tears, she tenderly speaks to you:

Just tell him. Tell my Son that you love him. Thank him for what he is suffering right now out of love for you. Smile at him. Give him what you can. Here, I will help you. I will hold you up to him.

Mary takes you into her arms and lifts you close to the broken face of the Savior. He seems dazed and still doesn't see you — he only sees the rejection of the crowd. You touch his cheek with your hand and direct his face toward yours. Now he sees you. You smile and speak to him from your heart:

Lord, don't look at them. Look at me. ... Lord Jesus, even though my sins are many, I know the mercy of your Heart. I'm sorry I was afraid to go to you. I'm so sorry I left you alone. But look, here I am. Please forgive me my sins. I'm going to try to do better. Please forgive them their sins, too. Lord, if only they knew you, they'd love you.

Lord, I can't offer much right now except for my weak trust and love. Jesus, I do trust in you, and I love you. Praise you, Jesus, and thank you for everything, especially for what you're suffering right now out of love for me. I've come to be with you, my friend. Don't be sad. I love you, and there's nowhere else I'd rather be than right here, praising you, thanking you, and consoling your broken Heart.

As you go on in this way, even singing your praise and thanks to Jesus, Mary joins her voice with yours.

These acts of love take the Lord by surprise. He was longing for love and he's found a return. The demons are howling and grinding their teeth, but they're a million miles away. In this one moment, as you come to Jesus as you are, you distract him from all the abuse, rejection, and sin that his Sacred Heart is always enduring.

Of course, Jesus still feels the pain of rejection and sin, but as he looks from the Cross and sees your confident love, you really do distract him from the circus of abuse that surrounds him. Suddenly, he says to you, "My beloved friend, seeing your great confidence and love, I wish I could suffer even more." Yes, seeing you here, loving him and thanking him, makes it all worth it to him. This is what he's been waiting and hoping for. Now his suffering is somehow relieved, and he continues speaking to you: "Child, you are a delight to my Heart. At last, I have found some rest. My friend, I have found rest in your heart. Thank you for being with me at this hour."

Hearing such words from the Lord is the greatest joy for those who have dedicated themselves to consoling him — and we can be assured that Jesus always speaks such words to us whenever we go to him with confidence. Let us be convinced that our little acts of love and trust give delight to Jesus. We may not always be able to hear him saying so, but we can believe that he does take delight in them. If we do believe it, then going to the Lord is a constant joy.

May we find this joy always as we visit Jesus and carry him in our hearts. May we also realize just how powerful our going to the Lord with joyful trust really is. It may seem like a little thing, but it amounts to a lot.

2. This Simple and Easy Way Is Powerful

At this point, we probably no longer fear consoling the Lord's Heart in the best possible way, because we've learned it's so simple and easy to do. So let's decide to strive to console Jesus in the best possible way by joyfully and trustingly accepting his will for us. But just in case the fear of suffering again tries to get us to abandon Jesus, let's strengthen our resolve to stay with him in his Passion by reflecting on just how powerful and fruitful this little way is. Saint Faustina, who lived the Little Way so well, will help us.

Before entering the convent, Faustina Kowalska didn't seem particularly special. She came from a poor family, didn't have much formal education, and was full of weaknesses. Yet the God who lifts up the lowly (see Lk 1:52) chose her to show what he can do (and what he wants to do) with all us little ones, if only we'll let him. On one occasion, Jesus spoke to Faustina about her weakness:

> You see what you are of yourself, but do not be frightened at this. If I were to reveal to you the whole misery that you are, you would die of terror. However, be aware of what you are. Because you are such great misery, I have revealed to you the whole ocean of My mercy. I seek and desire souls like you, but they are few. Your great trust in Me forces Me to continuously grant you graces. You have great and incomprehensible rights over My Heart, for you are a daughter of complete trust.

Like Faustina, we should strive to have "great trust." Jesus seeks and desires such trusting souls, but they are few. Why are they few? It can't be because only a few are strong, for Faustina herself was weak and full of "great misery." They're few because few people give Jesus their complete trust. Yet such trust is what he wants — and needs. Why does he desire and even need trusting souls so much? Because then he can work his miracles of mercy in them.

When we trust the Lord, he's free to form us into the great saints he longs for us to be. Remember how Jesus couldn't work a miracle in his hometown, Nazareth? (see Mk 6:1-6). He couldn't do it because of people's lack of faith. That's an amazing mystery. Jesus, the all powerful God-Man, is in a sense made powerless when we don't trust him. But when we do trust him, look out! For then he can act with his full power in our lives.

A trusting soul consoles Jesus so much. In such a soul, Jesus has free reign to live and work. He's free to live his life of love through it, through its deeds, words, and prayers. On the other hand, when people give themselves completely over to the power of evil, then evil has free reign to act in and through them, bringing tragic consequences. Unfortunately, it often seems there are many who, knowingly or unknowingly, have signed up to fight in the devil's army.

Well, how many have signed up with the Lord? How many have consciously chosen to give him free reign in their lives? As Jesus said to St. Faustina, they are few. Few people trustingly give themselves completely to the Lord, and that's just plain sad. But remember, the Lord can do a lot with just a little (see Jn 6:1-13), so let's each decide to be one of the Lord's few — let's join the Lord's little army!

Okay, great. So where do we sign up? We sign up at the foot of the Cross by giving Jesus our trust, our praise and thanks. Then, he does the rest.

Think back to our earlier meditation when Jesus was on the Cross. We learned from that scene that just one person full of trust can, in a sense, make Jesus forget about all the abuse he receives from the world at a certain time. As St. Faustina wrote, such a person becomes a "mist" before the eyes of Jesus that blocks from his view the terrible sins of the world.

Do we realize the power of this? If we simply live with an attitude of trust, if we go to Jesus full of confidence, then each of us can make him forget about the rejection he continually receives. Yes, he'll still feel the pain caused by humanity's sins, but it'll be like nothing to him, for, from the Cross, he'll say to us those remarkable words we heard earlier, "I wish I could suffer even more." He says this. He'll say it to you. Listen with your heart.

Let's frequently try to distract Jesus. That way, he won't have to constantly distract us. Isn't it the truth that, too often, Jesus has to distract us from the evil that tempts us to discouragement? For some reason, we tend to fixate on sin: sin in the world, sin in the Church, sin in our families, sin in ourselves. This fixation leads to no good. How often do we read the newspaper or hear of so much tragedy in the world and then become sad and depressed? How often do we get frustrated, bitter, and angry over the sin that surrounds us? This attitude won't cut it if we wish to live up to our decision to console the Lord's Heart. Let's decide to strive to distract *him*. He's tired enough to have to continually pull our gaze back to himself ... and why should he be the one always having to cheer *us* up? Let's give him a break. Let's cheer him up, and let's do it with our trust, with our constant praise and thanks.

"Come on," someone might say, "isn't this just a form of escapism for those who are too weak to face reality?" It is not. The attitude of focusing on Jesus, which I've just described, begins by seeing the world in its darkest reality. In fact, it requires that we first take a good, hard look at the reality of sin — but then we need to move on. We don't need to stay with it, and we shouldn't.

Too often we linger with bad news. We allow ourselves to be seduced by juicy gossip, gory details, and shocking scandal. Or, as we continually hear of the triumph of evil, we brood over it. Yet all that bad news is empty, nothing, and only a small slice of reality. In fact, it's often just a distraction, a waste of time, or worse. Dwelling on evil leads to evil. It leads to anger, envy, bitterness of spirit, lust, discouragement, and despair — but there's another way. We can avoid the bankruptcy of such hopelessness. There's something we can do.

Instead of looking at the bad news, we can turn to the good news, to Christ's love, and we can love him even more than before. Others don't love Him? I'm going to love him even more than before. Others don't honor him? I'm going to honor him even more than before. You said, "That must break the Lord's Heart"? Then I'm going to console him, cheer him up, praise and thank him even more than before. It seems this is why God permits so much evil in the world: not so that we become discouraged and hopeless but so that the sight of it will help steel our wills to be more fully for Christ. A French priest, Fr. Jean C.J. d'Elbée, says something similar in the following reflection:

> Some are astonished when they see the number of unbelievers, the number of pagans, of impious and impenitent sinners in the world, compared to that of the faithful. There is a surprising disproportion there which is hard to explain. One might wonder whether the Redemption has not failed after all.
>
> I think Divine Providence has permitted this (I purposely say permitted and not willed) in order that fervent souls may live the apostolic spirit in a better way, with a greater desire to save unfaithful souls, seeing how many there are, and that they may share even more the thirst of Jesus on the Cross and his Heart which goes out to the multitude. And then because his chosen souls, his privileged, his elect, will love him with a greater love, Jesus himself will have mercy on others. You see your responsibility!

We who are making this retreat, we who have committed to console Jesus, we who, therefore, are among the "chosen souls" Fr. d'Elbée speaks about, let's recognize our responsibility! May we always look at Jesus, see the rejection he continually endures — "Behold this Heart which loves so much yet is so little loved" — and be enkindled with the desire to console his Heart. By doing this, we'll distract him and thereby make up for so much of the rejection he receives. By doing this, a whole ocean of mercy will open up on the world, including on our loved ones.

Jesus is not outdone in generosity. If we make efforts to console him, he'll take care of the rest. As he said to one mystic, Sr. Consolata Betrone, "You, worry only about loving me, and I will take care of everything else to the smallest detail." Yes. That's it. Focusing on consoling Jesus is not a waste of time or prayer. If we stay fixed on our goal, he'll take care of all our cares, all those who are dear to us, and much more than we can imagine. Yes, our efforts to console Jesus cause love and grace to multiply and flow out to the whole world — and it's so easy to do. We can focus on him by visiting him in the Most Blessed Sacrament or simply by being mindful of his true presence in our hearts through grace, even as we do things like mopping the floor or mowing the lawn. So what's stopping us from doing this most important work, even in the midst of our work? Truly, it can change the world.

So, let's fly past the demons and the miserable crowd and go straight to the foot of the Cross to console our Lord. As we begin, a little devil puts up yet another obstacle to trip us on our way.

Fourth Obstacle: The Sensitivity of the Lord's Heart

Recall how easy it is to console Jesus: It simply takes our trust. Now recall how easy it is to hurt the Lord: It simply takes our lack of trust. That last part often presents an obstacle to our going to Jesus.

The sensitivity of the Lord's Heart is like a double-edged sword. On the one side, it makes consoling him so simple and easy. On the other side, it makes hurting him just as simple and easy. Perhaps this sensitivity of the Lord's Heart has got us thinking: "Well, if it's so easy to hurt the Lord, especially for those who are closest to him, maybe I should keep my distance so as to avoid hurting him. After all, I'm weak, and I may begin to distrust. I don't want to hurt him like that, like Peter did during his trial." Our friend Joe was thinking something similar during one of his retreats. Hearing more of his story may help us overcome this obstacle.

Remember how at the end of his 30-day retreat, Joe heard the Lord say to him, "All I want is for you to be my friend"? Well, Joe took those words to heart. After the retreat, he put all his energy into just trying to be the Lord's friend by not being afraid to go to him. Still, the thought of how much he must have hurt the Lord during the retreat because of his lack of trust stayed on his mind. Therefore, when it came time for an eight-day retreat later in the year, and after he'd had a lot of practice trusting Jesus, Joe decided to make it up to the Lord by giving him his complete trust.

Joe began his eight-day retreat with one goal: to console Jesus by trusting him. He decided that no matter what happened, he would strive to keep his peace and simply enjoy the time with his friend. Not surprisingly, the retreat went amazingly well. Even during the times of dryness, Joe wasn't disturbed because he thought to himself: "Perhaps Jesus is too tired to give me consolation. Maybe he just needs me to be here with him to give him consolation." Joe knew he was consoling the Lord simply by being there with him during the meditations, and that was enough for him. Thus, the whole retreat had a tone of peace and joy. Even if he didn't always feel it, Joe knew he was a delight to the Lord, and that knowledge was Joe's greatest delight during those blessed eight days.

There was, however, one part of that beautiful retreat that threatened to take away Joe's peace and joy. It happened when Joe suddenly realized that because he was becoming the Lord's friend more and more, it would be easier to hurt him. After all, didn't Jesus tell St. Faustina it's the distrust of his closest friends that hurts him most? Joe felt that he might not always be able to trust, that he might sometimes fall into distrust, and he knew this would hurt the Lord. Because he didn't want to do this, he thought to himself, "Maybe it would be better if I keep a little distance from the Lord so my lack of trust won't hurt him so much."

Thus, just as happened during the last meditation of his 30-day retreat, Joe resisted entering into prayer. Once again, however, the Lord beautifully broke through. Joe believes he heard Jesus say to him, "Joseph, I am going to give you two ways by which, I assure you, you will always be a delight to my Heart." Joy filled Joe's heart as he felt the Lord inviting him to do the following two things.

1. A Special Marian Consecration

First, Joe believes that the Lord was asking him to renew his consecration to Mary, though with a particular emphasis. Before I explain what that particular emphasis was, I should first say something about Marian consecration for those who aren't familiar with it.

MARIAN CONSECRATION. According to St. Louis de Montfort, total consecration to Jesus through Mary (Marian consecration) is "the surest, easiest, shortest and the most perfect means" to becoming a saint. (No wonder it's part of this retreat.) To get the full story on Marian consecration, one should read de Montfort's classic work, *True Devotion to Mary*. Because we don't have time to read a whole book besides this one during a weekend retreat, I'll summarize it now.

To properly understand the essence of total consecration to Jesus through Mary, we'll first need to reflect on an important point: Jesus wants to include all of us in his work of salvation. In other words, he doesn't just redeem us and then expect us to kick back and relax. On the contrary, he puts us to work. He wants all of us to labor in his Father's vineyard in one way or another. Why he didn't just snap his fingers and make it so that everyone in the world would individually hear and understand the Gospel by some private, mystical revelation, we don't know. We do know that Jesus relies on others to spread his Gospel and that he commissions his disciples to preach the Gospel to all (see Mt 28:19-20). He basically says to them and to us, "Let's get to work!" Of course, that God wants to include us in his work of salvation is a great gift and glorious privilege. Truly, there's no more important work to be done.

While everyone is called to lend a hand in the great work of salvation, not everyone has the same task. For example, St. Paul says, "There are varieties of service and ... there are varieties of working" (1 Cor 12:5-6). He goes on to say that God has appointed to the work of salvation "first apostles, second prophets, third teachers, then workers of miracles, then healers, helpers, administrators" (v. 28). Whoever we are, God has appointed us to a special task in his great work.

Among the various tasks God has given to his children, there's one that's radically more important than all the others: the task he gave to Mary. We all know that God uniquely blessed Mary by choosing her to conceive, bear, and nurture Jesus Christ, our Savior. But do we also realize that her blessed work didn't end once Jesus left home and began his public ministry? After the three years of Mary's hidden life during Jesus' public ministry, Jesus brought her back into the picture of his work of salvation at its most crucial time, the "hour" of his Passion. At that hour, we might say he fully revealed Mary's special task — the same task she had begun some 33 years before and that she still continues.

Jesus fully revealed Mary's special task shortly before his death. It happened when he looked down from the Cross and said to Mary as she stood with the Apostle John, "Woman, behold your son," and to John, "Behold your mother" (Jn 19:26-27). At that moment, Jesus gave us one of his greatest gifts: his mother as our mother. Of course, Mary isn't our natural mother. She's our spiritual mother. In other words, just as it was once her task some 2,000 years ago to give birth to Christ, to feed and nurture him, and to help him grow and develop into a man, so also, from the time she first said yes to being the mother of Jesus until the end of time, Mary's task is to give spiritual birth to Christians, to feed and nurture them with grace, and to help them grow to full stature in Christ. In short, Mary's job is to help us grow in holiness. It's her mission to form us into saints.

"Now, wait just a minute," someone might say, "isn't it the job of the Holy Spirit to make us holy?" Indeed, it is. The Holy Spirit is the Sanctifier. It is he who transforms us at our baptism from being mere creatures into members of the Body of Christ and who helps us in our ongoing transformation into Christ through continued conversion. Great. So how does Mary come into all of this?

Mary is the spouse of the Holy Spirit. At the Annunciation, the angel Gabriel declared to Mary that she would conceive and bear a son and that the Holy Spirit would overshadow her (see Lk 1:31-35). When Mary said, "Behold, I am the handmaid of the Lord; let it be to me according to your word" (Lk 1:38), we can see most clearly that she's the spouse of the Holy Spirit, for at that moment she gave the Holy Spirit permission to conceive Christ in her womb. Thus, at that moment, the already unfathomably deep bond between Mary and the Holy Spirit that had begun (in time) at the first moment of her Immaculate Conception was revealed as nothing less than a two-become-one marital union (see Gen 2:24). As a result of that union, the Holy Spirit is pleased to work and act through his spouse, Mary, for the sanctification of the human race. Of course, he didn't *have* to be so united to Mary. It was his free choice (and that of the Father and the Son), and in that choice he takes delight.

So, it's Mary's great God-given task, in union with and by the power of the Holy Spirit, to form every human being into "another Christ," that is, to unite everyone to the Body of Christ and form each person into a fully mature member of this body. Therefore, every human being is invited to rest in the womb of Mary and be transformed there, by the power of the Holy Spirit, more perfectly into Christ's own image. Yes, if we want to become more fully Christ, then we need to belong more fully to Mary. By going to her and remaining with her, we allow her to accomplish her mission in us. We allow her to form us into other Christs, into great saints. But how do we do this? How do we belong more fully to Mary and allow her to fulfill her mission in us? Simple. We say yes.

Mary has a deep respect for human freedom. She knows from her own experience in Nazareth what a free yes to God can do (see Lk 1:38), and so she doesn't pressure us into giving her our yes. Of course, she always cares for her children, but she won't force us to enter into a deeper relationship with her. She surely invites us to such a relationship and patiently waits for us to accept her invitation, but she remains respectful. Still, if we could see how much longing hides behind her silence, we'd say yes to her if only to give her relief. In fact, saying yes to her gives her more than relief. It gives her joy. Great joy. And the more fully we say yes to Mary, the more joyful she becomes. For our yes gives her the freedom to complete her work in us, the freedom to form us into great saints. This brings us to the essence of what Marian consecration is all about.

Marian consecration, as I understand it, is to give Mary our full permission (or as much permission as we can) to complete her motherly task in us, which is to form us into other Christs. Thus, by consecrating ourselves to Mary, each of us is saying to her:

> Mary, I want to be a saint. I know that you also want me to be a saint and that it's your God-given mission to form me into one. So, Mary, at this moment, on this day, I freely choose to give you my full permission to do your work in me, with your Spouse, the Holy Spirit.

As soon as Mary hears us make such a decision, she flies to us and begins working a masterpiece of grace within our souls. She continues this work for as long as we don't deliberately choose to change our choice from a yes to a no, as long as we don't take back our permission and leave her. That being said, it's always a good idea for us to strive to deepen our yes to Mary. For the deeper our yes becomes, the more marvelously she can perform her works of grace in our souls.

One of the greatest aspects of being consecrated to Mary is that she's such a gentle mother. She makes the lessons of the

Cross into something sweet, and she pours her motherly love and solace into our every wound. Going to her and giving her permission to do her job truly is the "surest, easiest, shortest and the most perfect means" to becoming a saint. What joy it is to be consecrated to Jesus through Mary!

JOE'S SPECIAL CONSECRATION TO MARY. Having learned what Marian consecration is, we can now appreciate the special emphasis Joe gave to his consecration to Jesus through Mary during his retreat. Feeling moved by the Holy Spirit, he prayed the following:

> Today I renew my total consecration to you, Mary, my mother. I give you my whole being so you may lead me to console your Son with the perfect consolation you give to him.
>
> From this day forward, dear Jesus, whenever I embrace you, may it be with the arms of Mary. Whenever I kiss you, may it be with the lips of Mary. Whenever I sing to you, praise you, and thank you, may it be with the voice of Mary. Jesus, in short, every time I love you, may it be with the Heart of Mary.

We see in this prayer that Joe gave Mary his yes with a particular emphasis: He gave her permission to be with him in a special way in his mission of consoling Jesus. Still, why would Jesus teach this consecration to Joe as a way of being assured that he would always be a consolation to his Heart? More specifically, why would Jesus say that this consecration prevents Joe from wounding his Heart with distrust? Well, look at it this way: When we console Jesus with the Heart of Mary, our acts of trust and love go to Jesus through the perfect faith and love of his mother. Thus, even if our acts of trust are not so perfect — even if they're tainted with some distrust — they don't hurt Jesus, because Mary's faith makes up for what we lack.

To help us understand better something of the mystery of how Mary can make up for our lack, it might be helpful to meditate on a passage from *True Devotion to Mary.* In the context of explaining how Mary embellishes and adorns everything we give to Jesus, de Montfort writes:

> It is as if a peasant, wishing to gain the friendship and benevolence of the king, went to the queen and presented her with a fruit which was his whole revenue, in order that she might present it to the king. The queen, having accepted the poor little offering from the peasant, would place the fruit on a large and beautiful dish of gold, and so, on the peasant's behalf, would present it to the king. Then the fruit, however unworthy in itself to be a king's present, would become worthy of his majesty because of the dish of gold on which it rested and the person who presented it.

So, when we at least try to console Jesus with our trust (even if our whole bodies shake with anxiety), when we at least try to be full of praise and thanks (even if we look gloomy and sad), and when we at least try to remain with our friend (even if our minds are distracted by 1,000 different things), then we don't need to fear hurting our Lord. He sees that we want to console him, and because his mother makes up for what we lack (if we're consecrated to her), we always do console him as long as we keep trying. We ought to ponder this reality, for it's a truly great gift.

So that you don't pass by such a great gift as Marian consecration, I suggest setting aside some time during this retreat to make in a formal way the same consecration our friend, Joe, made. Perhaps you can prayerfully write it out on a piece of paper and sign it. Might I further suggest that someday you read *True Devotion to Mary* and make the 33-day preparation de Montfort proposes? People usually make such a consecration on their favorite Marian feast day, and then they later testify that that day was for them the beginning of a new and marvelous way of life in Christ.

2. *Spiritual Communion of Merciful Love*

After Joe renewed his Marian Consecration with its special emphasis on consoling Jesus with Mary, he believes that the Lord was showing him the second way by which he could always be a delight to his Sacred Heart. Specifically, he believes that the Lord was inviting him to renew his Offering to Merciful Love by making a spiritual communion. Before I explain this way of renewing the Offering to Merciful Love, I should say something about what this offering is for those who aren't familiar with it.

*T*HE OFFERING TO MERCIFUL LOVE. The Offering to Merciful Love is the glorious summit of St. Thérèse of Lisieux's whole spirituality. (For the actual text of the Offering, see "References and Notes.") It's something she constantly repeated, even on her deathbed. One of her sisters went so far as to say, "[H]er whole life revolved around it."

What is this offering that was so important to the "greatest saint of modern times"? We can begin to get an idea of what it is by first learning what it's not.

In the convent where St. Thérèse lived, one could sometimes hear animated talk about certain heroic nuns of the past who had offered themselves as victims to God's justice. These spiritual giants made shocking deals with God. They said to him, "Lord, I ask you to put me in the place of poor sinners as a substitute, so the punishments due to them will fall on me instead." Amazingly, the Lord accepted such deals. When he did, the big souls who made them would often come down with illnesses that caused them excruciating pain and even death, all of which they lovingly offered to the Lord for the conversion of the sinners who really deserved such punishment.

On hearing about these "super-nuns," we might imagine that St. Thérèse would have felt drawn to make such an offering. After all, she had said that she wanted to love God more than he'd ever been loved before (and the word around Thérèse's convent was that there's no greater love than to lay down one's life as a victim to God's justice). Yet Thérèse wasn't interested in making such an offering. She writes:

I was thinking about the souls who offer themselves as victims of God's Justice in order to turn away the punishments reserved to sinners, drawing them upon themselves. This offering seemed great and very generous to me, but I was far from feeling attracted to making it.

Perhaps we're like Thérèse. Perhaps we, too, are far from feeling attracted to offering ourselves to God's justice. Well, this doesn't have to mean our love is any less than that of the super-nuns. Why not? Because, here again, Thérèse has discovered an alternate route to the heights of holiness. Hers is not the unattractive route known as the offering to God's justice, but rather the marvelously beautiful *Offering to Merciful Love*. The following citation captures Thérèse's excitement and delight as she discovers and explains it:

> O my God! Will your Justice alone find souls willing to immolate themselves as victims? Does not Your *Merciful Love* need them too? On every side this love is unknown, rejected; those hearts upon whom You would lavish it turn to creatures ... [T]hey do this instead of throwing themselves into Your arms and of accepting Your infinite *Love*. O my God! Is Your disdained Love going to remain closed up within Your Heart? It seems to me that if You were to find souls offering themselves as victims of holocaust to Your Love, You would consume them rapidly; it seems to me, too, that You would be happy not to hold back the waves of infinite tenderness within You. If Your Justice loves to release itself, this Justice *which extends only over the earth*, how much more does Your Merciful Love desire to set souls on fire since Your Mercy *reaches to the heavens*. O my Jesus, let me be this happy victim; consume Your holocaust with the fire of Your Divine Love! (emphasis in original).

So, Thérèse offers herself not to God's justice but to his merciful love, an act that's just as pleasing to him as an offering to his justice. In fact, it may even be more pleasing to him. For, while an offering to justice has as its aim the alleviation of the suffering of sinners, the explicit aim of the Offering to Merciful Love is to alleviate the suffering of Jesus. (Thérèse specifically declares in the text of her offering that she makes it for the purpose of consoling Jesus' Sacred Heart.) Of course, Jesus is also consoled when sinners are consoled and converted, but there's something about the Offering to Merciful love that gets to the heart of what Jesus longs for, namely, people who will let him love them completely.

What's the Offering to Merciful Love? It's basically this. First, it's to see, like St. Thérèse saw, that the Heart of Jesus is sorrowful because so many people reject his merciful love. Then, for the purpose of consoling Jesus, it's to give him permission to fill us with all the mercy others have rejected. He surely does fill us if we give him permission, and this gives him great relief primarily because someone has chosen to receive his mercy fully and secondarily because the mercy that fills such a soul begins to overflow to others. At its core, the Offering to Merciful Love is simply to receive Jesus' rejected mercy. Words the Lord spoke to St. Faustina express well this essence of the offering:

My Heart overflows with great mercy for souls, and especially for poor sinners. ... I desire to bestow My graces upon souls, but they do not want to accept them. You, at least, come to Me as often as possible and take these graces they do not want to accept. In this way you will console My Heart.

That's all well and good, but what's the catch? After all, a *big* catch goes with offerings made to God's justice: lots of suffering! So what's the catch with the Offering to Merciful Love? Well, there is, indeed, a catch — but it's not a scary one. The catch is this: People who live the Offering to Merciful Love begin to experience greater heartache. That is, they feel in their hearts more acutely the sorrowful reality that "Love is not loved as He ought to be loved," that Jesus suffers terribly because so many do not know and love him. This kind of heartache isn't so intimidating. In fact, it fits perfectly with what this retreat is all about, namely, awakening our hearts to having compassion on the Sacred Heart of Jesus. This kind of heartache we want to have. It also fits perfectly with what I described earlier as loving Jesus with the Heart of Mary. Let's see how it does.

Imagine Jesus and Mary at Calvary. Look at Jesus, hanging there on the Cross. He's the one who has offered himself as a victim to God's justice. One might say he made a deal with God that he would take on all the punishment due to the sins of humanity so humanity might be saved. God seems to have taken him up on that deal, and we realize he suffers for it as we see him hanging there. Now look at Mary, standing there at the foot of the Cross. While we cannot fully understand her share in Christ's redemptive act by her being the New Eve associated with Jesus, the New Adam, and therefore also a "victim of justice," it could be said that she is also the one who lives the Offering to Merciful Love. She receives the rejected love and mercy that gushes forth from the Heart of Jesus, and she suffered because of it, a great *heart* suffering, a suffering of empathy and compassion, making her a "victim of mercy." (Remember Simeon's prophecy from Luke 2:35, "a sword shall pierce your heart"?) More than anyone, she knows the heartache of the Offering to Merciful Love, and she wants us to experience it, too — but don't worry. She's very gentle as she brings us into this heartache (she knows how much we can take) and we find that, with her, there's actually a beautiful sweetness to it.

This explains, in summary, the Offering to Merciful Love. Now, who wouldn't want to live such an offering? Still, if the idea that it greatly consoles Jesus, overflows to the good of others, and gives us a deeper sensitivity to the Lord's sorrow isn't enough to convince us to make it, then here's something else we might want to consider: According to St. Thérèse, those who live the Offering to Merciful Love need not fear purgatory! To spend one's life receiving God's rejected merciful love for the sake of consoling him apparently makes up for the punishment due to a multitude of sins. Thérèse writes to her sister, Mother Agnes, about this particular fruit of having offered herself to Merciful Love:

> You permitted me, dear Mother, to offer myself in this way to God, and you know the rivers or rather the oceans of graces that flooded my soul. Ah! since that happy day, it seems to me that Love penetrates and surrounds me, that at each moment this *Merciful Love* renews me, purifying my soul and leaving no trace of sin within it, and I need have no fear of purgatory. I know that of myself I would not merit even to enter that place of expiation since only holy souls can have entrance there, but I also know that the Fire of Love is more sanctifying than is the fire of purgatory. I know that Jesus cannot desire useless sufferings for us, and that He would not inspire the longings I feel unless He wanted to grant them (emphasis in original).

Joy to Jesus and Mary, a more compassionate heart, fullness of mercy, mercy for others, and no purgatory — the Offering to Merciful Love is a sweet deal, indeed! It's no wonder, then, that Jesus wanted Joe to renew it, but what's this business about renewing it within the context of a spiritual communion?

THE SPIRITUAL COMMUNION OF MERCIFUL LOVE. What's a spiritual communion? It basically consists of making a prayer of desire to receive Jesus in Holy Communion. For instance, one can simply pray: "Lord Jesus, I long to receive you in Holy Communion, but because I can't do so now, I ask you to come into my heart through spiritual communion." According to one of the greatest theologians in the Church, St. Thomas Aquinas, this kind of prayer can be amazingly powerful. He wrote that a person who fervently makes such a prayer of spiritual communion can receive the same grace as one who fervently receives Sacramental Communion! Now that we know what it is and its potential power, let's see how the Lord inspired Joe to make a spiritual communion.

During his retreat, Joe believed that the Lord wanted him to make a spiritual communion with a special emphasis. Specifically, he believed that the Lord wanted him to console him by making a spiritual communion with the intention of receiving the mercy that other people reject. Joe was to see the Eucharist (even spiritually received) as being the channel through which Jesus would pour out on him the superabundance of this rejected mercy.

So, Joe thought to himself, "Great!" And he made a spiritual communion right then and there. But then he began to think, "Well, it's easy to do this right now, while I'm on retreat, but I know I'm going to forget to do it later, when life gets busy again." With such a thought in mind, Joe asked the Lord to show him an easy-to-remember way by which he might frequently make such a spiritual communion. The Lord taught him a beautiful prayer in answer to his request.

As Joe was praying and reflecting on the words of the Offering to Merciful Love, he suddenly became aware of his breathing: in/out — in/out — in/out. After a while, he noticed that after he would exhale (out), for a brief moment, before the next inhale (in), his lungs were empty: empty/in/out — empty/in/out — empty/in/out. He reflected on that brief moment of "empty" and began to prolong it by not inhaling right after he exhaled. He would simply hold that moment of "empty lungs" for several seconds before inhaling. Sensing that this breathing exercise was not a distraction from his meditation (the Lord seemed to be leading), he further reflected on the moment of empty. He thought to himself: "This moment of empty is fragile. If I remained in it for long, I'd pass out." He tried to see how long he could hold it. Not long. (Don't worry, he didn't pass out.) He noticed that the inhale sure felt good after holding empty for a while.

Just as Joe began to think this breathing experiment was a waste of time (and a bit silly), three Latin words popped into his mind: *ecce, fiat,* and *magnificat.* Joe understood almost immediately. Each word fit with one of the three moments of breathing. Each word represented a word spoken by Mary in the Bible. Each word following the other was a way of continually making a spiritual communion of merciful love with the Heart of Mary. The Lord answered Joe's request. He not only taught him an easy-to-remember way of continually making a spiritual communion, but he also taught him to do so with Mary. Now I'm going to teach this prayer by explaining two things: first, the three words of Mary and, second, how each of these words corresponds to one of the three moments of breathing.

The Latin word *ecce* means "behold." Mary spoke this word at the Annunciation when the angel Gabriel announced to her that she would be the mother of the Messiah. Mary said, "Behold (*Ecce*), I am the handmaid of the Lord." In other words, she presented herself to the Lord just as she was.

When we pray, God wants us to present ourselves to him as we are, like Mary did. He wants us to say, "*Ecce,*" that is, "Behold, here I am, O Lord." Yet there's obviously something very different about Mary and us: We sin; Mary never sinned. Does this fact mean we're unacceptable to the Lord? Absolutely not. Quite the contrary, in fact.

As we learned earlier in this retreat, we may be tempted to avoid going to Jesus because of our weaknesses, sinfulness, and attachments. This is the temptation of Jansenist fear, but there's no need to be afraid. We console Jesus' Heart when we go to him just as we are — it breaks his Heart when we don't. We don't have to be perfect to go to him. In fact, the weaker and more sinful we are, the more he wants us to go to him and present ourselves with complete honesty and truth, "*Ecce ...* behold, Lord, here I am, sinfulness and all." If only we would always remember how much this pleases him! May we not be afraid to pray, "*Ecce,* here I am, O Lord." May we not give in to the lie that says we're ugly to the Lord. We are not. We're so beautiful to him just as we are! In fact, his merciful Heart is particularly attracted to the weakest, most sinful souls. My explanation of the next word will say more about this.

The Latin word *fiat* comes from *Fiat mihi*, "Let it be done to me." At the Annunciation, Mary spoke this word after she presented herself to the Lord (*ecce*). Jesus also wants us to speak this word after we present ourselves to him. Yet, when we speak it, it has a bit of a different meaning than Mary's *fiat*. When Mary said, "Let it be done to me," she was allowing the Incarnation of the Word to take place in her immaculate soul. When we say, "Let it be done to me," we're allowing God's merciful love to come pouring down into our weak, sinful souls.

It might be helpful to think of our *fiat* in the following way. First, imagine that the heavens above are an infinite ocean. Next, imagine that this ocean is held back from emptying out onto the earth by a giant floodgate. Well, when we say "*fiat*," it's the magic word that unlocks the gate, and once this gate is unlocked, look out! The waters of the heavenly ocean burst through and pour down into our souls like a great cascading waterfall. But don't be afraid, for as we'll now see, this ocean is a wonderful thing to experience.

As you might have guessed, the ocean I just described is the ocean of God's merciful love. Remember, merciful love is that particular kind of love that seeks out brokenness, suffering, sin, and weakness. Do we understand, then, why Jesus loves it when we go to him as we are, sinfulness and all? It's because weakness and wretchedness is precisely what attracts his merciful love. Thus, he simply (and eagerly) awaits our *fiat*. When we give it, look out! We get washed in the wonderful flood of his merciful love. Now, to the third word spoken by Mary.

The word *magnificat* comes from Mary's exclamation in Latin, *Magnificat anima mea Dominum*, "My soul magnifies the Lord." This is Mary's song of praise when she went to her cousin Elizabeth after giving her *fiat* to the Lord (see Lk 1:46-55). Mary was full of praise because of the "great things" God had done for her. After our *fiat*, after we've experienced the power of God's merciful love, we, too, will want to give praise to God. We, too, will want to sing out, "*Magnificat!*"

Earlier in this retreat, I said that the best way to console the Heart of Jesus is by trusting him. I also said, thanks to Fr.

Seraphim, that the concrete expression of that trust is praise and thanksgiving. Well, because *magnificat* basically means the same as praise and thanksgiving, when we give our *magnificat* to the Lord, we're consoling him in the best possible way. Of course, sometimes it's easier to praise and thank the Lord than at other times. Moreover, sometimes our praise will have no outward expression at all. It'll just be an act of the will in the depths of our hearts — and that's just fine with Jesus. We give him what we can, and he's happy with that. Nonetheless, when we consider the merciful love that God pours into our hearts, it tends to be much easier to let out an outward song of praise.

Having explained the meaning of the three words, *ecce*, *fiat*, and *magnificat*, now I'm going to apply them to the three moments of our breathing: empty, in, and out.

Recall that Joe thought of "empty" as that brief, fragile moment in between an exhale and an inhale and that he realized if he held it too long, he might pass out. Well, that moment of empty illustrates for us our utter *ecce*. In other words, it shows us what we are of our own sinful selves: empty, weak, and on the verge of passing out. In fact, we can only remain in the moment "empty lungs" for a short time before we pass out and die. This is exactly what we are at *ecce*. We're saying, "Behold, Lord, here I am — without your mercy, I'll collapse and die." Of course, when we present ourselves to the Lord like this, he rushes to us with his mercy, and we take a deep breath in.

The moment "in" obviously refers to inhale and follows the moment of empty lungs. This moment "in" feels great, especially if we've held empty lungs for 10 to 20 seconds. Go ahead. Try it. Inhale after doing about 20 seconds of empty lungs. Doesn't the inflow of air feel great? Savor it for a moment before you let it go. Hold it for a few moments and enjoy.

What you've just experienced (inhaling) illustrates what happens when we say "*fiat*." For, when we say it, we allow God's merciful love to flow into our hearts, and it feels great. It's exactly what we need, namely, his mercy entering into our emptiness. Breathe it in.

Now realize this: Each inhale can be a spiritual communion. It becomes one if we make it our intention when we inhale to receive God's rejected merciful love into our emptiness. It's especially like receiving Sacramental Communion if we imagine that the merciful love we inhale is coming down from the pierced side of Christ as blood and water. (More on this later.)

Obviously, after we inhale, we'll need to blow the air back out (exhale). This is the "out" moment of breathing. Similarly, after we "inhale" God's merciful love, because it was so good and refreshing, we'll "need" to praise and thank him for the gift of his mercy. This praise and thanks is signified by the air we exhale from our lungs. We give it back to God as an exhaled *magnificat*.

Okay, having explained the meaning of *ecce*, *fiat*, and *magnificat* and having further explained how each of these three words apply to the three moments of our breathing (*ecce*/empty, *fiat*/in, *magnificat*/out), it might be helpful to put it all together with a meditation. For, if we live this breathing exercise as a prayer, then we can constantly be making a spiritual communion, renewing the Offering to Merciful Love, and living praise and thanks. To make our meditation, let's go to the foot of the Cross just before Jesus dies.

Almost everyone else has abandoned him, but Mary is here with you. She puts her words on your lips, "*Ecce* ... Here I am, Lord." You continue: "Here I am, Lord, with all my sinfulness, weaknesses, and attachments. I don't deserve to be here, but I've learned this pleases you. So, behold, O Lord, I come here to console you, even as you are about to die." This humble confidence consoles Jesus right at the moment he breathes his last.

As you pause here in the *ecce* moment with empty lungs, the soldier's lance thrusts through Jesus' side and into his Heart, causing blood and water to flow out and down like a waterfall, down into your heart and soul. As the first drops of this blood and water touch your face, you take a deep breath in, *fiat*. This blood and water (which is his mercy) and this wonderful air (which is also his mercy) fills your soul. After your soul has filled, after your lungs have filled, you linger at the end of the *fiat* moment as you simply enjoy and take delight in his merciful love.

Ah, but after having rested for a brief time in the *fiat* moment, your heart and lungs are ready to release what you've just enjoyed. You're ready to breathe back out to the Lord your love and mercy, your praise and thanks. And so, although he seems to be dead (because this is a meditation, you actually still console him), Mary gently raises you to his lips. You breathe into him your praise and thanks, the love and mercy that his blood and water have given you. In this *magnificat* moment, Jesus' lungs slowly fill with your praise and thanks. Yet his Heart can't hold this returned love, for it's been pierced, and now your lungs are empty. Don't worry. Mary gently lowers you to the foot of the Cross where the blood and water again begin to flow down from the Lord's pierced side and into your emptiness, into the poverty of your *ecce*. And so begins again that wonderful cycle of love and mercy: *ecce*/empty — *fiat*/in — *magnificat*/out — *ecce*/empty — *fiat*/in — *magnificat*/out.

If we live this attitude of presenting our wretchedness to the Lord (*ecce*), receiving his mercy (*fiat*), and then praising and thanking him for his saving mercy (*magnificat*), we can be assured that we won't seriously be wounding the Lord by our lack of trust — for trust is not only praise and thanks, it's also to receive God's mercy. Remember how Fr. Seraphim said that to live trust means to praise and thank God for everything? Some people might have read that and thought, "Hmmm. That's all well and good, but I don't always feel full of praise and thanks, especially when it's hard to be grateful because of life's hurts." Isn't that the truth? But look at what we've just learned from the *ecce, fiat, magnificat* movement: The path to praise begins with the *ecce* moment. Moreover, while we're in the *ecce* moment, we normally don't feel like praising and thanking, and that's all right. For, from the *ecce* moment, we eventually move to the *fiat* moment, that is, we call down (*fiat*) the Lord's blood and water (mercy) into our emptiness. Then, that *fiat* moment eventually leads to *magnificat*, to praise and thanks.

Don't worry if you're in the *ecce* moment for a long time. For the simple act of presenting yourself to the Lord as you are, sinfulness and all, is itself an act of trust. Furthermore, the act of receiving God's merciful love (*fiat*) is also an act of trust, and both these acts of trust (*ecce* and *fiat*) tend to lead to a further act of trust, namely, praise and thanks (*magnificat*).

Congratulations. At this point in the retreat, you've overcome all the main obstacles to consoling Jesus (directly) as the Head of the Mystical Body. Yet there's one more obstacle. This one has to do with giving consolation to Christ in the members of his body. Get ready, because this isn't an easy obstacle to overcome. You might say I've saved the best obstacle (as in the hardest to overcome) for last.

Fifth Obstacle: The Insensitivity of Our Hearts

When I finished writing the first version of this retreat in early 2002, this section did not exist. Although I knew I'd eventually have to write it, I didn't do so at the time because I wasn't ready. As the years passed, I still wasn't ready. Then, in 2008, I heard a remarkable talk. Shortly after hearing it, I was ready.

The talk was given by the kindhearted Cardinal from Vienna, Christoph Schönborn. In fact, it was more than just a talk. It was the opening address of the first World Apostolic Congress on Mercy in Rome delivered in the Pope's "home parish" (the St. John Lateran Basilica) to a standing-room-only crowd of more than 5,000 people. Of course, the Cardinal spoke of Divine Mercy.

I loved everything the Cardinal said in the first part of his address. With a gentle voice and powerful words, he praised the great apostle of Divine Mercy, Pope John Paul II, and described how this pope's teaching on God's mercy is an authoritative mandate to the Church to spread the message of mercy to the world. As I listened to the Cardinal's words, my heart burned within me, because, for many years, my great desire has been to make known the Lord's amazing mercy. In the second part of his address, though, something changed for me. The Cardinal began to speak about the meaning of mercy — specifically, what it's not — and in doing so, his words hit me squarely in the chest, like so many piercing arrows:

> A hard heart is the opposite of mercy. How much we must implore God so our hearts do not become hardened like stone! Our hearts must not become insensitive! In fact, insensitivity is the primary sin of man against God and neighbor. Hardness of heart separates us from God, is the loss of our humanity, and causes so much suffering. It is also that which brought Jesus to the Cross and caused his death — it is that which crucified him! Only the love of God that reaches as far as the Cross can open a breach in our hardened hearts.

These words about insensitivity and hardness of heart deeply convicted me. There I was at the World Congress on Mercy, eager to spread the message of Divine Mercy, and yet, at the same time, I was suddenly realizing that part of my heart had become just the opposite of mercy: hard and insensitive. I hadn't really noticed the change before because it had happened so gradually. An ice-cold and steady stream of disappointments, misunderstandings, and various hurts over the years had tempted me to close my heart to others, and I'd responded, little by little, by closing it.

After the Cardinal's arrows hit me, I hardly heard the rest of his talk. I was too busy feeling depressed about the contradiction I'd discovered right at my core. Then, I remembered his words, "Only the love of God that reaches as far as the Cross can open a breach in our hardened hearts." Right there in the big Lateran Basilica, I begged God to come with his merciful love and heal my heart.

After making that prayer, I didn't feel any change inside me. However, in the days and weeks following the Cardinal's address, as I reflected on his words, I began to feel the inspiration to write this section, the Fifth Obstacle. As I mentioned earlier, I knew someday I'd have to write it, but I'd never felt ready to do so. It took the experiences of six heart-hardening years to get me ready.

Perhaps you've also experienced an ice-cold stream of disappointments, misunderstandings, and various hurts that have tempted you to close your heart to others. Perhaps you've also given in to some of those temptations, and you're heart has become insensitive and hard. If so, then this section is written especially for you. Actually, it's written for everyone. I say that because all of us, in one way or another, have let at least some hardness take hold of our hearts. May this section help us overcome this "primary sin of man," so we might better console Jesus in the members of his body.

A BRIEF LESSON ON MERCY. For me, the best part of Cardinal Schönborn's talk came when he spoke about the meaning of mercy. Now I'd like to do as he did by offering my own brief lesson on the topic. I think this will be helpful as we take on the Fifth Obstacle, because mercy has a great deal to do with being sensitive to the suffering of others.

Mercy is love when it encounters suffering. More specifically, it's two movements that take place within us when we see someone (or something) suffer. The first is an emotional movement, a movement of compassion that we feel in our hearts or even, when the suffering of the other is particularly intense, deep in our guts. The second is a movement of action. In other words, as we see someone suffering and feel compassion for him, we soon find ourselves reaching out to alleviate his suffering. In sum: Mercy is love that feels compassion for those who suffer (heart) and reaches out to help them (arm).

In case we didn't notice it before, I'll say it now: This whole retreat has been about mercy. Specifically, it's been about having mercy on the Sacred Heart of Jesus. In other words, we've been focusing on feeling compassion for Jesus' Heart

(Part One) and then on reaching out to alleviate his suffering, that is, seeking to console him (Part Two).

Now we're going to change our focus a bit. Instead of giving all our attention to the suffering of the Sacred Heart, we're going to take a close look at the suffering of our neighbor. Specifically, in keeping with the two movements of mercy, we're going to see (1) how we can become more sensitive to the suffering of our neighbor and (2) how we can reach out to our neighbor to help alleviate his suffering.

Before we begin, I'd like to make an important point. By turning our focus to our neighbor's suffering, we're not forgetting our principle and foundation of consoling the Heart of Jesus. This is because we console the Heart of Jesus not only when we trust him but also when we show mercy to our neighbor. If this connection isn't already clear, it'll become clearer as we continue.

1. Becoming Sensitive to the Suffering of Our Neighbor

There's nothing more inhuman than hardheartedness, nothing more against human nature than to be without a shred of compassion. How do we know this? Well, we don't know it so much as we feel it — and what do we feel? Horror. Yes, it's hellishly horrifying to encounter hardheartedness. Hollywood knows this well. I say that because horror movies almost always revolve around a character (or characters) whose defining trait is a complete lack of compassion. And what do we instinctively say of such a character? That's right, "What a monster!"

I've got some bad news. There's a bit of a monster in all of us. Unless we're already soaring on the heights of holiness, we all have at least some hardheartedness. As I mentioned earlier, all of us have at least some place in our hearts that's already turned to stone. This is simply one of the sad facts of sin in our lives; it hardens our hearts.

Unfortunately, I've got some more bad news. We live under the influence of a culture that's extremely successful at hardening peoples' hearts. This is why Pope John Paul II went so far as to call it a "culture of death."

"Wait," someone might say, "I thought he called it that because of all the abortions." Yes, that's part of the reason, but abortion is just a symptom of a more fundamental problem, namely, the hardening of so many hearts. Look at it this way: A lot of heart hardening had to take place before so many mothers and fathers decided to end the lives of their own unborn children. Hearts had to die before the babies did.

So, the culture of death in which we live is expert in killing not just babies but hearts, and it wants to kill ours. Thus, buyer beware! The fast food, consumer culture doesn't just cause heart attacks, it causes *heart* attacks. In other words, if we let it, the influence of the culture of death will kill that spiritual center we call "the heart." This kind of heart attack makes us incapable of true love and causes spiritual death. Such is the high-stakes battle we're in: The culture of death threatens to kill our hearts, to kill our ability to love, to kill our true humanity.

Now, here's some good news. There's hope for our hearts. The culture of death doesn't have to win; our hearts don't have to die. In fact, the heart-hardening process can be reversed. Put another way, we can get "new hearts" (Ez 36:26), hearts that feel true love and compassion, hearts that are sensitive to the suffering of others. We don't have to give in to the culture of death. We can be countercultural. We can help build up what Pope John Paul II called the "culture of life" and the "civilization of love."

I've got some more good news. For us, the heart-healing process has already begun. In case we didn't notice it before, I'll say it now: This whole retreat has been about the work of healing our hearts. You know all that obstacle jumping we've been doing throughout Part Two? Well, it's been strengthening our hearts to love. (These really are spiritual *exercises.*) In fact, most of what I've been saying about consoling the Heart of Jesus hasn't primarily been about his Heart at all. It's been about our hearts. For, while we've been busy consoling Jesus' Heart, he's been busy changing and healing ours, and that's good news.

"Great," someone might say, "but does this mean the idea of consoling Jesus' Heart has just been a ploy to get my heart into shape?" No. Not at all. Jesus really — and I do mean *really* — needs our consoling love. Yet he needs it not because he's some kind of emotionally needy weakling but because he's so powerful. Allow me to explain.

Jesus sees so many people dying the spiritual death of hardheartedness, and he calls out to them because he loves them and has the power to save them. Unfortunately, so many of them don't come. Jesus desperately wants them to come so he can save them, but such a great number of them don't even know they need saving. Moreover, many of them don't want anything to do with Jesus. They think he's the "Jansenist Jesus," the one who just wants to ruin their fun. Thus, they scorn him, run away, and harden their hearts to the God who is Love — and then they die (spiritually). This tragic reality breaks Jesus' Heart; it's why he needs us to console him.

Still, the truth remains. When we go to Jesus, we're not just doing something for him. He's doing something for us. In fact, that's how we "do for him," namely, by letting him "do for us." For the way we give him joy is by letting him be our Savior. As I mentioned earlier, although God didn't have to, he chose to put a fundamental need into his own beautiful Heart when he became man: the need to give us his saving love. Thus, Jesus loves us so much not because we're so good but because he's so good, and knowing that we need him, his joy is to use his power to save us. Clear? Great. Now let's get back to the idea that Jesus heals our hearts when we go to him.

First, let's review. What is it about our hearts that needs healing? That's right, they've become hard. In other words, they're slow to be moved to compassion by the suffering of others. Okay, so how do we soften 'em up? How do we make them more compassionate? (Hint: It has to do with what we keep before our eyes as part of our principle and foundation.) Answer: the Passion of Jesus. In other words, our hearts become softened when we listen to Jesus' plea, "Behold this Heart which loves so much yet is so little loved." This plea is simply a way for Jesus to state the essence of his suffering during the Passion, namely, the rejection of his love. This plea is simply an echo of some of his last words from the Cross, "I thirst" — not a thirst for water but a thirst for our love.

So, reflecting on the Passion of Jesus, seeing his suffering Heart, and hearing his cry from the Cross softens our hearts. Okay, but now let's see some evidence for this. Let's consider some testimony. Saint Faustina records that Jesus said to her: **"My daughter, your compassion for Me refreshes Me. By meditating on My Passion, your soul acquires a distinct beauty."** Notice two things here. First, Jesus is consoled ("refreshed") by Faustina's compassion. Second, Faustina is changed. That is, her soul "acquires a distinct beauty." What beauty? I suggest it's the beauty of a soul (heart) that's growing in compassion. And what's the means to such growth? According to Jesus, it's meditation on his Passion. So how does meditating on the Passion make us more compassionate? To answer this question, I think it'll be helpful if we first look at something I call "CEP."

CEP stands for "compassion-evoking power." And what has CEP? Of course, suffering. Seeing the suffering of others evokes our compassion. Now, in most cases, the principle holds that the greater the suffering the greater will be its CEP on us. For example, we would naturally feel more compassion for a starving child in Africa than for some chubby kid at McDonald's as he accidently drops his Big Macs.

Something else besides the "size" of suffering affects CEP: love. The greater love we feel for the one who suffers, the greater will be his suffering's CEP on us. So, for example, if the chubby kid at McDonald's is *your* kid, then you'll have a lot more compassion on him than the high school punks who, seeing the look of horror on his face as his burgers cascade to the floor, begin laughing their heads off.

In sum: CEP, which stands for suffering's "compassion-evoking power," is affected by at least two factors: (1) the size of the suffering and (2) the size of the love. Great. Now, let's see how paying attention to these two factors can help us better appreciate the CEP of the Passion of Jesus.

Regarding the first factor (size of suffering), Jesus' Passion contains the most suffering — period. In fact, it contains all the world's suffering and then some. How? Well, I can't explain it. It's a mystery. It's a mystery not in the sense that nobody can understand it but in the sense that we can never exhaust the meaning of it. In other words, we can always grasp more fully how much the Lord suffered — and still suffers — the more deeply he brings us into the mystery of his Passion. If we spend time meditating on it, if we spend time living the principle and foundation, we'll see for ourselves. Anyway, here's the main point: Because Jesus' Passion presents to us the greatest suffering, it has the potential to exercise the greatest CEP on us.

Now, regarding the second factor (the size of the love), let me put it this way: Jesus, especially during his Passion, is the most lovable being in the cosmos. He himself speaks to this mystery with regard to his Passion when he says, "Greater love has no man than this, that a man lay down his life for his friends. You are my friends ..." (Jn 15:13-14). During his Passion, Jesus manifested the greatest love when he gave up his life for us, his friends. Yet, even though he calls us his friends, we were actually his enemies because of our sins, and this fact shows his love even more, as St. Paul explains:

> While we were yet helpless, at the right time Christ died for the ungodly. Why, one will hardly die for a righteous man — though perhaps for a good man one will dare even to die. But God shows his love for us in that while we were yet sinners Christ died for us. ... [W]hile we were enemies we were reconciled to God by the death of his Son (Rom 5:6-8).

By our sins we offend not just any man but the God-Man, an offense that deserves the penalty of death. Yet, instead of destroying us ungrateful creatures as we deserved, God in Christ Jesus chose to suffer the death penalty for us, so we might be forgiven and have life with God. What unfathomable love and mercy! As the second factor is applied to the Passion, we again meet a great mystery: Christ's Passion reveals to us a love so deep that it's impossible to grasp fully. That being said, we can always delve deeper into the mystery of God's love for us in Christ Jesus, especially by reflecting on the Passion. As we do, it can have the greatest CEP on our hearts.

So, the Passion of Jesus contains the greatest suffering and the greatest love, and therefore, it can evoke our compassion more than anything else. This is important because our hearts have become hardened and need to be healed. Moreover, one of the most important ways they begin to be healed is when they come face-to-face (heart-to-face?) with the suffering of another. Thus, because the suffering of Christ has the greatest CEP, meditating on his Passion has the potential to heal our hardened hearts more than anything else. O wonderful Cross on which our Savior died for us!

As if this weren't enough, the Passion contains yet another gift. While the suffering of others evokes our compassion and thus helps heal our hearts, the suffering of Jesus carries with it an extraordinary gift of grace. When we prayerfully reflect on the Passion, God's grace powerfully works in our hearts to help us experience compassion and healing — but don't just take my word for it. After lamenting that few souls reflect on his Passion with true feeling, Jesus said to St. Faustina, **"I give great graces to souls who meditate devoutly on My Passion."**

With deep feeling (compassion) and devotion, may we contemplate the Lord's Passion, the suffering of his Heart, and his great love for us. In this way perhaps more than any other, our hearts become transformed from stony hearts into hearts of flesh. Of course, that's not the main reason why we do it (that would be putting a second thing first). We do it primarily to console Jesus (the "first thing"). Still, the effect ("second thing") is marvelous: Meditation on the Passion enables our hearts to see the suffering of others better and then be moved by their sufferings.

Even though contemplating Christ's Passion does so much to heal our hearts, it's not enough. We also need to reach out to others. When we do, our hearts continue to soften:

Compassion-in-action produces even deeper compassion. That's one of the laws of mercy. For instance, a person who actually goes to serve the poor comes away with a much more compassionate heart than the person who simply sees them on TV and says, "How sad." Still, compassion-in-action takes some know-how. That is, it can be helpful to learn (or at least have in mind) the ways by which we can reach out to others. The next section will talk about this.

Before we move on to the next section, I think it'll be good for us to take some time for prayer. Specifically, let's make an examination of conscience to help us become more aware of what sins in our lives might especially be hardening our hearts. For, if we truly want renewed hearts, we not only need to go to Jesus and reach out to others, but we also need to go away from sin.

All sin hardens our hearts, but some sins are particularly effective in doing so. Let's take a brief look at some specific kinds of sin that do the best job of hardening our hearts, and let's begin with a prayer to the Holy Spirit.

PRAYER. Come, Holy Spirit. Come, you who can open my eyes to the reality of sin. Help me to see the areas in my life that harden my heart and make it insensitive to the suffering of my neighbor. Holy Spirit, speak to me during this examination of conscience. Show me what's wounding my heart. Help me to overcome sin in my life that I may ponder Christ's Passion with true feeling, that my heart may be renewed, and that I may respond to my neighbor's suffering with deeper compassion and more generous mercy.

GOSSIP AND ENVY. Gossip and envy are especially effective at hardening hearts because of the way they twist our emotional responses to the suffering of others. So, for example, instead of feeling sorry for someone who suffers, gossip and envy get us to rejoice and delight over his suffering. In the case of gossip, this kind of emotional perversion may not happen immediately, but it leads in this direction. Envy is more directly destructive. By its very nature, it leads to a kind of wicked celebration over the misfortune of others whose goods we want for ourselves.

Regarding gossip: Do I have a morbid curiosity? For instance, when I watch the news, do I become interested in catastrophes, murders, or atrocities of war as a kind of entertainment? Or, when I hear of such sad situations, do I immediately pray for the people affected? Do I take delight in hearing of scandals? If I begin to feel an intense interest in some scandal, am I quick to mortify my curiosity? Do I engage in the kind of gossip that repeats the sins or misfortunes of others for no good reason? (detraction). Or worse, do I harm the reputation of others by speaking falsely about them? (calumny). Do I take too much interest in rumors and the doings of others? Do I choose as my friends people who like to gossip about others? Do I watch television shows, visit websites, or read magazines that tend toward gossip? Do I give some thought to what I say about others? Do I speak too much about others? Do I do some critical reflection after a conversation about others that has left me feeling uneasy?

Regarding envy: Do I become sad when I see the material or spiritual wealth of others? Do I rejoice or take delight in the misfortunes or falls of someone whom I envy? If I experience such emotions in myself, do I act against them by praying for the person and turning my thoughts to something else? Or do I linger with the perverted delight and nurture it by continually reflecting on the "good news" of someone else's misfortune? Do I take what I have for granted? Or am I aware of and thankful for what God has given to me and my family?

*L*UST *AND* *GREED.* Sins that habituate us to seeing our neighbor as an object (instead of as a person) are particularly good at making us blind to the suffering of others. Such sins include lust, whereby we see others simply as objects for sexual pleasure, and greed, whereby we see others merely as opportunities for (or obstacles to) making money.

Regarding lust: Do I tend to see others as sexual objects? Do I look at pornography? Do I keep a healthy custody of my eyes, especially during spring and summer months when people often dress immodestly? If I catch my eyes turning to where they shouldn't go, do I give the "second look" to God? Or do I allow my eyes to continue their pursuit? If I'm tempted with impure thoughts, do I turn to prayer? Or do I linger with them and their sinful delight? Do I avoid the near occasion of sin by avoiding forms of entertainment and places that might especially tempt me to impurity? Do I avoid idleness? Or do I waste time and give in to laziness? (Being idle and lazy invites temptations to impurity.)

Regarding greed: Do I see people only as potential clients and miss seeing them as persons? Are things more important to me than people? Am I driven to seek ways of making excessive amounts of money? If I'm married, am I open to life? Or do I have a contraceptive mentality, valuing a fancy car or exotic vacations more than having another child? Do I distinguish needs from wants? Do I always have to have the latest thing or a name brand? Can I enjoy the simple pleasures of life? Am I generous in giving to the poor?

*J*UDGMENTAL *ATTITUDE*. As Blessed Mother Teresa used to say, "If you take the time to judge, you don't have time to love." When we assume an attitude of judgment toward another, a gap yawns between us and them, and we can't connect. This is a diabolical attitude that stems from pride. It's subtle, but it does more damage to the heart than sins of the flesh — the very same sins over which it often sits in judgment.

Do I see myself as superior to others? Do I look down on particular groups of people because of their race, opinions, or ways of life? Do I impute motives to the actions of others, or do I leave such judgments to God? Am I quick to judge priests and bishops, or do I leave them, especially, to God's judgment? Do I pray for priests and bishops? Do I tend to make rash judgments of others? In other words, do I assume as true, without sufficient foundation, the moral faults of others? Do I realize rash judgment is grave matter when it rashly judges acts that are grave? To avoid rash judgment, am I careful, as the *Catechism* says, "to interpret insofar as possible [my] neighbor's thoughts, words, and deeds in a favorable way"? Am I insecure in my own life of faith and judge others out of a need to feel righteous? Or, while striving for holiness, do I recognize my own weaknesses, sinfulness, and attachments and go to Jesus, whom I know is rich in mercy? Do I relate to the older brother in the parable of the Prodigal Son? (see Lk 15:11-32). Do I believe in God's mercy? Do I realize that those who are merciful will obtain mercy (see Mt 5:7) and that the measure I give will be the measure I get back? (see Lk 6:38).

*U*NWILLINGNESS TO FORGIVE. Here I've saved what may be the "worst" for last. Nothing hardens a heart more than an unwillingness to forgive. When we cling to bitterness, resentment, grudges, and hate for those who have hurt us, our hearts quickly become as cold and hard as ice. When we don't forgive, we may think we're punishing the other person, but the reality is we're destroying ourselves. We often pray to our heavenly Father, "Forgive us our trespasses as we forgive those who trespass against us." Do we realize that if we don't forgive, we won't be forgiven? Still, we need not get discouraged or despair if we struggle in this area, for if we have even the slightest bit of good will, the Lord's mercy is there for us. Moreover, he knows that it often takes time for us to be able to forgive fully, and he's patient. O Lord, please give us the grace to forgive!

Are there people in my life whom I haven't forgiven? Do I hold on to bitterness over past wounds? Am I resentful toward anyone? Is there anyone to whom I give the silent treatment? Is there anyone I would refuse to help if he needed it? Do I pray for my enemies? Is there anyone for whom I would not pray? Do I need to ask anyone for forgiveness? Is there anyone with whom it might be helpful to talk regarding a past hurt that especially bothers me, and can I do so without being accusatory and with a readiness to forgive? Have I asked Jesus for the grace to forgive? Do I reflect on how often Jesus has forgiven me? Do I reflect on his example of forgiving those who crucified him? Do I realize my sins crucified him? Do I realize he still loves me when I choose to forgive but struggle with forgetting? Do I try to forget? Or do I continually replay in my mind past hurts? Do I try to give people a clean slate? Have I said, "I forgive you"? Do I try to forgive? Or do I give in to anger, which seeks to do evil to someone out of a desire for revenge? According to St. Faustina, "We resemble God most when we forgive our neighbors."

Okay, that examination of conscience might have been a bit heavy. If you want to go to confession soon, then by all means, go for it. (Before going, I suggest you read the section "Confession" in Appendix Two.)

Confession is great, but getting down on oneself is not. If the spiritual exercise we just read has got you beating yourself up, please stop. Yes, stop beating yourself and, instead, start reflecting on what we learned in the Second Obstacle about our weaknesses, sinfulness, and attachments. Also, before you start reading the next section, you might want to spend some time with the Lord — actually, that's a good idea for all of us. Even if we didn't start getting down on ourselves, let's all spend some time going to Jesus as we are with all our weaknesses, sinfulness, and attachments (*ecce*). Then, let's console Jesus (and ourselves) by allowing his merciful love to wash over us (*fiat*). Finally, after having spent some time praising him for his superabundant mercy (*magnificat*), let's get back to the retreat. See you in a little while.

2. Reaching Out to Our Neighbor to Help Alleviate His Suffering

Welcome back. Ready to begin some lessons on reaching out to our neighbor? Wonderful. Let's start with a little meditation.

Imagine a big, burning building. There it is, a raging inferno. Black smoke's bellowing up, flames flash forth from broken windows, and above the fire's low roar and constant crackling rise the faint voices of people inside crying out for help. As you're watching, smelling, and hearing this frightening scene, a new sound comes to your ears. At first, it's faint. Then, it gradually gets louder and louder. All right! Fire Department to the rescue! Racing out from around the corner suddenly appears a bright red fire truck with sirens blaring and lights flashing wildly. It arrives with a screeching halt. Immediately, six strong firemen rush out, unravel a huge hose, and stand in a line, hose in hand, ready to blast that fire into a puff of white smoke. They await their captain's command. It comes: "Let'er rip!" Down goes the switch that opens up the tank, and they're off. Hundreds of gallons of raging water race from the tank, through the hose, and then, right as they hit the nozzle, *poof!* A cloud of mist slowly spreads out and makes its lazy ascent up, up, and harmlessly away from the laughing flames. (Someone must have accidently left the nozzle setting on "mist.")

This brief meditation can teach us an important lesson about reaching out to our neighbor. The gallons of rushing water represent the compassionate force of feeling that flows from a healthy heart when it sees the suffering of others (represented by the people in the burning building). The water as it hits the nozzle set to mist represents what happens when we don't know what to do with our compassion: *Poof!* It ends up going off in different directions, like mist, and therefore isn't effective. Even worse, it becomes a spectacle of softness (like the mist in the meditation) that gets mocked by hostile spectators (the laughing flames) and sometimes even embarrasses, confuses, or offends those for whom it's intended (the people in the burning building). For example, there's that deep kind of compassion one might call "smother love," which, though well-intentioned, to the recipient feels overbearing and a bit too soft and gushy.

To prevent our compassion from hitting the mist setting, one virtue is extremely important: prudence. Prudence tightens the nozzle so compassion becomes a concentrated stream capable of reaching its target. In other words, it helps teach us how to reach out to our neighbor in ways that are effective (not all over the place) and truly consoling (not embarrassing, offensive, or confusing). Because prudence is more art than science, it can't easily be taught. Moreover, it usually requires experience and time spent with prudent people. Therefore, even if we need it, we can't get it in just a weekend retreat.

So what do we do now? Simple. The same thing we did in Part One when we didn't have enough time to learn something else important. We listened to a holy nun. Remember how God gave us (through St. Margaret Mary) a 30-day-retreat-sized principle and foundation in one shot? Well, now he'll give us (through St. Faustina) a lesson on prudent compassion ... in three shots. Here's what he said to the Mercy Saint:

> **I am giving you three ways of exercising mercy toward your neighbor: the first — by deed, the second — by word, the third — by prayer. In these three degrees is contained the fullness of mercy, and it is an unquestionable proof of love for Me. By this means a soul glorifies and pays reverence to My mercy.**

The saint herself elaborated (a little) on these three "degrees" of mercy in the following passage from her *Diary*:

> The first: the act of mercy, of whatever kind. The second: the word of mercy — if I cannot carry out a work of mercy, I will assist by my words. The third: prayer — if I cannot show mercy by deeds or words, I can always do so by prayer. My prayer reaches out even there where I cannot reach out physically.

So there we go: prudent compassion summarized in the "three shots" of deed, word, and prayer. I know, I know, it's still pretty sparse on detail, but it has to be because, again, prudence is an art, and one can't exactly nail down an art. Nonetheless, for those of us who are worried our compassion setting might still be left on "mist," I've got two suggestions.

First suggestion: Turn to the Holy Spirit. The Holy Spirit is always with us, and he can give us something called "infused prudence." In other words, he can enlighten us with inspirations on how to act in everyday situations with prudent compassion (compassion without the mist). Saint Faustina would turn to the

Holy Spirit whenever she needed such help. Calling the Holy Spirit by his name, "Love," she writes: "When I hesitate on how to act in some situations, I always ask Love. It advises best." Let's get in the habit of doing the same.

Second suggestion: Reflect on the three degrees of mercy. It's a great spiritual exercise to think of practical and prudent ways by which we might actually show mercy through deed, word, and prayer in daily life. Such an exercise goes a long way in helping us begin to "tighten the nozzle," so our compassion will be effective and appropriate. Because this is a retreat (a time for reflection), why don't we spend some time right now reflecting on the three degrees of mercy?

*M*ERCY IN DEED: THE MERCIFUL OUTLOOK. There are infinite ways of doing deeds of mercy. To give some organization to them, theologians have divided the "works of mercy" into two categories: spiritual and corporal. Each category, they say, contains seven works of mercy, making for a grand total of 14. Yet reflecting on 14 points is still a lot, especially if we've only got a weekend for this retreat. (Those who want to reflect on them after the retreat can find them in "References and Notes.") So, instead of fourteen points, I'd like to present just one simple and effective way of practicing deeds of mercy. I call it the "merciful outlook." I like this way a lot because it's a deed of mercy we can practice almost anytime (provided we're around other people). I also like it because it seems to fit so well with the Lord's strategy, as I'll now explain.

Earlier in the retreat, we learned that people in 17th century France used to see Jesus according to the frightening portraits painted by the Jansenists — the one's with the mean, bearded guy who looks ready to smack us. Well, people today often still see Jesus like that, so they steer clear of his supposed "smack zone." Yet, even if they've given up on Jesus, he hasn't given up on them. If they're too afraid to go to him, he's decided to go to them. In going to them, however, he's cautious, because he knows that at even the slightest sign of him, they'll bolt. So Jesus goes to them incognito. Can you guess what disguise he uses? That's right, you and me. Jesus wants to love them through the way we look at them, through our merciful outlook. They probably won't immediately recognize that it's Jesus behind such a look (if they did, they'd bolt), but it can still have its healing effect, and it prepares their hearts to eventually recognize his loving face. Thus, the merciful outlook truly is part of the Lord's patient and loving strategy.

Now that we know something about the Lord's strategy, it should make even more sense (as we learned in the previous section) why Jesus loves to heal our hearts, making them more compassionate. For, not only does such healing make us love him more, not only do we become much happier, but having a renewed heart helps us to develop a merciful outlook toward others. It helps us to look at others, especially at God's prodigal children, with Jesus' own love and compassion. Therefore, it's another way (along with trust) by which we can console Jesus. But developing the merciful outlook isn't easy. If we want to be good missionaries of the Lord's mercy and love, we need to come to a better understanding of what it is. Let's begin by considering what it's not.

The merciful outlook is not the "patronizing outlook." It's not about pitying people. Yes, mercy is love when it encounters suffering, but the merciful outlook is not about feeling sorry for people, and it's certainly not about looking down on them from some high pedestal of self-righteousness. As Pope John Paul II wrote in his encyclical letter *Dives in Misericordia*, true mercy is always a *bilateral* reality, a two-way street: As we give it, we also receive it. If we don't habitually realize this as we do deeds of mercy, then we just might be stuck in the patronizing outlook. To get unstuck (and thus to be free to live the merciful outlook), I recommend we spend some time pondering the pope's actual words on bilateral mercy:

> We must also continually purify all our actions and all our intentions in which mercy is understood and practiced in a unilateral way, as a good done to others. An act of merciful love is only really such when we are deeply convinced at the moment that

we perform it that we are at the same time receiving mercy from the people who are accepting it from us. If this bilateral and reciprocal quality is absent, our actions are not yet true acts of mercy, nor has there yet been fully completed in us that conversion to which Christ has shown us the way by His words and example, even to the cross, nor are we yet sharing fully in the magnificent source of merciful love that has been revealed to us by Him.

The merciful outlook is not the "over-spiritualized outlook." Sometimes people speak of loving Christ in others in a way that makes me a bit uncomfortable. Here's why. Imagine your spouse or a close friend seems especially kind and loving toward you, so you ask them, "Why do you love me so much?" And they reply, "Oh, I was loving Jesus *in* you." That sounds awfully close to, "I wasn't loving you. I was loving Jesus." Which might as well be, "You're chopped liver, but Jesus is lovable even in dead meat." If that's what's meant, then something is surely missing.

The merciful outlook is not the "proselytizing outlook." For example, the approach of those who wear a salesman's smile and a slick badge that says "Elder Smith" is exactly what I do not mean by the merciful outlook. I'm not talking about phony friendliness that sees others through the agenda of winning converts. No, the merciful outlook, as we'll see, has to do with evangelization — not proselytization. It has to do with proclaiming the good news of Christ's love through an authentic love for the other as a person. We'll get to that in due time. For now, having learned something of what the merciful outlook is not, let's explore what it is.

The outlook I'm describing is merciful because it responds to suffering. In fact, it's a compassionate response to what's probably the most universal and deepest human suffering, namely, existential loneliness. This needs some more explaining.

I think the best way to describe man's existential loneliness (and man in general) is with one simple word: thirst. Man is a "thirst," and his thirst, unlike that of animals, is not fully quenched by the things of this world. For example, let's say we give Fido the dog a nice yard, food, water, and lots of affection. Of course, his tail will just keep on wagging. It's not so with us. We can have everything and still be depressed, still be thirsting for what we can't quite put into words.

St. Augustine, brilliant writer that he was, could put the problem into words. In one of the most famous lines in Christian literature, he wrote, "You made us for Yourself, O Lord, and our hearts are restless until they rest in You." We all have restless hearts, a seemingly unquenchable thirst, because we're made for God. We're made to be with him in heaven. We're made to see him face-to-face. Right now, however, we're not there. We're not fully with him, and we can't fully see him. So, in this land of exile, we experience a deep and sometimes agonizing existential loneliness.

Like St. Augustine, the French philosopher Blaise Pascal had an amazing way with words. Also like Augustine, he explained man's existential loneliness with astonishing clarity. Writing in the 17th century at a time when kings held absolute power in their dominions and everyone seemed to envy them, Pascal came up with an insightful theory to explain why everyone wants to be king. He said everyone wants to be king because kings can wage wars, conduct the affairs of state, throw big parties, and always be surrounded by a whirlwind of people. In other words, the king gets to be perpetually distracted. Distracted from what? Distracted from the fact of his unhappiness, his existential loneliness.

Pascal held that the worst torture for modern man is to be quiet and alone in his own room. Why? Because solitude brings out the beast of our loneliness. Of course, even in the midst of distraction, the beast is still there gnawing at our hearts. (Even in the middle of a crowd, we can often feel him chewing away.) But distraction helps numb us to his constant gnawing. Thus, people in Pascal's day envied the king, and in our day, people still want to live like kings. Yes, with our cell phones, iPods, and e-mail, some might say we've become "royally good" at distracting ourselves.

Christ teaches another way. He tells us we don't have to numb the pain of our loneliness. He calls out to us, "I can quench your thirst! I can give your hearts rest!" (see Jn 7:47; Mt 11:28). He can say this in full truth because he's God, the one for whom we're made, the one for whom we thirst. Specifically, he's Jesus Christ, God the Son become flesh, and he's been sent by God the Father through the power of God the Holy Spirit to bring us into their Family of Love, the Holy Trinity.

Jesus says to us: "I did not create you to be alone. I created you for communion in my Family of Love." Such words are not pie in the sky, not a future fulfillment we only get when we die. No. Christ comes now in Word and Sacrament — especially in the Sacrament of Holy Communion — to give us the joy the world cannot give. Christ also comes now through you and through me, through communion with friends and family, thus giving us a real (though limited) satisfaction to our longing, quench to our thirst, and rest to our hearts. It's precisely here that the merciful outlook comes in as a response to people's loneliness.

The merciful outlook is a way of giving drink to the thirsty. It gives a cup of love to another and to ourselves as we make our pilgrimage through this desert of life to the Ocean of Love, the Holy Trinity. I said it provides a cup. The merciful outlook is not a gushing bucket of smother love. It's a cup. It's a simple thing but beautiful to a thirsty heart. It's a subtle way of seeing others — not an intense staring — that communicates to them a simple and sincere message, "I delight that you exist." This modest expression of real delight in the very existence of the other will often be for them a refreshing cup of love, a cup that helps to quench their thirst and point them along the way to the Eternal Fountain of delight-filled Love that alone truly satisfies.

Now, some people may be getting troubled at this point. They may be honing in on how the merciful outlook is a way of seeing others with delight, which may cause them to think, "Wait a minute, delight is a feeling." (People often get nervous about feelings.) In fact, they may be saying to themselves: "He's not suggesting we're always supposed to be feeling delight in others, is he? After all, what matters is not what we feel anyway, right? What truly matters is simply that we choose to love, that we will it." In response to such thoughts, I'd say, "Yes, it's true that sometimes love must be expressed without feeling. Sometimes it's simply a dry but firm decision of the will." (Thus, we've all probably heard the expression, "Love is a choice.") However, I'd also say that love simply as a choice is not the ideal. Ideally, love ought to be felt.

Think about it. Unless we ourselves feel love for the other, will our love still carry the warmth that touches hearts? I don't think so. People are good at distinguishing felt love from forced love. The merciful outlook just doesn't work without true feeling — and it can't be faked. Phony smiles that say "You're just so special!" (gag) do not work. Thus, an important question arises, "How do we feel delight in others?" This question brings us to the essence of the merciful outlook.

Felt delight in others, expressed in the merciful outlook, stems from grasping the truth and beauty of who the other authentically is. And who is the other? The other is Christ. Yet I don't mean the other is Christ in an over-spiritualized kind of way. (There's no ghost-like Christ hiding behind the other's ear.) No, the other is Christ. Christ is not hiding. The other is Christ insofar as he's a member of Christ's Mystical Body (or, if he's not a Christian, he's a prospective member of Christ by virtue of his being made in the image of God and called to full membership in Christ's Body). Of course, the other is not the same as Christ the *Head* of the Body. Still, to be a member of Christ's Body is truly to be Christ. Regarding this point, it's helpful to reflect once again on Christ's startling words to Saul (later St. Paul), who had been persecuting Christians, "Saul, Saul, why are you persecuting me?" (Acts 9:4). The Lord didn't say, "Hey, Saul, why are you persecuting my followers?" Rather, he said "Why are you persecuting *me*?"

So, the member of Christ's Body *is* Christ. The word "is" here is important. The merciful outlook I'm proposing takes it seriously. For this outlook aims to discover the other person as a unique member of the Body of Christ. As a member (or potential member) of Christ's Body, the other person shows forth an utterly unique facet of the mystery of Christ. I'll now say more about this, for this is precisely that in which we should feel our delight when we delight in another person. It's also what helps turn the over-spiritualized outlook into the merciful outlook.

A Christian ought to delight in Christ. He ought to have drunk deeply of the beauty, goodness, and glory of Christ Jesus. He ought always to be eager to have more of Christ, that is, to know him more fully so as to love him more deeply. Well, the members of the Body of Christ help us to know and love Christ more. I say that because each and every human being is created in the image of God and given a vocation to manifest by his redeemed existence a facet of the beauty of Christ in a way that no other being in the cosmos is capable of doing. What an amazing vocation each person has! No wonder Christ longs for us to become saints, for a saint is someone who most perfectly fulfills this vocation. A saint manifests the unique face of Christ he or she is called to be. Thus, a saint helps reveal Christ to us, and Christ is so beautiful in his saints.

"But wait just a minute," someone might say, "Isn't Christ enough? Why do I need other people to show me Christ?" Yes, Christ is enough. That is, the full Christ is enough, Christ head and members (see Eph 4:13). For Christ and the members of his body truly are one (see 1 Cor 12:12-27), and to know and love Christ is not only to know and love Christ the Head but also to know and love his members. Those other people *are* him. They're his body. Clearly, we don't express true love for some-one by saying, "From the neck up, I'm in love with you. As for the rest, well, all I feel is hate." Similarly, we don't love Christ if we say, "I love Christ the Head of the Mystical Body but despise the members of his body." Saint John calls such a person "a liar" (1 Jn 4:20). Love, then, is of the whole body, head and members. We can't truly love the one without also loving the others.

Now, let's address from a different angle the question, "Why do I need other people to show me Christ?" Look at it this way: Christ is like the sun. His brightness, like the sun's, is so great that we may only be able to gaze on his full glory for a short while. Yet, just as we can easily take in the sun's marvelous light as it bathes the beauties of creation and thus have a better appreciation and gratitude for the gift of the sun, so also we can easily see the marvelous beauty of Christ in his saints and thus have a better appreciation, knowledge, and love of Christ. In the Christian dispensation, more is not less. Rather, more is more! And the beauty of Christ in his members gives us limited beings even more ways to take in and contemplate his infinite richness.

Still, it's true that God didn't have to make things this way. Christ didn't have to invite us to such close intimacy with himself that we become his very body. God could have forgiven our sins but then left us as mere creatures and slaves — thank God that's not what he did. Thank God that God in Christ Jesus no longer calls us creatures but "children of God" (1 Jn 3:1), no longer calls us slaves but "friends" (Jn 15:15). Thank God he not only forgives our sins but raises us up to his own divine life and makes us members of his body. This, thanks be to the unfathomable mercy of God, is now the way things are. No, it didn't have to be this way. God didn't have to do it like this, but it's how he did do it. By God's good pleasure and design, it *is* reality. Christ is now glorious not only in himself but in his members, and this doesn't take anything away from him. In fact, it helps us to appreciate him all the more not only for the superabundant mercy that created this new situation but for the amazing richness of Christ that this situation reveals.

"Okay, fine," someone may say, "I can accept that the saints reveal Christ's glory. Yes, Christ is beautiful in his saints ... but not in everyday people." Not true. The glory of God and the beauty of Christ fill all creation. It's just more of a challenge to see this glory in those people who don't manifest it as overwhelmingly as do the saints. This is the challenge of living the merciful outlook. It takes practice. It takes grace. It takes begging for the gift of grace.

We really can have the merciful outlook. The saints have it, and we're called to be saints. We're called to see as they see. And how do they see? They see as God sees. And how does

God see? He sees the beauty of what he created (see Gen 1:31). In an unrepentant sinner, he still sees a vocation to greatness even if it's tragically entombed in a hardened heart. Amazingly, when such a sinner recognizes that God sees this greatness in him, he begins to come alive. Such is the gaze of God. Such is the power of mercy. Such is the meaning and power of the merciful outlook. It draws out the good and brings back to life. It's a God-like gazing on others that draws out their good and brings them into the new and more abundant life.

Sometimes this God-like gaze is terrible. It's terrible not in the sense of "that movie was terrible" but in the weighty sense of that "terrible day" when Christ comes again on the clouds of heaven with trumpet blasts (see Mt 24:30-31). For the merciful outlook does indeed bring with it a kind of reckoning. It's not yet the "terrible day of reckoning" — thank God — but it's like it. For the person who receives the merciful outlook from another sees reflected in the eyes of the other the words, "You are great." However, these words are also a call to greatness. For, while the greatness is truly there — the other person sees it! — it's not fully there.

The person who receives the merciful outlook knows that the greatness he sees reflected back at him in the eye of the other is tragically not all there in him, because he can also feel the gaze of his own "inner eye," his conscience. This inner eye makes him tragically aware of not being who he's meant to be, which is terrible. Yet it's not despairingly terrible. For there's still the gaze of the other, at least in memory, constantly echoing the words, "You are great." So the person feels himself in the midst of the terrible drama of having to choose either to be the person he presently is or the person he's called to become, either the person of mediocrity or the awe-inspiring person he was destined to be from before the foundation of the world (see Mt 25:34; Eph 1:4).

The terrible aspect of the merciful outlook leads us to an important point: It's not our job to see in the other what the other's own inner eye sees. In fact, we can't do it. Our gaze can't penetrate to the inner sanctuary of another's conscience, and we ought not to try. For not only are we incapable of doing it, but there's a penalty if we try. Another's conscience is sacred space the Lord himself guards. If we try to enter it — for instance, with our rash judgments — we pay a heavy price. We pay the price of losing some, if not all, of our ability to exercise the merciful outlook, and our own hearts harden.

Sadly, the other person also pays a price when we presume to know how his conscience convicts him. For just as the merciful outlook can give life and draw out the good, the judgmental outlook can draw darkness out of the other and even destroy him. It can crushingly magnify his inner eye's verdict of guilt. It can help tempt him to believe that who he is at his core is really the evil the judgmental outlook thinks it's discovered there, and thus it can extinguish hope. In fact, seeing the other's look of disdain, the person living under the harsh stare of the judgmental outlook will often say to himself, "Well, I guess that's just who I am." And then he'll stop striving for the greatness that's his call.

When we look at others with the judgmental outlook, we abandon our part in the Lord's patient and loving strategy, which I mentioned earlier. We go, instead, to assist in someone else's strategy, a sinister, destructive strategy. Although we don't want to do this, how can we avoid it? For surely there are signs in others of what's inconsistent with their vocation in Christ — and at least we can point to things about them that annoy us.

Can people be annoying? Yes. Do people sin? Yes. As for the annoying stuff, we need to deal with it, look past it, or maybe even rediscover it as treasure. As for the sinful stuff, we leave that up to the Lord and them — unless, of course, we have a clear responsibility to confront or correct them, in which case we need to beg the Holy Spirit for grace and prudence and then do our duty lovingly. Most of the time, however, I think our responsibility lies in deep-sea diving.

In overcoming temptations to go from the merciful to the judgmental outlook, it's good to be like a deep-sea diver who searches for sunken treasure. Such a diver knows there's treasure down there, and he goes for it. Sometimes he has to swim through dark, murky water and even fend off underwater beasts, but he keeps going. He knows the treasure's worth.

As we've already learned, in each person there's an invaluable treasure, a facet of the face of Christ that can't be found in anyone else. In the saints, no diving is necessary to find it — at some point a volcano of love erupted in them and pushed its way up to the surface, becoming a beautiful tropical island that displays its abundant treasure right there on the sun-swept beach. In most of us, however, the treasure is still underwater, and it may even be lying on the ocean floor. But it's down there, and it's worth diving for. We need not fear the murky water (the hardness of the other's heart) nor pay attention to the sea monsters (the other's annoying personality traits). If the sharks come out (meanness or signs of certain kinds of inappropriateness), we don't have to stay (and sometimes we shouldn't), but the little bites from the other sea monsters are nothing compared to the delight that comes from finding the treasure that lies on the ocean floor.

Some people don't like this kind of talk. They think we should be harder on others. They think diving for underwater treasure isn't worth it. They think it's better to come crashing down on people with constant corrections. Well, they're free to have their own opinions, and maybe that's the way to go for drill sergeants and parents with teenagers. (Yes, parents, I'm kidding.) But this retreat is about mercy, and it includes the merciful outlook as part of the program. Nevertheless, while this program is for little souls, it definitely doesn't take the soft approach that sees no evil. The merciful outlook doesn't pretend that sin and annoyances aren't there. They're there. We all know they're there. The merciful outlook just makes a strategic choice to go past them. It makes a strategic choice to go for what St. Ignatius would call "the greater good." It chooses mercy over justice and trusts in the power of mercy to bring an even greater good out of evil.

While we're on the topic of cynical objections, let's take another one. Some people will complain that all this talk of finding people's treasure and delighting in their good is all too "romantic." They'll say we just need to do our duty, not hurt anyone, and not get too excited. That last part, I think, is the most revealing: Don't get too excited. Now, there's something to this objection. For, if the merciful outlook is exercised imprudently, if the nozzle isn't properly tightened, if our compassion becomes misty, gushy, clingy, and overbearing, then, yes, it's definitely not perfect. But that's to be expected. Loving is messy business, and it takes time to get it right.

Actually, it's not business at all. It's art. And great artists begin by making mistakes. Even Michelangelo must have started out with his share of messy canvases and broken statues, but God bless the one who tries! For loving is everything, and God is pleased with the person who doesn't lose heart after embarrassing himself trying to love. He's so happy when we don't give up after learning firsthand what it means to be a "fool for Christ's sake" (1 Cor 4:10).

Yet how many people — people who had such beautiful, loving, and compassionate hearts! — have already given up? How many people, after feeling embarrassed, foolish, or hurt because their love came out messy or was misunderstood, have then said to themselves, "That's the last time I'm opening up"? How many people close up their hearts and decide to take the safe route of "not getting too excited"? Cynicism and hardness of heart are not signs of prudence. They're signs of quitting, cowardice, buried talents, and hidden light. But Jesus doesn't want our light hidden. He wants it shining for all to see (see Mt 5:14-16), and even if we burn down a few fields on our way to the lampstand, there's no need to worry — they'll grow back.

One last cynical objection (cynicism dies hard):

> Yeah, that's just great. Set people up for a big fall. Lift those ideals so high that when people come crashing back down to reality, the impact's sure to break their necks (and hearts) — because that's what's going to happen. They'll climb up that high lampstand, find out their lamp was never even lit, and then jump off in despair.

There's something to this objection, too. The merciful outlook ideal is definitely high: to delight in each person we meet. That's not easy. It's not easy to delight in the people we see every day. It's not easy to find treasure in people day in and day out, especially when there's a lot going on. It's not easy, and we often don't do it. Of course we'll fail — but we'll also succeed, and the successes are worth the pain of failure. So, yes, to the extent that our duties allow us, we should try to reach our ideal. It's not possible to live perfectly, but it is possible to live. Why? Because people really do have an amazing beauty that comes from being the unique members of the Body of Christ they are (or are called to be). Even if we see them every day for the rest of our lives, there's no exhausting their richness.

But how do we know this? How do we know all that beauty is really there? After all, most of the time it might seem like it's not there. People are people — and, frankly, we do seem to be a motley crew. Moreover, the day-in, day-out people, especially those we live with and love, quickly seem to lose their mystery.

One test shows that each person is an inexhaustible beauty: death. Someone we know and love suddenly dies. Just as suddenly, they're not so mundane. Suddenly, we easily see past their annoying aspects and remember the irreplaceable gift that they were — and, in fact, as we remember them, we often find we love those aspects that annoyed us and wish we could experience them again. When someone we love dies, there's no question of consoling ourselves with the thought, "Oh, don't be so sad, there are plenty of other people in the world." We all intuitively understand why that's so ridiculous. Even though many other people in the world are funnier, better looking, kinder, more athletic — whatever — none of that matters. That wasn't the point. There was a treasure in the beloved that no one can replace no matter how talented or gifted, and we rightfully mourn the fact that this side of heaven, we'll never encounter it again. We rightfully weep because there's a hole in the cosmos, a reflection of Christ's face that, here, we behold no more.

So, wonder and delight at the beauty of another is something real — we surely feel its absence after someone we love has just died. It's not something too "romantic," though we may indeed be setting ourselves up for disappointment if we expect to feel it all the time. Still, we can try. We can ask for the grace. We can continue to draw close to Christ, especially to the suffering of his Heart, and hope that he'll make our hearts more like his.

The Heart of Christ. Yes, that's the goal. As members of his body, we share his Heart. We can love with his Heart, the Heart that always sees the treasure (and the suffering) of each person, the Heart that always sees his image in another, the pierced Heart that knows at what terrible price the other has been made so beautiful.

Before closing this long but important section (for a summary, see "References and Notes"), there's one last issue that still needs to be addressed. It's the issue raised by the question, often timidly asked, "What do we do when we see 'too much' beauty in the other?" In other words, "What do we do if our hearts become attached to someone?" This is a real possibility. For Christ is indeed beautiful in his saints — even in the not-yet-saints. It would be strange if sometimes, as a relief from our own existential loneliness, our hearts were not tempted to find "too much" fulfillment in the other.

Of course, in a certain sense, our hearts should be attached to people. (This especially applies to spouses.) Yet sometimes we can be too attached or attached to the wrong person. What then? That's a big question. Unfortunately, the full answer is too long to include in a weekend-length retreat, so we'll have to settle for a summary.

While Christ is beautiful in his saints, each saint is but a pale reflection of the beauty of Christ, the Head of the Mystical Body. Each person does indeed have a unique sharing in Christ's beauty, but Christ is beauty in its fullness. He *is* Beauty. Yes, we should love the beauty in which he has created and re-created each person. For, again, he gives them a share in his very own beauty, and they're his gifts to us. However, we mustn't confuse the gift for the Giver, and if we find ourselves doing so, we need to go back to him. We need to get back to "first things first" and give primacy to some contemplation.

So, the short answer to the delicate problem of being too attached to others is to continually go to Jesus as we are, even when we're desperately gripping our beloved attachment. Sometimes Jesus may say to us, "Well, you're not ready to let go of that just yet, but please sit here a while with me." At other times, he resorts to the strategy I recommended earlier for painlessly retrieving a tennis ball from a stubborn dog. In other words, when we act like a stubborn dog that grips its beloved ball firmly in its teeth, we just might begin to feel an affectionate pat on the head followed by gentle, coaxing words: "Nice doggie. ... That's a *good* dog. ..."

*W*ORD: *THE MERCIFUL QUESTION.* Just as there are infinite ways of doing deeds of mercy, so also there are infinite ways to speak a merciful word. Unfortunately, theologians haven't categorized these ways (as they have deeds of mercy), thus we'll have to settle for a simple definition and a few examples. A merciful word is anything written or said with the intention of alleviating the suffering of another. For example, a word that aims to give hope to the despairing, tries to get the sad to laugh, attempts to help the fearful to trust in Jesus, or seeks to make the lonely feel less alone is a word of mercy. Here, I'd like to focus on one specific word of mercy. It's actually a question. I call it the "merciful question."

The merciful question goes with the merciful outlook. Recall that the merciful outlook responds to the suffering of another's existential loneliness by expressing delight in him. Well, the merciful question is simply a way of helping us to experience this delight in the other. It does so by inviting the other (by means of a question) to open up, reveal his treasure, and show who he is.

I said earlier that prudence tightens the nozzle of our compassion, so it'll be effective. This also applies to when we want to show compassion through the merciful question. In other words, we need to be prudent in asking the merciful question — it's not a gushing bucket of questions; it's not an interrogation. It's a simple question or two at the right time and place that invites the other to disclose his treasure, so we might delight in him (or, perhaps, even feel sorrow with him). For instance, after small talk and the usual cordialities that help establish trust with another (and if our duties allow us to take the time), we can ask a question about the other's hopes, joys, fears, or sorrows and then simply listen. If the other wants to share and has the time for it, great. If not, that's fine, too. Simply having asked the merciful question is an act of mercy — but be prepared. Just as a lot of people out there starve to be delighted in, so there are perhaps just as many who long to be listened to.

Because so many people long to be listened to, we can be sure that our merciful questions will meet with responses. Sometimes the responses will be a gently trickling stream. At other times, they'll be like a dam bursting, and we'll get flooded. If that happens, don't worry. As we advance in prudence, we'll learn how and when to lovingly bring things to a close, if need be. Of course, if we're beginners, we just might frequently get flooded. If that happens, don't worry. It gives us practice in learning how to swim through the sometimes messy waters of love, and the next time we'll be able to do better. Speaking of practice, it might be helpful if I relate something of my own experience of learning to ask the merciful question.

For me, the best school for learning to ask the merciful question was the seminary. Several factors made it a particularly good school: There were many seminarians, we had to meet for conversation frequently (at least three times a day during mealtimes), and we were often different in age, temperament, and background. In such an environment, there were lots of opportunities to ask merciful questions, but that's not to say it was easy. It didn't take long for me to discover that the merciful question often needs to take different forms, depending on the person to whom it's addressed.

With some of the guys in the seminary, I learned it's best not to prod. Showing mercy to them usually meant keeping things light, for example, by talking sports or weather and by doing a lot of joking. Interestingly enough, after spending some time on the superficial, they appreciated a merciful question now and then, as long as an injection of humor quickly followed their sharing. Other guys were starving for deeper conversation. They were the ones who felt most consoled by any question that asked about their joys and sorrows, hopes and fears. They were also the ones who gave me the most practice in learning to lovingly manage floods. Then there were the intellectuals who were eager to delve into questions of philosophy or the mysteries of faith. With them, the merciful question was easy. I'd simply ask, "So, what'd you learn in class today?" Then it would begin. Once we got into it, and I was asked my opinion, I have to confess that I was usually the one responsible for doing the flooding (especially if the topic was Divine Mercy or Ignatian spirituality), which brings me to one last point about the merciful question.

We ourselves should be open to answering the merciful questions others pose to us. Once again, as Pope John Paul II wrote, mercy is a bilateral reality. Thus, while the one who shares receives the gift of being listened to, there's also a gift for the person who gets to listen, who gets to see the treasure of the other open up. We all have inner riches, and we shouldn't be afraid to share them with others. However, we might want to make sure that the other really is open (maybe their question was just small talk), and we might want to strive not to flood them. If we're not sure how open the other is, before we begin, it doesn't hurt to ask something like, "Well, how much time do you have?" If we end up flooding them anyway, at least we're giving them an opportunity to learn to swim, and we can make a mental note to do better the next time.

*P*RAYER: *THE PRAYERS OF MERCY.* According to St. Faustina, if we can't do a deed of mercy or speak a word of mercy, we can always reach out to others spiritually through our prayers. How do we do this, specifically? From among the infinite ways of offering prayers of mercy, I'd like to make two recommendations: the Chaplet of Divine Mercy and a modified "breathing prayer."

In the context of the First Obstacle, I spoke about the power of the Chaplet of Divine Mercy (see page 72). Because it's so mighty, I suggest we adopt it as one of our prayers of mercy. Building on what I said earlier, I'd like to explain further why the chaplet is so awesome.

I said earlier that the chaplet is particularly effective as a prayer, because through it we offer the suffering of Jesus to the Father. In fact, because of this action, the chaplet is the most powerful prayer there is. On hearing this, perhaps someone might say, "Wait a minute. I thought the Mass was the most efficacious prayer." That's right. It is — and that's the whole point. The chaplet is a kind of extension of the prayer of the Mass. For, in the chaplet, as in the Mass (and in union with the Mass), we offer the Body and Blood of Christ to the Father — along with our own joys, sorrows, sufferings, and prayers. Because of this connection between the chaplet and the Mass, I recommend that whenever we pray the chaplet, we consciously unite our praying of it to the prayer of all the Masses being said throughout the world.

To help us appreciate better the power of the chaplet, I'd now like to present a few selections from the *Diary of St. Faustina*. The first selection provides an instance of how the chaplet can help those who face material evils. Faustina writes:

> Today I was awakened by a great storm. The wind was raging, and it was raining in torrents, thunderbolts striking again and again. I began to pray that the storm would do no harm, when I heard the words: **Say the chaplet I have taught you, and the storm will cease.** I began immediately to say the chaplet and hadn't even finished it when the storm suddenly ceased, and I heard the words: **Through the chaplet you will obtain everything, if what you ask for is compatible with My will.**

The second selection has to do with the power of the chaplet to help those in spiritual need. In the following, St. Faustina describes what happened after Jesus asked her to help him save a certain despairing soul by praying the chaplet for him:

> Suddenly, I found myself in a strange cottage where an elderly man was dying amidst great torments. All about the bed was a multitude of demons and the family, who were crying. When I began to pray [the chaplet], the spirits of darkness fled, with hissing and threats directed at me. The soul became calm and, filled with trust, rested in the Lord.
>
> At the same moment, I found myself again in my own room. How this happens ... I do not know.

In relating events like this, St. Faustina was simply following the instructions of the Lord, who had said to her: "**My daughter, encourage souls to say the chaplet which I have given to you. It pleases Me to grant everything they ask of Me by saying the chaplet.**" May St. Faustina's testimony to the power of the chaplet encourage us to pray it with greater fervor and bolder confidence. (To read more of her testimony on the power of the chaplet, see the section "Chaplet of Divine Mercy" in Appendix Two.)

Okay, so we realize the Chaplet of Divine Mercy is a powerful prayer. Yet, as we begin to pray it, some of us might wonder, "Well, for whom should I pray?" Of course, prayers of mercy are for anyone who's in need of mercy ... but that's everyone! Moreover, maybe you're one of those people who, like me, finds it difficult to pray for general things (like "the whole world"). For those of us who run into such problems with intercessory prayer, I have two bits of advice.

First, give "first rights" to the grace (merit) of your prayers to Mary (which, by the way, is part of what it means to be consecrated to her). In other words, tell her, "Mary, I give you the right to distribute the grace of my prayers as you see fit." Making such a gift to her ensures that the grace of our prayers will be used in the best possible way, and thus it can relieve our anxiety about who to pray for.

It works like this: Because of her unique vantage point from heaven, Mary can best determine which people are most in need of our prayers. For instance, seeing some forgotten person in China about to die in despair, she can take the grace of our prayers (and "offered up" sufferings) and use it to help that dying person to trust in God and accept salvation.

Now, perhaps this idea has got some of us thinking:

Well, that's great. I'm happy to help the dying person in China, whom I don't know, but I'd be disappointed if I therefore couldn't use the grace of my prayers to help the people I do know, like my family and friends. I'm worried that if I give Mary "first rights," then I'll lose the right to pray for those whom I especially love, even if they're less in need than other people in the world.

This is a legitimate concern, but there's no need to worry. Remember how we read earlier that Mary makes the good things we give to her more perfect? (see pages 114-115). Well, it's true. She increases the grace of such good things as our prayers, and she works to make sure there's enough to go around. Moreover, we should keep in mind that Mary is not outdone in generosity. If we're so generous as to give her first rights to the grace of our prayers, she'll surely be especially generous to our loved ones. In fact, she'll take even better care of our loved ones than we ourselves can. For instance, let's say one of our family members or friends is in need of prayer, and we don't know it. Well, Mary knows it, and she'll make sure that that person doesn't go without.

Giving Mary first rights to the grace of our prayers doesn't mean we can't still pray for our loved ones. We can and should pray for them. It's just that we reserve to Mary the first right to distribute the grace of our prayers. Now then, if we can and should still pray for others, the question remains, "For whom should I pray the Chaplet of Divine Mercy?" This brings us to my second bit of advice: If you're looking for specific mercy intentions, you might want to begin to pray a continuous Novena to Divine Mercy. Allow me to explain.

In the Novena to Divine Mercy, Jesus asked St. Faustina to pray for nine different groups of people (see the section "Novena to Divine Mercy" in Appendix Two). To pray a continuous Novena to Divine Mercy simply means praying for one of those nine groups of people each day while reciting the chaplet, and then, after nine days, starting over. I find this a helpful way to focus my prayer. Along with or instead of this, I suggest praying for the people who are most in need of mercy, namely, unrepentant sinners, especially for those who are dying. Jesus told Faustina that prayer for sinners is the most pleasing to him and that nobody is more in need of trust than the dying. As we learned from the story about the man dying in the cottage, great battles are waged for despairing souls at the hour of death. Let's help Jesus save them by praying the chaplet.

Having spent some time reflecting on the Chaplet of Divine Mercy as a way of showing mercy through prayer, we're now ready to turn our attention to my next suggestion for doing prayers of mercy. Like the chaplet, the prayer I'm now going to suggest is based on a prayer that Jesus taught St. Faustina. Also, it includes the "breathing prayer" we learned earlier. In order to explain it, I'm going to start with the prayer that Jesus taught Faustina. He said to her:

> **Call upon My mercy on behalf of sinners; I desire their salvation. When you say this prayer, with a contrite heart and with faith on behalf of some sinner, I will give him the grace of conversion. This is the prayer: "O Blood and Water, which gushed forth from the Heart of Jesus as a fount of mercy for us, I trust in You."**

Did you catch the Lord's promise? He said, "**When you say this prayer, with a contrite heart and with faith on**

164 CONSOLING THE HEART OF JESUS

behalf of some sinner, *I will give him the grace of conversion.*"
That's quite a promise. Because this "O Blood and Water"
prayer is so powerful, I suggest we make a deal with the Lord
by praying the following:

> Lord, you can understand people in any language,
> including sign language. Well, I'd like to translate the
> "O Blood and Water" prayer into sign language. So,
> Lord, I propose the following deal. Anytime I con-
> sciously inhale with the intention of receiving the
> blood and water that gushed forth from your pierced
> side [recall the *fiat* moment of the breathing prayer,
> which implies contrition], I ask you to fill me with
> your merciful love. Then, when I exhale with the
> intention of giving this mercy to others, I ask you to
> give them the grace of the "O Blood and Water"
> prayer, namely, the grace of conversion.

Does this deal seem too bold? When it comes to asking for
graces for sinners, nothing is too bold for the soul that trusts in
God's mercy. In fact, we can read example after example from
the lives of saints such as Faustina and Thérèse of mind-blowing
boldness in prayer. The Lord accepted their bold petitions,
because he was so pleased with the trust in his mercy that
inspired them. To Faustina, he even emphasized that anything
she might say to express the generosity of his mercy would
always fall well short of the reality. Moreover, he also emphasized
that the more a soul trusts in his mercy the more it will receive.

Okay, so it's not too bold to make the sign-language prayer
deal with Jesus. Therefore, let's make the deal and begin
exhaling God's mercy. The best part about the prayer is that it
isn't complicated. It's as straightforward as breathing. We can
simply walk down the street and pray for everyone we pass,
trustfully exhaling superabundant mercy on them. Still, simple
doesn't mean easy. Such intercession does take concentration
and a spirit of prayer. Speaking of prayer, let's now close our
reflection on the three degrees of mercy by making a meditation.

A MEDITATION WITH JESUS AND AN OLD FRIEND. We're sitting at the back of a creaky, little chapel in an old retreat house. There's no one else here except for Jesus in the Eucharist and some guy sitting in one of the front pews. Hey, wait a minute — yes, I recognize him — it's our old friend, Joe. I'd go over and say hello to him, but it looks like he's deep in meditation. He also seems a bit agitated. That's strange. It seems like I've seen him this way before. Ah, yes, now I remember. We're here, again, for the last meditation of his 30-day retreat. Let's listen once more to the last part of his conversation with the Lord:

> Joseph, Joseph ... All I want is for you to be my friend. All I want is for you not to be afraid of me and to come to me.
> That's all, Lord?
> That's all.

After this conversation, Joe doesn't look so agitated anymore. Indeed, his face is full of peace. Unfortunately, we may not be as peaceful. In fact, now we might be feeling agitated. For, if Jesus said to Joe and to us that "all he wants" is that we not be afraid of him and go to him, then why did we just spend so many pages focusing on showing mercy to our neighbor? That sure makes it seem like "all Jesus wants" is not just that we not be afraid of him and go to him, but a whole lot more. Everything seemed simple before — "All I want is for you to be my friend. All I want is for you not to be afraid of me and to come to me" — but now there's all this other stuff to do. Did Joe misunderstand the Lord? Was the voice he heard simply a product of his own wishful thinking? How could the Lord say at one point, "All I want ... " and then add something later as if it hadn't really been "all" in the first place?

These questions bothered me for some time. Then, one day, as I was reflecting on the Lord's words to Joe, I got an answer. Unlike Joe, I didn't hear a voice. Rather, two insights gently came into my mind and gave me peace.

Through the first insight, I realized that so much of what Jesus wants from us truly is simply that we not be afraid of him and go to him, for this gives him consolation. Part of the reason this consoles him is that when we're with him — especially when we reflect on his Passion — he begins to heal our hearts, making them more sensitive and compassionate. (Remember CEP?) Then, this readies our hearts to be moved by the suffering of our neighbor. Still, Jesus didn't say to Joe that showing mercy to one's neighbor is part of the "all" that he wants — or did he?

Through the second insight, I realized that reaching out to one's neighbor is indeed part of the all that Jesus said he wants. It's like this: When Jesus says "All I want is for you to be my friend," it seems he doesn't simply mean he wants us to be a friend to him by trustfully going to meet him in prayer. He also seems to mean he wants us to be a friend to him by being merciful to our neighbor. In other words, as we've already heard a few times earlier in this retreat, Jesus is one body, head *and* members. So when he says "I," he's referring to the whole Christ, head and members.

With this insight in mind, let's take some time now to reflect on the Lord's words to Joe and to us once again: "All I want is for you to be my friend. All I want is for you not to be afraid of me and to come to me. ... That's all." As we reflect, let's think not only about how Jesus (the head) is asking us to trust in him and go to him in prayer but also about how he's calling us to have the courage to lovingly go to him (the body) in the person of our neighbor. This truly is all he wants from us. In fact, it's simply an expression of the two great commandments to love God and neighbor. After reflecting on this fuller "all" for five-to-ten minutes, close this meditation by speaking to the Lord from your heart, telling him that you choose, once again, to be his friend and to console him.

*C*ONCLUSION TO *F*IFTH *O*BSTACLE. Having learned (1) how we can become more sensitive to the suffering of our neighbor and (2) how we can reach out to our neighbor to help alleviate his suffering, we've covered everything we need to overcome the Fifth Obstacle to consoling Jesus. I hope we'll now be able to put it into practice and thus console our Lord's Heart by consoling our neighbor.

I don't know about you, but after reading this section, I have a lot more hope for change in my sometimes stony heart than I did during those depressing moments after it first got hit with the arrows from Cardinal Schönborn's talk at the Mercy Congress. Of course, the Lord has much more work to do in healing my heart and, perhaps, your heart as well — but at least now we know how to cooperate in the healing process. May the Lord give us the grace to cooperate well. May he give us the grace to trust him and go to him, the Head of the Mystical Body, and also as he's truly present in the members of his body. May he heal our hearts and make them loving like his.

[Note: No review questions follow Part Two because the next section (Conclusion) includes a general review of the retreat.]

CONCLUSION

Congratulations! We've covered all the main obstacles to living our principle and foundation of consoling the Heart of Jesus. Yet we're still not finished. While now we may have everything we need to become great saints, this doesn't mean we already are. Before it can happen, each of us needs to ask himself a crucial question, "Will I live what I've learned and experienced this weekend?" To those who might be thinking, "Well, I'd like to, but I'm afraid I'll forget," I say, "Don't worry." Don't worry, because this conclusion is designed to help us keep the graces of the retreat in our hearts, so that they might transform us into great saints, that is, into people who give tremendous consolation to the Heart of Jesus. Do you want to be this kind of saint? If so, then I invite you to make the following three promises to yourself, strive with God's grace to keep them, and you will be.

[Note: Much of what follows repeats what we've already covered during the retreat. This is intentional. According to St. Ignatius, repetition is crucially important for storing up and living out the graces of a retreat.]

1. I will live my principle and foundation of consoling Jesus, with Mary, by giving him my trust and acts of mercy.

*B*EGINNING OF OUR PRINCIPLE AND FOUNDATION. Let's review. What's our principle and foundation? It begins (first part) with being sensitive to the suffering of the Heart of Jesus. In other words, it begins by hearing his sorrowful words, "Behold this Heart which loves so much yet is so little loved." Or, more simply put, it begins by hearing his cry from the Cross, "I thirst." However you want to remember the Lord's lament is fine. The important thing is that you remember it.

The members of the Missionaries of Charity, the congregation founded by Blessed Mother Teresa of Calcutta, have a good way of remembering the first part of their principle and foundation (which happens to be the same as ours). First, they get a crucifix that clearly depicts Jesus' sorrow. Next, they put it up someplace where they'll see it every day (in the chapel of their houses). Finally, they write the words "I Thirst" right below one of the arms of the Cross. (See photo on the inside front cover of this book.) This combination of word and symbol reminds them to always keep the sorrow of Jesus before their eyes, for they've consecrated their lives for the purpose of consoling him, of quenching his thirst for love.

I suggest we follow the example of the Missionaries of Charity. Specifically, I suggest each of us get a crucifix (or a picture of one), write the words "I Thirst" (or "Behold this Heart ... ") below one of its arms, and then put it someplace where we'll see it frequently. Or, if you can think of a better way to remember the sorrowful cry of Jesus addressed personally to you, inviting you to console him, then go with that. For instance, instead of a crucifix, maybe you have an image of Jesus crowned with thorns that particularly speaks to you. This will work just as well. Simply add the words "I Thirst" or "Behold this Heart ... ," and put it someplace where you'll see it often.

LIVING THE FOUNDATION: TRUST. Seeing the sorrow of Jesus' Heart is just the beginning of living our principle and foundation. For, as we know, after seeing the sorrow of his Heart, we then ought to respond with mercy. In other words, we ought to console him. After having finished reading the Fifth Obstacle, we now know that there are at least two ways we can console the Heart of Jesus. The first and foundational of these ways is through our basic spiritual attitude of trust. Now, let's review. What is trust?

Thanks to Fr. Seraphim, we learned earlier that trust is praise and thanksgiving, to praise and thank God for all things. It's to praise and thank him for those things that make praise and thanks easy to do: for instance, family, friends, food, shelter, and so on. It's also to strive to praise and thank him for those things that often make praise and thanks difficult, namely, the crosses in our lives. This attitude of trust is primarily all Jesus wants from us little souls. Thus, may we always have the trustful attitude of the child who knows that God the Father lovingly watches over him always because he's so little. Let's strive to accept everything from his loving hands with trust, with praise and thanksgiving.

When we discover that sometimes we don't trust the Lord, we need not get discouraged. Rather, we simply need to turn back to him and give him our worries, surrendering whatever situation or difficulty might be oppressing us. A great prayer for this besides "Jesus, I trust in you" is "O Jesus, I surrender this to you. You take care of it." By praying like this, we console Jesus and receive his grace. On this topic, Jesus himself told St. Faustina: **"You will give Me pleasure if you hand over to Me all your troubles and griefs. I shall heap upon you the treasures of My grace."**

There's nothing to fear. Even if we ourselves cause a bad situation because of our sins, we can still make another marvelous prayer, "Jesus, I trust in your mercy so much that I believe you can bring an even greater good out of the evil I've done." Of course, when and how Jesus will bring the greater good is up to him, but he can and will do it if we ask him with trust. There's no problem his mercy can't fix. Certainly, we still need to strive to do what we can, but we should do so peacefully, trusting that Jesus is helping us with his amazing mercy.

Because the spiritual attitude of trust is so important, during the course of the retreat, I've presented several meditations or images to help us live it better. We might want to remember at least two of them. The first comes from the meditation we made at the foot of the Cross, when we went to Jesus with Mary past the hateful crowd (see pages 100-103). That meditation helps teach us that we need not fear going to Jesus because of our sins. In fact, it helps teach us, as did Jesus' words to our friend Joe, that the Lord simply wants us to go to him as we are, "All I want is for you to be my friend. All I want is for you not to be afraid of me and to come to me. ... That's all."

Another good way to remember the attitude of going to Jesus as we are with complete trust is the other meditation we made at the foot of the Cross, the one with the three words of Mary: *ecce, fiat, magnificat*. These three words as three spiritual moments are a complete summary of the whole spiritual attitude of trust. Moreover, we should be consoled to know that each one of these three moments consoles Jesus. Thus, we need not worry when we experience times when praise and thanks just don't seem to come. Sometimes our trust is simply expressed by going to Jesus as we are with all our problems and brokenness (*ecce*) and by receiving his mercy (*fiat*). Make no mistake about it: This kind of trust truly consoles Jesus. Still, we should also be open to being moved to praise and thanks (*magnificat*). I suggest we memorize the three words of Mary and pray them with her often.

*L*IVING THE *F*OUNDATION: *A*CTS OF *M*ERCY. While reading the Fifth Obstacle, we learned that there's another way to console Jesus besides by giving him our trust. It involves reaching out to our neighbor through acts of mercy. Recall that Jesus taught St. Faustina three "degrees" of performing an act of mercy: deed, word, and prayer. Among the infinite number of deeds of mercy, let's especially do that deed of mercy I called the "merciful outlook." As we learned, the merciful outlook is to delight in each person we meet, seeing each one as the unique face of Christ he presently is and is called to be. Then, regarding words of mercy, we can ask the merciful question, and regarding prayers of mercy, we can pray the Chaplet of Divine Mercy and modified "breathing prayer."

*C*ONSOLER *P*RINCIPLE AND *F*OUNDATION. Now that we've reviewed our principle and foundation, I'd like to make the following recommendation: As a way of concluding the retreat, I suggest you write out on a piece of paper your principle and foundation. I offer what follows as a model. You can either copy it down exactly as it is, or use your own words. Under the title, "My Principle and Foundation," here's how it might look:

I _____ , on this day _____ , choose as my principle and foundation to console the Heart of Jesus.

Dear Jesus, relying on your grace and the prayers of Mary and of all the angels and saints, I will strive to keep before my eyes the deep sorrow of your Heart and respond, with Mary, by consoling you in the following two ways:

First, I will give you my trust. Jesus, I trust in you. I will try not to be afraid of going to you as I am (*ecce*), even when my sins and weaknesses weigh heavily upon me. With an open heart, I choose to accept your mercy (*fiat*), even all that mercy other souls reject. Finally, I will do my best to praise and thank you in all things (*magnificat*), even when you give me the privilege of sharing in your Cross.

Second, I will strive to show mercy to my neighbor through my deeds, words, and prayers, remembering that by consoling others, I am also consoling you.

Heavenly Father, for the sake of the sorrowful Passion of your Son, I beg you: Send forth your Holy Spirit to help me fulfill this choice.

After writing out your principle and foundation, you might want to put it in a place where you'll easily find it and then take it out to review from time to time. I propose prayerfully reviewing it at least once a month, for instance, on your "birthday day." For example, if your birthday is on September 8, I recommend that you prayerfully review your mission statement on the eighth day of each month. This is a good way of keeping clear and gripping what the first secretary of the Jesuits called the "clarity that grips us and leads us on."

2. I will keep a simple schedule of daily prayer

A schedule of daily prayer? I hope there's no screeching of the brakes at this point. Really, there's no need to worry. What I'm about to propose is not difficult. Remember, I wrote this retreat for people who don't have time to make a longer retreat, so I'm especially gearing this part for busy people. Of course, one can always add other prayers to the following program, such as the Rosary, but I think it's a manageable minimum for the busy layperson.

I propose as a simple schedule of daily prayer the following three prayer practices, which even the busiest people can keep: (a) morning offering, (b) three o'clock hour devotion, (c) examination of conscience.

(a) *MORNING OFFERING.* When you wake up in the morning or when you're on your way to work or school, I suggest getting in the habit of making a morning offering. It doesn't have to be long. I propose the following (ideally prayed before your image of "I Thirst" Jesus):

> Dear Jesus, I know that your Sacred Heart is sorrowful because so many people neither love you nor trust in you. Behold, Lord, here I am. Though weak and sinful, I love you and I trust in you. I intend that all my actions this day be for the purpose of consoling you.
>
> Heavenly Father, in union with all the Masses being offered today, I give you praise and thanks for the many gifts you will send me, including the gift of my small sharing in the Cross. May this my prayer glorify you and console your Son. With the help of your grace, I resolve to remain all day in this prayerful spirit of praise and thanks and, further, to console Jesus by being merciful to my neighbor through my deeds, words, and prayers.
>
> Mary, my mother, come with your spouse, the Spirit. Make my sacrifice of praise, thanks, and mercy a most pleasing consolation to your Son. Behold, I present to you all I am and have. Take my offering so it may pass through your Immaculate Heart, to Jesus' Sacred Heart, and on to the Father, for his greater glory. Amen.

(b) *THREE O'CLOCK HOUR*. Three to four o'clock in the afternoon is the Hour of Great Mercy. Jesus promised St. Faustina that during this hour he would give extraordinary graces to whomever might ask for them. So that we don't let such an amazing opportunity pass us by, I propose we get the "three o'clock habit" and tap into these great graces. Before I offer suggestions for how we might do this, let's first read Jesus' actual words to Faustina on this topic.

Jesus spoke to Faustina about the Hour of Great Mercy on two separate occasions. On the first occasion, he said:

> **At three o'clock, implore My mercy, especially for sinners; and, if only for a brief moment, immerse yourself in My Passion, particularly in My abandonment at the moment of agony. This is the hour of great mercy for the whole world. I will allow you to enter into My mortal sorrow. In this hour, I will refuse nothing to the soul that makes a request of Me in virtue of My Passion.**

On the second occasion, Jesus spoke at greater length about this special time of grace:

> **I remind you, My daughter, that as often as you hear the clock strike the third hour, immerse yourself completely in My mercy, adoring and glorifying it; invoke its omnipotence for the whole world, and particularly for poor sinners; for at that moment mercy was opened wide for every soul. In this hour you can obtain everything for yourself and for others for the asking; it was the hour of grace for the whole world — mercy triumphed over justice.**
>
> **My daughter, try your best to make the Stations of the Cross in this hour, provided that your duties permit it; and if you are not able to make the Stations of the Cross, then at least step**

into the chapel for a moment and adore, in the Blessed Sacrament, My Heart, which is full of mercy; and should you be unable to step into the chapel, immerse yourself in prayer there where you happen to be, if only for a very brief instant.

In light of these two passages, I'd like to propose three ways by which we can take advantage of the amazing graces available to us every day during the Hour of Great Mercy. We can choose the way or ways that work best for us.

First way: We can immerse ourselves in the Lord's Passion, especially in his abandonment on the Cross. We can do this briefly, even "for an instant" or a longer period of time. If our duties allow us only a brief moment, we can simply call to mind an image of Jesus on the Cross or look at a crucifix or a picture of Jesus. We can also pray the "Three O'clock Hour Prayer" from the *Diary of St. Faustina*:

> You expired, Jesus, but the source of life gushed forth for souls, and the ocean of mercy opened up for the whole world. O Fount of Life, unfathomable Divine Mercy, envelop the whole world and empty Yourself out upon us. ... O Blood and Water, which gushed forth from the Heart of Jesus as a fount of mercy for us, I trust in You.

If we have more time, we can pray the sorrowful mysteries of the Rosary or make the Stations of the Cross. Jesus told St. Faustina to try her best to make the Stations of the Cross during the three o'clock hour. Here's an idea for those who want to make the stations but don't have time because of other duties. First, pick one of the fourteen stations and keep it at the back of your mind as you work during the three o'clock hour, thinking about it from time to time. Then, meditate on the next station during the next day in the same way, and so on. The following "map," which assigns a day of the week to each station (in two cycles), may be helpful to those who want to use this method:

Sunday	Monday	Tuesday	Wednesday	Thursday	Friday	Saturday
I. Jesus is condemned to death.	II. Jesus takes up his Cross.	III. Jesus falls the first time.	IV. Jesus meets his blessed mother.	V. Simon of Cyrene helps Jesus to carry the Cross.	VI. Veronica wipes the face of Jesus.	VII. Jesus falls a second time.

Sunday	Monday	Tuesday	Wednesday	Thursday	Friday	Saturday
VIII. Jesus consoles the women of Jerusalem.	IX. Jesus falls the third time.	X. Jesus is stripped of his garments.	XI. Jesus is nailed to the Cross.	XII. Jesus dies on the Cross.	XIII. Jesus is laid in the arms of his blessed mother.	XIV. Jesus is laid in the tomb.

Second way: We can confidently present our petitions to the Father by virtue of his Son's Passion. In particular, we can invoke God's mercy on the whole world and especially on unrepentant sinners. The Lord's promise that he would grant everything we ask for ourselves and for others during the three o'clock hour should help us to pray during it with great boldness and confidence. Of course, God always hears our prayers, but during the three o'clock hour, he has promised to be especially generous. It's a perfect time to pray for others and a great idea to do so through the Chaplet of Divine Mercy, which only takes about seven minutes. While we can surely pray for ourselves and for our family and friends during the Hour of Great Mercy, let's not forget to pray also for those who need it most: unrepentant sinners and the dying.

Third way: We can visit Jesus, truly present in the Blessed Sacrament. Jesus asked St. Faustina (provided that her duties allowed it) to go to the chapel during the Hour of Great Mercy and adore his Eucharistic Heart, which is full of mercy. Of course, for most of us, it won't always be easy to visit a church or chapel during this hour. Still, if we have the time and an opportunity — for example, if while running errands we pass by a Catholic church — we just might want to pay Jesus a visit.

(c) *EXAMINATION OF CONSCIENCE: B-A-K-E-R*. For many people, making an examination of conscience seems the same as drawing up a laundry list of sins. It's not that. What I mean by an examination of conscience (also called an "examen") is a powerful spiritual exercise that can help us live our principle and foundation perhaps better than any other form of personal prayer — and it only takes about ten minutes.

The method of examination of conscience I'll be presenting here is based on the one taught by St. Ignatius of Loyola to his Jesuits. Recall that Ignatius founded the Jesuits as one of the first religious communities that decisively left the walls of the monastery and went out into the world. Further recall that in going out into the world, the Jesuits set it on fire with love for God. I said earlier that the secret to the early Jesuits' success was their First Principle and Foundation. Well, their secret was also faithfulness to making the daily examination of conscience.

Saint Ignatius reportedly told his Jesuits that if ever they had to omit one of their spiritual exercises, they should make sure it not be the examen. Why did he give so much importance to it? Probably because the examen is the most effective tool for being formed into a contemplative-in-action, that is, a person who can easily find God in all things, even amid the hustle and bustle of the world. It was of the utmost importance that the Jesuits have this kind of spiritual vision. For it allowed them to remain in close communion with God even during the most rigorous apostolic labors. Thus, thanks to the examen, they could be contemplative (like monks) but without having to spend long hours of prayer in the chapel.

Like the early Jesuits, after this retreat you'll be going back out into the world. Also like those Jesuits, you probably won't have hours to spend in the chapel, and that's all right. If you're faithful to making an examination of conscience every day, you can quickly become a contemplative-in-action. More to the point: By being faithful to the daily examen, you'll be able to live out your principle and foundation with ease. Sound good? Good. Then let's learn how to make an examination of conscience. As we proceed, I'll explain why it's effective in helping us to live our principle and foundation.

The examination of conscience should be made sometime toward the end of the day. Most people make it shortly before going to bed. It's basically a mental review of the previous 16 hours or so of consciousness — thus, some people prefer to call the examination of conscience an examination of *consciousness*. This mental review can be done by oneself or, if one is married (and daring), in conversation with one's spouse. If it's done by oneself, some people find it helpful to write in a notebook or on note cards because (1) writing helps jog the mind and (2) it provides a record of one's spiritual life, which can then easily be reviewed before going to confession or spiritual direction.

Okay, so it's the end of the day, and we're ready to make our examination of conscience. Now what? First, we should put ourselves in the presence of God. In other words, we should begin with the attitude that the examen is a time of prayer, not just a mental exercise. Devoutly making the sign of the Cross may be enough to do this. Next, we just have to remember one word: baker, B-A-K-E-R, baker. Actually, we also have to remember what each letter of this word stands for. Let's start with "B."

B stands for "blessings." According to St. Ignatius, this is the most important of the five points. (See, it's not just a laundry list of sins.) Here we simply review our day, survey the many blessings God has given us throughout it, and then praise and thank him for these blessings. For instance, maybe we had a great conversation with someone at lunch. During the examen, we might want to reflect on that gift and praise and thank God for it. Of course, we don't have to go through every single blessing of the day. That would take way too much time. The key is to let one's heart roam about and settle on the particular peaks of joy and blessing of the day, what Ignatius calls "consolation." One more thing: We shouldn't forget to thank God for the crosses of the day, which are also blessings.

Already after the first point, we can see how the examen helps us to live our principle and foundation. After all, this first point is simply a call to the prayer of praise and thanksgiving, which, as we already know, greatly consoles Jesus. Furthermore, if we get into the habit of praising and thanking God like this every day during our examen, then we'll begin to better recognize the blessings of our day as they happen, and thus, we'll develop a continual attitude of gratitude. In other words, our praise and thanks won't begin to flow simply when we make our examen — it'll flow all day long. Furthermore, as God sees our efforts to recognize and thank him for his many gifts, he'll send us more and more. But be careful, for if we keep it up, we might end up like St. Ignatius.

Because he was so faithful to the examen, St. Ignatius developed an attitude of gratitude to a remarkably high degree. He became so sensitive to the countless blessings God constantly poured out on him that he was always on the verge of tears. Mind you, Ignatius was a former soldier and had a will of iron. He was no wimp. Nevertheless, he was always on the brink of being overwhelmed by the immense love that he recognized God was always showering down upon him. It got so "bad" that when he was in public, he would sometimes have to distract himself from seeing the blessings to prevent his torrents of tears from flowing. But don't worry. We're still far behind Ignatius, as the next two points may remind us.

A stands for "Ask." Although we already placed ourselves in the presence of God when we began the examen, here we need to ask for a special grace from the Holy Spirit, the grace to recognize our sins. Without the help of the Holy Spirit, we'll remain blind to our sinfulness. Thus, when we get to this second point, we need to ask the Holy Spirit to help us recognize our sinfulness, which brings us to the next point.

K stands for "Kill." Why "kill"? Because it was our sins that killed and crucified Jesus. During this third point, we look at our sinfulness (weaknesses and attachments, too). So, again, we gaze across the conscious hours of our day. This time, however, we look not for peaks but valleys, what Ignatius calls "desolation." In other words, we pay attention to those times during our day when our hearts dropped. Why might they have dropped?

Maybe because of someone else's sin. Maybe someone said something unkind to us. Fine. Did we forgive them? If so, good. If not, well, the examen is a good time to deal with it.

Now, let's keep looking. Here's another time our hearts dropped. It was this afternoon at work, standing by the water cooler. Hmmm. Why did our hearts drop then? Ah, yes (thanks, Holy Spirit), that's when we stuck Bob with a verbal barb. Let's see, anything else? Yes, there's another heart dropper: We didn't accept the traffic jam on our way home as a small sharing in the Cross. We should have been more peaceful about it and offered it up as a prayer for others.

Okay, so after remembering all those heart dropping moments, we may feel pretty down. In the past, such feelings might have made us want to run away from Jesus. But now it's different, right? Now we know that when the weight of our sinfulness drags us down, that's the best time to go to Jesus, sinfulness and all — which brings us to the next point.

E stands for "embrace." This is to allow Jesus to embrace us, sinners that we are, with the rays of his merciful love. While praying over this point, it may be helpful to think of the Image of Divine Mercy. I like to imagine the rays of this image embracing me with forgiveness. I also like to remember Jesus' words that it rests his Heart to forgive and that when I go to him with my sinfulness, I give him the joy of being my Savior. I believe that at this point of the examen, we greatly console Jesus when we simply let him embrace us with his merciful love — and of course, we, too, are consoled. I recommend spending some time lingering on this point (in the embrace) before moving on to the next.

R stands for "Resolution." During this last point of the examen, we take what we've learned from the previous points and look ahead to the next day, ready to make resolutions. For instance, having recognized during "K" that we stuck Bob with a verbal barb at the office today, we might resolve that tomorrow morning we'll make it up to him by going to his cubicle, slapping him on the back, and congratulating him on how his football team did earlier this evening. Also, having remembered that we were impatient during the traffic jam today, we can resolve to bite our tongues if the sea of brake lights appears again tomorrow. Finally, because during "B" we realized that God was speaking to us during our lunchtime conversation with Sally, giving light on a certain problem, we can resolve to act on that light by looking up the online article she recommended. (I think we get the idea.)

So, the examen is a great way to live our principle and foundation, because it helps us to see God in all things, particularly in the many blessings he sends us daily. As we learn to recognize the blessings ("B"), we grow in having an attitude of gratitude, in having a readiness to praise and thank God for all. This attitude, as we know, is the same as the attitude of trust, which is what consoles Jesus most.

The examen also helps us to console Jesus by training us not to be afraid of going to him with our sinfulness (remember "K"?), and it gives us an opportunity every day to let him embrace us ("E") with his merciful love, which is a mutual delight for him and for us.

Finally, the examen helps us to live our principle and foundation with Mary. Why? Because the prayer of the examen is a great way to imitate Mary's attitude of constantly pondering in her heart the good things the Lord was doing in her life (see Lk 2:19, 51). Of course, her examen would only have been "B-E-R," because she had no sin. Our examen ("B-A-K-E-R") is basically an imitation of her heart-pondering attitude. May she help us to live the examen well, along with the other two points of our daily schedule of prayer — and she probably wouldn't mind if we threw in the Rosary as a fourth point.

3. I will frequent the Sacraments and take time for spiritual reading

Okay, so we've promised ourselves that we'll live our principle and foundation and keep to a simple schedule of daily prayer. Now, as the last of our three promises to ourselves, I propose that we promise to frequent the Sacraments and take time for spiritual reading. Allow me to explain each of these two points.

*F*REQUENT THE SACRAMENTS. Some Sacraments we can't frequent. They're one-time deals (Baptism and Confirmation). Others we can experience more than once, but because they often follow some kind of misfortune — our spouse died, we're sick, or we've been chosen to be Bishop — we probably wouldn't want to (Matrimony, Anointing of the Sick, Holy Orders). Then, there are those Sacraments we really should receive frequently: the Eucharist and Confession. Regarding such Sacraments, it's probably already obvious, but I'll say it anyway: Catholics are obliged to attend Mass every Sunday and to go to confession at least once a year. This is basically what I mean when I say we're promising ourselves that we'll frequent the Sacraments, namely, that we'll keep our Sunday obligation and go to confession at least once a year. Still, I'm not letting us off so easily.

The promise to frequent the Sacraments should also mean that we'll try to attend daily Mass, if we have time, and try to go to confession at least once a month. Daily Mass or going to Mass at least a few times during the week is a great way to console Jesus (and be consoled). Frequent confession is also a great way to console him. Of course, by frequent confession, I'm not advocating committing frequent mortal sins. God forbid! Contrary to what people sometimes think, confession is not just for mortal or serious sins. In other words, we can go to confession even if we "only" have everyday faults (venial sins) to confess, and it's a good idea to go. It's a good idea because whenever we confess our sins in the Sacrament of Confession, we receive sacramental graces to overcome them. If we ever commit a mortal sin, we should go to confession as soon as possible, but for venial sins, it's a good practice to go at least once a month, even if it's not obligatory.

By the way, those making this retreat who think they might have committed a mortal sin but who are stymied from going to confession sooner rather than later might want to make a perfect act of contrition to put their minds at rest. A perfect act of contrition, or perfect contrition, is an act of sorrow for our sins together with the intention not to sin again that's done out of love for God above all else and not out of fear of punishment. "Such contrition," says the *Catechism*, "obtains forgiveness of mortal sins if it includes the firm resolution to have recourse to sacramental confession as soon as possible." (To learn more about mortal sin, see "References and Notes.")

I'm also recommending that by our promising to frequent the Sacraments, we seriously consider going regularly to spend time praying before Jesus, truly present in the Blessed Sacrament. Spending time in Eucharistic Adoration is a great way to console Jesus. All those times during this retreat when we read about not being afraid of going to Jesus as we are, include not being afraid of going to him in the Blessed Sacrament. He loves it when we do. Pope John Paul II wrote, "Jesus waits for us in the Sacrament of Love." He also encouraged us to be generous with our time "in going to meet him in adoration."

Yes, if our duties allow, let's be generous in going to visit Jesus. Perhaps we can make a weekly (or even daily) Holy Hour of prayer before Jesus in the Blessed Sacrament. If a local parish has perpetual adoration, we might want to begin there. I say that because, while it's great to pray before Jesus in the Blessed Sacrament at any Catholic church, there's something extra special about when he's brought out and placed in the monstrance for all to see and adore. Moreover, perpetual adoration means we can go to the church that has it at any time, 24 hours a day. Once we start going, we might even be inspired to sign up for a time slot of adoration. Still, the most important thing is not where we go but that we go if we have the time.

Of course, some might be thinking, "Yeah, but I really don't have time." That's all right. Visiting Jesus in the Blessed Sacrament isn't an obligation. If we can't go to visit Jesus in the Blessed Sacrament (and even if we can), I propose that we frequently visit him in the tabernacle of our hearts.

Jesus is truly present in our hearts through sanctifying grace. This is true, provided that we're baptized and haven't committed a mortal sin — but if we have committed a mortal sin, Jesus returns to our hearts the moment we make a perfect act of contrition and intend to go to confession or the moment the priest absolves us in the Sacrament of Confession. One of the best ways to develop a deeper life of prayer is to begin to pay attention to this real presence of Jesus in our hearts. He loves it when we do. There's really no excuse for us not to visit Jesus in the tabernacle of our hearts. (If you're interested in learning more about how to do this, see "References and Notes.")

Still, some might be thinking: "I've got an excuse. Life's so busy it's extremely difficult to slow down long enough to realize Jesus is truly present in my heart." Okay. That's a good point, but I still say we should visit Jesus in the tabernacle of our hearts frequently, no matter how busy we are. Now, don't worry. I'm going to close this section by explaining a method by which we can slow ourselves down enough to be present and recollected to Jesus in our hearts, even in the midst of chaos.

We can become recollected fairly easily with the help of what I like to call the "two movements" of the Image of Divine Mercy. All we need is the image — either an actual one (in our hands) or a virtual one (in our imagination) — and an understanding of the two movements that go forth from and return to it. To get this understanding, I invite you to make the following meditation.

*M*EDITATION: *THE TWO MOVEMENTS OF THE DIVINE MERCY IMAGE.* Look at the Image of Divine Mercy. See Jesus stepping toward you. Do you know what scene from the Gospel this image depicts? It's John 20:19-31, the same reading the Church uses for the liturgy of Divine Mercy Sunday. The setting is the upper room where Jesus and his disciples ate the Last Supper. The reading tells the story of what happened about three days later, three days after Jesus was brutally tortured, killed, and buried.

Imagine the scene. The disciples are all huddled together in the upper room where they've locked the doors out of fear. It seems they have good reason to be afraid. After all, their master has just been killed — might they be next? Imagine their fear and shame. Yes, shame. Each one of them abandoned the Lord in his time of need, the same Lord who had called them friends. Some of them, remembering how Jesus so lovingly, humbly washed their feet in this very room only three days before, are beginning to feel the weight of their betrayal. Despair begins to creep into their hearts. See the darkness in the room. Feel the coldness of the fear, sadness, and shame.

Suddenly, in the midst of such darkness and despite the locked doors, there appears the figure of a man clothed in radiant white. Some of the disciples fearfully conclude, "The ghost of the Master has come to punish us for abandoning him." Then Jesus acts. He clears away the darkness of fear and shame with a gentle gesture of blessing and one simple word, "Peace."

Imagine this word tenderly but powerfully rolling off the Lord's lips, "Peace." Feel its strength. Here he is, the Word himself, proclaiming the word "peace" with power. Here he is whose voice calmed the seas (see Mk 4:39). Here he is whose reply to the soldiers sent them sprawling to the ground. Remember that? Remember how just a few nights before, that crowd of soldiers with clubs, swords, and lanterns was no match for two simple words from Jesus? Let's take a brief side trip to that scene (see Jn 18:1-6).

See and hear how the soldiers march into the garden of Gethsemane with all their ruckus of shouts, clanging swords, and curses. Watch as the Lord comes forward, and listen as he asks them, "Whom do you seek?" Instead of seeking the Son of God come down from heaven, Jesus Christ the Savior, the soldiers reply that they've come for Jesus the Nazarene. The Lord responds to this earthly title with his divine name, "I AM." This divine name, so full of might and spoken by the Word himself, sends the soldiers collapsing to the ground.

Now go back to the upper room. During this Easter Sunday scene, Jesus speaks with the same power he revealed in the garden but with different words, "Peace be with you." These words send fear, shame, and worry falling to the ground, just as the divine name had earlier sent the soldiers down. Here in this room, as Jesus appears, he gives his peace.

Now look at Jesus in the Image of Divine Mercy. Hear him say to you, "Peace." Hear your name as it follows this word, "Peace, ..." Do you feel the pulse of power?

Now go to the shore of the ocean. You're alone on a beach, facing the open sea. Watch the swells rolling in toward you. While you stand on the shore, the swells, though still far out, gather in size and strength as they approach. Walk out into the water to meet them. Stand in the warm, refreshing water. You're in up to your waist. The swells build as they come nearer. Closer and closer they come: 50 yards, 40 yards, 30 ... . The lead swell forms into a wave, and now, finally, it washes over you, pulling on you. Somehow, you remain standing in the bubbling, white water. Wave after wave comes in and washes over you. These are the waves of the Lord's peace. Over and over he says to you through the waves, "Peace ... peace ... peace."

Now look at the Image of Divine Mercy again. See the Ocean of Mercy before you, Mercy Incarnate. Hear him say to you, "Peace," and let the waves of peace wash over you and over all your attachments and worries. These waves of peace and mercy calm you, allowing you to let go of everything you were so tightly clinging to before, "Peace ... peace ... peace." The peace comes through these pale and red rays. You let go of more and more anxiety and fear until, finally, you're free.

This is the first movement of the Image of Divine Mercy, the outgoing waves of peace. Your job is to let go in trust. This is what the Lord puts on your lips and in your heart as you pray the words, "Jesus, I trust in you." When you let go in trust, that's when you experience the fruit of the first movement: peace. The fruit of trust is peace. Let go in trust and experience the peace. Now, to the second movement.

What happens after a wave crashes? It washes up on the shore. Then what? It pulls back into the ocean. If you stand in the wash that pulls back into the ocean, what do you feel? You feel it pulling the sand out from under your toes. This is like the second movement of the Divine Mercy Image.

After you let go in trust and experience the peace of the first movement, then you can be carried out into the Ocean of

Mercy. The rays that go out from Jesus' Heart also pull you back in when you let go and let them. This second movement toward the Lord is to fix on him in love. It means taking your eyes off your fears, problems, and distractions, and then fixing them on the Lord, on his Heart. (Remember "first things first" and the primacy of contemplation?) When you fix on the Lord in love, on he who is your true treasure, Beauty himself, and the fulfillment of all desire, then you have joy.

Let go in trust, experience the peace. Fix on the Lord in love, experience the joy. As you're caught up in these two movements, it's just you and Jesus, trust and love, peace and joy. When you spend time with the Image of Divine Mercy and feel the push and pull of its rays, it becomes an oasis of peace and joy in the midst of a life of busyness. Feeling frazzled, over-worked, and burdened? Hear him say to you, "Peace." Let go. Feel his peace. Then, let the rays draw you in. Fix on him in love. Experience the joy. After becoming recollected like this, you'll be free to feel (or at least to know) that Jesus is resting in the tabernacle of your heart. Then you'll find it much easier to visit him there, which consoles him.

SPIRITUAL READING. I didn't put the idea of visiting Jesus in the tabernacle of our hearts as one of the points of our daily schedule of prayer, because it's something we should do when-ever we can and not just once a day. I didn't put taking time for spiritual reading into our daily schedule of prayer for a different reason: Busy people might not have time to do spiritual read-ing every day. Yet we should take time for it at least once in a while. It keeps the flame of devotion burning and can even bring it back if it peters out. It's also a great aid to prayer. Saint Teresa of Avila wrote that she couldn't pray without a spiritual book (and she was an all-star prayer-pro).

In this section, I'm going to recommend some books that will help reinforce what we've learned in this retreat. You might want to buy some of them and keep them on hand for rainy days or lazy Sunday afternoons when you could use a little spir-itual boost. That being said, the more often you can keep them not just on hand but *in* hand the better, for we probably need spiritual book boosts a lot more often than we think.

Before giving my recommendations, I'd first like to say one thing about spiritual reading: Make it spiritual. In other words, when you read a spiritual book, don't just read. Take time to talk with Jesus. For example, if something stirs your heart while you're reading, enkindling desire and love — pause. Take it in. Thank the Lord. Tell him about your desires. Ask for the grace. Or, if something makes your heart drop, that can be a good thing, too. Stop. Don't run from it by rushing on ahead. Stop. Pay attention to what you're feeling. Why did your heart drop? Are you afraid of something you read? Let the Lord speak to you. Maybe he'll put you at ease, "Don't worry, my little one, I'm not calling you to that." (It seems that because little souls are prone to freaking out when they read things intended for big souls, Jesus is usually quick to calm them, if they'll pause and let him.) However, sometimes he'll confirm what we've read, "Yes, my friend, that's something we need to work on." If he does, then ask him for the grace. By the way, the Lord rarely speaks to people in audible words. I think most of the time his words are waves of peace in our hearts or thoughts that pop into our minds. So don't worry if you don't hear actual words.

Here's a loose formula for spiritual reading: Pause, reflect, speak, now listen (PRSNL — the word "personal" without the vowels). Speak from the heart, and don't be afraid to ask for what's in your heart. Spiritual reading isn't about the quantity of pages read but the quality of the conversation it inspires. By the way, I didn't say all this at the beginning of the retreat, so you'd be able to finish it in a weekend!

*B*OOK RECOMMENDATIONS. The first book I'd like to recommend is the Bible, but I don't recommend starting with Genesis. Now, don't get me wrong. Genesis is wonderful to read — it's the inspired Word of God, after all. However, if your time is limited (and I assume it is because you're making this kind of retreat), I recommend going straight to the heart of it all, the Gospels. The Gospel of Luke is known as the "Gospel of Mercy" because of its particular emphasis on mercy. Since mercy is the central theme of this retreat, Luke is especially appropriate for reinforcing what we've learned.

Maybe you've recently read the Gospel of Luke or one of the other two Gospels that stick to the same story line (Matthew and Mark), and you want to try something different. Well, if you're feeling adventurous and ready to mine for the deepest spiritual riches, I recommend plunging into the Gospel of John, the Gospel of the Heart of Jesus. Now, if you want to get to the heart of this Gospel of the Lord's Heart, I strongly recommend reading Chapters 14-17, especially chapter 17. These are the chapters of the "Farewell Discourse," the chapters in which Jesus says goodbye to his disciples as he enters the hour of his Passion. These chapters can be challenging, but they're well worth the effort it takes to read them. In my opinion, nothing more beautiful has ever been written.

I can't move on to my next book recommendation without saying something about the Psalms. The Psalms are a great way to reinforce central themes from this retreat, because they're largely songs of praise and thanksgiving to God for his tender mercy and steadfast love. In fact, the *Catechism* describes the prayer of the Psalms as the great school of trust in God. Although there are 150 of them, there's no need to feel overwhelmed because most of them are short. I recommend reading through them, making a list of your favorite ones as you go, and then going back regularly to pray from the Psalms on your list.

The second book that will help reinforce what we've learned is the *Diary of St. Faustina*. Here's a personal testimony: After the Bible, no spiritual book has nourished my soul more. It's amazing. It's also very big. In fact, I'm afraid people won't read it because of its sheer size. Therefore, I've made a summary. Although it's a much longer summary than the other ones I gave earlier in the retreat, I think you'll like it. (See Appendix Two, which is the summary.) Basically, it's a compilation of various citations from the *Diary* organized according to categories that harmonize with themes from this retreat.

You probably won't have time during this retreat weekend to read through them all. In fact, as I mentioned in the introduction, Appendix Two is not part of the retreat. Rather, it's meant as an aid to help deepen the graces of the retreat during later times of spiritual reading.

My third book recommendation, as you might have guessed, is the spiritual autobiography of St. Thérèse of Lisieux, *Story of a Soul*. Earlier in the retreat, I summarized Thérèse's spirituality by selecting a few citations from it. Well, there's much more. It wasn't an accident that the Church made her a Doctor of the Church, and it's not an accident that her *Story of a Soul* is one of the most beloved Christian writings ever. Although she was only 24 when she died, her wisdom is well beyond her years. Actually, you might say it's well *under* her years, because she had the wisdom of a child, the wisdom of those to whom the Father is pleased to reveal the mysteries of the kingdom (see Mt 11:25). Little souls will easily understand her wisdom.

The fourth book I'd like to recommend is St. Louis de Montfort's *True Devotion to Mary*. Earlier in the retreat, I gave a summary of the essence of the devotion to Mary that de Montfort taught. Well, *True Devotion* gives the whole thing. Although it's written in a outdated style that sometimes grates on modern ears, it's worth reading because of the deep spiritual riches it contains on how to live a total consecration to Jesus through Mary — but be careful. It tends to be life-changing. Pope John Paul II succinctly describes the impact it had on him, "The reading of [de Montfort's book] was a decisive turning point in my life."

My fifth book recommendation is actually one you're not supposed to read. In fact, I discourage you from reading it. It's the book, the *Spiritual Exercises of St. Ignatius*. The book is actually an instruction manual for one who directs the *Spiritual Exercises* retreat. So, what I'm really recommending is that you reinforce the graces of this weekend retreat by actually making the *Spiritual Exercises* — if you can find the time and resources for making it.

There are many other books I could recommend about the message of Divine Mercy (St. Faustina), St. Thérèse's Little Way, consecration to Mary, and the *Spiritual Exercises.* However, since you're just about to finish reading a book (making a retreat) that introduces you to all these things, why not first try diving right into the real things themselves? They're not so difficult, and they're worth the time it takes to read them.

Speaking of time, it looks like our time together has come to an end, but what would a retreat be without a closing prayer? Moreover, what would an Ignatian-inspired retreat be without a concluding "Contemplation to Attain Divine Love"?

I wrote the following "Contemplation to Attain Divine Love" for little souls. May it and everything you've learned during this retreat inspire you to great sanctity (according to the Little Way), and thus, may you be a tremendous consolation to the Heart of Jesus. Please pray for me that I might be the same. Please offer an ardent prayer for the other people who will make this retreat. And please consider coming again, even annually, for another *Consoling* weekend. God bless you.

[Note: After the closing meditation, some readers may want to spend half hour to an hour in quiet prayer with the Lord, if possible, in Eucharistic Adoration.]

Closing Meditation: A Contemplation to Attain Divine Love

You're the Lord's disciple. You've been following him through the lands of Israel. From the place where you first responded to his call, through the deserts, grassy plains, mountains, valleys, and that beautiful Sea of Galilee where he walked on the water, you've been with him.

Now it's late at night. The campfire still blazes. Its soft crackling mixes with the sound of muffled snores and chirping crickets. The few disciples who still haven't fallen asleep after the long day's journey linger on mats, whispering and occasionally laughing quietly.

There is the Lord, alone, sitting before the fire, gazing beyond its flames, lost in prayer. You feel an urge to go to him.

Pushing aside the covers, you rise from your mat and approach him. The others fall silent and begin to watch you. You can feel their eyes following you, but your attention goes back to the Lord as you draw closer to him.

The Lord still doesn't see you. You sit next to him. He gazes beyond the fire, its light dancing on his face. Sitting here, so close to him, you can see it more clearly than ever: profound sorrow. Something in your heart convinces you that this sorrow comes from his not being understood. So what are you doing approaching him? After all, he's a mystery to you, too. He's from somewhere else. How can you relate to him? Perhaps you should go back to sleep — it seems he still hasn't seen you. Despite these thoughts, something urges you to speak to him. Something inside you wants to console him even though he seems unreachable.

"Jesus," you begin with a whisper, "I see you're sorrowful, Lord." He still gazes beyond the fire, motionless, eyes glistening. Should you continue? You do:

> Lord, here I am. I don't know exactly why you're so full of sorrow, but I'm here to console you. Jesus, I'm very weak. I don't have much to offer. In fact, too often I've been distant as I've followed you — and yet ... behold, here I am, Lord. Take me and use me as you desire. Use me to make you known and loved, weak though I am. Help me to love you. Jesus, I see how gentle you are, and I trust you. I know that you know me better than I know myself. You know what I can take. I put myself completely into your hands. Use me to help you, weak though I am. You may not be able to do much with me ... then again, I've seen you work miracles before. Do with me what you can. Behold, I believe. Help my unbelief. I trust in you.

As you were speaking, other disciples awoke and now they're all upset with you. As soon as you finish, you're distracted by them. You see their frowns and hear some of their angry whispers: "Who does he think he is? Does he think he's better than we are? Is he trying to get a special place with the Master?"

These words hurt you, and you continue looking at the other disciples, all of whom are staring at you with fierce eyes. Finally, you turn back to the Lord, expecting to see him still gazing toward the fire. But now, as you turn back to him, your eyes meet his. He's looking directly at you. What's this?! He's surprised ... and *joyful*. His face is all awe and amazement as he gazes on you with wonder. His mouth is open and slightly smiling. You feel embarrassed that he looks at you in this way. You think to yourself, "What was it I said? Didn't he hear the part about how I'm weak and don't have much to offer?" As these thoughts begin to swarm your mind, he suddenly exclaims in a loud voice, startling you and the others:

> My child! This is what I've been waiting for! This is the faith I longed for as I sat here. Never mind your weakness — I can take care of that! You've given me the freedom to work in your soul, the freedom I've been waiting for. Now, here. Receive my blessing.

He reaches over to you, places his hand on your head, and proclaims to the astonishment of all present: "You, my child, shall be called prophet of the Most High, for you will go before me to prepare my way. You will give my people knowledge of my mercy and love, and you shall continually delight my Heart."

Still confused, you ask, "But how can this be, Lord? I'm so weak."

He continues, "Here, behold." He pulls back his garment at the breast, and you see a burning flame there. You can hear his Heart crying out in its anguished thirst for a return of his love. He puts that into your heart. You feel in your heart a burning thirst to make him loved, to alleviate his sorrow. You're impelled to speak from a pulsing force within:

Lord, my one desire is to console you. I trust in you to use me. Mary, I put myself into your hands. Help me. Teach me to console Jesus. Lord, if I have any desire other than to console you, please change my desire. I go from here, Lord, with you in my heart. I love you, I praise you, and I thank you for whatever you do with my life. All is your grace. I love you, Lord Jesus, with the heart of your mother. I love you! I praise you! I thank you! I love you!

Jesus, so pleased with these words of humble confidence and love, cries out to all present, flashing you an unforgettable glance as he begins: "I have come to cast fire on the earth. How I wish it were already burning! Set this fire, my friends. Set this fire! Console me."

APPENDIX
ONE

Rules for the Discernment of Spirits
(for Little Souls)

In the Battle for Spiritual Joy

Some people are particularly prone to feeling sad, desolate, and downright depressed. I'm one of them. I'm a "melancholic," and I write this appendix especially for my fellow melancholics. As I write, I'm wondering if some of them having finished this retreat, tried to live its central attitude of trust as "praise and thanksgiving," fell flat on their faces, and now feel even more depressed than before. To them, I say, Cheer up! This appendix is for you. It's meant to give you hope that you truly can be a great consolation to the Heart of Jesus, even if the battle for spiritual joy seems unwinnable.

As for all the bubbly, happy-go-lucky types, you, too, may find this appendix helpful, since even the bubbliest of people surely have their down days. (In fact, "bubbles" can be a mask that hides desolation.) As for everyone in between, you, too, may want to read this appendix, because you have to deal with feeling desolate at one time or another. Yes, desolation comes for us all.

So, how do we deal with desolation when it comes? How do we still live our principle and foundation of "praise and thanks" when we don't see, hear, or feel a thing? How do we console Jesus when we ourselves need to be consoled? Answering these questions is what this appendix is all about. It's about winning the battle for spiritual joy.

In order to win a battle, it's important to have the right weapons. Our old friend, the former soldier, St. Ignatius of Loyola, has for us some devastatingly powerful weapons as we fight in the battle for spiritual joy. He calls his arsenal, "The Rules for the Discernment of Spirits."[1] Yet, because this retreat

---

1. The Rules for the Discernment of Spirits can be found in the *Spiritual Exercises*, 331-336. (Hereafter, the book *Spiritual Exercises* is abbreviated in these footnotes as *SpirEx*.) Saint Ignatius divides the Rules into two "weeks," with fourteen rules for the First Week and eight for the Second Week. To simplify things, I'll refer to the eight rules of the Second Week as rules 15-22. For a more detailed and complete treatment of the rules of the First Week, I recommend *The Discernment of Spirits: An Ignatian Guide for Everyday Living* (New York: Crossroad Publishing Company, 2005) by Timothy Gallagher, OMV. For a more detailed and complete treatment of the rules of the Second Week, I recommend *Spiritual Consolation: An Ignatian Guide for the Greater Discernment of Spirits* (New York: Crossroad Publishing Company, 2007) by the same author.

is for little souls, I'm not going to deal with all 22 of his "big guns" here. For trying to master such firepower here and now just might blow us away — believe me, I know. As a seminarian first learning to fire these guns in battle, I got knocked out by the force of their recoil. In other words, there were so many things to remember, so many nuances to each point, and so much I just didn't get that I lost my joy right from the start. So that you, too, don't get blown away by the back-fire of all 22 of Ignatius's big guns, I'm going to give a simplified "little soul" version of them.

My simplified version of the Rules for the Discernment of Spirits attempts to organize and streamline the combined forces of St. Ignatius's ideas, St. Faustina's experience, and Consoling spirituality.[2] It may not pack the full punch of Ignatius's 22-gun arsenal, but thanks to the extra boost from Faustina, you just might find that firing my lower caliber "little shots" is just as deadly to the enemy of our joy.

AIR: Awareness, Identify, Respond

The key to wielding the weapons that follow is a seemingly harmless word: *AIR*. As **A**wareness, **I**dentify, **R**espond, however, it's not so harmless. In fact, as we head into the battle for spiritual joy, this kind of AIR is like a mighty wind at our backs, pushing us forward and blowing sand into our enemy's eyes.

A = Awareness: *The spiritual life is a roller coaster.*

A big part of the battle for spiritual joy is won simply when we become aware that we're in a battle — and that the battle takes place on a roller coaster.

The spiritual life (as well as the emotional life, to which it's closely tied) is a series of ups, downs, and somewheres-in-between. Saint Ignatius calls the ups "consolation" and the

---

2. Since my simplified version does all this, it's much longer than Ignatius's Rules. Yet I still call mine a "simplified version," because I think little souls will find that reading my text makes it easier for them to remember and digest the information about the Rules than simply reading the Rules themselves. For those who would like to see how my rules connect with those of Ignatius, see the many notes that follow in which I cite Ignatius's text.

downs "desolation."[3] The ups are basically when we feel, well, like saints. In other words, it's when we eagerly run to prayer, overflow with empathy and compassion for all, practice virtues with the greatest of ease, and seem to walk hand-in-hand with God himself.[4] At some point, however, our high-riding coaster

3. Some authors who offer more thorough commentaries on the Rules for the Discernment of Spirits (Gallagher, for instance) are careful to distinguish *spiritual* consolation and desolation from "*unspiritual*" consolation and desolation. For the sake of simplicity, that is, so as not to have to constantly qualify my use of the terms "consolation" and "desolation," hereafter, whenever I use either term, I mean the spiritual form of it. Instead of using the terms "unspiritual consolation" and "unspiritual desolation," I will use the terms "emotional high" and "emotional low," respectively. (In a later section, "Ask, Why?," I will go into some of the details regarding the differences between the spiritual and "unspiritual" versions of desolation.) I feel justified in making this simplifying move, because in everyday language, it's not common for people to describe their emotional highs as "consolation" or their emotional lows as "desolation." Thus, when we hear such terms, it's not difficult to understand them as having the specific meaning Ignatius gives them. I feel further justified in this move because in his text on the Rules, Ignatius himself doesn't get into this distinction. (He never uses the term "unspiritual" to describe consolation or desolation.) He seems to assume that when we read "consolation" or "desolation," we understand them to have the spiritual meaning he intends.

4. Ignatius says it's characteristic of the good spirit, who causes consolation, "to give courage and strength, consolations, tears, inspirations, and peace. This He does by making all easy, by removing all obstacles so that the soul goes forward in doing good" (*SpirEx*, 315, Rule 2). Ignatius then offers the following definition of consolation: "I call it consolation when an interior movement is aroused in the soul, by which it is inflamed with love of its Creator and Lord, and as a consequence, can love no creature on the face of the earth for its own sake, but only in the Creator of them all. It is likewise consolation when one sheds tears that move to the love of God, whether it be because of sorrow for sins, or because of the sufferings of Christ our Lord, or for any other reason that is immediately directed to the praise and service of God. Finally, I call consolation every increase of faith, hope, and love, and all interior joy that invites and attracts to what is heavenly and to the salvation of one's soul by filling it with peace and quiet in its Creator and Lord" (Ibid., 316, Rule 3). Later, he writes, "It is characteristic of God and His Angels, when they act upon the soul, to give true happiness and spiritual joy, and to banish all the sadness and disturbances which are caused by the enemy" (Ibid., 329, Rule 19).

Saint Faustina's *Diary* is filled with clear descriptions of consolation. Here are a few examples: "I understood how much God loves us, how simple He is, though incomprehensible, and how easy it is to commune with Him, despite His great majesty. With no one do I feel as free and as much at ease as with Him" (603). And later, "My soul was filled with peace and love, and the more I come to know the greatness of God, the more joyful I become that He is as He is. And I rejoice immensely in His greatness and am delighted that I am so little because, since I am

cars come to the "big drop," and down we go to the depths of desolation. Desolation is basically when prayer feels like eating dust, people easily irritate us, God seems light-years away, and we wonder, "Why the heck was I wasting my time with all that religious stuff?" Throw in nagging regret, self-loathing, sadness, fear, lack of energy for anything "spiritual," and a burning urge for whatever distracts the mind, feeds the belly, or arouses the senses, and we've got ourselves a good dose of desolation.[5]

little, He carries me in His arms and holds me close to His Heart" (779). Elsewhere, she says that Jesus' gaze "filled my soul with strength and power, courage and extraordinary trust that I would carry out everything He was demanding of me, despite such tremendous difficulties, and ... that with Him I can do all things" (858). A final example shows how consolation builds up charity and service for neighbor: "My life at present flows on in peaceful awareness of God. ... I feel a certain need to share myself with others" (887).

5. Ignatius says it is characteristic of the bad spirit, who causes desolation, "to harass with anxiety, to afflict with sadness, to raise obstacles backed by fallacious reasonings that disturb the soul. Thus, he seeks to prevent the soul from advancing." Ignatius then offers the following definition of desolation: "I call desolation what is entirely the opposite of what is described in [consolation], as darkness of soul, turmoil of spirit, inclination to what is low and earthly, restlessness rising from many disturbances and temptations which lead to want of faith, want of hope, want of love. The soul is wholly slothful, tepid, sad, and separated, as it were, from its Creator and Lord" (Ibid., 317, Rule 4).

In her *Diary*, Faustina gives many vivid descriptions of particularly deep desolation. She writes: "Darkness began to cast its shadow over my soul. I felt no consolation in prayer; I had to make a great effort to meditate; fear began to sweep over me. Going deeper into myself, I could find nothing but great misery. I could also clearly see the great holiness of God. I did not dare to raise my eyes to Him, but reduced myself to dust under His feet and begged for mercy. ... I did not understand what I was reading; I could not meditate; it seemed to me that my prayer was displeasing to God. ... The simple truths of the faith became incomprehensible to me. My soul was in anguish, unable to find comfort anywhere. At a certain point, there came to me the very powerful impression that I am rejected by God" (23). On another occasion, she writes: "When people spoke to me about God, my heart was like a rock. I could not draw from it a single sentiment of love for Him. ... More than once, all through Holy Mass, I had to struggle against blasphemous thoughts which were forcing themselves to my lips. I felt an aversion for the Holy Sacraments, and it seemed to me that I was not profiting from them in any way. ... [My confessor] explained to me that these were trials sent by God and that, in the situation I was in, not only was I not offending God, but I was most pleasing to Him. 'This is a sign,' he told me, 'that God loves you very much and that He has great confidence in you, since He is sending you such trials.' But these words brought me no comfort; it seemed to me that they did not apply to me at all. ... Then other thoughts came to me: why strive to acquire virtues and do good works? ... what good is it to take vows? to pray?" (77).

Again, the first step to victory in the battle for spiritual joy is to become aware that the spiritual life is a roller coaster, rolling on through the ups and downs of consolation and desolation. Put a little differently, this first point "Awareness" is a simple exhortation: "Keep your eyes open on the roller coaster of life!" This is an exhortation we may often need to hear. I say that because just as people tend to keep their eyes closed when they ride a normal roller coaster, so also do they tend to keep them closed as they ride the roller coaster of life. But this won't do. We can't fight well with our eyes closed, especially in those bizarre battles that take place on a roller coaster.

I = Identify: *Where am I on the ride?*

Okay, so our eyes are wide open. Now what? Well, look around. Where are we on the ride? Are we up, down, or somewhere in the middle? The main idea with the point "Identify" is that we identify what kind of spiritual state we're in. We've already learned what consolation and desolation are. Now we continually need to ask ourselves, "Well, which one is it? Which state am I in right now?" These questions aren't always easy to answer, especially because spiritual movements of consolation and desolation often get stirred up with the natural movements of our moods and emotions. Without getting into the mind-numbing nuances of, for example, a spiritual consolation and an emotional high, let's focus on asking ourselves a few simple questions: How's our faith, hope, and charity? Is prayer easy? Are things light and clear or heavy and confusing? Do we have peace and joy? In my experience, that last question is the golden key that often unlocks the mystery of whether I'm in consolation, desolation, or somewhere in the middle. Coincidentally, it also gets to the core of Consoling spirituality.

In a certain sense, *Consoling the Heart of Jesus* is all about striving to remain at peace and in spiritual joy, striving to stay in a spirit of praise and thanksgiving throughout good times and bad. In a certain sense, this is also how St. Ignatius sees the whole spiritual life, namely, as one great effort to keep on keeping on in consolation.[6] Of course, he knows that every-one's coaster car eventually hits the big drop and dives down to desolation. Yet, when this happens, he tells us not to give up. In fact, he encourages us to marshal our efforts and strive to get back to consolation. Such striving is what the next point is all about.

R = Respond: *What we can **do** in consolation and desolation.*

I mentioned that I'm writing this appendix especially for my fellow melancholics, to give them hope. Well, here's where the hope comes in: There's a lot you can *do* to enter and remain in the peaceful, joyful land of consolation! Ignatius isn't a defeatist who thinks we're doomed to be dominated by dark emotions and desolate spiritual states. Of course, he recognizes that consolation is a gift from God, and yet he also believes there's much we can do to prepare ourselves for this gift (and to keep it when it comes). The following rules are simple things we can do to win the battle for spiritual joy.

By the way, before we begin reading the "response rules," it's important to keep in mind the last point, namely, that we need to try to identify whether we're in consolation, desolation, or somewhere in between. That point was crucially important, because what we do as our response depends on what spiritual state we're in. So, one set of response rules covers our conduct in consolation and the other set advises us in desolation. (There's only one rule for when we're in the middle: "Stay vigilant with your eyes open, for an up or down will surely come soon.") Let's begin with the response rules for times of consolation because they're the most straightforward.

Response Rules for Times of Consolation

Three main response rules should direct us during times of consolation. In other words, we should strive to do three

---

6. That Ignatius sees the spiritual life in this way should become clear in the next section.

things when prayer is easy, all seems clear, and we're filled with peace and joy because of the closeness we feel to God: (1) Eat it up! (2) Humble yourself, and (3) Listen.

1. Eat it up!

Have you ever been offered a big, tasty slice of chocolate cake and then said, "Oh, no thanks." Dieting aside, why might we say that? Why do at least some of us sometimes say "no thanks" to the good things people offer us? While all little souls may not have this problem, some surely do. Moreover, in my experience, little souls often have great difficulty not only accepting things from people but also from God. In other words, when God offers them a big, tasty slice of spiritual consolation, they sometimes say, "Oh, no thanks ... I don't deserve that. I'm not good enough." Well, whatever the reasons for this strange but all-too-common behavior, here's a bit of advice for such souls: When God offers you a big slice of consolation, take it. Eat it up![7] It's not humility to refuse it. In fact, such refusals might even be a lack of humility. That's because when God gives his consolation, it's often for a reason. It's often because he sees we need to be strengthened. Perhaps there's an upcoming battle, and he wants us to withstand it. Well, if we refuse the extra help of his consolation, when the battle comes, we just might get routed. So it's a humble thing to accept God's gifts and wisely to store up strength for the future.[8] Such readiness to

---

7. Regarding accepting God's gifts, Jesus gives the following instruction to Faustina: "**Act like a beggar who does not back away when he gets more alms** [than he asked for], **but offers thanks the more fervently. You, too, should not back away and say that you are not worthy of receiving greater graces when I give them to you. I know you are unworthy, but rejoice all the more and take as many treasures from My Heart as you can carry, for then you will please Me more**" (*Diary*, 294).

8. Regarding the idea of storing up for the future the strength that comes from accepting God's gifts, Ignatius says, "When one enjoys consolation, let him consider how he will conduct himself during the time of ensuing desolation, *and store up a supply of strength as a defense against that day*" (emphasis added; *SpirEx*, 323, Rule 10). Similarly, Faustina writes that during times when she experienced deep consolation, she often heard the following words in her soul repeated over and over, "**Strengthen yourself for combat.**" She went on to say, "I regard the time of [consolation] as a time of preparation for victory" (*Diary*, 145).

accept means we realize, "I'm not Superman" and that we need to rely on God for everything. Let's stay on the topic of humility as we turn to the second response rule for times of consolation.

2. Humble yourself.

God's consolation is powerful. Yet, sometimes as we "eat it up" and begin to experience its strength, we may be tempted to think we're the cause of it. Whereas, we may not have felt much like Superman before the consolation came, after it comes we often do. I say that because deep consolation can give us the ability to leap tall vices in a single bound, to be bulletproof against Satan's salvos, and seemingly to fly up, up, and away on the heights of holiness with the superhero saints we read about in books. Now, before we begin planning our own canonizations, we need to realize there's one big chunk of kryptonite that quickly puts an end to our delusions of grandeur, namely, the truth. What truth? The truth that the super strength we experience in times of consolation is God's gift. It's his to give and to take away.

One of the reasons God might begin to pull away the grace of his consolation is that he sees it's going to our heads. Because he loves us, he doesn't want us to live the illusion that we're super saints, so he'll withdraw consolation to keep us little and in his love and truth.[9] Thus, Ignatius's advice to someone in

---

9. According to Ignatius, one reason God allows us to suffer desolation is because "God wishes to give us a true knowledge and understanding of ourselves, so that we may have an intimate perception of the fact that it is not within our power to acquire and attain great devotion, intense love, tears, or any other spiritual consolation; but that all this is the gift and grace of God our Lord. God does not wish us to build on the property of another, to rise up in spirit in a certain pride and vainglory and attribute to ourselves the devotion and other effects of spiritual consolation" (*SpirEx*, 322, Rule 9). Faustina learned the truth of this rule from the Lord himself when, after she had experienced an extremely dark desolation, he said to her, **"My daughter, know that of yourself you are just what you have gone through, and it is only by My grace that you are a participant in eternal life and all the gifts I lavish on you."** Then, she commented, "And with these words of the Lord, there came to me a true knowledge of myself. Jesus is giving me a lesson in deep humility ..." (*Diary*, 1559).

consolation is this: "Humble yourself."[10] In other words, "Put yourself in the truth." While some of us may be thinking, "Easier said than done," I don't fully agree. I would agree if we hadn't already been formed during the retreat in the three words of Mary (*ecce*, *fiat*, and *magnificat*), but now we're trying to know and live the spiritual attitude those three words represent. The more we live it, the easier it will be for us to humble ourselves. I say that especially because of the first word of our Marian trio, *ecce*.

The *ecce* moment is crucially important. It's the starting point of our relationship with God. It's to recognize the truth of who we are, namely, sinners who can do no good on our own. Yet the word *ecce* also implies a confidence in going to God as we are, sinfulness and all, because of another truth: God's infinite mercy. These two truths (our misery and God's mercy) should always be kept together. If we do keep them together, then we'll be free to eat up plate after plate of God's consolation without getting fat (heads). Unfortunately, people often don't keep these truths together. Little souls especially get tempted to stay stuck in their wretchedness without having confidence in God's mercy. I should say a bit more about this very real danger before moving on to the third rule.

It often happens that little souls see themselves as repulsive and unlovable, especially to God. This is one of the most vicious lies told by the enemy of our joy. If there's one thing the retreat tried to emphasize, it's God's mercy and the truth that he most especially loves the littlest souls (because of his mercy). It's therefore crucially important that we never separate *ecce* from *fiat*. Of course, it sometimes happens that we remain in the *ecce* moment, head down and full of tears, for a long time. I beg all little souls who feel this way to please realize that the loving embrace of God's mercy is already surrounding you and patiently awaiting the signal — *fiat* — that you'll allow him to fill your heart and soul. Attention little souls: He loves you. He

---

10. See *SpirEx*, 324, Rule 11: "He who enjoys consolation should take care to humble himself and lower himself as much as possible. Let him recall how little he is able to do in time of desolation, when he is left without such grace or consolation."

loves you. He loves you most especially. Don't believe Satan's lies to the contrary. If his lies keep running through your head, please make the retreat again and see the sections in Appendix Two entitled "Divine Mercy — Misery" and "Divine Mercy — For Sinners." Until then, ponder some of Jesus' words to you from one of those sections:

> **Be not afraid of your Savior, O sinful soul. I make the first move to come to you, for I know that by yourself you are unable to lift yourself to me. Child, do not run away from your Father; be willing to talk openly with your God of mercy who wants to speak words of pardon and lavish his graces on you. How dear your soul is to Me! I have inscribed your name upon My hand; you are engraved as a deep wound in My Heart. ...**
>
> **My mercy is greater than your sins and those of the entire world. Who can measure the extent of My goodness? For you I descended from heaven to earth; for you I allowed Myself to be nailed to the Cross; for you I let My Sacred Heart be pierced with a lance, thus opening wide the source of mercy for you. Come, then, with trust to draw graces from this fountain. I never reject a contrite heart. Your misery has disappeared in the depths of My mercy. Do not argue with Me about your wretchedness. You will give Me pleasure if you hand over to Me all your troubles and griefs. I shall heap upon you the treasures of My grace.**[11]

3. *Listen.*

St. Ignatius teaches that the thoughts and ideas that come to our minds during times of consolation tend to originate from

---

11. Ibid., 1485.

the "good spirit," that is, from God.[12] Therefore, when we're in a time of consolation, it's important to strive to pay attention to what God may be saying to us. This is important for winning the battle for spiritual joy not only because God's voice brings sweetness but also because following his will for us is our joy and deepest happiness.

Contrary to a popular lie, God's will is not bent on causing his creatures the most misery possible. No, he has a marvelous plan for each one of us, the following of which is our greatest happiness. To follow it well, it's helpful to continually strive to listen to his voice, especially during times of consolation.

At this point, some might be saying, "How do I listen? I don't hear anything in prayer." I wonder if these same people also became a bit discouraged when they read during the retreat about how clearly God spoke to our friend, Joe. They may have thought, "Well, I guess I'm just not as special or holy as Joe." Now's a good time to reflect on how God might speak to us that, I hope, will also take care of any discouragement that reading Joe's story might have caused.

God speaks to us all. He constantly speaks to us through Sacred Scripture, liturgy, people, circumstances, events, and in many other ways, such as when he speaks to us more directly during times of quiet prayer. While it's possible for him to speak to us at such times in audible words, that seems rare. More often, he speaks with inaudible, interior words (or ideas, called "lights"), like he did to our friend, Joe. Such interior words are often delicate and quiet — at least according to Joe.

Joe once gave a talk about his 30-day retreat. When someone asked him exactly how he had heard God's voice during it, he answered with an analogy. He said he heard God's voice in a way similar to how we experience dreams when we're asleep. (Though, he insisted, what happened during the retreat

---

12. Ignatius writes, "For just as consolation is the opposite of desolation, so the thoughts that spring from consolation are the opposite of those that spring from desolation" (*SpirEx*, 317, Rule 4). On this topic, he also says, "For just as *in consolation the good spirit guides and counsels us*, so in desolation the evil spirit guides and counsels" (emphasis added; Ibid., 318, Rule 5).

was not a dream, and he was not asleep.) He said that when he heard the words during the meditations of his retreat, they were vivid and clear, but then, after the meditations, it sometimes seemed that he could have forgotten them had he not reflected on his meditations immediately after they finished. (St. Ignatius recommends a review of the time of meditation after it's finished.)[13] He said this is like what often happens in the case of dreams when we're asleep. Sometimes we have dreams that are quite vivid and clear, but then, when we wake up and jump into the bustle of our day, their content just as quickly jumps out of our consciousness. For instance, it sometimes happens, Joe said, that when he wakes up in the morning, apart from the usual drowsiness, he has a vague sense of lightness or heaviness, depending on the nature of his dreams the night before. Those dreams, he said, often only come into focus in his memory when he makes a deliberate effort to remember them. Without such effort, he said, the memory of them often slips into oblivion.

In light of Joe's description of how he heard God's voice, I'd like to make some comments. It seems to me that the center of our hearts, where God speaks to us most intimately, is a place where we're truly conscious but with a consciousness that's not exactly the same as our everyday consciousness. That place of prayer consciousness, where we meet God in our hearts, seems to belong to another realm.[14] In that realm, we

---

13. Ibid., 77.

14. To what realm does prayer consciousness belong? Because of the comparison Joe made between prayer states and dream states, one might think that prayer states, like dream states, belong primarily to the realm of the subconscious. However, I think that's a mistake. For, while it's true that the subconscious can be vigorous and active during times of prayer (especially during imaginative meditation), in my experience, I'm much more active and aware — that is, my heart is more active and aware — during a state of prayer consciousness than during a dream state. Thus, I think it's better to think of prayer consciousness as belonging not to a subconscious realm, but rather to a kind of super-conscious realm.

While it's true, at least according to the great mystics, that during the deepest forms of prayer, the faculties of the soul (e.g., reason and will) are "put to sleep" by the activity of grace, this doesn't mean one's heart is also napping at such times. On the contrary, during deep prayer, it seems that one's heart is most engaged by God and that, although it remains passive in relation to him, it's somehow taken up into his own divine activity. Because of this, a person at

truly are conscious of what happens as it happens, but when we leave it, we often easily forget what happened there. In fact, it sometimes takes effort (like Ignatius's review) to bring with us what we hear during prayer consciousness as we step back into our everyday consciousness. Moreover, the voice that speaks to us in that other realm is gentle, mysterious, and delicate. It's so delicate, in fact, we can easily miss it, even while we're praying. To hear this voice, it often takes the practice of listening, interior quiet, and simply spending time in the other realm of prayer. (Perhaps that's why Joe heard the Lord's voice so clearly, namely, because his 30-day retreat helped him to be silent and to listen closely.)

That our souls need to be still in order to hear God's voice explains for me why words or ideas (lights) that come during my own meditations often come at the very end, that is, after I've had time to quiet down, enter my heart, and listen. I wonder if this is at least part of the reason why Jesus said to St. Faustina, **"I often wait with great graces until towards the end of prayer."**[15] Perhaps he said that because we're not usually ready to receive such great graces until after we've quieted down and entered our hearts. This may also be why, as St. Ignatius points out, the bad spirit makes every effort while we meditate to get us to shorten the time we've decided beforehand to devote to our meditation.[16]

such times of prayer may be even more radically active and even aware (though in a different way) than during his everyday conscious states. (Yet, as I'll soon explain in the text, it's not always easy to bring the memory of what happens at such times of prayer into everyday consciousness.)

15. *Diary*, 268.

16. Ignatius gives this advice in the twelfth of his "Introductory Observations" to the *Exercises*. He writes: "He who is giving the Exercises must insist with the exercitant that since he is to spend an hour in each of the five exercises or contemplations which are made every day, he must always take care that he is satisfied in the consciousness of having persevered in the exercise for the full hour. Let him rather exceed an hour than not use the full time. For the enemy is accustomed to make every effort that the hour to be devoted to a contemplation, meditation, or prayer should be shortened." In the observation that follows (13), he gives more explicit directions as to how to deal with such temptations: "We must remember that during the time of consolation it is easy, and requires only a slight effort, to continue a whole hour in contemplation, but in time of

I should mention that the great graces God gives to us in prayer don't always come in the form of words or ideas. He can also communicate to our hearts in the wordless language of what I call the "waves of peace." Sometimes such waves don't seem to have any special content or message other than that of being an experience of God's love and care. At other times, they do have a special kind of content or message. For instance, let's say we're praying about some decision and, as we began to focus our attention on one option, we begin to feel the waves of peace. When this happens, it may indicate that such a choice is the right one. Sometimes, however, God can speak through a lack of peace. For instance, if, during our prayer, we begin to focus our attention on the second option and begin to feel a lack of peace, this is often a sign that such an option isn't what God wants for us.[17] Here's an example from St. Faustina's life of how her experience of a lack of peace and then a subsequent sense of peace helped her to recognize God's will:

> On the eve of the retreat, I started to pray that the Lord Jesus might give me just a little health so that I could take part in the retreat, because I was feeling so ill that I thought perhaps it might be my last. However, as soon as I had started praying I felt a strange dissatisfaction. I interrupted the prayer of supplication and began to thank the Lord for everything He sends me, submitting myself completely to His holy will. Then I felt profound peace of soul.[18]

Such "prayer surfing," as I like to call it, where we ride the waves of peace, takes practice, but it's not as difficult as we

desolation it is very difficult to do so. Hence, in order to fight against the desolation and conquer the temptation, the exercitant must always remain in the exercise a little more than the full hour. Thus he will accustom himself not only to resist the enemy, but even to overthrow him."

17. Please note an important difference: lack of peace as a sign from the Lord vs. lack of peace as a result of our own resistance. Sometimes we resist a decision because it goes against our sinful nature. Such resistance isn't the same as feeling the kind of lack of peace that alerts us that something isn't pleasing to God.

18. *Diary*, 724. For more examples, see 18, 42, 45, 143, 155, and 359.

might think. In fact, with continued practice, we might find that we're able to surf these waves not only during our set times of prayer but even in the midst of a busy day. For instance, let's say we have to make an important decision and after thinking about it a while, we're not sure what the right choice is. Well, we might try conferring with God in the midst of a busy day by pausing, entering into our hearts, and getting a feel for what the surf's like there.[19] Is it peaceful or turbulent? Often the answer to this question can give us an idea of what decision to make. It's like the idea of going with your gut, but it's deeper because it's a "going with your heart," particularly with that place in our hearts where we've learned to meet God in prayer. Getting into this habit helps one to live a life of discernment, that is, a life of attentive listening to the voice of the Lord.

I have to bring up St. Faustina again, because she provides us with such an excellent example of someone who lived a life of discernment by always conferring with Jesus in her heart. In fact, one of the reasons I love her *Diary* so much is that simply reading it is a school of this kind of prayer. I say that because when someone reads the many times and ways that Jesus spoke to Faustina (for example, through words, ideas or lights, and by waves of peace), it's like one's own soul becomes attuned to listening for the same kinds of voices. Of course, Jesus probably won't speak to us in as radical a way as he sometimes did to Faustina — after all, she had the extraordinarily important vocation of communicating to the whole world Jesus' desire in our day for a renewed and deeper devotion to his mercy. Nevertheless, I believe that Jesus truly does speak to us in many of the same ways he spoke to her. We simply need to make the effort to listen, but don't just take my word for it. Let's consider again words from Faustina's *Diary*.

St. Faustina wrote, "If only souls would become recollected, God would speak to them at once, for dissipation drowns out the word of the Lord."[20] Later, Jesus himself told

---

19. This idea of "entering into our hearts" is similar to what I said during the retreat on the topic of visiting Jesus in the "tabernacle of our hearts," pages 184-185.
20. Ibid., 452.

her, "**Strive for a life of recollection so that you can hear My voice, which is so soft that only recollected souls can hear it.**"[21] Jesus' words here indicate that it's not always easy to hear his voice. Yet it's worth the effort. He said to Faustina:

> **When you reflect upon what I tell you in the depths of your heart, you profit more than if you had read many books. Oh, if souls would only want to listen to My voice when I am speaking in the depths of their hearts, they would reach the peak of holiness in a short time.**[22]

Before moving on to the next section, there's one last point I should make about listening to God's voice during times of consolation: The words, thoughts, or inspirations we receive in prayer, even those that come during times of deep consolation, are *not* infallible. In other words, we can make mistakes. We can make mistakes not only in interpreting the words, but also in making judgments about their origin.[23] For sometimes the

21. Ibid., 1779.

22. Ibid., 584.

23. I say this, even as I'm well aware that Ignatius says, "God alone can give consolation to the soul without any previous cause" (*SpirEx*, 330, Rule 16). This rule isn't the same as saying that we always have certainty regarding the origin of a consolation without previous cause. I say that because we can't always be sure there *wasn't* a previous cause — maybe there was a previous cause that we didn't recognize. Moreover, Ignatius later explains the difficulties that come from interpreting consolation without previous cause: "When consolation is without previous cause, as was said, there can be no deception in it, since it can proceed from God our Lord only. But a spiritual person who has received such a consolation must consider it very attentively, and must cautiously distinguish the actual time of the consolation from the period which follows it. At such a time the soul is still fervent and favored with the grace and aftereffects of the consolation which has passed. In this second period the soul frequently forms various resolutions and plans which are not granted directly by God our Lord. They may come from our own reasoning on the relations of our concepts and on the consequences of our judgments, or they may come from the good or evil spirit. Hence, they must be carefully examined before they are given full approval and put into execution" (Ibid., 336, Rule 22). I think it's best to have a skeptical attitude, or at least one of detachment, with regard to extraordinary consolations received in prayer. Even when she felt sure something came from God, St. Faustina always submitted it to the judgment of her confessor. She once wrote: "In the depths of my soul, I was so very sure that these things came from God, that I would lay down my life for

movements that take place in our souls are simply the activities of our own psychological processes. On the other hand, the bad spirit, that is, the devil or a demon, can appear as an "angel of light" (2 Cor 11:14) and communicate things to us even when we're in a time of consolation.[24] Thus, I say with St. Ignatius that the words, thoughts, or inspirations that come to us in times of consolation tend to come from the good spirit but not that they always or certainly do.[25] Thus, we all should say with St. Faustina: "I attach greater importance to the words of my confessor than to all the lights taken together that I receive interiorly."[26] Truly, we should be ready to humbly submit our judgment about the origin of what we receive in prayer to a spiritual director and, ultimately, to the Church. Speaking of the Church, we have in her a great help in our discernment of spirits. One reason I say that is if something someone were to receive in prayer were to go against the Church's moral or doctrinal teaching, then he would be certain it did not come from God.

---

this. However, I placed the confessor's opinion above all" (*Diary*, 131). We will hear more from Faustina about this detached attitude in a forthcoming note.

24. See *SpirEx*, 331-332, Rules 17-18.

25. Ignatius writes, "For just as consolation is the opposite of desolation, so the thoughts that spring from consolation are the opposite of those that spring from desolation" (SpirEx, 317, Rule 4). On this topic, he also says, "For just as *in consolation the good spirit guides and counsels us*, so in desolation the evil spirit guides and counsels" (emphasis added; Ibid., 318, Rule 5). However, he also makes the point that it's possible for the bad spirit, acting as an angel of light, to give consolation to the soul (Ibid., 331-332, Rules 17-18).

26. *Diary*, 680. In another passage on the same topic, Faustina gives the following advice: "Few are the souls that are always watchful for divine graces, and even fewer of such souls who follow those inspirations faithfully. Still, a soul which is faithful to God cannot confirm its own inspirations; it must submit them to the control of a very wise and learned priest; and until it is quite certain, it should remain distrustful. It should not, on its own initiative alone, put its trust in these inspirations and all other higher graces, because it can thus expose itself to great losses. Even though a soul may immediately distinguish between false inspirations and those of God, it should nevertheless be careful, because many things are uncertain. God is pleased and rejoices when a soul distrusts Him for His own sake; because it loves Him, it is prudent and itself asks and searches for help to make certain that it is really God who is acting within it. And once a well-instructed confessor has confirmed this, the soul should be at peace and give itself up to God, according to His directions; that is, according to the directions of the confessor" (Ibid., 138-139).

Our lack of certainty regarding words, thoughts, and inspirations we receive in prayer is a good thing. It's a healthy reminder that in our life of prayer we're not lone rangers who have no need of others. Truly, we need to rely on others and on the Church. That being said, we can go a long way by using our own properly formed sense of discernment. For, while we may not have certainty regarding the origin of something we receive during a specific time of prayer, we can become more and more certain of its origin as coming from God if we receive the same word, thought, or inspiration again and again during times of consolation.[27] This should put us at ease, because it means that if God wants us to hear something important, and yet we're not quite sure it was him, he'll often repeat it during times of consolation. Furthermore, St. Ignatius offers an advanced set of his rules (of the Second Week) for helping us distinguish between the good spirit and the bad spirit when he appears as an angel of light and tempts us with good things.[28]

If my having mentioned the bad spirit appearing as an angel of light, the value of a spiritual director, and advanced rules for discernment has started to get you worried, don't let it. There's no need to be afraid. Allow me to put you at ease.

Regarding the bad spirit appearing as an angel of light, know this: He can "appear" through words, thoughts, or inspirations that come in prayer but not in the peace and joy of consolation itself. Therefore, we don't have to be afraid or skeptical of simple experiences of God's love and the peace and joy they bring. Remember what I said earlier regarding consolation: Eat it up! Caution and discernment comes in when experiences of love are accompanied by words, thoughts, or inspirations (especially those that try to get us to do something) or by more extraordinary mystical experiences such as visions or locutions. In sum: Eat up the chocolate cake of consolation (peace and joy). Be picky about eating the letters in yellow frosting (words, thoughts, or inspirations).

---

27. See *SpirEx*, 176.

28. For more information on this advanced set of rules, see the first footnote of this appendix.

Be especially careful with the birthday candles and their burning flames (visions and the like).

Regarding spiritual directors, I don't think having one is absolutely necessary for spiritual growth. (If I were of that opinion, I probably wouldn't have written a do-it-yourself retreat.) I don't think they're absolutely necessary, because I know many people who want a spiritual director but who, after a reasonable amount of prayer and effort to find one, still haven't been able to. I don't believe the Lord abandons them. For, while it's a great, great gift to have a good spiritual director[29] — a gift for which we should earnestly pray — the Lord can still lead souls to the heights of holiness without one if they strive to remain humble and confident in the Lord (if they stay on the Little Way). Saint Faustina surely strove for humility and trusted the Lord. Thus, she could write:

> During those times I had no spiritual director; I was without any kind of guidance whatever. I begged the Lord, but He did not give me a director. Jesus Himself has been my Master from the days of my infancy up to the present moment. He accompanied me across all the deserts and through all dangers. I see clearly that God alone could have led me through such great perils unharmed. ... Later on, the Lord did give me a director.[30]

St. Thérèse of Liseux, the very one who pioneered the Little Way, was even less reliant on a spiritual director than St. Faustina. Part of the reason for this was that Faustina, unlike Thérèse, had to deal with visions, extraordinary mystical experiences, and direct instructions from the Lord to do things like

---

29. Faustina writes: "Oh, how great a grace it is to have a spiritual director! One makes more rapid progress in virtue, sees the will of God more clearly, fulfills it more faithfully, and follows a road that is sure and free of dangers. The director knows how to avoid the rocks against which the soul could be shattered. The Lord gave me this grace rather late, to be sure, but I rejoice in it greatly, seeing how God inclines His will to my director's wishes" (*Diary*, 331).

30. Ibid., 108.

have images painted. (Thus, for Faustina, having a spiritual director became a kind of necessity.[31]) Thérèse's way was much simpler and ordinary. Because our own paths probably more closely resemble that of Thérèse than Faustina (thank God), we'd do well to read and reflect on some of her reflections on spiritual direction:

> [My Novice Mistress's] kindness toward me was limitless and still my soul did not expand under her direction. It was only with great effort that I was able to take direction, for I had never become accustomed to speaking about my soul and I didn't know how to express what was going on within it. One good old Mother understood one day what I was experiencing, and she said laughingly during recreation: "My child, it seems to me you don't have very much to tell your Superiors." "Why do you say that, Mother?" "Because your soul is extremely *simple*, but when you will be perfect, you will be even *more simple*; the closer one approaches to God, the simpler one becomes."
>
> ... I have said that Jesus was "my Director." Upon entering Carmel, I met one who was to serve me in this capacity, but hardly had I been numbered among his children when he left for exile. [He was sent from France to Canada.] Thus I came to know him only to be deprived of him. Reduced to receiving one letter a year from him to my twelve, my heart quickly turned to the Director of directors, and it was He who taught me that science hidden from the wise and prudent and revealed to *little ones* (emphasis in original).[32]

31. Having a spiritual director becomes more important for a person who feels called to the consecrated life and/or to the priesthood or to some extraordinary mission. Also, if a person begins to regularly experience higher forms of mystical prayer, then that person, too, will have greater need to find a good spiritual director. All such people should especially pray for and seek out a good spiritual director. By the way, higher forms of spiritual prayer don't necessarily mean a person is holier than others. The Little Way teaches us that.

32. *Story of a Soul*, p. 151.

Thérèse's wisdom about being simple and little brings comfort to those who haven't been able to find a suitable spiritual director. It might also comfort those who became worried when they heard me mention Ignatius's more advanced rules for the discernment of spirits. Thérèse's wisdom helps such souls realize that they need not worry if they can't master òr even understand such rules. For, while it's a good thing to know and apply them, the Lord surely doesn't abandon little souls who aren't able to do so. In fact, with a tender and marvelous care, the Lord truly guides, protects, and provides for little souls who humbly trust in him and simply strive to follow his will. I should add that those who have consecrated themselves to Mary especially need not worry. For, from her, they enjoy a particularly tender care and powerful protection. Truly, she has a way of protecting them from the damaging deceptions of the enemy and of finding the right spiritual directors for those who need them.[33]

---

33. According to St. Louis de Montfort in his book *True Devotion to Mary* (Charlotte, NC: TAN Books, 1941): "[Mary] is on the lookout ... for favorable occasions to do [her true children] good, to advance and enrich them. She sees clearly all good and evil, all prosperous and adverse fortunes, the blessings and the cursings ... and then she disposes things from afar that she may except her servants from all sorts of evils, and obtain for them all sorts of blessings. ... 'She herself takes care of our interests,' says a certain saint" (p. 127). And elsewhere he writes: "[Mary] conducts and directs [her devotees] according to the will of her Divine Son. ... She shows them the paths of eternal life. She makes them avoid the dangerous places. ... 'If you follow her,' says St. Bernard, 'you cannot wander from the road.' Fear not, therefore, that a true child of Mary can be deceived by the evil one, or fall into any formal heresy. There where the guidance of Mary is, neither the evil spirit with his illusions, nor the heretics with their subtleties, can ever come" (pp. 131-132). And later he says: "[Mary] puts herself around [her true children], and accompanies them 'like an army in battle array' (Cant 6:3). Shall a man who has an army of a hundred thousand soldiers around him fear his enemies? A faithful servant of Mary, surrounded by her protection ... has still less to fear. This good Mother ... would rather dispatch battalions of millions of angels to assist one of her servants than that it should ever be said that a faithful servant of Mary, who trusts in her, had had to succumb to the malice, the number and the vehemence of his enemies" (pp. 132-133).

Response Rules for Times of Desolation

Three main response rules should direct us during times of desolation. In other words, we should strive to do three things when we have little or no peace and joy, when praise and thanks is far from our lips, and when it seems we're in a dark, dry desert far from God: (1) Ask, "Why?" (2) Fight. (3) Don't listen.

1. Ask, "Why?"

After identifying that we're in a time of desolation, our first move for winning the battle for spiritual joy is to try to discover why the desolation happened. A good starting point is to ask ourselves, "When did this desolation begin?" Often we can think of a specific moment or period when the fountain of our peace and joy began to dry up. To find it, we may have to do the work of reflecting back on the previous hours, days, weeks, or even months. If we're in the habit of making a daily examination of conscience (B-A-K-E-R), this shouldn't be too difficult. Still, even if we've gotten used to examining our consciences, we may find that sometimes it's not so easy to figure out when and why desolation began. To make us more prepared for such times, it may be helpful to reflect on some of the natural contributing factors and supernatural causes of desolation.

While desolation is a spiritual reality, it's closely linked to our natural feelings and moods. In fact, it easily sprouts up in the fertile soil of our dark and down emotional states. Factors such as an unhealthy diet, extraordinary or prolonged stress, disappointments, failures, bumps or breaks in relationships, too much television, too little exercise, lack of sunshine, sleep, or recreation can contribute to emotional lows that, in turn, can easily lead to spiritual desolation. Once we identify something that's made us feel emotionally down or depressed, it's usually much easier to deal with it. For example, once we realize we've gotten depressed because we're so overworked and exhausted, then we can make an effort to find time to relax and get more sleep. So, recognizing the natural causes of our emotional lows can often help us to understand why we may be in a time of desolation. Moreover, striving to prevent such emotional lows and dealing with them when they occur may also prevent and put an end to the desolation that gets triggered by them. Supernatural causes of desolation are not as easy to discover as the natural causes of emotional lows. Still, with the help of the Holy Spirit, we can get light on them. One cause of desolation might be our sins, especially neglect of prayer, lack of humility during times of consolation, and being uncharitable to our neighbor. Another cause might be that God wants to train us in virtues such as patience, perseverance, and trust. A third cause might be that God wants to give us the valuable (humbling) self-knowledge of who we are without his grace.[34] Whatever the cause of desolation might be, we shouldn't think God directly causes it — he permits it but doesn't directly cause it.[35] Furthermore, we shouldn't look at it as a punishment from God as if he were mad at us. To receive training in virtues is not punishment. Still, some may be thinking, "But what about when desolation comes as a result of my sins? Isn't that punishment?"

If God didn't allow desolation because of our sins, *that* would be punishment, for then he'd be "giving us up" to sin in our lives (see Rom 1:18-32). So, when God allows us to experience desolation as a result of our sins, it's a mercy. It's a way he gets our attention. It's a merciful wake-up call by which he says to us: "All right, time to wake up! You're not aware of something you're doing (or not doing) that's hurting you. Please examine your conscience." If we then examine our consciences and discover a sin that's causing the desolation, we know what to do. (Repent of it and move on.) If, however, it's not clear that a specific sin is causing our desolation, then we

---

34. For Ignatius's full treatment of the causes of spiritual desolation, see *SpirEx*, 322, Rule 9.

35. In a letter to Teresa Rejadell, reproduced by William Young, SJ, in *Letters of Saint Ignatius of Loyola* (Chicago: Loyola University Press, 1959), pp. 21-22 and cited by Gallagher in *Discernment of Spirits*, p. 67, Ignatius makes the important distinction that while God "*gives*" spiritual consolation, he "*permits*" spiritual desolation, which is given by the enemy.

should simply fight the desolation, which is the topic of the next point. Before moving on to the next point, I'd like to emphasize something extremely important.

After reading that our sins can be a cause of desolation, some little souls may get caught in the trap of thinking that anytime they're in desolation it must be their own fault. Thus, desolation for them will be a slippery slope that leads to deeper and deeper desolation as they continually blame themselves for the darkness they feel. I have some advice for such souls: If it becomes clear that there's some specific thing you've done to bring on the desolation, then deal with it. For instance, if, as you examine your conscience, you realize the darkness you're in started when you were particularly unkind to someone, then tell Jesus (and perhaps the person involved) you're sorry, and resolve to be kind in the future. Or, to use another example, if you realize that the time of desolation started when you stopped praying, then start praying again. However, if it's not clear to you that there's some specific thing you did to bring on the desolation, don't torture yourself trying to figure it out. God may have allowed the desolation for another reason, namely, to help you grow in virtue.

If you're worried there's some hidden sin that's the cause of your desolation, stop worrying. God will show it to you if in his presence, you make a reasonable effort to examine your conscience. If he doesn't reveal it to you or if you're not sure about it, then don't worry. You might say the ball's in God's court. If he wants you to see a sin, he'll show you. But if he doesn't, then, again, don't worry. Simply treat the desolation as a call to engage in the battle for spiritual joy, and begin to fight it. As for any lingering fears that a hidden sin might be causing the desolation, give them to our merciful Lord, and trust that he'll reveal to you what you need to see when you need to see it.

2. *Fight.*

Again, apart from being a wake-up call regarding sin in our lives, God may allow desolation to help us grow in humility[36] or to help us become better soldiers. I say "better soldiers" because engaging in the battle for spiritual joy trains us in the soldier-like virtues of patience, perseverance, and especially trust. At first, maybe trust doesn't seem like much of a soldier-like virtue, but it is. In fact, in spiritual battles, it's probably the most important virtue. Before looking at trust in the battle for spiritual joy, let's first turn our attention to fighting with patience and perseverance in the context of hope.

(a) FIGHT ANCHORED IN HOPE. In order to grow in patience and perseverance as we fight desolation, we need to be anchored in hope. Without hope, it's not possible to fight desolation with those other two virtues. Without hope, all is lost. Yet, with hope, we're strong, and as hope grows, so does our ability to be patient and persevering in the midst of battle. It's not surprising, therefore, that the enemy tries everything in his attempts to overcome our hope.

To help us fortify our hope against the enemy's attacks, St. Ignatius gives three important instructions before battle begins. First, he says we should consider that God never allows more than we can take.[37] In other words, even if we don't feel it, God's grace upholds us during times of desolation. Thus, Jesus said to St. Faustina, **"I am always with you, even if you don't feel My presence at the time of battle."**[38] Moreover, the grace God gives us during the time of battle is always more than enough to defeat our enemy. No matter how strong the enemy force, God always gives us stronger grace. It's amazing how this simple thought can give us hope, patience, and perseverance to stand strong against seemingly relentless attacks of desolation.

---

36. Regarding desolation as a lesson in humility, see the earlier section entitled "Humble yourself."

37. *SpirEx*, 320, Rule 7: "When one is in desolation, he should be mindful that God has left him to his natural powers to resist the different agitations and temptations of the enemy. ... He can resist with the help of God, which always remains, though he may not clearly perceive it. For though God has taken from him the abundance of fervor and overflowing love and the intensity of His favors, nevertheless, he has sufficient grace for eternal salvation." See also 1 Cor 10:13.

38. *Diary*, 1499.

Such thoughts made St. Faustina fearless in battle:

> I see that God never tries us beyond what we are able
> to suffer. Oh, I fear nothing; if God sends such great
> suffering to a soul, He upholds it with an even
> greater grace, although we are not aware of it.[39]

Ignatius's second instruction for helping us to fortify our
hope is as follows: During desolation we should be patient,
knowing that the time of consolation will return soon.[40] This is
great hope. Consolation will come *soon*. Tired soldiers fighting
what seems like a losing battle immediately find new strength
when, from a distance, they see reinforcements racing to their
aid. To prevent the birth of such renewed hope, the bad spirit
tries to hide from us the fact that reinforcements are racing
toward us. In other words, he makes us think our desolation
will never end. Not only that, he sometimes even tries to make
us think we've always been in desolation. Thus, he creates the
illusion that desolation is a bottomless pit from which we'll
never escape and, perhaps, in which we've always been
trapped. By such tactics, he expects us to give up hope even as
our reinforcements (consolation) are about to arrive. What a
tragedy it would be to give up right on the verge of winning
the battle! To prevent such a terrible mistake, we need to keep
a look out for consolation. Curiously, we do this primarily by
looking back, which is Ignatius's third instruction for helping
us to fortify our hope.[41]

---

39. Ibid, 78.

40. *SpirEx*, 321, Rule 8: "When one is in desolation, he should strive to
persevere in patience. This reacts against the vexations that have overtaken him.
Let him consider, too, that consolation will soon return."

41. While Ignatius never explicitly says in his rules that during times of desolation one should "look back" to times of consolation, I think it's implied in at
least three of them. It seems to be implied in Rule 5, because remaining firm
and constant in decisions made during consolation requires thinking back to the
time of consolation. Also, it seems to be implied in Rule 6, which calls for an
intensification of activity against desolation by means of further meditation and
examination. I think Ignatius would agree that a fruitful meditation during
times of desolation is to think back to times of consolation. Furthermore, by its
very nature, the examen prayer involves a looking back. Finally, Rule 8 seems to

Thinking back to times of consolation as we fight desolation not only aids our hope but sometimes even wins the battle right then and there. Because of the effectiveness of this tactic, many people find it helpful to write in a journal during times of particularly strong consolation. This practice is useful for at least two reasons. First, the very act of writing out the time of consolation helps impress it more firmly on one's mind. Second, when times of desolation return, one can then read from his journal as an aid to jogging his memory to recall past times of consolation. Such recalling of consolation in one's life often increases hope. While this journaling idea may seem like overkill to some, I don't think it is. Allow me to explain why.

During times of great consolation, it often seems that we'll never forget it. After all, everything at such times is so vivid and clear. However, one of the first weapons desolation fires at us as it begins its attacks is a special kind of smoke bomb. The smoke from this bomb creates a surprisingly effective screen that prevents us from easily looking back to the vivid and clear times of consolation. Reading something like a journal or a "list of blessings" can be like a blast of fresh air that dispels desolation's smoke, allowing us to see more clearly. Moreover, the very act of writing in a journal about times of consolation strengthens the eye of one's memory to see through the smoke. Still, sometimes desolation's smoke screens are so incredibly thick that we

---

call for a looking back to times of consolation during desolation when it says, "Let him consider, too, that consolation will soon return."

In the letter addressed to Teresa Rejadell already mentioned in a previous footnote, Ignatius explains to her that the bad spirit "places obstacles and impediments in the way of those who love and begin to serve God our Lord" and "*fails to remind us* of the great comfort and consolation which our Lord is wont to give to such souls, who, as new recruits in our Lord's service, surmount these obstacles and choose to suffer with their Creator and Lord." This letter is reproduced by Young, in *Letters of Saint Ignatius*, p. 19. I found the citation in Gallagher, *Discernment of Spirits*, p. 102. Fr. Gallagher goes on to write that in times of such spiritual desolation "our part is to *remember*, as Ignatius writes to Teresa Rejadell, 'the great comfort and consolation which our Lord is wont to give to such souls' who seek to love and serve … . This 'remembering' fortifies us, as it does the whole people of God (Deut 32:7; Ps 105:5; Ps 143:5), to progress with courage on our spiritual journey" (p. 103).

can't see a thing. What do we do then? How do we keep up hope when all we see is a dense, dark smoke?

While St. Faustina never wrote about desolation's smoke screens, she did describe desolation as thick clouds that cover the sun.[42] I'd like to borrow her imagery as a way of preparing us for those times when the clouds (smoke) of desolation are so thick that they blind us to even the smallest rays of consolation. Moreover, I'd like to use her imagery within the context of my own experience.

Growing up in Southern California, I was spoiled by innumerable sunny days. I loved to sit out in the front yard of my parents' home with the warm sun on my face and the ever present ocean breeze blowing through my hair. Since the time I was 18, though, I've lived in places that had a lot less sunshine. The most difficult for me was Boston, where I lived for too many years. Boston seemed to have about as many cloudy days as California had days of sun. This often got me depressed. With a shiver, I remember the long winters with day after day of cold, dark clouds that made my previous life in California seem like a distant dream. Some melancholy afternoons, I'd look up at the endless grey blanket above and think to myself, "How is it possible that just above that blanket the sun really shines?" Then I'd get depressed. It seemed like I'd never see the sun again. Obviously, my mind knew the sun was somewhere up there and that I'd see it again, but my heart refused to believe it.

When our spiritual lives are like a Boston winter, we need to give primacy to facts over feelings. We need to listen to our reason, which tells us there truly were times when we sat out in the front yard, soaking in the warm California sun. In other words, we've all experienced times of consolation, times when we've basked in the rays of God's love and mercy. Well, one of the most important things we can do to win the battle for spiritual joy during the darkest desolation is to cling to the fact of the sun (that is, to God). It's there beyond the clouds. We know it. We've experienced it. May we not give in to our feel-

42. See *Diary*, 73, 385, 507, 697, 862, 1040, 1333.

ings when, during times of desolation, they protest that it no longer exists. Instead, with St. Faustina, may we strive to cling to what we know, "O my Jesus, despite the deep night that is all around me and the dark clouds which hide the horizon, I know that the sun never goes out."[43]

I love the idea of "clinging to the fact of the sun," that is, to God. Even when the darkness is so thick that it numbs our minds and makes it almost impossible to think, we can still cling to God and to his mercy.

This is one truth we can always cling to: God's mercy, that God *is* Mercy, and that no one who trusts in his mercy has ever been disappointed.[44] In times of deep desolation, even though there may be many things about God we don't understand, the truth of his mercy is always within our reach. It's the *Great Truth* to which, with St. Faustina, we should always tenaciously cling, "O Lord, though I cannot comprehend You and do not understand Your ways, I nonetheless trust in Your mercy."[45] Trusting in this truth, trusting the God of Mercy, can keep our hope alive no matter how deep the darkness gets.[46] Because such trust is so powerful a force against desolation, we'd do well to spend some time learning about it as a "secret weapon."

43. Ibid., 73.
44. Ibid., 1541.
45. Ibid., 73.
46. Some may say, "Ah, yes, but God is also a God of justice." That's true. Yet I'm of the opinion that we have a choice regarding which of two rulers God will measure us with: the ruler of his justice or the ruler of his mercy. For the measure with which we measure will be measured back to us (see Lk 6:38) and the merciful will be shown mercy (see Mt 5:7). What does it mean to measure with the ruler of mercy? It means to be merciful to others, which begins when we understand God as a God of mercy. Saints such as Faustina and Thérèse saw God through the lens of his mercy and then chose to measure others according to the ruler of his mercy. What it means to see God through the lens of his mercy can be gathered from their words. For Faustina's words, see Appendix Two under the section, "Divine Mercy — And Justice." Thérèse's words now follow: "To me [God] has granted *His infinite Mercy*, and *through it* I contemplate and adore the other divine perfections! All of these perfections appear to be resplendent *with love*; even His Justice (and perhaps this even more so than the others) seems to me clothed in *love*. What a sweet joy it is to think that God is *Just*, i.e., that He takes into account our weakness, that He is perfectly aware of our fragile nature. What should I fear then?" (emphasis in original. *Story of a Soul*, p. 180). Describing her

(b) FIGHT WITH THE SECRET WEAPON OF TRUST. During her life-and-death struggles with desolation, St. Faustina frequently fired something I like to call the "secret weapon of trust."[47] Such trust is an invincible weapon whose power to gain the victory is impossible to underestimate. It's also relatively easy to wield. Even at the moment when the enemy prepares to deal the final, lethal blow, the secret weapon of trust is always loaded, aimed, and ready to fire. All we need to do is pull the trigger or simply give the word.

We shouldn't confuse the secret weapon of trust with normal trust as *ecce, fiat, magnificat.* While these three words truly are a kind of summary of trust (as we learned during the retreat), they don't exhaust the full meaning of this amazing virtue.

Offering to Merciful Love, Thérèse writes: "O my God! Will Your Justice alone find souls willing to immolate themselves as victims? Does not Your Merciful Love need them too? On every side this love is unknown, rejected; those hearts upon whom You would lavish it turn to creatures ... they do this instead of throwing themselves into Your arms and of accepting Your infinite *Love.* O my God! Is Your disdained Love going to remain closed up within Your Heart? It seems to me that if You were to find souls offering themselves as victims of holocaust to Your Love, You would consume them rapidly; it seems to me, too, that You would be happy not to hold back the waves of infinite tenderness within You. If Your Justice loves to release itself, this Justice *which extends only over the earth,* how much more does Your Merciful Love desire to *set souls on fire* since Your Mercy *reaches to the heavens.* O my Jesus, let me be this happy victim; consume Your holocaust with the fire of Your Divine Love" (Ibid., p. 164). Finally, one of Thérèse's sisters, Mother Agnes (Pauline), begins her testimony for the process of Thérèse's beatification with these words: "I want to see her beatified because she will bring God great glory, and will make his mercy known especially. *People will put more trust in his mercy and fear his justice less:* that is the secret of the 'humble path of trust and self-surrender' that she hoped to make known to everybody once she was dead" (emphasis added; O'Mahoney, p. 21).

47. Although none of Ignatius's rules mention a "secret weapon of trust," the main idea behind this secret weapon is related to Rule 7 and the second half of Rule 11. Rule 7 reads: "When one is in desolation, he should be mindful that God has left him to his natural powers to resist the different agitations and temptations of the enemy in order to try him. He can resist with the help of God, which always remains, though he may not clearly perceive it. For though God has taken from him the abundance of fervor and overflowing love and the intensity of His favors, nevertheless, he has sufficient grace for eternal salvation." The second half of Rule 11 reads: "One who suffers desolation should remember that by making use of the sufficient grace offered him, he can do much to withstand all his enemies. Let him find his strength in his Creator and Lord."

The secret weapon of trust doesn't look like trust. In fact, on the outside, it may not look like anything but discouragement and despair. Yet, despite appearances, the secret weapon of trust is in some ways the golden crown of trust and its deepest expression. By the way, this kind of trust can be wielded by anyone, including melancholics. In fact, melancholics may have to wield the secret weapon of trust more often than others, and I hope they'll soon realize that by doing so they give some of the greatest consolation to Jesus and glory to God.

During the retreat, I said that sometimes when we practice *ecce, fiat,* and *magnificat,* we only get as far as *ecce* — and that that's quite all right. *Ecce* is like the secret weapon of trust insofar as it doesn't exactly look like trust, as I explained during the retreat. Yet the secret weapon of trust is a little different. It's the prayer "Jesus, I trust in you" when the darkness is so deep and our minds so numb that we can't even remember what *ecce* stands for, let alone anything else. It's our weapon when the enemy has tied us up, gagged our mouths, beaten us on the head, and begun dragging us down to his hellish camp. At such times, when we're all bound up and to all appearances look like we've fully given in to discouragement and despair, the secret weapon of trust begins to glow in the deepest recess of our hearts in the form of the prayer, "Jesus, I trust in you."

Jesus, I trust in you. Even if we express these words wordlessly — as might very well be the case because of the gag in our mouths — they are total victory. Even if we pray them simply as an act of the will without any emotion and in a way that seems to be "only words," we give great glory to God. In fact, such prayer is to his greatest glory. We may not feel it, but to pray "Jesus, I trust in you" during the deepest darkness is the triumph of mercy. Whenever we pray it, the enemy has lost. Of course, he may think he's won when he drags us to the outskirts of his dark camp, nails us to wooden beams, and raises us up naked, broken, and bloody before his mocking, blaspheming army. Then, he may especially think he's won when we cry out, "My God, my God why have you forsaken me?"

The problem for our enemy is this: He doesn't hear the rest of the words this psalm, Psalm 22, introduces. For the Psalm continues with the firing off of the secret weapon of trust. The Psalmist declares: "In you [my God] our fathers trusted; they trusted, and you delivered them. To you they cried, and were saved; in you they trusted, and were not disappointed ..." (vv. 4-5). If, like "our fathers" (and "sisters" such as Faustina), we place our trust in the Lord during our most desperate moments, we will be saved. We will not be disappointed, and we will live on to praise the Lord and glorify his name (vv. 22-23). In such moments, though, broken and seemingly dying in the midst of the enemy's taunting army, we may not be able to say a word, and singing may be the farthest thing from our lips. Still, if we cling to the secret weapon of trust — again, even if it be silently, in the secret recesses of our hearts — we thereby offer to God the greatest song of praise and thanksgiving, the greatest trust. Thus, our darkest moments become our greatest glory, just as they were for our Savior on Calvary. Faustina helps confirm it, "One act of trust at such moments gives greater glory to God than whole hours passed in prayer filled with consolations."[48]

Even though this is just an appendix and no longer a retreat, I'd still like to invite those who haven't yet done so to make a retreat-like promise to the Lord always to cling to the truth of his mercy with trust — no matter what. For it's a great idea to decide to trust in God's infinite mercy always, no matter how deep the darkness gets. To help us remember such a promise, I'd like to share a rather strange image that came to me during a meditation one day. It helps me remember my promise. Maybe it will help you remember yours.

During my meditation, as my mind wandered from the topic I'd chosen, I began to imagine a big, brown dog. I got closer and closer to this dog until my eyes were just a few inches from the hair on the back of its neck. Then, as I got still closer, I suddenly shrank to the size of a flea and found myself right in the midst of the dog's hair. A forest of tall, brown, branchless hair trunks surrounded me. Bewildered, I stood there

48. Ibid., 78.

on the forest floor of the dog's bare skin. After a little while, the forest began to shake. Although the shaking started gently, it wasn't long before the trunks were swaying wildly back and forth. I figured the dog was going from a walk to a run. To prevent myself from sliding around the fur forest and off the dog's back, I clung to a trunk of its hair with all my might and resolved not to let go. I had a good grip on it and decided I wouldn't let go even if the dog's run turned into a wild sprint after some cat. "No matter what," I said to myself, "I won't let go."

It may come as a surprise that after this meditation, during the time of review, I didn't scold myself for giving in to what might seem like a silly distraction. Instead, I thought to myself, "That dog is like God ... and I'm the flea." Then, I thought about the dog's hair and said, "That hair is God's love and mercy." I concluded my review of the meditation by promising myself: "Like the flea, I will never let go of my grip on God's love and mercy. I will always cling to him with trust." Bizarre meditation? Yes, but it helps me to remember my promise. If it helps you, too — good. If not, well, just try not to forget your resolution to cling with trust to God's mercy no matter what (even if he goes sprinting after some cat).

So as not to end such an important section of this appendix with my strange meditation, why don't we listen to St. Faustina as she wields the secret weapon of trust. In other words, let's take a nice, close, many-angled look at her grip on God's mercy during some extremely difficult times of desolation. Although we may never experience darkness to the same degree she did, her example can still teach us a lot about how to act when our deepest times of darkness come.

In the first passage, Faustina writes in her *Diary*:

During the evening service, my soul began to agonize again in a terrible darkness. ... During these terrible moments I said to God, "Jesus, who in the Gospel compare Yourself to a most tender mother, I trust in Your words because You are Truth and Life. In spite of everything, Jesus, I trust in You in the face of every interior sentiment which sets itself against hope. Do what You want with me; I will never leave You, because You are the source of my life."[49]

On another occasion of excruciatingly deep darkness, Faustina again reflects on Sacred Scripture (see Is 49:15) as a way of helping her to trust:

Jesus, You said that a mother would sooner forget her infant than God His creature, and that "even if she would forget her infant, I, God, will never forget My creature." O Jesus, do You hear how my soul is moaning? Deign to hear the painful whimpers of Your child. I trust in You, O God, because heaven and earth will pass, but Your word will last forever.[50]

During a time when the desolation made her feel especially distant from God, Faustina said to him:

Your mercy surpasses the understanding of all Angels and people put together; and so, although it seems to me that You do not hear me, I put my trust in the ocean of Your mercy, and I know that my hope will not be deceived.[51]

Shortly after writing these words, Faustina went on to pray using the images of clouds and sun that I cited earlier. It's worth it to read her prayer again:

O my Jesus, despite the deep night that is all around me and the dark clouds which hide the horizon, I know that the sun never goes out. O Lord, though I cannot comprehend You and do not understand Your ways, I nonetheless trust in Your mercy.[52]

---

49. Ibid., 24.
50. Ibid., 23.
51. Ibid., 69.
52. Ibid., 73.

Faustina's experience of darkness eventually made her feel so desolate that she thought she might die from it. Despite that, she cried out with a trust that seems to go to the very limits of trust, "Even if You kill me, still will I trust in You!"[53] Finally, in the midst of horrible temptations to despair, the Mercy Saint expresses the heart of the secret weapon of trust when she exclaims to Jesus, "I trust in Your mercy!"[54]

If reading about these intense trials has got us feeling discouraged and desolate, we should remember that Jesus doesn't allow more than we can bear. Still, if our own experience of darkness ever does feel like more than we can bear, we can take courage that even St. Faustina prayed: "When the burden of the battle becomes too much for me, I throw myself like a child into the arms of the heavenly Father and trust I will not perish."[55] There's no dishonor in this battlefield maneuver. In fact, it may be the most effective maneuver in the whole battle for spiritual joy, for by it we're assured that the Lord himself will guard us "even jealously" because we choose to remain little.[56] In the powerful arms of the Lord, little souls need not feel overwhelmed or discouraged by the sight of any enemy army.

3. Don't listen.

We've heard a couple of times now that deep desolation can be like dark clouds. Well, there's something else. While it's true that during the cloudiest periods of desolation we can't see a thing, we often do hear a great deal, and what we hear during such times is rarely the consoling sweetness of God's voice. Instead, we get barraged by the dark words and sinister suggestions of the enemy.[57] If that seems scary, it is — but probably

---

53. Ibid., 77.

54. Ibid., 101.

55. Ibid., 606.

56. Ibid., 1440.

57. Ignatius writes, "For just as consolation is the opposite of desolation, so the thoughts that spring from consolation are the opposite of those that spring from desolation" (*SpirEx*, 317, Rule 4). On this topic, he also says, "For just as in consolation the good spirit guides and counsels us, *so in desolation the evil spirit guides and counsels*" (emphasis added; *SpirEx*, 318, Rule 5).

not for the reason one might think. The enemy's voice that comes to us in desolation isn't creepy like a villain's voice in some movie. Rather, his voice takes the form of interior words and ideas similar in "sound" to those we hear during times of consolation. In fact, we don't recognize them so much by their sound as by the content of what's communicated. For instance, if our minds fill with thoughts of accusation and judgment against someone with whom we live, this may very well be the bad spirit's voice. In themselves, such thoughts don't sound any different from our normal, everyday thoughts, but we know where they come from because of where they lead, namely, to sin and the loss of our peace and joy.

While the words and thoughts that come from the bad spirit are innumerable, three classic phrases seem to come up again and again during times of desolation. Let's explore these phrases now so we'll be ready to recognize and reject them in real life. They are: (a) "Keep it a secret," (b) "Change your decision," and (c) "Run!"

(a) DON'T "KEEP IT A SECRET." In the last point of the previous section, we read that during times of desolation, we have a secret weapon. Well, so does the bad spirit. His secret weapon, however, isn't invincible like ours. In fact, it's incredibly weak and easy to defeat, if only we have the courage to fight against it. What's his secret weapon? It's the words, "Keep it a secret." Keep what a secret? His many little temptations, especially those that might embarrass us and that we don't want to reveal.

The enemy's secret temptations are like little wounds he inflicts on us that we easily ignore. Because they're so little, we may think: "Ah, what's the big deal? Why should I worry about a little paper cut?" The big deal is that even the littlest wound, if left uncared for and dirty, quickly gets infected, festers, and can eventually kill. So it is with the bad spirit's hidden, little temptations. When we're not attentive to them and bury them under the soil of silence, they can get infected, fester, and eventually lead to spiritual sickness and death. What a clever strategy from such a weak enemy! Because he's so weak, he has to rely on such little tricks. Let's not fall for them. Here's how.

Little wounds, especially those that become red and irritating with infection, should be shown to a doctor. This is because a doctor knows how to properly clean them and prescribe the right medication, if need be. Often a simple cleaning is enough to take care of the situation and prevent infection. Similarly, little temptations, especially those that become red (they embarrass us) and irritating (they constantly fill our minds), should be shown to a doctor. By a doctor, I mean a priest in the Sacrament of Confession, a spiritual director, or a trusted friend. It's amazing how the simple act of revealing temptations and difficulties to such doctors is often enough to bring total health and an end to the enemy's little tricks.[58]

I can think of many times in my own life when a temptation persistently filled my thoughts (irritating) and made me feel embarrassed (red) to reveal it. However, whenever I eventually told the priest in confession or my spiritual director, time and time again the temptation literally disappeared. It was kind of eerie, as if I'd been under a spell. One minute, I couldn't get the thoughts out of my head. The next minute (after I spoke about them), they totally dissipated. Simply saying the temptation broke the spell and spoiled the bad spirit's trick. Because such temptations are still embarrassing to share, I think I'll give an example from someone else's life.

Saint Faustina knew how to spoil Satan's little tricks. One day, while getting ready to go to confession, she was assailed by temptations against revealing "the most secret

---

58. On this topic of revealing the bad spirit's temptations, Ignatius writes: "Our enemy may also be compared in his manner of acting to a false lover. He seeks to remain hidden and does not want to be discovered. If such a lover speaks with evil intention to the daughter of a good father, or to the wife of a good husband, and seeks to seduce them, he wants his words and solicitations kept secret. He is greatly displeased if his evil suggestions and depraved intentions are revealed by the daughter to her father, or by the wife to her husband. Then he readily sees he will not succeed in what he has begun. In the same way, when the enemy of our human nature tempts a just soul with his wiles and seductions, he earnestly desires that they be received secretly and kept secret. But if one manifests them to a confessor, or to some other spiritual person who understand his deceits and malicious designs, the evil one is very much vexed. For he knows that he cannot succeed in his evil undertaking, once his evident deceits have been revealed" (*SpirEx*, 326, Rule 13).

depths of my heart" and speaking about "all that goes on between God and myself." Recognizing that Satan was at work, she opened up to her confessor about the difficulties she was having. After that, the difficulties "took to flight," and her soul was put at peace.[59] Thus, she faithfully followed the instructions Jesus had given her earlier: **"Do not fight against a temptation by yourself, but disclose it to the confessor at once, and then the temptation will lose all its force."**[60] May we also remember to reject the enemy's words "keep it a secret" by revealing our temptations and difficulties to the right spiritual doctors.

Sometimes, Satan's little trick of trying to get us to keep his temptations hidden isn't so little. For example, he once played a very big form of this trick on St. Thérèse of Lisieux on the evening before she was to make her final profession of religious vows — her "wedding day," as she called it. Because hers is a classic example of how to fight the temptation to "keep it a secret" and also because it serves as a kind of introduction to the next point, I cite it at length:

> The *beautiful day* of my wedding finally arrived. It was without a single cloud; however, the preceding evening a storm arose within my soul the like of which I'd never seen before. Not a single doubt concerning my vocation had ever entered my mind until then. ... In the evening, while making the Way of the Cross after Matins, my vocation appeared to me as a *dream*, a chimera. I found life in Carmel [the convent] to be very beautiful, but the devil inspired me with the assurance that it wasn't for me and that I was misleading my Superiors by advancing on this way to which I wasn't called. The darkness was so great that I could see and understand one thing only: I didn't have a vocation. Ah! how can I possibly describe the anguish of my soul? It appeared to

59. *Diary*, 1715.
60. Ibid., 1560.

me (and this is an absurdity which shows it was a temptation from the devil) that if I were to tell my Novice Mistress about these fears, she would prevent me from pronouncing my Vows. And still I wanted to do God's will and return to the world rather than remain in Carmel and do my own will. I made the Mistress come out of the choir and, filled with confusion, I told her the state of my soul. Fortunately, she saw things much clearer than I did, and she completely reassured me. The act of humility I had just performed put the devil to flight since he had perhaps thought that I would not dare admit my temptation. My doubts left me completely as soon as I finished speaking.[61]

The evening before her profession, Thérèse experienced sure signs of desolation: doubt, darkness, anguish of soul, fears, and confusion. Notice that the thoughts that came to her in that state immediately went for the jugular vein, "The darkness was so great that I could see and understand one thing only: I didn't have a vocation." That was no little trick. The bad spirit tried to get Thérèse to keep secret a temptation to change the biggest decision of her life. It's crucially important that we be aware of this big trick. We'll hear more about it in the following point.

(b) DON'T "CHANGE YOUR DECISION." When we're in the darkness of desolation, we should be on guard against the suggestion, "change your decision." Such a suggestion can come up regarding any thoughtful decision we made before the desolation came, especially decisions we made during a time of consolation. For instance, during a time of consolation, let's say you decide to make a *Consoling* retreat weekend. Well, don't be surprised if, when the weekend approaches, clouds of

---

61. *Story of a Soul*, p. 166. I first heard this story used as an example of how to fight the temptation to keep the bad spirit's temptations a secret during a talk given by Fr. Timothy Gallagher, OMV.

desolation come, and you get harassed by the idea of going back on your decision. When the bad spirit tries this kind of trick on you, don't fall for it. Stay the course. Stick to what you've decided before the desolation came. Ignatius states his rule on this topic in strong terms, "In time of desolation, we should never make any change."[62] He puts it this way because he knows that the thoughts that come to us in times of desolation tend to come from the bad spirit.[63] Thus, following such thoughts leads to problems, sometimes big problems.

Never change a decision during a time of desolation. I wish this exhortation were painted above the exits of seminaries and novitiates and engraved on engagement rings. I say that because, as happened to St. Thérèse on the evening before her vows, the bad spirit's big trick is to tempt people to change important decisions, such as those regarding a state of life, while they're in a time of desolation. People tempted in this way should be patient, stay the course, and listen to their thoughts and feelings when the time of consolation returns. Thus, I used to give the following advice to my fellow seminarians who seemed to be struggling with their vocations:

> Look, if you're thinking about leaving the seminary, make your decision only after feeling at peace about it in prayer [consolation] several times over a period of time and after speaking with your spiritual director. If it's the Lord's will that you leave the seminary, he'll let you know during the peace and clarity of consolation. Don't decide to leave because of the thoughts that come up when you're sad and things are all stirred up. I say that because the bad spirit does most of the talking during desolation, and what he says is usually the opposite of what

---

62. *SpirEx*, 318, Rule 5.

63. Ignatius writes, "For just as consolation is the opposite of desolation, so the thoughts that spring from consolation are the opposite of those that spring from desolation" (Ibid., 317, Rule 4). On this topic, he also says, "For just as in consolation the good spirit guides and counsels us, so in desolation the evil spirit guides and counsels" (*SpirEx*, 318, Rule 5).

God wants. Do what God wants. That's what will make you (and him) happy.

By the way, if you're one of those people who have already fallen for the bad spirit's big trick, please don't get discouraged. Leave the past to God's mercy and ask the Lord to bring an even greater good out of the decision. As I said during the retreat, God's mercy can truly work such miracles of mercy if we ask him with trust and patiently persevere in hope.

(c) DON'T "RUN!" I think the bad spirit probably got the idea for one of his tricks from watching old cowboy movies. He seems to copy the bad guy in those movies who slaps the rear of one of the good guys' horses, which sends the horse off on a fierce gallop without its rider. When the bad spirit plays this trick on us, instead of a slap on the rear, he shouts, "Run!" — which seems to work just as well. His goal in sending us off and running is to keep us without the benefit of one of two riders: our reason or our Lord. He knows that if we run off without being guided by at least one of them, we'll end up discouraged and sad and thus lose the battle for spiritual joy. To prevent this from happening, let's first look at how the bad spirit tries to send us off and running without our reason and then how he tries to send us off and running without the Lord.

The bad spirit's attempt to send us off and running without our reason can come not only during times of desolation but at any moment. (This part of my "response rules" doesn't exclusively fit a time of desolation or consolation.)[64] Thus, we should always be ready for this trick, especially if we're zealous. The bad spirit knows that zealous people fall for it most easily. He also knows that such people can do a

---

64. I decided to put the material for this kind of temptation here, because it's related to the temptation to run without the Lord, at least insofar as both temptations share an excited, compulsive tone, which is indicated by the exclamation, "Run!" The temptation to run without the Lord applies especially to those times when we're in desolation, as I'll explain later, which is why it's under the category "Response Rules for Desolation."

242 CONSOLING THE HEART OF JESUS

great deal of good for the kingdom of God. Therefore, he tries this trick on them whenever he can not only because they easily fall for it but also because it makes their efforts in God's service much less effective.

The bad spirit has to be clever in his dealings with zealous people. He knows that their fervent love for God and ardent desire to do good prevents them from falling for his more obvious temptations to do something evil, like rob a bank. So he wisely tempts them not with bad things but good things.[65] In other words, he points out to them some good thing and then shouts, "Run after it!" Unfortunately, zealous people often immediately obey. I say "unfortunately," because the good things the bad spirit proposes to them are usually lesser goods than the good the Lord wants them to do. Thus, the bad spirit's trick distracts such people from doing God's more perfect will, making them less effective in God's service. Moreover, the lesser goods the bad spirit proposes sometimes even end up destroying the greater good. At this point, an example may be helpful.

During my early days in the seminary, I remember being tempted to leave, because I wasn't allowed to go pray at the local abortion clinic on Saturday mornings, as had been my practice before entering the seminary. The bad spirit knew

---

65. Ignatius wrote a whole set of his rules for the discernment of spirits — the rules of the Second Week — for those people whom the bad spirit tempts with goods. He writes in the tenth of his "Introductory Observations" the following: "When the one who is giving the Exercises perceives that the exercitant is being assailed and tempted under the appearance of good, then is the proper time to explain to him the rules of the Second Week." The Second Week rules, which I earlier called Ignatius's "advanced set of rules," can be found in *SpirEx*, 328-336. I should point out that these Second Week rules seem to deal exclusively with when the bad spirit appears as an angel of light and brings consolation to the soul for his evil purposes (see ibid., 331, Rule 3). My treatment of the topic "running off without our reason" seems to be slightly different. As I'll soon explain, the bad spirit's shout at us to run without our reason isn't exactly consolation, for it has a different tone. In fact, such shouts can come at any time: during consolation, desolation, or the middle periods. Thus, the treatment that follows is not exactly a commentary on the Second Week rules, though it does use some of their principles, as I'll point out. For a strict commentary on the Second Week rules, see the book recommendation I gave in the first note of this appendix.

that my pro-life zeal made me prone to running off to the clinic despite the greater good God was asking of me. God wanted me to obey the decision of my superiors that Saturday morning was the time to clean the bathrooms. He wanted me to pray for the unborn and their mothers and fathers as I cleaned toilets and not while standing in front of the clinic. Above all, he wanted me to continue following my vocational path, which I would have had to give up had I decided to run after the good of praying at the clinic. Public witness to the sanctity of human life combined with intercessory prayer truly is a good. However, in my case, sticking with my vocation was a much greater good. Thankfully, I took the time to reflect, and instead of running off at the bad spirit's shout, I decided to stay home, clean the toilets, and follow my vocation.

So, the bad spirit tends to tempt zealous people to run after good things that are usually lesser goods than the good God wants them to do. Because those who make retreats have to have at least some zeal (otherwise they wouldn't make a retreat), all of us ought to reflect on what greater goods we might be sacrificing before we decide to run after an opportunity to do something good. This doesn't mean we always have to be hesitating whenever we have such opportunities. I'm just suggesting that we not run after them. In other words, if it feels like we're being shouted at to do something, then that should make us cautious.

At this point, if not earlier, some people may be saying, "Wait a minute, I never hear any voice shouting at me, 'Run!'" That's probably because the bad spirit doesn't exactly shout with words. In my experience, his shouting at me comes in the form of sense of urgency and compulsion that makes me feel frantic and rushed: "I've got to do this *now*. Come on, come on. Let's go, let's go!" That's a lot different from my experience of the good spirit who, even when something is urgent, always prompts me in a patient, gentle way that makes me feel confident and peaceful: "This is important. It's time to get to work, and I'm going to have to give it my all. Still, I don't have to worry, for if it's truly something God wants, he'll give me the time and the strength I need to accomplish it." So, especially when we contrast the two "voices," the influence of the bad spirit really does make us feel as if someone were shouting at us, "Run after it!"[66]

Before we turn our attention to how the bad spirit tries to send us off and running without the Lord, I'd like to make one more point about how he tries to send us off and running without our reason.

Sometimes, instead of getting people running after lesser goods, the bad spirit tries to get them running after true goods in an extreme way. His intention in playing this version of his trick is eventually to leave his victims feeling tired and discouraged. After all, people can only live life to the extreme for so long. Let's look at a few examples.

The bad spirit may try to get us to run after the good of being detached from possessions in an extreme way. For instance, he may command a person who, before a conversion, often listened to violent, impure, and hateful music, "Throw out all your CDs *now*!" That makes sense with regard to the gangster rap CDs, but does the uplifting music on the Jack Johnson CD really deserve the trash can? If this sounds like a joke, it's not. The bad spirit knows that good, uplifting music at the right time and place can be a great ally to us in the battle for spiritual joy. Therefore, he sometimes tries to trick us into getting rid of good music or other legitimate natural consolations. Remember, we're not Superman. God provides us not only with supernatural but also natural consolations, and it can be a good and humble thing to accept them.

The bad spirit may also try to get us to run after such goods as prayer and fasting in an extreme way. For instance, he may push us into the chapel and down on our knees so often

---

66. Regarding the contrast between the action of the good spirit and the bad spirit on a soul who is striving for holiness, Ignatius says: "[T]he action of the good angel is delicate, gentle, delightful. It may be compared to a drop of water penetrating a sponge. The action of the evil spirit upon such souls is violent, noisy, and disturbing. It may be compared to a drop of water falling upon a stone" (*SpirEx*, 335, Rule 21).

that the spiritual life begins to seem like nothing but a joyless drag. Or he may make us feel that the salvation of the whole world depends on the rigors of our fasts, thus causing us to fast in a way that makes us irritable, joyless zombies who hardly have the energy to do our daily duty and who live our lives secretly dreading every fast day. Or he may make us think we have to be perfect as our Heavenly Father is perfect *right now*, thus causing us to zealously dissipate our spiritual energies as we try to put out the fires of our every vice and imperfection all at once. None of this is the way of the good spirit.

The good spirit takes us where we are and gently leads us to a life of prayer, sacrifice, and conversion that's balanced and appropriate to the kind of souls we are. During the retreat, we learned that the good spirit leads little souls by little steps and helps them to attain all through humble confidence. Thus, he's not like the bad spirit who tries to send us off on a wild run that leaves prudence and reason behind.

Finally, we come to the second rider. The bad spirit not only tries to send us off and running without our reason but also without the Lord. Such temptations come up a lot during one type of spiritual darkness. Sometimes it's desolation, and then again, sometimes it's a strange kind of darkness that may or may not be desolation. This peculiar darkness is something we all feel (though with varying degrees of intensity). It's our spiritual thirst, our longing to be free from loneliness and to enter into communion. I treated this topic during the retreat in the section on the merciful outlook that talked about existential loneliness.[67] Here, I'd just like to point out from that earlier treatment that this thirst is a basic and often deep pain in our lives, and whether it's the natural longing that simply makes us feel bored and lonely or the more ardent, supernatural longing for God who paradoxically seems farther away the closer he comes, it's definitely not easy to endure.

During those times when we're burning with "the thirst," be sure the bad spirit is nearby and ready to let out an unpleasant shout: "Run! Run away from the pain! Escape!"

---

67. See pages 145-146

He shouts at us like this because he sees the pain of our thirst as an opportunity to get us running to things that distract us from the pain. Sometimes such distractions aren't necessarily bad in themselves, for example, TV, food, the telephone, and music. At other times, they are bad in themselves, for instance, sins of impurity, drug abuse, or suicide. Of course, we should always reject the seduction of distractions that are bad in themselves, and we shouldn't overdo the neutral ones. Still, even legitimate distractions temperately used can hurt us when they distract us from the invitation of the Lord who, through our thirst, calls us to deeper intimacy with himself. The bad spirit especially doesn't want us to hear this call, so he shouts, "Run! Run! Run!"

I think many little souls are like horses that easily get spooked by the pain of "the thirst" and the bad spirit shouting at them to run. In fact, I bet most of us little souls probably have dozens of distraction habits already deeply ingrained in our lives. For instance, when we begin to feel lonely, we probably have a regular routine like checking e-mail, calling someone on the phone, or watching a movie. The problem with this is that if we always run to such things when we feel the pain of spiritual thirst, we might never hear and respond to the Lord's invitation to deeper intimacy, which comes through it. We might completely miss his voice. We might lose the chance to let the Lord transform our heartache and loneliness into spiritual joy, which is exactly what the Lord's invitation means. He wants us to discover joy in the midst of darkness, joy with him.

Yet how can we experience the joy of solitude with the Lord if we're used to always running away? Don't worry. The Lord has a strategy. He's so good and merciful he comes after us even when we run — at least that's what he did with me.

The Lord came after me when I was on my skateboard. (Yes, one of my favorite distractions is a skateboard.) Next to the seminary where I used to live, there's a big college campus that was like my own private skate park. In the evenings, when the thirst of my heart was often particularly strong, I got in the habit of grabbing my skateboard, running out the door, and riding like the wind. Sometimes, instead of reaching for my board, I'd go to the chapel and pray. Most of the time, however, I just went for the distraction.

One day, when I was riding like the wind, I noticed that Jesus seemed to be following me. I don't know how to explain that except to say that I sensed his presence. At first, it kind of annoyed me. I wanted to say, "Please leave me alone!" He must have known what I wanted to say, but he still kept silently following. I kept riding, and he kept following. At one point, I stopped riding. By then, the sun had gone down, and it was rather dark except for a few street lights. I stood there in the darkness. It was quiet. What I experienced next came as a shock — although it shouldn't have. I suddenly understood that Jesus wasn't there to scold me. He just wanted me to let him come along as I rode. So I let him, and it was actually kind of fun.

Every evening after that, I invited Jesus to come with me as I passed the chapel on my way out the door for my evening ride, and he always came. Sometimes I'd stop riding and watch the sunset, and his presence would be right there with me. Eventually, I started talking with him during such breaks. I talked with him about the painful longing in my heart, and he listened. At one point, I realized he not only listened but really understood — from his own experience. In fact, I saw that the painful longing of my heart was similar to his. He also was thirsting. He also felt, in a certain sense, lonely. That was a big breakthrough for me: My loneliness was like a small slice of his own lonely longing, and thus, I could truly understand him. In that discovery, I realized that my thirst wasn't an impossible burden but a gift that united me in deeper friendship with Jesus.

Whenever we burn with longing, it may be Jesus inviting us to deeper friendship. Such an invitation seems to come through his gaze, a loving gaze from the Cross, a somewhat sorrowful gaze that says, "I thirst for you." In fact, I wonder if the thirst we sometimes experience is his gaze, such that when it's especially strong, it's simply him gazing on us with longing and love. Whether or not that's true, I at least know this much: When we feel "the thirst" and realize that the Lord's loving gaze is on us — and especially if we allow our gaze to meet his — then our thirst can become a kind of joy.[68] I say a "kind" of joy because we'll surely still feel the pain, but it becomes something beautiful. We may indeed continue to feel alone, but it will be like we're "together alone" with him.

I still ride my skateboard, but now it's not so much a distraction from my thirst as part of my response to the Lord's invitation to deeper intimacy with him. In fact, when I feel "the thirst" now, I usually don't listen to the bad spirit telling me to run away. Rather, I try to become quiet, listen, and reflect on the Lord's loving, compassionate gaze on me. Then I run (ride) to him — or, at least with him — and he loves it. He loves it for two reasons. First, as it changes my painful longing into spiritual joy, it consoles me. Second, as it quenches his thirst for love, it consoles him.

Jesus calls us to a deeper intimacy with him through the longing of our hearts. All he wants is for us to be his friends, to trust him enough to share our joys and sorrows with him, and to let him share his with us. When we do, we become a great delight to him, a fact that quickly becomes our great delight. Saint Faustina testifies to the beauty of this kind of friendship:

> There is no greater happiness than when God gives me to know interiorly that every beat of my heart is pleasing to Him, and when He shows me that He loves me in a special way. This strong inner conviction, by which God assures me of His love for me and of how much my soul pleases Him, brings deep peace to my soul.[69]

---

68. This mutual gaze is what Faustina describes in the following passage as a "higher form of prayer." She writes: "Under His loving gaze my soul gains strength and power and an awareness that it loves and is especially loved. It knows that the Mighty One protects it. Such prayer, though short, benefits the soul greatly, and whole hours of ordinary prayer do not give the soul that light which is given by a brief moment of this higher form of prayer" (*Diary*, 815).

69. Ibid., 1121.

Before concluding, I want to address an important question this whole section may have raised, a question little souls frequently ask, "But does God love *me* like that?" In other words, I think little souls might have read my skateboarding story or St. Faustina's words above and thought, "Well, that may be true for them, but it's not so for me."

I've already addressed this difficulty earlier in this appendix when I wrote to all little souls, "He loves you. He loves you. He loves you most especially." I also addressed it time and time again during the retreat. However, this issue is like the obstacle "fear of suffering": It keeps coming up again and again. Yes, little souls often have a hard time believing and accepting that God loves them and especially that he loves them in a special way — but this won't do. Believing and accepting God's love for us is a crucially important part of consoling Jesus. So what do we do? Well, during the retreat, I tried to knock out "fear of suffering" with a one-two punch. Now I'd like to try something similar. I'd like to share one last part of Joe's story that contains a one-two punch, which, I hope, will help knock out the enemy of our spiritual joy.

A FINAL TESTIMONY FROM JOE. Like most little souls, Joe had a difficult time believing in God's love for him. Thankfully, for Joe and us, he was able to make Ignatian retreats every year for many years. During those retreats, it would be more or less the same. Joe would have some doubt about God's love for him, and the Lord would reassure him not only of his love for him but that he has a particularly tender love for him (because Joe is such a little soul). Well, during his last Ignatian eight-day retreat, Joe asked the Lord to somehow give him something that would serve as a constant reminder to him not only of the Lord's tender love for him but also of his special care. The Lord graciously gave him such a reminder during the last meditation of the retreat. Joe relates the experience as follows:

At the very last moment of the meditation, after having asked the Lord at the beginning to somehow summarize for me all the promises of his special love and care for me, the Lord brought before my mind's eye the Image of Divine Mercy. Then, it was like he was saying to me that the two rays that go forth from his Heart in that image are like his twofold "covenant" with me, a covenant that never changes. First, I understood the red ray to be his promise of a particular love for me. In other words, he was saying that because I'm such a weak and little soul, his merciful love reaches out to me with a particular tenderness and that it never changes. He also seemed to say that at times I may choose not to accept it but that, nevertheless, this particular love will always be there for me. Second, I understood the pale ray to be his promise of a special and tender care for me. In other words, he was saying that because I'm such a weak and little soul, his loving providence and protective arm will always care for and shield me in a special way. Again, he seemed to emphasize that these two promises of a particular love and special care (because I'm so little) will always be there. They'll never change. They don't depend on me. I might choose not to accept them, but they'll still be there for me.

After the retreat, the grace of that meditation has stayed with me more powerfully than any other grace I've ever received, at least as far as I'm aware. Wherever I am, even when darkness assails me, I only need to think of the "covenant" of the two rays and an inner joy and peace come to me. The joy comes from the promise of particular love represented by the red ray. The peace comes from the promise of a special care represented by the pale ray. Thus, the heart of my prayer since my last eight-day retreat has simply been to accept the Lord's love and care for me, to live under the rays of his mercy, and to let the joy and peace they bring take deeper and deeper root in my soul. It's all very simple. It makes me happy and, best of all, it makes him happy, too.[70]

I'm convinced the "covenant" promised to Joe is also promised to us, provided we choose to remain little souls.[71] If we do, then this covenant can be yet another great weapon for us in the battle for spiritual joy, and it can begin to knock out the doubts we might have about God's love and care for us. Moreover, all this makes even clearer the crucially important point that consoling Jesus is just as much about letting him console us. For, if we simply accept his love and care, then this brings peace and joy, which overflows into praise and thanks, which, as we know, is the trust that greatly consoles him.

On to Joyful Victory

At the beginning of this appendix, I mentioned that I was writing it especially for my fellow melancholics. I hope that after reading it, they now realize they truly can be a great consolation to Jesus and win the battle for spiritual joy. For, while it's true that we should strive to praise and thank the Lord always, sometimes it's not easy to be bubbly about it, and that's all right. In fact, those times when we're in deep darkness and cling to Jesus

---

70. That Jesus would make such a promise of particular love and special care is not so surprising to those who have read the *Diary of St. Faustina*. I say that because this book is full of such promises from the Lord. For examples of his promise of particular love to certain souls, see Appendix Two under the section "Divine Mercy — For Sinners." For an example of his promise of a special care, read the following: "**Souls who spread the honor of My mercy I shield through their entire lives as a tender mother her infant, and at the hour of death I will not be a Judge for them, but the Merciful Savior**" (1075).

71. How do we choose to remain little souls? That's what the whole retreat was about. If we try to live our three promises (especially the first one), then there's no need to worry. Our promises meet the Lord's, and his covenant with Joe becomes a covenant with us. (In case you forgot our three promises, see the first side of the Consoler Cheat Sheet under the heading "A Consoler's Three Promises.")

only with the secret weapon of trust are precisely the times when we give him the greatest glory. Still, we should strive to remember that St. Ignatius teaches us there's so much we can do to get out of times of desolation, such as by asking, "Why?," fighting it, and not listening to the voice of the bad spirit. We should also strive to remember that there's a lot we can do to stay in consolation when it comes, such as by eating it up, humbling ourselves, and listening to the inspirations of the good spirit. If, with eyes wide open, we stay in the battle for spiritual joy and fight with these weapons, we'll win battle after battle. In fact, if we firmly resolve not to give up the fight no matter what, then we can confidently and joyfully declare victory as we make St. Faustina's courageous prayer our own:

> I know that I am under Your special gaze, O Lord. I do not examine with fear Your plans regarding me; my task is to accept everything from Your hand. I do not fear anything, although the storm is raging, and frightful bolts strike all around me, and I then feel quite alone. Yet, my heart senses You, and my trust grows, and I see all Your omnipotence which upholds me. With You, Jesus, I go through life, amid storms and rainbows, with a cry of joy, singing the song of Your mercy. I will not stop singing my song of love until the choir of Angels picks it up. There is no power that can stop me in my flight toward God.[72]

---

72. Ibid., 761. The certainty of victory comes from Jesus' own words, **"If only you are willing to fight, know that the victory is always on your side"** (Ibid., 1560).

APPENDIX
TWO

Diary of St. Faustina
(Selections)

Chaplet of Divine Mercy

(For instructions on how to pray the Chaplet of Divine Mercy, see the citation that follows.)

In the evening, when I was in my cell, I saw an Angel, the executor of divine wrath. He was clothed in a dazzling robe, his face gloriously bright, a cloud beneath his feet. From the cloud, bolts of thunder and flashes of lightning were springing into his hands; and from his hand they were going forth, and only then were they striking the earth. When I saw this sign of divine wrath which was about to strike the earth, and in particular a certain place, which for good reasons I cannot name, I began to implore the Angel to hold off for a few moments, and the world would do penance. But my plea was a mere nothing in the face of the divine anger. Just then I saw the Most Holy Trinity. The greatness of Its majesty pierced me deeply, and I did not dare to repeat my entreaties. At that very moment I felt in my soul the power of Jesus' grace, which dwells in my soul. When I became conscious of this grace, I was instantly snatched up before the Throne of God. Oh, how great is our Lord and God and how incomprehensible His holiness! I will make no attempt to describe this greatness, because before long we shall all see Him as He is. I found myself pleading with God for the world with words heard interiorly.

As I was praying in this manner, I saw the Angel's helplessness: he could not carry out the just punishment which was rightly due for sins. Never before had I prayed with such inner power as I did then.

The words with which I entreated God are these: **Eternal Father, I offer You the Body and Blood, Soul and Divinity of Your dearly beloved Son, Our Lord Jesus Christ for our sins and those of the whole world; for the sake of His sorrowful Passion, have mercy on us.**

The next morning, when I entered chapel, I heard these words interiorly: **Every time you enter the chapel, immediately recite the prayer which I taught you yesterday.** When

I had said the prayer, in my soul I heard these words: **This prayer will serve to appease My wrath. You will recite it for nine days, on the beads of the rosary, in the following manner: First of all, you will say one OUR FATHER and HAIL MARY and the I BELIEVE IN GOD.** Then on the OUR FATHER beads you will say the following words: "Eternal Father, I offer You the Body and Blood, Soul and Divinity of Your dearly beloved Son, Our Lord Jesus Christ, in atonement for our sins and those of the whole world." On the HAIL MARY beads you will say the following words: "For the sake of His sorrowful Passion have mercy on us and on the whole world." In conclusion, three times you will recite these words: "Holy God, Holy Mighty One, Holy Immortal One, have mercy on us and on the whole world" (474-476).

Say unceasingly the chaplet that I have taught you. Whoever will recite it will receive great mercy at the hour of death. Priests will recommend it to sinners as their last hope of salvation. Even if there were a sinner most hardened, if he were to recite this chaplet only once, he would receive grace from My infinite mercy (687).

The souls that say this chaplet will be embraced by My mercy during their lifetime and especially at the hour of their death (754).

The following afternoon, when I entered the ward, I saw someone dying, and learned that the agony had started during the night. ... [T]hen, I heard a voice in my soul: **Say the chaplet which I taught you.** I ran to fetch my rosary and knelt down by the dying person and, with all the ardor of my soul, I began to say the chaplet. Suddenly the dying person opened her eyes and looked at me; I had not managed to finish the entire chaplet when she died, with extraordinary peace. I fervently asked the Lord to fulfill the promise He had given me for the recitation of the chaplet. The Lord gave me to know that the soul had been granted the grace He had promised me. That was the first soul to receive the benefit of the Lord's promise. I could feel the power of mercy envelop that soul.

When I entered my solitude, I heard these words: **At the hour of their death, I defend as My own glory every soul that will say this chaplet; or when others say it for a dying person, the pardon is the same. When this chaplet is said by the bedside of a dying person, God's anger is placated, unfathomable mercy envelops the soul, and the very depths of My tender mercy are moved for the sake of the sorrowful Passion of My Son** (810).

Oh, what great graces I will grant to souls who say this chaplet; the very depths of My tender mercy are stirred for the sake of those who say the chaplet (848).

"Jesus, I have so much to tell You." And the Lord said to me with great love, **Speak, My daughter.** And I started to enumerate the pains of my heart; that is, how greatly concerned I am for all mankind, that "they all do not know You, and those who do know You do not love You as You deserve to be loved. I also see how terribly sinners offend You; and then again, I see how severely the faithful, especially Your servants, are oppressed and persecuted. And then, too, I see many souls rushing headlong into the terrible abyss of hell. You see, Jesus, this is the pain that gnaws at my heart and bones. And, although You show me special love and inundate my heart with streams of Your joys, nevertheless, this does not appease the sufferings I have just mentioned, but rather they penetrate my poor heart all the more acutely. Oh, how ardently I desire that all mankind turn with trust to Your mercy. Then, seeing the glory of Your name, my heart will be comforted."

Jesus listened to these outpourings of my heart with gravity and interest, as if He had known nothing about them, and this seemed to make it easier for me to talk. And the Lord said to me, **My daughter, those words of your heart are pleasing to Me, and by saying the chaplet you are bringing humankind closer to Me** (929).

The heat is so intense today that it is difficult to bear. We are all thirsting for rain, and still it does not come. For several days the sky has been overcast, but there is no rain. When I looked at the plants, thirsting for the rain I was moved with pity, and I decided to say the chaplet until the Lord would send us rain. Before supper, the sky covered over with clouds, and a heavy rain fell on the earth. I had been saying this prayer without interruption for three hours. And the Lord let me know that everything can be obtained by means of this prayer (1128).

My daughter, encourage souls to say the chaplet which I have given to you. It pleases Me to grant everything they ask of Me by saying the chaplet. When hardened sinners say it, I will fill their souls with peace, and the hour of their death will be a happy one (1541).

Write that when they say this chaplet in the presence of the dying, I will stand between My Father and the dying person, not as the just Judge but as the merciful Savior (1541).

My daughter, help Me to save a certain dying sinner. Say the chaplet that I have taught you for him. When I began to say the chaplet, I saw the man dying in the midst of terrible torment and struggle. His Guardian Angel was defending him, but he was, as it were, powerless against the enormity of the soul's misery. A multitude of devils was waiting for the soul. But while I was saying the chaplet, I saw Jesus just as He is depicted in the image. The rays which issued from Jesus' Heart enveloped the sick man, and the powers of darkness fled in panic. The sick man peacefully breathed his last. When I came to myself, I understood how very important the chaplet was for the dying. It appeases the anger of God (1565).

Today I was awakened by a great storm. The wind was raging, and it was raining in torrents, thunderbolts striking again and again. I began to pray that the storm would do no harm, when I heard the words: **Say the chaplet I have taught you, and the storm will cease.** I began immediately to say the chaplet and hadn't even finished it when the storm suddenly ceased, and I heard the words: Through the chaplet you will obtain everything, if what you ask for is compatible with My will (1731).

When a great storm was approaching, I began to say the chaplet. Suddenly I heard the voice of an angel: "I cannot approach in this storm, because the light which comes from her mouth drives back both me and the storm." Such was the angel's complaint to God. I then recognized how much havoc he was to have made through this storm; but I also recognized that this prayer was pleasing to God, and that this chaplet was most powerful (1791).

Today, the Lord came to me and said, **My daughter, help Me to save souls. You will go to a dying sinner, and you will continue to recite the chaplet, and in this way you will obtain for him trust in My mercy, for he is already in despair.**

Suddenly, I found myself in a strange cottage where an elderly man was dying amidst great torments. All about the bed was a multitude of demons and the family, who were crying. When I began to pray, the spirits of darkness fled, with hissing and threats directed at me. The soul became calm and, filled with trust, rested in the Lord.

At the same moment, I found myself again in my own room. How this happens ... I do not know (1797-1798).

Confession

The confessor will sometimes say something he had never intended to say, without even realizing it himself. Oh, let the soul believe that such words are the words of the Lord Himself! Though indeed we ought to believe that every word spoken in the confessional is God's, what I have referred to is something that comes directly from God. And the soul perceives that the priest is not master of himself, that he is saying things that he would rather not say. That is how God rewards faith (132).

Pray for souls that they be not afraid to approach the tribunal of My mercy [i.e., the Sacrament of Confession] (975).

Write, speak of My mercy. Tell souls where they are to look for solace; that is, in the Tribunal of Mercy [i.e., the Sacrament of Confession]. There the greatest miracles take place [and] are incessantly repeated. To avail oneself of this miracle, it is not necessary to go on a great pilgrimage or to carry out some external ceremony; it suffices to come with faith to the feet of My representative and to reveal to him one's misery, and the miracle of Divine Mercy will be fully demonstrated. Were a soul like a decaying corpse so that from a human standpoint, there would be no [hope of] restoration and everything would already be lost, it is not so with God. The miracle of Divine Mercy restores that soul in full (1448).

Daughter, when you go to confession, to this fountain of My mercy, the Blood and Water which came forth from My Heart always flows down upon your soul and ennobles it. Every time you go to confession, immerse yourself entirely in My mercy, with great trust, so that I may pour the bounty of My grace upon your soul. When you approach the confessional, know this, that I Myself am waiting there for you. I am only hidden by the priest, but I myself act in your soul. Here the misery of the soul meets the God of mercy. Tell souls that from this fount of mercy souls draw graces solely with the vessel of trust. If their trust is great, there is no limit to My generosity (1602).

My daughter, just as you prepare in My presence, so also you make your confession before Me. The person of the priest is, for Me, only a screen. Never analyze what sort of a priest it is that I am making use of; open your soul in confession as you would to Me, and I will fill it with My light (1725).

Consoling Spirituality

O my Jesus, I will console You for all the ingratitude, the blasphemies, the coldness, the hatred of the wicked, the sacrileges (80).

As often as you want to make Me happy, speak to the world about My great and unfathomable mercy (164).

My child you are My delight, you are the comfort of My Heart (164).

My daughter, your heart is My heaven (238).

It seems to me as though Jesus could not be happy without me, nor could I, without Him. Although I understand that, being God, He is happy in Himself and has absolutely no need of any creature, still, His goodness compels Him to give Himself to the creature, and with a generosity which is beyond understanding (244).

O Jesus, if only I could become like mist before your eyes, to cover the earth so that You would not see its terrible crimes (284).

I am giving you a share in the redemption of mankind. You are solace in My dying hour (310).

I was reflecting on how much God had suffered and on how great was the love He had shown for us, and on the fact that we still do not believe that God loves us so much. O Jesus, who can understand this? What suffering it is for our Savior! How can He convince us of His love if even His death cannot convince us? (319).

My daughter, your heart is My repose; it is My delight. I find in it everything that is refused Me by so many souls (339).

I am consumed with sorrow at the sight of those who are cold and ungrateful; and I then try to have such a love for God that it will make amends for those who do not love Him, those who feed their Savior with ingratitude at its worst (481).

I have ever before my eyes His sorrowful Face, abused and disfigured, His divine Heart pierced by our sins and especially by the ingratitude of chosen souls (487).

[Mary:] *You give Me great joy when you adore the Holy Trinity for the graces and privileges which were accorded Me* (564).

My Jesus, I would rather not exist than make You sad (571).

[Regarding Fr. Sopocko:] **His heart is, for Me, a heaven on earth** (574).

I do not fear anything in the world, but fear only lest I make Jesus sad (610).

I try always to be a Bethany for Jesus, so that He may rest here after all His labors (735).

My daughter, I want to repose in your heart, because many souls have thrown Me out of their hearts today. I have experienced sorrow unto death (866).

Although the desert is fearful, I walk with lifted head and eyes fixed on the sun; that is to say, on the merciful Heart of Jesus (886).

Do not grow weary of praying for sinners. You know what a burden their souls are to My Heart. Relieve My deathly sorrow; dispense My mercy (975).

Beloved daughter of My Heart, you are My solace amidst terrible torments (1058).

I do not know how to live without God, but I also feel that

God, absolutely self-sufficient though He is, cannot be happy without me (1120).

[See the text of the Novena to Divine Mercy (1209-1228). The relevant excerpts from the novena, that is, those parts that specifically have to do with Consoling spirituality, can be found on pages 51-52. The full citation of the novena can be found in this appendix under the heading "Novena to the Divine Mercy."]

The loss of each soul plunges Me into mortal sadness. You always console Me when you pray for sinners. The prayer most pleasing to Me is prayer for the conversion of sinners. Know, My daughter, that this prayer is always heard and answered (1397).

You will give me pleasure if you hand over to me all your troubles and griefs. I shall heap upon you the treasures of My grace (1485).

O my Jesus, ... Your Divine Heart was filled with bitterness throughout Your life, and in return for Your love You received ingratitude. You were in such pain that a sorrowful complaint escaped Your lips when You said that You were looking for someone to console You and You found none [cf. Ps. 68:21] (1609).

My daughter, your compassion for Me refreshes Me. By meditating on My Passion, your soul acquires a distinct beauty (1657).

My daughter, know that your ardent love and the compassion you have for Me were a consolation to Me in the Garden [of Olives] (1664).

When on Holy Thursday I left Myself in the Blessed Sacrament, you were very much on My mind (1774).

Your love compensates Me for the coldness of many souls (1816).

Conversation with a Despairing Soul*

Jesus: **O soul steeped in darkness, do not despair. All is not yet lost. Come and confide in your God, who is love and mercy.**

— But the soul, deaf even to this appeal, wraps itself in darkness.

Jesus calls out again: **My child, listen to the voice of your merciful Father.**

— In the soul arises this reply: "For me there is no mercy," and it falls into greater darkness, a despair which is a foretaste of hell and makes it unable to draw near to God.

Jesus calls to the soul a third time, but the soul remains deaf and blind, hardened and despairing. Then the mercy of God begins to exert itself, and, without any co-operation from the soul, God grants it final grace. If this too is spurned, God will leave the soul in this self-chosen disposition for eternity. This grace emerges from the merciful Heart of Jesus and gives the soul a special light by means of which the soul begins to understand God's effort; but conversion depends on its own will. The soul knows that this, for her, is final grace and, should it show even a flicker of good will, the mercy of God will accomplish the rest.

My omnipotent mercy is active here. Happy the soul that takes advantage of this grace.

Jesus: **What joy fills My Heart when you return to me. Because you are weak, I take you in My arms and carry you to the home of My Father.**

Soul (as if awaking, asks fearfully): Is it possible that there yet is mercy for me?

---

* For the four conversations of the Merciful God with a sinful soul, suffering soul, soul striving after perfection, and perfect soul, see *Diary* entries 1485, 1487, 1488, 1489, respectively.

Jesus: **There is, My child. You have a special claim on My mercy. Let it act in your poor soul; let the rays of grace enter your soul; they bring with them light, warmth, and life.**

Soul: But fear fills me at the thought of my sins, and this terrible fear moves me to doubt Your goodness.

Jesus: **My child, all your sins have not wounded My Heart as painfully as your present lack of trust does — that after so many efforts of My love and mercy, you should still doubt My goodness.**

Soul: O Lord, save me Yourself, for I perish. Be my Savior. O Lord, I am unable to say anything more; my pitiful heart is torn asunder; but You, O Lord ...

Jesus does not let the soul finish but, raising it from the ground, from the depths of its misery, He leads it into the recesses of His Heart where all its sins disappear instantly, consumed by the flames of love.

Jesus: **Here, soul, are all the treasures of My Heart. Take everything you need from it.**

Soul: O Lord, I am inundated with Your grace. I sense that a new life has entered into me and, above all, I feel Your love in my heart. That is enough for me. O Lord, I will glorify the omnipotence of Your mercy for all eternity. Encouraged by Your goodness, I will confide to You all the sorrows of my heart.

Jesus: **Tell me all, My child, hide nothing from Me, because My loving Heart, the Heart of your Best Friend, is listening to you.**

Soul: O Lord, now I see all my ingratitude and Your goodness. You were pursuing me with Your grace, while I was frustrating Your benevolence. I see that I deserve the depths of hell for spurning Your graces.

Jesus (interrupting): **Do not be absorbed in your misery —
you are still too weak to speak of it — but, rather, gaze on
My Heart filled with goodness, and be imbued with My
sentiments. Strive for meekness and humility; be merciful
to others, as I am to you; and, when you feel your strength
failing, if you come to the fountain of mercy to fortify your
soul, you will not grow weary on your journey.**

Soul: Now I understand Your mercy, which protects me, and
like a brilliant star, leads me into the home of my Father,
protecting me from the horrors of hell that I have deserved,
not once, but a thousand times. O Lord, eternity will hardly
suffice for me to give due praise to Your unfathomable mercy
and Your compassion for me (1486).

Distrust

**Distrust on the part of souls is tearing at My insides. The
distrust of a chosen soul causes Me even greater pain;
despite My inexhaustible love for them they do not trust
Me. Even My death is not enough for them. Woe to the
soul that abuses these [gifts] (50).**

**O, how much I am hurt by a soul's distrust! Such a soul
professes that I am Holy and Just, but does not believe that
I am Mercy and does not trust in my Goodness. Even the
devils glorify My Justice but do not believe in My
Goodness (300).**

My Heart is sorrowful, Jesus said, **because even chosen
souls do not understand the greatness of My mercy. Their
relationship [with Me] is, in certain ways, imbued with
mistrust. Oh, how much that wounds My Heart!
Remember My Passion, and if you do not believe My
words, at least believe My wounds (379).**

God is very displeased with lack of trust in Him, and this is
why some souls lose many graces. Distrust hurts His most

sweet Heart, which is full of goodness and incomprehensible love for us (595).

On the evening of the last day before my departure from Vilnius, an elderly sister revealed the condition of her soul to me. She said that she had already been suffering interiorly for several years, that it seemed to her that all her confessions had been bad, and that she had doubts as to whether the Lord Jesus had forgiven her. I asked her if she had ever told her confessor about this. She answered that she had spoken many times about this to her confessors and ... "the confessors are always telling me to be at peace, but still I suffer very much, and nothing brings me relief, and it constantly seems to me that God has not forgiven me." I answered, "You should obey your confessor, Sister, and be fully at peace, because this is certainly a temptation."

But she entreated me with tears in her eyes to ask Jesus if He had forgiven her and whether her confessions had been good or not. I answered forcefully, "Ask Him yourself, Sister, if you don't believe your confessors!" But she clutched my hand and did not want to let me go until I gave her an answer, and she kept asking me to pray for her and to let her know what Jesus would tell me about her. Crying bitterly, she would not let me go and said to me, "I know that the Lord Jesus speaks to you, Sister." Since she was clutching my hand and I could not wrench myself away, I promised her I would pray for her. In the evening, during Benediction, I heard these words in my soul: **Tell her that her disbelief wounds My Heart more than the sins she committed.** When I told her this, she began to cry like a child, and great joy entered her soul. I understood that God wanted to console this soul through me. Even though it cost me a good deal, I fulfilled God's wish (628).

How painfully distrust of My goodness wounds Me! Sins of distrust wound Me most painfully (1076).

My child, all your sins have not wounded My Heart as painfully as your present lack of trust does — that after so

many efforts of My love and mercy, you should still doubt My goodness (1486).

Jesus complained to me of how painful to Him is the unfaithfulness of chosen souls, **and My Heart is even more wounded by their distrust after a fall. It would be less painful if they had not experienced the goodness of My Heart** (1532).

Divine Mercy

I am Lord in My essence and am immune to orders or needs. If I call creatures into being — that is the abyss of My mercy (85).

I see now that the work of Redemption is bound up with the work of mercy requested by the Lord (89).

The greatest attribute [of God] is love and mercy. It unites the creature with the Creator (180).

Proclaim that mercy is the greatest attribute of God. All the works of My hands are crowned with mercy (301).

Praise the Lord, my soul, for everything, and glorify His mercy, for His goodness is without end. Everything will pass, but His mercy is without limit or end. And although evil will attain its measure, in mercy there is no measure (423).

Mercy is the greatest attribute of God; everything that surrounds me speaks to me of this (611).

O my Jesus, Your goodness surpasses all understanding, and no one will exhaust Your mercy. Damnation is for the soul who wants to be damned; but for the one who desires salvation, there is the inexhaustible ocean of the Lord's mercy to draw from. How can a small vessel contain the unfathomable ocean? (631).

O incomprehensible God, how great is Your mercy! It surpasses the combined understanding of all men and angels. All the angels and all humans have emerged from the very depths of Your tender mercy. Mercy is the flower of love. God is love, and mercy is His deed. In love it is conceived; in mercy it is revealed. Everything I look at speaks to me of God's mercy. Even God's very justice speaks to me about His fathomless mercy, because justice flows from love (651).

Satan hates mercy more than anything else. It is his greatest torment (764).

I am giving mankind the last hope of salvation; that is, recourse to My mercy (998).

Saint Joseph urged me to have a constant devotion to him. ... He looked at me with great kindness and gave me to know how much he is supporting this work [of mercy] (1203).

My daughter, do you think you have written enough about My mercy? What you have written is but a drop compared to the ocean. I am Love and Mercy itself (1273).

Love God, because He is good and great is His mercy! (1372).

Oh, how great is the mercy of God, who allows man to participate in such a high degree in His divine happiness! (1439).

I received a deeper understanding of divine mercy. Only that soul who wants it will be damned, for God condemns no one (1452).

Your mercy runs through our life like a golden thread and maintains in good order the contact of our being with God. For He does not need anything to make Him happy; so everything is solely the work of His mercy (1466).

Everything begins with Your mercy and ends with Your mercy (1506).

Lord, my heart is filled with amazement that You, absolute Lord, in need of no one, would nevertheless stoop so low out

272   CONSOLING THE HEART OF JESUS

of pure love for us. I can never help being amazed that the Lord would have such an intimate relationship with His creatures (1523).

No mind, either of angel or of man, will ever fathom the mysteries of Your mercy, O God. The angels are lost in amazement before the mystery of divine mercy, but cannot comprehend it. Everything that has come from the Creator's hand is contained in this inconceivable mystery; that is to say, in the very depths of His tender mercy (1553).

O inconceivable goodness of God, which shields us at every step, may Your mercy be praised without cease. That You became a brother to humans, not to angels, is a miracle of the unfathomable mystery of Your mercy. All our trust is in You, our first-born Brother, Jesus Christ, true God and true Man. My heart flutters with joy to see how good God is to us wretched and ungrateful people. And as a proof of His love, He gives us the incomprehensible gift of Himself in the person of His Son. Throughout all eternity we shall never exhaust that mystery of love. O mankind, why do you think so little about God being truly among us? O Lamb of God, I do not know what to admire in You first: Your gentleness, Your hidden life, the emptying of Yourself for the sake of man, or the constant miracle of Your mercy, which transforms souls and raises them up to eternal life. Although You are hidden in this way, Your omnipotence is more manifest here than in the creation of man. Though the omnipotence of Your mercy is at work in the justification of the sinner, yet Your action is gentle and hidden (1584).

I often communicate with persons who are dying and obtain the divine mercy for them. Oh, how great is the goodness of God, greater than we can understand. There are moments and there are mysteries of the divine mercy over which the heavens are astounded. Let our judgment of souls cease, for God's mercy upon them is extraordinary (1684).

I often attend upon the dying and through entreaties obtain for them trust in God's mercy, and I implore God for an abundance of divine grace, which is always victorious. God's mercy sometimes touches the sinner at the last moment in a wondrous and mysterious way. Outwardly, it seems as if everything were lost, but it is not so. The soul, illumined by a ray of God's powerful final grace, turns to God in the last moment with such a power of love that, in an instant, it receives from God forgiveness of sin and punishment, while outwardly it shows no sign either of repentance or of contrition, because souls [at that stage] no longer react to external things. Oh, how beyond comprehension is God's mercy! But — horror! — there are also souls who voluntarily and consciously reject and scorn this grace! Although a person is at the point of death, the merciful God gives the soul that interior vivid moment, so that if the soul is willing, it has the possibility of returning to God. But sometimes, the obduracy in souls is so great that consciously they choose hell; they [thus] make useless all the prayers that other souls offer to God for them and even the efforts of God Himself (1698).

GOD'S INFINITE GOODNESS IN CREATING MANKIND. God, who in Your mercy have deigned to call man from nothingness into being, generously have You bestowed upon him nature and grace. But that seemed too little for Your infinite goodness. In Your mercy, O Lord, You have given us everlasting life. You admit us to Your everlasting happiness and grant us to share in Your interior life. And You do this solely out of Your mercy. You bestow on us the gift of Your grace, only because You are good and full of love. You had no need of us at all to be happy, but You, O Lord, want to share Your own happiness with us. But man did not stand the test. You could have punished him, like the angels, with eternal rejection, but here Your mercy appeared, and the very depths of Your being were moved with great compassion, and You promised to restore our salvation. It is an incomprehensible abyss of Your compassion that You did not punish us as we deserved. May Your mercy be glorified, O

Lord; we will praise it for endless ages. And the angels were amazed at the greatness of the mercy which You have shown for mankind ... (1743).

THE INFINITE GOODNESS OF GOD IN SENDING US HIS ONLY-BEGOTTEN SON. God, You did not destroy man after his fall, but in Your mercy You forgave him, You forgave in a divine way; that is, not only have You absolved him from guilt, but You have bestowed upon him every grace. Mercy has moved You to deign to descend among us and lift us up from our misery. God will descend to earth; the Immortal Lord of lords will abase Himself. ... [T]he inconceivable miracle of Your mercy takes place, O Lord. The Word becomes flesh; God dwells among us, the Word of God, Mercy Incarnate. By Your descent, You have lifted us up to Your divinity. Such is the excess of Your love, the abyss of Your mercy. Heaven is amazed at the superabundance of Your love. No one fears to approach You now. You are the God of mercy. You have compassion on misery. You are our God, and we are Your people. You are our Father, and we are Your children by grace. Praise be to Your mercy, that You have deigned to descend among us (1745).

Heaven is astounded that God has become man ... .
Why is it that You do not unite Yourself with a Seraph,
but with a sinner, O Lord?
Oh, because, despite the purity of the virginal womb,
this is a mystery of Your mercy.
O mystery of God's mercy, O God of compassion,
That You have deigned to leave the heavenly throne
And to stoop down to our misery, to human weakness,
For it is not the angels, but man who needs mercy (1746).

GOD'S INFINITE GOODNESS IN REDEEMING MAN. God, You could have saved thousands of worlds with one word; a single sigh from Jesus would have satisfied Your justice. But You Yourself, Jesus, purely out of love for us, underwent such a terrible Passion. Your Father's justice would have been propiti-ated with a single sigh from You, and all Your self-abasement is solely the work of Your mercy and Your inconceivable love. On leaving the earth, O Lord, You wanted to stay with us, and so You left us Yourself in the Sacrament of the Altar, and You opened wide Your mercy to us. There is no misery that could exhaust You; You have called us all to this fountain of love, to this spring of God's compassion. Here is the tabernacle of Your mercy, here is the remedy for all our ills. To You, O living spring of mercy, all souls are drawn; some like deer, thirsting for Your love, others to wash the wound of their sins, and still others, exhausted by life, to draw strength. At the moment of Your death on the Cross, You bestowed upon us eternal life; allowing Your most holy side to be opened, You opened an inexhaustible spring of mercy for us, giving us Your dearest possession, the Blood and Water from Your Heart. Such is the omnipotence of Your mercy. From it all grace flows to us (1747).

GOD'S INFINITE GOODNESS IN ADORNING THE WHOLE WORLD WITH BEAUTY IN ORDER TO MAKE MAN'S STAY ON EARTH PLEASANT. O God, how generously Your mercy is spread everywhere, and You have done all this for man. Oh, how much You must love him, since Your love is so active on his behalf. O my Creator and Lord, I see on all sides the trace of Your hand and the seal of Your mercy, which embraces all created things. O my most compassionate Creator, I want to give You worship on behalf of all creatures and all inanimate creation; I call on the whole universe to glorify Your mercy. Oh, how great is Your goodness, O God! (1749).

Before I made the world, I loved you with the love your heart is experiencing today and, throughout the centuries, My love will never change (1754).

Divine Mercy — And Justice

O, how much I am hurt by a soul's distrust! Such a soul professes that I am Holy and Just, but does not believe that I am Mercy and does not trust in my Goodness. Even the devils glorify My Justice but do not believe in My Goodness (300).

I do not fear the blows, blows of divine justice, because I am united with Jesus. ... I hope against all hope in the ocean of Your mercy (309).

Even if I were to hear the most terrifying things about God's justice, I would not fear Him at all, because I have come to know Him well. God is love, and His Spirit is peace. ... I have placed my trust in God and fear nothing (589).

O my Jesus, I implore You by the goodness of Your most sweet Heart, let Your anger diminish and show us Your mercy. May Your wounds be our shield against Your Father's justice. I have come to know You, O God, as the source of mercy that vivifies and nourishes every soul. Oh, how great is the mercy of the Lord; it surpasses all His other qualities! Mercy is the greatest attribute of God; everything that surrounds me speaks to me of this. Mercy is the life of souls; His compassion is inexhaustible. O Lord, look on us and deal with us according to Your countless mercies, according to Your great mercy (611).

Love has overtaken my whole heart, and even if I were to be told of God's justice and of how even the pure spirits tremble and cover their faces before Him, saying endlessly, "Holy," which would seem to suggest that my familiarity with God would be to the detriment of His honor and majesty, [I would reply,] "O no, no, and once again, no!" (947).

I cannot punish even the greatest sinner if he makes an appeal to My compassion, but on the contrary, I justify him in My unfathomable and inscrutable mercy. Write: before I come as a just Judge, I first open wide the door of My mercy. He who refuses to pass through the door of My mercy must pass through the door of My justice (1146).

I often pray for Poland, but I see that God is very angry with it because of its ingratitude. I exert all the strength of my soul to defend it. I constantly remind God of the promises of His mercy. When I see His anger, I throw myself trustingly into the abyss of His mercy, and I plunge all Poland in it, and then He cannot use His justice (1188).

I remind you, My daughter, that as often as you hear the clock strike the third hour, immerse yourself completely in My mercy, adoring and glorifying it; invoke its omnipotence for the whole world, and particularly for poor sinners; for at that moment mercy was opened wide for every soul. In this hour you can obtain everything for yourself and for others for the asking; it was the hour of grace for the whole world — mercy triumphed over justice (1572).

In the Old Covenant I sent prophets wielding thunderbolts to My people. Today I am sending you with My mercy to the people of the whole world. I do not want to punish aching mankind, but I desire to heal it, pressing it to My Merciful Heart. I use punishment when they themselves force Me to do so; My hand is reluctant to take hold of the sword of justice. Before the Day of Justice I am sending the Day of Mercy (1588).

Tell sinners that no one shall escape My Hand; if they run away from My Merciful Heart, they will fall into My Just Hands. Tell sinners that I am always waiting for them, that I listen intently to the beating of their heart ... when will it beat for Me? (1728).

God, You could have saved thousands of worlds with one word; a single sigh from Jesus would have satisfied Your justice. But You Yourself, Jesus, purely out of love for us, underwent such a terrible Passion. Your Father's justice would have been propitiated with a single sigh from You, and all Your self-abasement is solely the work of Your mercy and Your inconceivable love (1747).

Divine Mercy — And Misery

At the beginning of my religious life, suffering and adversities frightened and disheartened me. So I prayed continuously, asking Jesus to strengthen me and to grant me the power of His Holy Spirit that I might carry out His holy will in all things, because from the beginning I have been aware of my weakness. I know very well what I am of myself, because for this purpose Jesus has opened the eyes of my soul; I am an abyss of misery, and hence I understand that whatever good there is in my soul consists solely of His holy grace. The knowledge of my own misery allows me, at the same time, to know the immensity of Your mercy. In my own interior life, I am looking with one eye at the abyss of my misery and baseness, and with the other, at the abyss of Your mercy, O God (56).

Truly, Jesus, I become frightened when I look at my own misery, but at the same time I am reassured by Your unfathomable mercy, which exceeds my misery by the measure of all eternity (66).

Of myself I can do nothing, but when You sustain me, all difficulties are nothing for me (91).

[One of the sisters in the convent said to Faustina:] "Get it out of your head, Sister, that the Lord Jesus might be communing in such an intimate way with such a miserable bundle of imperfections as you! Bear in mind that it is only with holy souls that the Lord Jesus communes in this way!" [Faustina then comments:] I acknowledged that she was right, because I am indeed a wretched person, but still I trust in God's mercy. When I met the Lord I humbled myself and said, "Jesus it seems that You do not associate intimately with such wretched people as I." **Be at peace, My daughter, it is precisely through such misery that I want to show the power of My mercy** (133).

It is with just such miserable souls that the Lord Jesus communes in this intimate way. And the more you humble yourself, the more the Lord Jesus will unite Himself with you (174).

My daughter, all your miseries have been consumed in the flame of My love, like a little twig thrown into a roaring fire. By humbling yourself in this way, you draw upon yourself and upon other souls an entire sea of My mercy (178).

I saw the abyss of my misery: whatever there is of good in me is Yours, O Lord. But because I am so small and wretched, I have a right to count on Your boundless mercy (237).

Thank You, Jesus, for the great favor of making known to me the whole abyss of my misery. I know that I am an abyss of nothingness and that, if Your holy grace did not hold me up, I would return to nothingness in a moment. And so, with every beat of my heart, I thank You, my God, for Your great mercy towards me (256).

O my Jesus, keep me near to You! See how weak I am! I cannot go a step forward by myself; so You, Jesus, must stand by me constantly like a mother by a helpless child — and even more so (264).

My Heart was moved by great mercy towards you, My dearest child, when I saw you torn to shreds because of the great pain you suffered in repenting for your sins. I see your love, so pure and true that I give you first place among the virgins. You are the honor and glory of My Passion. I see every abasement of your soul, and nothing escapes my attention. I lift up the humble even to My very throne, because I want it so (282).

My happiest moments are when I am alone with my Lord. During these moments I experience the greatness of God and my own misery (289).

O Christ, O Jesus, I want to surpass [the Seraphim] in my love for You! I apologize to you, O pure spirits, for my boldness in comparing myself to you. I, this chasm of misery, this abyss of misery; and You, O God, who are the incomprehensible abyss of mercy, swallow me up as the heat of the sun swallows up a drop of dew! A loving look from You will fill up any abyss (334).

You are My delightful dwelling place; My Spirit rests in you. After these words, I felt the Lord looking into the depths of my heart; and seeing my misery, I humbled myself in spirit and admired the immense mercy of God, that the Most High Lord would approach such misery (346).

Holy Trinity, One God, incomprehensible in the greatness of Your mercy for creatures, and especially for poor sinners, You have made known the abyss of Your mercy, incomprehensible and unfathomable [as it is] to any mind, whether of man or angel. Our nothingness and our misery are drowned in Your greatness. O infinite goodness, who can ever praise You sufficiently? Can there be found a soul that understands You in Your love? O Jesus, there are such souls, but they are few (361).

O good Jesus, thank You for the great grace of making known to me what I am of myself: misery and sin, and nothing more. I can do only one thing of myself, and that is to offend You, O my God, because misery can do no more of itself than offend You, O infinite Goodness! (363).

I am very much aware of His greatness and my misery (432).

O my Creator and Lord, my entire being is Yours! Dispose of me according to Your divine pleasure and according to Your eternal plans and Your unfathomable mercy. May every soul know how good the Lord is; may no soul fear to commune intimately with the Lord; may no soul use unworthiness as an excuse, and may it never postpone [accepting] God's invitations, for that is not pleasing to the Lord. There is no soul more wretched than I am, as I truly know myself, and I am astounded that divine Majesty stoops so low. O eternity, it seems to me that you are too short to extol [adequately] the infinite mercy of the Lord! (440).

God usually chooses the weakest and simplest souls as tools for His greatest works ... for it is just in this way that God's works are revealed for what they are, the works of God (464).

Lay your head on my shoulder, rest and regain your strength. I am always with you. Tell the friend of My Heart that I use such feeble creatures to carry out My work (498).

You are my great joy; your love and your humility make Me leave the heavenly throne and unite myself with you. Love fills up the abyss that exists between My greatness and your nothingness (512).

My Jesus, You see how weak I am of myself. Therefore, You Yourself direct my affairs (602).

You see what you are of yourself, but do not be frightened at this. If I were to reveal to you the whole misery that you are, you would die of terror. However, be aware of what you are. Because you are such great misery, I have revealed to you the whole ocean of My mercy. I seek and desire souls like yours, but they are few. Your great trust in Me forces Me to continuously grant you graces. You have great and incomprehensible rights over My Heart, for you are a daughter of complete trust. You would not have been able to bear the magnitude of the love which I have for you if I had revealed it to you fully here on earth. I often give you a glimpse of it, but know that this is only an exceptional grace from Me. My love and mercy knows no bounds (718).

And your heart is My constant dwelling place, despite the misery that you are. I unite Myself with you, take away your misery and give you My mercy (723).

Today the Lord's gaze shot through me suddenly, like lightning. At once, I came to know the tiniest specks in my soul, and knowing the depths of my misery, I fell to my knees and begged the Lord's pardon, and with great trust I immersed myself in His infinite mercy. Such knowledge does not depress me nor keep me away from the Lord, but rather it arouses in my soul greater love and boundless trust. The repentance of my heart is linked to love. These extraordinary flashes from the Lord educate my soul. O sweet rays of God, enlighten me to the most secret depth, for I want to arrive at the greatest possible purity of heart and soul (852).

My daughter, why are you giving in to thoughts of fear? I answered, "O Lord, You know why." And He said, **Why?** "This work frightens me. You know that I am incapable of carrying it out." And He said, **Why?** "You see very well that I am not in good health, that I have no education, that I have no money, that I am an abyss of misery, that I fear contacts with people. Jesus, I desire only You. You can release me from this." And the Lord said to me, **My daughter, what you have said is true. You are very miserable, and it pleased Me to carry out this work of mercy precisely through you who are nothing but misery itself. Do not fear; I will not leave you alone. Do whatever you can in this matter; I will accomplish everything that is lacking in you. You know what is within your power to do; do that.** The Lord looked into the depth of my being with great kindness; I thought I would die for joy under that gaze (881).

Jesus ... I always remain in holy amazement when I sense that You are approaching me, You, the Lord of the awesome throne; that You descend to this miserable exile and visit this poor beggar who has nothing but misery! ... Although we are separated by a great chasm, for You are the Creator and I am Your creature, nevertheless, love alone explains our union. Without it, all is incomprehensible. Only love makes it possible to understand these incomprehensible intimacies with which You visit me. O Jesus, Your greatness terrifies me, and I would be in constant astonishment and fear, if You Yourself did not set me at peace (885).

There are moments when I mistrust myself, when I feel my own weakness and wretchedness in the most profound depths of my own being, and I have noticed that I can endure such moments only by trusting in the infinite mercy of God. Patience, prayer and silence — these are what give strength to the soul. There are moments when one should be silent, and when it would be inappropriate to talk with creatures; these are the moments when one is dissatisfied with oneself, and when the soul feels as weak as a little child. Then the soul clings to God with all its might. At such times, I live solely by faith, and when I feel strengthened by God's grace, then I am more courageous in speaking and communicating with my neighbors (944).

Sometimes there are whole hours when my soul is lost in wonder at seeing the infinite majesty of God abasing Itself to the level of my soul. Unending is my interior astonishment that the Most High Lord is pleased in me and tells me so Himself. And I immerse myself even deeper in my nothingness, because I know what I am of myself (947).

When one day I resolved to practice a certain virtue, I lapsed into the vice opposed to that virtue ten times more frequently than on other days. In the evening, I was reflecting on why, today, I had lapsed so extraordinarily, and I heard the words: **You were counting too much on yourself and too little on Me.** And I understood the cause of my lapses (1087).

This grace [of purity] from God was given to me precisely because I was the weakest of all people; this is why the Almighty has surrounded me with His special mercy (1099).

In the last evening conference, which was a preparation for the renewal of vows, Father was speaking about the happiness that flows from the three vows, and about the reward that comes from observing them faithfully. Suddenly, my soul was thrown into great interior darkness. My soul was filled with bitterness instead of joy, and my heart was pierced with a sharp pain. I felt so miserable and unworthy of this grace and, conscious of my misery and unworthiness, I would not have dared to so much as approach the feet of the youngest postulant to kiss them. I saw the postulants, in spirit, beautiful and pleasing to the Lord; and myself, an abyss of misery. After the conference, I flung myself at the feet of the hidden God, midst tears and pain. I threw myself into the sea of God's infinite mercy, and only there did I experience relief and feel that all of His omnipotent mercy was enveloping me (1108).

There is no misery that could be a match for My mercy, neither will misery exhaust it, because as it is being granted — it increases. The soul that trusts in My mercy is most fortunate, because I Myself take care of it (1273).

If it hadn't been for this small imperfection, you wouldn't have come to Me. Know that as often as you come to Me, humbling yourself and asking My forgiveness, I pour out a superabundance of graces on your soul, and your imperfection vanishes before My eyes, and I see only your love and your humility. You lose nothing but gain much (1293).

O Omnipotent, ever-merciful God,
Your compassion is never exhausted.
Although my misery is as vast as the sea,
I have complete trust in the mercy of the Lord (1298).

My daughter, you have not offered Me that which is really yours. I probed deeply into myself and found that I love God with all the faculties of my soul and, unable to see what it was that I had not yet given to the Lord, I asked, "Jesus, tell me what it is, and I will give it to You at once with a generous heart." Jesus said to me with kindness, **Daughter, give Me your misery, because it is your exclusive property.** At that moment, a ray of light illumined my soul, and I saw the whole abyss of my misery. In that same moment I nestled close to the Most Sacred Heart of Jesus with so much trust that even if I had the sins of all the damned weighing on my conscience, I would not have doubted God's mercy but, with a heart crushed to dust, I would have thrown myself into the abyss of Your mercy. I believe, O Jesus, that You would not reject me, but would absolve me through the hand of Your representative (1318).

With one eye, I gaze on the abyss of my misery and with the other, on the abyss of Your mercy (1345).

This great misery of mine does not deprive me of trust. On the contrary, the better I have come to know my own misery, the stronger has become my trust in God's mercy (1406).

O my Lord, my soul is the most wretched of all, and yet You stoop to it with such kindness! I see clearly Your greatness and my littleness, and therefore I rejoice that You are so powerful and without limit, and so I rejoice greatly at being so little (1417).

Though my miseries be great, I have great trust in the power of Your mercy (1479).

Your misery has disappeared in the depths of My mercy. Do not argue with Me about your wretchedness. You will give me pleasure if you hand over to Me all your troubles and griefs. I shall heap upon you the treasures of My grace. ... Child, speak no more of your misery; it is already forgotten. Listen, My child, to what I desire to tell you. Come close to My wounds and draw from the Fountain of Life whatever your heart desires. Drink copiously from the Fountain of Life and you will not weary on your journey. Look at the splendors of My mercy and do not fear the enemies of your salvation. Glorify My mercy (1485).

Do not be absorbed in your misery — you are still too weak to speak of it — but, rather, gaze on My Heart filled with goodness, and be imbued with My sentiments (1486).

You see, My child, what you are of yourself. The cause of your falls is that you rely too much upon yourself and too little on Me. But let this not sadden you so much. You are dealing with the God of mercy, which your misery cannot exhaust. Remember, I did not allot only a certain number of pardons (1488).

You know, Lord, how weak I am. I am an abyss of wretchedness, I am nothingness itself; so what will be so strange if You leave me alone and I fall? I am an infant, Lord, so I cannot get along by myself. However, beyond all abandonment I trust, and in spite of my own feeling I trust, and I am being completely transformed into trust — often in spite of what I feel (1489).

O Greatly Merciful God, Infinite Goodness, today all mankind calls out from the abyss of its misery to Your mercy — to Your compassion, O God; and it is with its mighty voice of misery that it cries out. Gracious God, do not reject the prayer of this earth's exiles! O Lord, Goodness beyond our understanding, Who are acquainted with our misery through and through, and know that by our own power we cannot ascend to You, we implore You: anticipate us with Your grace and keep on increasing Your mercy in us, that we may faithfully do Your holy will all through our life and at death's hour. Let the omnipotence of Your mercy shield us from the darts of our salvation's enemies, that we may with confidence, as Your children, await Your final coming — that day known to You alone. And we expect to obtain everything promised us by Jesus in spite of all our wretchedness. For Jesus is our Hope: Through His merciful Heart, as through an open gate, we pass through to heaven (1570).

Know, My daughter, that between Me and you there is a bottomless abyss, an abyss which separates the Creator from the creature. But this abyss is filled with My mercy. I raise you up to Myself, not that I have need of you, but it is solely out of mercy that I grant you the grace of union with Myself (1576).

I have seen the way in which I adore God; oh, how miserable it is! And what a tiny drop it is in comparison to that perfect heavenly glory. O my God, how good You are to accept my praise as well, and to turn Your Face to me with kindness and let us know that our prayer is pleasing to You (1604).

Without You, I am weakness itself. What am I without Your grace if not an abyss of my own misery? Misery is my possession. ... Eternal Love, do You Yourself form my soul that it be made capable of returning Your love. ... Bring me into an intimacy with You so far as is possible for human nature to be brought (1630-1631).

I spent the whole day in thanksgiving, and gratitude kept flooding my soul. O my God, how good You are, how great is Your mercy! You visit me with so many graces, me who am a most wretched speck of dust. Prostrating myself at Your feet, O Lord, I confess with a sincere heart that I have done nothing to deserve even the least of Your graces. It is in Your infinite goodness that You give Yourself to me so generously. Therefore, the greater the graces which my heart receives, the deeper it plunges itself in humility (1661).

Your mercy abolishes the chasm which separates the Creator from the creature (1692).

I am mercy itself; therefore I ask you to offer Me your misery and this very helplessness of yours and, in this way, you will delight My Heart (1775).

One day during Holy Mass, the Lord gave me a deeper knowledge of His holiness and His majesty, and at the same time I saw my own misery. This knowledge made me happy, and my soul drowned itself completely in His mercy. I felt enormously happy (1801).

Although I am such misery, I do not fear You, because I know Your mercy well. Nothing will frighten me away from You, O

God, because everything is so much less than what I know [Your mercy to be] — I see that clearly (1803).

When I received Jesus [in Holy Communion], I threw myself into Him as into an abyss of unfathomable mercy. And the more I felt I was misery itself, the stronger grew my trust in Him. In this abasement, I passed the whole day (1817).

Today, my soul is preparing for Holy Communion as for a wedding feast, wherein all the participants are resplendent with unspeakable beauty. And I, too, have been invited to this banquet, but I do not see that beauty within myself, only an abyss of misery. And, although I do not feel worthy of sitting down to table, I will however slip under the table, at the feet of Jesus, and will beg for the crumbs that fall from the table. Knowing Your mercy, I therefore approach You, Jesus, for sooner will I run out of misery than will the compassion of Your Heart exhaust itself. That is why during this day I will keep arousing trust in The Divine Mercy (1827).

Divine Mercy — For Sinners

O Jesus, when I consider the great price of Your Blood, I rejoice at its immensity, for one drop alone would have been enough for the salvation of all sinners. Although sin is an abyss of wickedness and ingratitude, the price paid for us can never be equaled. Therefore, let every soul trust in the Passion of the Lord, and place its hope in His mercy. God will not deny His mercy to anyone. Heaven and earth may change, but God's mercy will never be exhausted (72).

I would like to be a priest, for then I would speak without cease about Your mercy to sinful souls drowned in despair (302).

My Heart overflows with great mercy for souls, and especially for poor sinners. If only they could understand that I am the best of Fathers to them and that it is for them that the Blood and Water flowed from My Heart as from a

fount overflowing with mercy. For them I dwell in the tabernacle as King of Mercy (367).

Heartfelt repentance immediately transforms the soul (388).

O God, You are compassion itself for the greatest sinners who sincerely repent. The greater the sinner, the greater his right to God's mercy (423).

All you souls, praise the Lord's mercy by trusting in His mercy all your life and especially at the hour of your death. And fear nothing, dear soul, whoever you are; the greater the sinner, the greater his right to Your mercy, O Lord. O Incomprehensible Goodness! God is the first to stoop to the sinner (598).

I perform works of mercy in every soul. The greater the sinner, the greater the right he has to My mercy. My mercy is confirmed in every work of My hands. He who trusts in My mercy will not perish, for all his affairs are Mine, and his enemies will be shattered at the base of My footstool (723).

You are a bottomless sea of mercy for us sinners; and the greater the misery, the more right we have to Your mercy (793).

Love and sorrow go hand in hand (881).

I desire trust from My creatures. Encourage souls to place great trust in My fathomless mercy. Let the weak, sinful soul have no fear to approach Me, for even if it had more sins than there are grains of sand in the world, all would be drowned in the unmeasurable depths of My mercy (1059).

[Let] the greatest sinners place their trust in My mercy. They have the right before others to trust in the abyss of My mercy. My daughter, write about My mercy towards tormented souls. Souls that make an appeal to My mercy delight Me. To such souls I grant even more graces than they ask. I cannot punish even the greatest sinner if he

makes an appeal to My compassion, but on the contrary, I justify him in My unfathomable and inscrutable mercy. Write: before I come as a just Judge, I first open wide the door of My mercy. He who refuses to pass through the door of My mercy must pass through the door of My justice (1146).

My daughter, write that the greater the misery of a soul, the greater its right to My mercy; [urge] all souls to trust in the unfathomable abyss of My mercy, because I want to save them all. On the Cross, the fountain of My mercy was opened wide by the lance for all souls — no one have I excluded! (1182)

My Secretary, write that I am more generous toward sinners than toward the just. It was for their sake that I came down from heaven; it was for their sake that My Blood was spilled. Let them not fear to approach Me; they are most in need of My mercy (1275).

Oh, if sinners knew My mercy, they would not perish in such great numbers. Tell sinful souls not to be afraid to approach Me; speak to them of My great mercy (1396).

Be not afraid of your Savior, O sinful soul. I make the first move to come to you, for I know that by yourself you are unable to lift yourself to Me. Child, do not run away from your Father; be willing to talk openly with your God of mercy who wants to speak words of pardon and lavish His graces on you. How dear your soul is to Me! I have inscribed your name upon My hand; you are engraved as a deep wound in My Heart (1485).

My mercy is greater than your sins and those of the entire world. Who can measure the extent of My goodness? For you I descended from heaven to earth; for you I allowed Myself to be nailed to the Cross; for you I let My Sacred Heart be pierced with a lance, thus opening wide the source of mercy for you. Come, then, with trust to draw graces from this fountain. I never reject a contrite heart. Your misery has disappeared in the depths of My mercy. Do not argue with Me about your wretchedness. You will give Me pleasure if you hand over to Me all your troubles and griefs. I shall heap upon you the treasures of My grace (1485).

O soul steeped in darkness, do not despair. All is not yet lost. Come and confide in your God, who is love and mercy (1486).

What joy fills My Heart when you return to Me. Because you are weak, I take you in My arms and carry you to the home of My Father (1486).

Do not lose heart in coming for pardon, for I am always ready to forgive you (1488).

All grace flows from mercy, and the last hour abounds with mercy for us. Let no one doubt concerning the goodness of God; even if a person's sins were as dark as night, God's mercy is stronger than our misery. One thing alone is necessary: that the sinner set ajar the door of his heart, be it ever so little, to let in a ray of God's merciful grace, and then God will do the rest. But poor is the soul who has shut the door on God's mercy, even at the last hour. It was just such souls who plunged Jesus into deadly sorrow in the Garden of Olives (1507).

Write this for the benefit of distressed souls: when a soul sees and realizes the gravity of its sins, when the whole abyss of the misery into which it immersed itself is displayed before its eyes, let it not despair, but with trust let it throw itself into the arms of My mercy, as a child into the arms of its beloved mother. These souls have a right of priority to My compassionate Heart, they have first access to My mercy. Tell them that no soul that has called upon My mercy has been disappointed or brought to shame. I delight particularly in a soul which has placed its trust in My goodness (1541).

Even if I had had the sins of the whole world, as well as the sins of all the condemned souls weighing on my conscience, I would not have doubted God's goodness but, without hesitation, would have thrown myself into the abyss of the divine mercy, which is always open to us; and, with a heart crushed to dust, I would have cast myself at His feet, abandoning myself totally to His holy will, which is mercy itself (1552).

O soul, whoever you may be in this world,
Even if your sins were as black as night,
Do not fear God, weak child that you are,
For great is the power of God's mercy (1652).

You see My mercy for sinners, which at this moment is revealing itself in all its power. See how little you have written about it; it is only a single drop. Do what is in your power, so that sinners may come to know My goodness (1665).

There are souls who thwart My efforts, but I have not given up on them; as often as they turn to Me, I hurry to their aid, shielding them with My mercy, and I give them the first place in My compassionate Heart (1682).

Write: I am Thrice Holy, and I detest the smallest sin. I cannot love a soul which is stained with sin; but when it repents, there is no limit to My generosity toward it. My mercy embraces and justifies it. With My mercy, I pursue sinners along all their paths, and My Heart rejoices when they return to Me. I forget the bitterness with which they fed My Heart and rejoice at their return.

Tell sinners that no one shall escape My Hand; if they run away from My Merciful Heart, they will fall into My Just Hands. Tell sinners that I am always waiting for them, that I listen intently to the beating of their heart ... when will it beat for Me? Write, that I am speaking to them through their remorse of conscience, through their failures and sufferings, through thunderstorms, through the voice

of the Church. **And if they bring all My graces to naught, I begin to be angry with them, leaving them alone and giving them what they want** (1728).

O God of compassion, You alone can justify me, and You will never reject me when I, contrite, approach Your Merciful Heart, where no one has ever been refused, even if he were the greatest sinner (1730).

Write, My daughter, that I am mercy itself for the contrite soul. A soul's greatest wretchedness does not enkindle Me with wrath; but rather, My Heart is moved towards it with great mercy (1739).

How very much I desire the salvation of souls! My dearest secretary, write that I want to pour out My divine life into human souls and sanctify them, if only they were willing to accept My grace. The greatest sinners would achieve great sanctity, if only they would trust in My mercy (1784).

Divine Mercy — Way of Life

A noble and delicate soul ... sees God in everything, finds Him everywhere, and knows how to find Him in even the most hidden things. It finds all things important, it highly appreciates all things, it thanks God for all things, it draws profit for the soul from all things, and it gives all glory to God. It places its trust in God (148).

I went across the garden one afternoon and stopped on the shore of the lake; I stood there for a long time, contemplating my surroundings. Suddenly, I saw the Lord Jesus near me, and He graciously said to me, **All this I created for you ... and know that all this beauty is nothing compared to what I have prepared for you for in eternity** (158).

I want to be completely transformed into Your mercy and to be Your living reflection, O Lord. May the greatest of all divine attributes, that of Your unfathomable mercy, pass through my heart and soul to my neighbor.

Help me, O Lord, that my eyes may be merciful, so that I may never suspect or judge from appearances, but look for what is beautiful in my neighbors' souls and come to their rescue.

Help me, that my ears may be merciful, so that I may give heed to my neighbors' needs and not be indifferent to their pains and moanings.

Help me, O Lord, that my tongue may be merciful, so that I should never speak negatively of my neighbor, but have a word of comfort and forgiveness for all.

Help me, O Lord, that my hands may be merciful and filled with good deeds, so that I may do only good to my neighbors and take upon myself the more difficult and toilsome tasks.

Help me, that my feet may be merciful, so that I may hurry to assist my neighbor, overcoming my own fatigue and weariness. My true rest is in the service of my neighbor.

Help me, O Lord, that my heart may be merciful so that I myself may feel all the sufferings of my neighbor. I will refuse my heart to no one. I will be sincere even with those who, I know, will abuse my kindness. And I will lock myself up in the most merciful Heart of Jesus. I will bear my own suffering in silence. May Your mercy, O Lord, rest upon me (163).

You Yourself command me to exercise the three degrees of mercy. The first: the act of mercy, of whatever kind. The second: the word of mercy — if I cannot carry out a work of mercy, I will assist by my words. The third: prayer — if I cannot show mercy by deeds or words, I can always do so by prayer. My prayer reaches out even there where I cannot reach out physically (163).

My daughter, I desire that your heart be formed after the model of My merciful Heart. You must be completely imbued with My mercy (167).

The soul must divert the stream of its love, but not into the mud or into a vacuum, but into God. How I rejoice when I reflect on this, for I feel clearly that He Himself is in my heart. Just Jesus alone! I love creatures insofar as they help me to become united to God. I love people because I see the image of God in them (373).

I received an inner understanding of the great reward that God is preparing for us, not only for our good deeds, but also for our sincere desire to perform them. What a great grace of God this is! (450).

One must first live in You in order to recognize You in others (503).

When I see someone else's good, I rejoice as if it were mine. The joy of others is my joy, and the suffering of others is my suffering (633).

Everything I look at speaks to me of God's mercy (651).

I ask You to make my heart so big that there will be room in it for the needs of all the souls living on the face of the earth ... . O Jesus, make my heart sensitive to all the sufferings of my neighbor, whether of body or of soul. O my Jesus, I know that You act toward us as we act toward our neighbor.

My Jesus, make my heart like unto Your merciful Heart. Jesus, help me to go through life doing good to everyone (692).

I understood that it is not possible for a person to act in the same manner towards everyone ... . Your love, Jesus, gives the soul this great prudence in its dealings with others (695).

My daughter, if I demand through you that people revere My mercy, you should be the first to distinguish yourself by this confidence in My mercy. I demand from you deeds of mercy, which are to arise out of love for Me. You are to show mercy to your neighbors always and everywhere. You must not shrink from this or try to excuse or absolve yourself from it.

I am giving you three ways of exercising mercy toward your neighbor: the first — by deed, the second — by word, the third — by prayer. In these three degrees is contained the fullness of mercy, and it is an unquestionable proof of love for Me. By this means a soul glorifies and pays reverence to My mercy. Yes, the first Sunday after Easter is the Feast of Mercy, but there must also be acts of mercy, and I demand the worship of My mercy through the solemn celebration of the Feast and through the veneration of the image which is painted. By means of this image I shall grant many graces to souls. It is to be a reminder of the demands of My mercy, because even the strongest faith is of no avail without works. O my Jesus, You Yourself must help me in everything, because You see how very little I am, and so I depend solely on Your goodness, O God (742).

I shall fight all evil with the weapon of mercy (745).

O my Jesus, teach me to open the bosom of mercy and love to everyone who asks for it. Jesus ... teach me so that all my prayers and deeds may bear the seal of Your mercy (755).

O my Jesus, you know what efforts are needed to live sincerely and unaffectedly with those from whom our nature flees, or with those who, deliberately or not, have made us suffer. Humanly speaking, this is impossible. At such times more than at others, I try to discover the Lord Jesus in such a person and for this same Jesus, I do everything for such people. In such acts, love is pure, and such practice of love gives the soul endurance and strength. I do not expect anything from creatures, and therefore I am not disappointed. I know that a creature is poor of itself, so what can one expect from it? God is everything for me; I want to evaluate everything according to God's ways (766).

I must always have a heart which is open to receive the sufferings of others, and drown my own sufferings in the Divine Heart so that they would not be noticed on the outside, in so far as possible (792).

My Master, cause my heart never to expect help from anyone, but I will always strive to bring assistance, consolation and all manner of relief to others. My heart is always open to the sufferings of others; and I will not close my heart to the sufferings of others, even though because of this I have been scornfully nicknamed "dump"; that is, [because] everyone dumps his pain into my heart. [To this] I answered that everyone has a place in my heart and I, in return, have a place in the Heart of Jesus. Taunts regarding the law of love will not narrow my heart. My soul is always sensitive on this point, and Jesus alone is the motive for my love of neighbor (871).

There is a woman here who was once one of our students. Naturally, she puts my patience to the test. She comes to see me several times a day. After each of these visits I am tired out, but I see that the Lord Jesus has sent that soul to me. Let everything glorify You, O Lord. Patience gives glory to God (920).

The knowledge of God's will came to me; that is to say, I now see everything from a higher point of view and accept all events and things, pleasant and unpleasant, with love, as tokens of the heavenly Father's special affection (956).

I suffer great pain at the sight of the sufferings of others. All these sufferings are reflected in my heart. I carry their torments in my heart so that it even wears me out physically. I would like all pains to fall upon me so as to bring relief to my neighbor (1039).

When I went out into the garden, I saw how everything was breathing the joy of spring. The trees, adorned with flowers, gave off an intoxicating odor. Everything was throbbing with joy, and the birds were singing and chirping their adoration of God and said to me, "Rejoice and be happy, Sister Faustina;" but my soul remains in torment and darkness. My soul is so sensitive to the rustle of grace [that] it knows how to talk with all created things and with everything that surrounds me, and I know why God has adorned the earth in this way (1120).

We resemble God most when we forgive our neighbors (1148).

My Jesus, penetrate me through and through so that I might be able to reflect You in my whole life. Divinize me so that my deeds may have supernatural value. Grant that I may have love, compassion and mercy for every soul without exception. O my Jesus, each of Your saints reflects one of Your virtues; I desire to reflect Your compassionate Heart, full of mercy; I want to glorify it. Let Your mercy, O Jesus, be impressed upon my heart and soul like a seal, and this will be my badge in this and the future life. Glorifying Your mercy is the exclusive task of my life (1242).

The Lord gave me to know how much He desires a soul to distinguish itself by deeds of love. And in spirit I saw how many souls are calling out to us, "Give us God." (1249).

O Jesus, I see so much beauty scattered around me, beauty for which I give You constant thanks. But I see that some souls are like stone, always cold and unfeeling. Even miracles hardly move them. Their eyes are always fixed on their feet, and so they see nothing but themselves (1284).

During meditation, the sister on the kneeler next to mine keeps coughing and clearing her throat, sometimes without a break. It occurred to me once that I might take another place for the time of the meditation, because Mass had already been offered. But then I thought that if I did change my place, the sister would notice this and might feel hurt that I had moved away from her. So I decided to continue in prayer in my usual place, and to offer this act of patience to God. Toward the end of the meditation, my soul was flooded with God's consolation, and this to the limit of what my heart could bear; and the Lord gave me to know that if I had moved away from that sister I would have moved away also from those graces that flowed into my soul (1311).

I understand that mercy is manifold; one can do good always and everywhere and at all times. An ardent love of God sees all around itself constant opportunities to share itself through deed, word and prayer (1313).

[Many souls] **are often worried because they do not have the material means with which to carry out an act of mercy. Yet spiritual mercy, which requires neither permissions nor storehouses, is much more meritorious and is within the grasp of every soul. If a soul does not exercise mercy somehow or other, it will not obtain My mercy on the day of judgment. Oh, if only souls knew how to gather eternal treasure for themselves, they would not be judged, for they would forestall My judgment with their mercy** (1317).

When I hesitate on how to act in some situations, I always ask Love. It advises best (1354).

It should be of no concern to you how anyone else acts; you are to be My living reflection, through love and mercy. I answered, "Lord, but they often take advantage of my goodness." **That makes no difference, My daughter. That is no concern of yours. As for you, be always merciful toward other people, and especially toward sinners** (1446).

O God, give me a deeper faith that I may always see in [my neighbor] Your Holy Image which has been engraved in [his] soul (1522).

Have great love for those who cause you suffering. Do good to those who hate you. I answered, "O my Master, You see very well that I feel no love for them, and that troubles me." Jesus answered, **It is not always within your power to control your feelings. You will recognize that you have love if, after having experienced annoyance and contradiction, you do not lose your peace, but pray for those who have made you suffer and wish them well** (1628).

My daughter, look into My Merciful Heart and reflect its compassion in your own heart and in your deeds, so that

you, who proclaim My mercy to the world, may yourself be aflame with it (1688).

Be always merciful as I am merciful. Love everyone out of love for Me, even your greatest enemies, so that My mercy may be fully reflected in your heart (1695).

Know that whatever good you do to any soul, I accept it as if you had done it to Me (1768).

My daughter, I desire that your heart be an abiding place of My mercy. I desire that this mercy flow out upon the whole world through your heart. Let no one who approaches you go away without that trust in My mercy which I so ardently desire for souls (1777).

Divine Mercy Sunday*

I am very surprised that You bid me to talk about this Feast of Mercy, for they tell me that there is already such a feast and so why should I talk about it? And Jesus said to me, **And who knows anything about this feast? No one! Even those who should be proclaiming My mercy and teaching people about it often do not know about it themselves. That is why I want the image to be solemnly blessed on the first Sunday after Easter, and I want it to be venerated publicly so that every soul may know about it** (341).

This Feast emerged from the very depths of My mercy, and it is confirmed in the vast depths of My tender mercies. Every soul believing and trusting in My mercy will obtain it (420).

My daughter, tell the whole world about My inconceivable mercy. I desire that the Feast of Mercy be a refuge and

---

* On April 30, 2000, Divine Mercy Sunday, Pope John Paul II canonized Sr. Faustina Kowalska as the first saint of the Great Jubilee Year. During his homily, the pope announced that the Second Sunday of Easter would now be celebrated as Divine Mercy Sunday throughout the universal Church.

shelter for all souls, and especially for poor sinners. On that day the very depths of My tender mercy are open. I pour out a whole ocean of graces upon those souls who approach the fount of My mercy. The soul that will go to Confession and receive Holy Communion shall obtain complete forgiveness of sins and punishment. On that day all the divine flood-gates through which graces flow are opened. Let no soul fear to draw near to Me, even though its sins be as scarlet. My mercy is so great that no mind, be it of man or of angel, will be able to fathom it throughout all eternity. Everything that exists has come forth from the very depths of My most tender mercy. Every soul in its relation to Me will contemplate My love and mercy throughout eternity. The Feast of Mercy emerged from My very depths of tenderness. It is My desire that it be solemnly celebrated on the first Sunday after Easter. Mankind will not have peace until it turns to the Fount of My Mercy (699).

The Feast of My Mercy has issued forth from My very depths for the consolation of the whole world (1517).

Faithfulness to God's Will

Few are the souls that are always watchful for divine graces, and even fewer of such souls who follow those inspirations faithfully (138).

Now I understand what it means to be faithful to a particular grace. That one grace draws down a whole series of others (263).

True love of God consists in carrying out God's will (279).

Faithfulness to the inspirations of the Holy Spirit — that is the shortest route [to holiness] (291).

[Mary:] *I am Mother to you all, thanks to the unfathomable mercy of God. Most pleasing to Me is that soul which faithfully carries out the will of God* (449).

My daughter, you give Me the greatest glory by faithfully fulfilling My desires (500).

The souls in purgatory told Faustina: "Do the will of God; we are happy in the measure that we have fulfilled God's will." (518).

All creatures, whether they know it or not, and whether they want to or not, always fulfill My will (586).

Jesus bent toward me, looked at me kindly and spoke to me about the will of the Heavenly Father. He told me that the most perfect and holy soul is the one that does the will of the Father, but there are not many such, and that He looks with special love upon the soul who lives His will. And Jesus told me that I was doing the will of God perfectly ... **and for this reason I am uniting Myself with you and communing with you in a special and intimate way** (603).

A strange power entered my soul, and a strange light as to what our love for God consists in; namely, in doing His will (616).

[Mary:] *Oh, how pleasing to God is the soul that follows faithfully the inspirations of His grace* (635).

There is one word I heed and continually ponder; it alone is everything to me; I live by it and die by it, and it is the holy will of God. It is my daily food. My whole soul listens intently to God's wishes. I do always what God asks of me (652).

I understood that all striving for perfection and all sanctity consists in doing God's will. Perfect fulfillment of God's will is maturity in sanctity (666).

The essence of the virtues is the will of God. He who does the will of God faithfully, practices all the virtues. In all the events and circumstances of my life, I adore and bless the holy will of God. The holy will of God is the object of my love. In the most secret depths of my soul, I live according to His will. I act exteriorly according to what I recognize inwardly as the will of God. Sweeter to me are the torments, sufferings, persecutions, and all manner of adversities by divine will than popularity, praise, and esteem by my own will (678).

Faithful submission to the will of God, always and everywhere, in all events and circumstances of life, gives great glory to God. Such submission to the will of God carries more weight with Him than long fasts, mortifications and the most severe penances. Oh, how great is the reward for one act of loving submission to the will of God! (724).

We should take great heed of our interior inspirations and follow them faithfully, and that faithfulness to one grace draws down others (756).

Although the chosen ones in heaven see God face to face and are completely and absolutely happy, still their knowledge of God is not the same. God has given me to understand this. This deeper knowledge begins here on earth, depending on the grace [given], but to a great extent it also depends on our faithfulness to that grace (771).

My daughter, you give Me most glory by patiently submitting to My will, and you win for yourself greater merit than that which any fast or mortification could ever gain for you. Know, My daughter, that if you submit your will to Mine, you draw upon yourself My special delight. This sacrifice is pleasing to Me and full of sweetness. I take great pleasure in it; there is power in it (904).

I demand of you a perfect and whole-burnt offering; an offering of the will. No other sacrifice can compare with this one. I Myself am directing your life and arranging things in such a way that you will be for Me a continual sacrifice and will always do My will. And for the accomplishment of this offering, you will unite yourself with Me on the Cross. I know what you can do. I Myself will give you many orders

directly, but I will delay the possibility of their being carried out and make it depend on others. But what the superiors will not manage to do, I Myself will accomplish directly in your soul. And in the most hidden depths of your soul, a perfect holocaust will be carried out, not just for a while, but know, My daughter, that this offering will last until your death. But there is time, so that I the Lord will fulfill all your wishes. I delight in you as in a living host; let nothing terrify you; I am with you (923).

My daughter, My delight is to unite myself with you. It is when you submit yourself to My will that you give Me the greatest glory and draw down upon yourself a sea of blessings (954).

Let all my desires, even the holiest, noblest and most beautiful, take always the last place and Your holy will, the very first. The least of Your desires, O Lord, is more precious to me than heaven, with all its treasures (957).

My sanctity and perfection consist in the close union of my will with the will of God (1107).

My path is to be faithful to the will of God in all things and at all times, especially by being faithful to inner inspirations in order to be a receptive instrument in God's hands for the carrying out of the work of His fathomless mercy (1173).

I want to look upon everything, from the point of view that nothing happens without the will of God (1183).

Nothing under the sun happens without Your will (1208).

[Mary:] *My daughter, I strongly recommend that you faithfully fulfill all God's wishes, for that is most pleasing in His holy eyes. I very much desire that you distinguish yourself in this faithfulness in accomplishing God's will. Put the will of God before all sacrifices and holocausts* (1244).

Jesus gave me to know that even the smallest thing does not happen on earth without His will (1262).

ACT OF TOTAL ABANDONMENT TO THE WILL OF GOD, WHICH IS FOR ME, LOVE AND MERCY ITSELF. Jesus-Host, whom I have this very moment received into my heart, through this union with You I offer myself to the heavenly Father as a sacrificial host, abandoning myself totally and completely to the most merciful and holy will of my God. From today onward, Your will, Lord, is my food. Take my whole being; dispose of me as You please. Whatever Your fatherly hand gives me, I will accept with submission, peace and joy. I fear nothing, no matter in what direction You lead me; helped by Your grace I will carry out everything You demand of me. I no longer fear any of Your inspirations nor do I probe anxiously to see where they will lead me. Lead me, O God, along whatever roads You please; I have placed all my trust in Your will which is, for me, love and mercy itself.

Bid me to stay in this convent, I will stay; bid me to undertake the work, I will undertake it; leave me in uncertainty about the work until I die, be blessed; give me death when, humanly speaking, my life seems particularly necessary, be blessed. Should You take me in my youth, be blessed; should You let me live to a ripe old age, be blessed. Should You give me health and strength, be blessed; should You confine me to a bed of pain for my whole life, be blessed. Should you give only failures and disappointments in life, be blessed. Should You allow my purest intentions to be condemned, be blessed. Should You enlighten my mind, be blessed. Should You leave me in darkness and all kinds of torments, be blessed.

From this moment on, I live in the deepest peace, because the Lord Himself is carrying me in the hollow of His hand. He, Lord of unfathomable mercy, knows that I desire Him alone in all things, always and everywhere.

Prayer. O Jesus, stretched out upon the Cross, I implore You, give me the grace of doing faithfully the most holy will of Your Father, in all things, always and everywhere. And when this will of God will seem to me very harsh and difficult to fulfill, it is then I beg You, Jesus, may power and strength flow upon me from Your wounds, and may my lips keep repeating, "Your will be done, O Lord." O Savior of the world, Lover of man's salvation, who in such terrible torment and pain forget Yourself to think only of the salvation of souls, O most compassionate Jesus, grant me the grace to forget myself that I may live totally for souls, helping You in the work of salvation, according to the most holy will of Your Father (1264-1265).

I want the eyes of your soul to be always fixed on My holy will, since it is in this way that you will please Me most. No sacrifices can be compared to this (1327)

The Mother of God gave me to experience the anxious concern she had in Her heart because of the Son of God. But this anxiety was permeated with such fragrance of abandonment to the will of God that I should call it rather a delight than an anxiety. I understood how my soul ought to accept the will of God in all things. It is a pity I cannot write this the way I experienced it (1437).

So today I submit myself completely and with loving consent to Your holy will, O Lord, and to Your most wise decrees, which are always full of clemency and mercy for me, though at times I can neither understand nor fathom them. O my Master, I surrender myself completely to You, who are the rudder of my soul; steer it Yourself according to Your divine wishes. I enclose myself in Your most compassionate Heart, which is a sea of unfathomable mercy (1450).

Entrust yourself completely to My will saying, "Not as I want, but according to Your will, O God, let it be done unto me." These words, spoken from the depths of one's heart, can raise a soul to the summit of sanctity in a short time. In such a soul I delight (1487).

Be at peace, My child; nothing can oppose My will. ... My will shall be done in you in all its fullness, down to the last detail of My wishes and My designs (1531).

I want to live in the spirit of faith. I accept everything that comes my way as given me by the loving will of God, who sincerely desires my happiness. And so I will accept with submission and gratitude everything that God sends me (1549).

The Lord acts toward me in a mysterious manner. There are times when He Himself allows terrible sufferings, and then again there are times when He does not let me suffer and removes everything that might afflict my soul. These are His ways, unfathomable and incomprehensible to us. It is for us to submit ourselves completely to His holy will. There are mysteries that the human mind will never fathom here on earth; eternity will reveal them (1656).

I only want to do Your holy will. Although I have great enthusiasm, and the desires burning in my heart are immense, they are never above Your will (1729).

Faustina's Mission

I feel certain that my mission will not come to an end upon my death, but will begin. O doubting souls, I will draw aside for you the veils of heaven to convince you of God's goodness, so that you will no longer continue to wound with your distrust the sweetest Heart of Jesus. God is Love and Mercy (281).

It is my greatest desire that souls should recognize You as their eternal happiness, that they should come to believe in Your goodness and glorify Your infinite mercy (305).

My chosen one, I will give you even greater graces that you may be the witness of My infinite mercy throughout all eternity (400).

When I became aware of God's great plans for me, I was frightened at their greatness and felt myself quite incapable of fulfilling them, and I began to avoid interior conversations with Him, filling up the time with vocal prayer. I did this out of humility, but I soon recognized it was not true humility, but rather a great temptation from the devil. When, on one occasion, instead of interior prayer, I took up a book of spiritual reading, I heard these words spoken distinctly and forcefully within my soul, **You will prepare the world for My final coming.** These words moved me deeply, and although I pretended not to hear them, I understood them very well and had no doubt about them. Once, being tired out from this battle of love with God, and making constant excuses on the grounds that I was unable to carry out this task, I wanted to leave the chapel, but some force held me back and I found myself powerless. Then I heard these words, **You intend to leave the chapel, but you shall not get away from Me, for I am everywhere. You cannot do anything of yourself, but with Me you can do all things** (429).

O my God, I am conscious of my mission in the Holy Church. It is my constant endeavor to plead for mercy for the world. I unite myself closely with Jesus and stand before Him as an atoning sacrifice on behalf of the world. ...

O God, how I desire that souls come to know You and to see that You have created them because of Your unfathomable love. O my Creator and Lord, I feel that I am going to remove the veil of heaven so that earth will not doubt Your goodness.

... O Eternal God, an unquenchable fire of supplication for Your mercy burns within me. I know and understand that this is my task here and in eternity. You Yourself have told me to speak about this great mercy and about Your goodness (482-483).

My name is host — or sacrifice, not in words but in deeds, in the emptying of myself and in becoming like You on the Cross, O good Jesus, my Master! (485).

I desire to go throughout the whole world and speak to souls about the great mercy of God. Priests, help me in this; use the strongest words [at your disposal] to proclaim His mercy, for every word falls short of how merciful He really is (491).

Your assignment and duty here on earth is to beg for mercy for the whole world (570).

[Mary:] *I gave the Savior to the world; as for you, you have to speak to the world about His great mercy and prepare the world for the Second Coming of Him who will come, not as a merciful Savior, but as a just Judge. Oh, how terrible is that day! Determined is the day of justice, the day of divine wrath. The angels tremble before it. Speak to souls about this great mercy while it is still the time for* [granting] *mercy. If you keep silent now, you will be answering for a great number of souls on that terrible day. Fear nothing. Be faithful to the end. I sympathize with you* (635).

I desire to glorify Your infinite mercy during my life, at the hour of death, in the resurrection and throughout eternity (697).

[Your Mercy] is the guiding thread of my life, O Lord (697).

On [the last day of my life], for the first time, I shall sing before heaven and earth the song of the Lord's fathomless mercy. This is my work and the mission which the Lord has destined for me from the beginning of the world (825).

Sinners have taken everything away from me. But that is all right; I have given everything away for their sake that they might know that You are good and infinitely merciful (893).

I desire to draw aside the veils of heaven, so that the earth would have no doubts about The Divine Mercy. My repose is in proclaiming Your mercy (930).

I feel that I am being completely transformed into prayer in order to beg God's mercy for every soul (996).

What is it you desire, My daughter? And I answered, "I desire worship and glory be given to Your mercy" (1048).

Father of great mercy, I desire that all hearts turn with confidence to Your infinite mercy (1122).

Apostle of My mercy, proclaim to the whole world My unfathomable mercy. ... My daughter, be diligent in writing down every sentence I tell you concerning My mercy, because this is meant for a great number of souls who will profit from it (1142).

My daughter, secretary of My mercy, your duty is not only to write about and proclaim My mercy, but also to beg for this grace for them, so that they too may glorify My mercy (1160).

I desire to adore Your mercy with every beat of my heart and, to the extent that I am able, to encourage souls to trust in that mercy (1234).

Glorifying Your mercy is the exclusive task of my life (1242).

O my God, let everything that is in me praise You, my Lord and Creator; and with every beat of my heart I want to praise Your unfathomable mercy. I want to tell souls of Your goodness and encourage them to trust in Your mercy. That is my mission, which You Yourself have entrusted to me, O Lord, in this life and in the life to come (1325).

O my Jesus, I have only one task to carry out in my lifetime, in death, and throughout eternity, and that is to adore Your incomprehensible mercy (1553).

My daughter, I demand that you devote all your free moments to writing about My goodness and mercy. It is your office and your assignment throughout your life to continue to make known to souls the great mercy I have for them and to exhort them to trust in My bottomless mercy (1567).

I claim veneration for My mercy from every creature, but above all from you, since it is to you that I have given the most profound understanding of this mystery (1572).

O my Jesus, I now embrace the whole world and ask You for mercy for it. When You tell me, O God, that it is enough, that Your holy will has been completely accomplished, then, my Savior, in union with You, I will commit my soul into the hands of the Heavenly Father, full of trust in Your unfathomable mercy. And when I stand at the foot of Your throne, the first hymn that I will sing will be one to Your mercy. Poor earth, I will not forget you. Although I feel that I will be immediately drowned in God as in an ocean of happiness, that will not be an obstacle to my returning to earth to encourage souls and incite them to trust in God's mercy. Indeed, this immersion in God will give me the possibility of boundless action (1582).

In the Old Covenant I sent prophets wielding thunderbolts to My people. Today I am sending you with My mercy to the people of the whole world. I do not want to punish aching mankind, but I desire to heal it, pressing it to My Merciful Heart. I use punishment when they themselves force Me to do so; My hand is reluctant to take hold of the sword of justice. Before the Day of Justice I am sending the Day of Mercy. I replied, "O my Jesus, speak to souls Yourself, because my words are insignificant" (1588).

Write down everything that occurs to you regarding My goodness. I answered, "What do You mean, Lord, what if I write too much?" And the Lord replied, **My daughter, even if you were to speak at one and the same time in all human and angelic tongues, even then you would not have said very much, but on the contrary, you would have sung in only a small measure the praises of My goodness — of My unfathomable mercy.**

O my Jesus, You Yourself must put words into my mouth, that I may praise You worthily.

My daughter, be at peace; do as I tell you. Your thoughts are united to My thoughts, so write whatever comes to your mind. You are the secretary of My mercy.

I have chosen you for that office in this life and the next life. That is how I want it to be in spite all the opposition they will give you. Know that My choice will not change (1605).

Adore, my soul, the mercy of the Lord,
O my heart, rejoice wholly in Him,
Because for this you have been chosen by Him,
To spread the glory of His mercy (1652).

In eternal happiness, I will not forget those on earth, I will obtain God's mercy for all (1653).

Be at peace, My daughter. This Work of mercy is Mine; there is nothing of you in it. It pleases Me that you are carrying out faithfully what I have commanded you to do, not adding or taking away a single word. And He gave me an interior light by which I learned that not a single word was mine (1667).

My daughter give Me souls. Know that it is your mission to win souls for Me by prayer and sacrifice, and by encouraging them to trust in My mercy (1690).

Secretary of My most profound mystery, know that yours is an exclusive intimacy with Me. Your task is to write down everything that I make known to you about My mercy, for the benefit of those who by reading these things will be comforted in their souls and will have the courage to approach Me. I therefore want you to devote all your free moments to writing (1693).

"For Your Sake ..."

For your sake I will withhold the hand which punishes; for your sake I bless the earth (431).

Know, my child, that for your sake I grant blessings to this whole vicinity. But you ought to thank Me on their behalf, as they do not thank Me for the kindnesses I extend to them. **For the sake of your gratitude, I will continue to bless them** (719).

I have offered this day for Russia. I have offered all my sufferings and prayers for that poor country. After Holy Communion, Jesus said to me, **I cannot suffer that country any longer. Do not tie My hands, My daughter.** I understood that if it had not been for the prayers of souls that are pleasing to God, that whole nation would have already been reduced to nothingness. Oh, how I suffer for that nation which has banished God from its borders! (818).

I interceded before Him for the whole world. At such moments I have the feeling that the whole world is depending on me (870).

In one instant the Lord gave me a knowledge of the sins committed throughout the whole world during these days. I fainted from fright, and even though I know the depth of God's mercy, I was surprised that God allows humanity to exist. And the Lord gave me to know who it is that upholds the existence of mankind: it is the chosen souls. When the number of the chosen ones is complete, the world will cease to exist (926).

For your sake I bless the world (1061).

Host, dear to My Heart, for your sake I bless the earth (1078).

My daughter, delight of My Heart, it is with pleasure that I look into your soul. I bestow many graces only because of you. I also withhold My punishments only because of you. You restrain Me, and I cannot vindicate the claims of My justice. You bind My hands with your love (1193).

Today, the Lord gave me knowledge of His anger toward mankind which deserves to have its days shortened because of its sins. But I learned that the world's existence is maintained by chosen souls (1434).

For the sake of your love, I withhold the just chastisements, which mankind has deserved (1489).

I feel interiorly as if I were responsible for all souls (1505).

I unite Myself with you more closely than with any other creature (1546).

My gaze rests kindly upon you before any other creature (1700).

If you did not tie My hands, I would send down many punishments upon the earth. My daughter, your look disarms My anger. Although your lips are silent, you call out to Me so mightily that all heaven is moved. I cannot escape from your requests, because you pursue Me, not from afar but within your own heart (1722).

Gratitude/Ingratitude

Above all, O my Jesus, I thank You for Your Heart — it is all I need (240).

A terrible pain immediately filled my soul because of the ingratitude of so many souls living in the world; but particularly painful was the ingratitude of souls especially chosen by God. There is no notion or comparison [which can describe it]. At the sight of this blackest ungratefulness I felt as though my heart were torn open; my strength failed me completely, and I fell on my face, not attempting to hide my loud cries. Each time I thought of God's great mercy and of the ingratitude of souls, pain stabbed at my heart, and I understood how painfully it wounded the sweetest Heart of Jesus (384).

Oh, how sorely Jesus is hurt by the ingratitude of a chosen soul! (698).

I ran the length and breadth of the whole world and thanked the unfathomable mercy of God for all the graces granted to people, and I begged pardon for everything by which they have offended Him (857).

The Lord gave me knowledge of the graces which He has been constantly lavishing on me. This light pierced me through and through, and I came to understand the inconceivable favors that God has been bestowing on me. I stayed in my cell for a long act of thanksgiving, lying face down on the ground and shedding tears of gratitude. I could not rise from the ground because, whenever I tried to do so, God's light gave me new knowledge of His grace. It was only at the third attempt that I was able to get up (1279).

I desire that my whole life be but one act of thanksgiving to You, O God (1285).

[See "Hymn to Gratitude" (1286).]

Your thanksgiving opens up new treasures of graces (1489).

In return for My blessings, I get ingratitude. In return for My love, I get forgetfulness and indifference. My Heart cannot bear this (1537).

I will accept with submission and gratitude everything that God sends me (1549).

When I entered my room, I steeped myself in prayer of thanksgiving for everything the Lord had been sending me throughout my whole life, surrendering myself totally to His most holy will (1679).

Be grateful for the smallest of My graces, because your gratitude compels Me to grant you new graces (1701).

I saw all the ingratitude of creatures toward their Creator and Lord; I asked God to protect me from spiritual blindness (1766).

Holy Communion

Oh, what awesome mysteries take place during Mass! A great mystery is accomplished in the Holy Mass. With what great devotion should we listen to and take part in this death of Jesus. One day we will know what God is doing for us in each Mass, and what sort of gift He is preparing in it for us. Only His divine love could permit that such a gift be provided for us. O Jesus, my Jesus, with what great pain is my soul pierced when I see this fountain of life gushing forth with such sweetness and power for each soul, while at the same time I see souls withering away and drying up through their own fault. O Jesus, grant that the power of mercy embrace these souls (914).

Today I felt the nearness of my Mother, my heavenly Mother, although before every Holy Communion I earnestly ask the Mother of God to help me prepare my soul for the coming of Her Son, and I clearly feel Her protection over me. I entreat Her to be so gracious as to enkindle in me the fire of God's love, such as burned in Her own pure heart at the time of the Incarnation of the Word of God (1114).

After Communion today, Jesus told me how much He desires to come to human hearts. **I desire to unite Myself with human souls; My great delight is to unite Myself with souls. Know, My daughter, that when I come to a human heart in Holy Communion, My hands are full of all kinds of graces which I want to give to the soul. But souls do not even pay any attention to Me; they leave Me to Myself and busy themselves with other things. Oh, how sad I am that souls do not recognize Love! They treat Me as a dead object** (1385).

All the good that is in me is due to Holy Communion. I owe everything to it. I feel that this holy fire has transformed me completely. Oh, how happy I am to be a dwelling place for You, O Lord! (1392).

When I was receiving Holy Communion today, I noticed in the cup a Living Host, which the priest gave to me. When I returned to my place I asked the Lord, "Why was one Host alive, since You are equally alive under each of the species?" The Lord answered me, **That is so. I am the same under each of the species, but not every soul receives Me with the same living faith as you do, My daughter, and therefore I cannot act in their souls as I do in yours** (1407).

I saw the Lord Jesus, exposed in the monstrance. In place of the monstrance, I saw the glorious face of the Lord, and He said to me, **What you see in reality, these souls see through faith. Oh, how pleasing to Me is their great faith! You see, although there appears to be no trace of life in Me, in reality it is present in its fullness in each and every Host. But for Me to be able to act upon a soul, the soul must have faith. O how pleasing to Me is living faith!** (1420).

Oh, how painful it is to Me that souls so seldom unite themselves to Me in Holy Communion. I wait for souls, and they are indifferent toward Me. I love them tenderly and sincerely, and they distrust Me. I want to lavish My graces on them, and they do not want to accept them. They treat Me as a dead object, whereas My Heart is full of love and mercy. In order that you may know at least some of My pain, imagine the most tender of mothers who has great love for her children, while those children spurn her love. Consider her pain. No one is in a position to console her. This is but a feeble image and likeness of My love (1447).

When the chaplain brought me Holy Communion, I had to control myself by sheer effort of will to keep from crying out at the top of my voice, "Welcome, my true and only Friend!" (1509).

After Holy Communion, when I had welcomed Jesus into my heart, I said to Him, "My Love, reign in the most secret recesses of my heart, there where my most secret thoughts are conceived, where You alone have free access, in this deepest sanctuary where human thought cannot penetrate. May You alone dwell there, and may everything I do exteriorly take its origin in You. I ardently desire, and I am striving with all the strength of my soul, to make You, Lord, feel at home in this sanctuary." (1721).

Consider My love in the Blessed Sacrament. Here, I am entirely yours, soul, body and divinity, as your Bridegroom. You know what love demands: one thing only, reciprocity (1770).

The most solemn moment of my life is the moment when I receive Holy Communion. I long for each Holy Communion, and for every Holy Communion I give thanks to the Most Holy Trinity.

    If the angels were capable of envy, they would envy us for two things: one is the receiving of Holy Communion and the other is suffering (1804).

I want to tell you that eternal life must begin already here on earth through Holy Communion. Each Holy Communion makes you more capable of communing with God throughout eternity (1811).

When Jesus came [in Holy Communion], I threw myself into His arms like a little child. I told Him of my joy. Jesus listened to these outpourings of my love. When I asked pardon of Jesus for not preparing myself for Holy Communion, but for continually thinking of sharing in this joy as soon as possible, He answered that **Most pleasing to Me is this preparation with which you have received Me into your heart. Today, in a special way I bless this your joy. Nothing will disturb that joy throughout this day** (1824).

My soul draws astonishing strength from Holy Communion (1826).

Humility/Littleness

I keep company with you as a child to teach you humility and simplicity (184).

He who wants to learn true humility should reflect upon the Passion of Jesus (267).

Although My greatness is beyond understanding, I commune only with those who are little. I demand of you a childlike spirit (332).

Faustina's Confessor told her: "In practice, this spiritual childhood should manifest itself in this way: a child does not worry about the past or the future, but makes use of the present moment. I want to emphasize that spiritual childlikeness in you, Sister, and I place great stress upon it" (333).

True greatness of the soul is in loving God and in humility (427).

Know that a pure soul is humble. When you lower and empty yourself before My majesty, I then pursue you with My graces and make use of My omnipotence to exalt you (576).

O my Jesus, nothing is better for the soul than humiliations. In contempt is the secret of happiness, when the soul recognizes that, of itself, it is only wretchedness and nothingness, and that whatever it possesses of good is a gift of God. When the soul sees that everything is given it freely and that the only thing it has of itself is its own misery, this is what sustains it in a continual act of humble prostration before the majesty of God. And God, seeing the soul in such a disposition, pursues it with His graces. As the soul continues to immerse itself more deeply into the abyss of its nothingness and need, God uses His omnipotence to exalt it. If there is a truly happy soul upon earth, it can only be a truly humble soul. At first, one's self-love suffers greatly on this account, but after a soul has struggled courageously, God grants it much light by which it sees how wretched and full of deception everything is. God alone is in its heart. A humble soul does not trust itself, but places all its confidence in God. God defends the humble soul and lets Himself into its secrets, and the soul abides in unsurpassable happiness which no one can comprehend (593).

Without special help from Me, you are not even capable of accepting My graces. You know who you are (738).

God allows the soul to know how much He loves it, and the soul sees that better and holier souls than itself have not received this grace. Therefore, it is filled with holy amazement, which maintains it in deep humility, and it steeps itself in its own nothingness and holy astonishment; and the more it humbles itself, the more closely God unites himself with it and descends to it (771).

Oh, how happy is the soul who already here on earth enjoys His special favors! And of such are the little and humble souls (778).

The more I come to know the greatness of God, the more joyful I become that He is as He is. And I rejoice immensely in His greatness and am delighted that I am so little because, since I am little, He carries me in His arms and holds me close to His Heart (779).

The Lord, so very great though He is, delights in humble souls. The more a soul humbles itself, the greater the kindness with which the Lord approaches it (1092).

Your humility draws Me down from My lofty throne, and I unite myself closely with you (1109).

O humility, lovely flower, I see how few souls possess you. Is it because you are so beautiful and at the same time so difficult to attain? O yes, it is both the one and the other. Even

God takes great pleasure in her. The floodgates of heaven are open to a humble soul, and a sea of graces flows down upon her. O how beautiful is a humble soul! From her heart, as from a censer, rises a varied and most pleasing fragrance which breaks through the skies and reaches God Himself, filling His Most Sacred Heart with joy. God refuses nothing to such a soul; she is all-powerful and influences the destiny of the whole world. God raises such a soul up to His very throne, and the more she humbles herself, the more God stoops down to her, pursuing her with His graces and accompanying her at every moment with His omnipotence. Such a soul is most deeply united with God. O humility, strike deep roots in my whole being. O Virgin most pure, but also most humble, help me to attain deep humility. Now I understand why there are so few saints; it is because so few souls are deeply humble (1306).

[Mary:] *I desire, My dearly beloved daughter, that you practice the three virtues that are dearest to Me — and most pleasing to God. The first is humility, humility, and once again humility; the second virtue, purity; the third virtue, love of God* (1415).

Although You are great, Lord, You allow Yourself to be overcome by a lowly and deeply humble soul. O humility, the most precious of virtues, how few souls possess you! I see only a semblance of this virtue everywhere, but not the virtue itself. Lord, reduce me to nothingness in my own eyes that I may find grace in Yours (1436).

Oh, how good the Lord is in not letting me go astray! I know that He will guard me, even jealously, but only as long as I remain little, because it is with such that the great Lord likes to commune. As to proud souls, He watches them from afar and opposes them (1440).

"Although You are so little, I know that You are God. Why do You take the appearance of such a little baby to commune with me?" **Because I want to teach you spiritual childhood.**

I want you to be very little, because when you are little, I carry you close to My Heart (1481).

Because you are weak, I take you in My arms and carry you to the home of My Father (1486).

Little matter that often I hear people say that I am proud, for I know that human judgment does not discern the motives for our actions (1502).

When, at the beginning of my religious life, following the novitiate, I began to exercise myself particularly in humility, the humiliations that God sent me were not enough for me. And so, in my excessive zeal, I looked for more of them on my own, and I often represented myself to my superiors other than I was in reality and spoke of miseries of which I had no notion. But a short time later, Jesus gave me to know that humility is only the truth. From that time on, I changed my ideas, faithfully following the light of Jesus. I learned that if a soul is with Jesus, He will not permit it to err (1503).

I have learned that the greatest power is hidden in patience. I see that patience always leads to victory, although not immediately; but that victory will become manifest after many years. Patience is linked to meekness (1514).

O my Jesus, my only mercy, allow me to see contentment in Your face as a sign of reconciliation with me, because my heart cannot bear Your seriousness; if this continues a moment longer my heart will burst with grief. You see that I am even now crushed to dust.

And at that very moment I saw myself in some kind of a palace; and Jesus gave me His hand, sat me at His side, and said with kindness, **My bride, you always please Me by your humility. The greatest misery does not stop Me from uniting Myself to a soul, but where there is pride, I am not there** (1562-1563).

My daughter, the Lord said, **know that of yourself you are just what you have gone through** [an excruciating spiritual darkness], **and it is only by My grace that you are a participant of eternal life and all the gifts I lavish on you.** And with these words of the Lord, there came to me a true knowledge of myself. Jesus is giving me a lesson in deep humility and, at the same time, one of total trust in Him. My heart is reduced to dust and ashes, and even if all people were to trample me under their feet, I would still consider that a favor.

I feel and am, in fact, very deeply permeated with the knowledge that I am nothing, so that real humiliations will be a refreshment for me (1559).

Because you are a child, you shall remain close to My Heart. Your simplicity is more pleasing to Me than your mortifications (1617).

Strive to make your heart like unto My humble and gentle Heart. Never claim your rights. Bear with great calm and patience everything that befalls you. Do not defend yourself when you are put to shame, though innocent. Let others triumph. Do not stop being good when you notice that your goodness is being abused. I Myself will speak up for you when it is necessary (1701).

When I was left alone with the Blessed Virgin, She instructed me concerning the interior life. She said, *The soul's true greatness is in loving God and in humbling oneself in His presence, completely forgetting oneself and believing oneself to be nothing; because the Lord is great, but He is well pleased only with the humble; He always opposes the proud* (1711).

O my Jesus, You know that there are times when I have neither lofty thoughts nor a soaring spirit. I bear with myself patiently and admit that that is just what I am, because all that is beautiful is a grace from God. And so I humble myself profoundly and cry out for Your help; and the grace of visitation is not slow in coming to the humble heart (1734).

Image of Divine Mercy

Paint an image according to the pattern you see, with the signature: Jesus, I trust in You. I desire that this image be venerated, first in your chapel, and [then] throughout the world.

I promise that the soul that will venerate this image will not perish. I also promise victory over [its] enemies already here on earth, especially at the hour of death. I Myself will defend it as My own glory (47-48).

The two rays denote Blood and Water. The pale ray stands for the Water which makes souls righteous. The red ray stands for the Blood which is the life of souls ... .

These two rays issued forth from the very depths of My tender mercy when My agonized Heart was opened by a lance on the Cross.

These rays shield souls from the wrath of My Father. Happy is the one who will dwell in their shelter, for the just hand of God shall not lay hold of him (299).

Not in the beauty of the color, nor of the brush lies the greatness of this image, but in My grace (313).

My gaze from this image is like My gaze from the Cross (326).

I am offering people a vessel with which they are to keep coming for graces to the fountain of mercy. That vessel is this image with the signature: "Jesus, I trust in You" (327).

By means of this Image I shall be granting many graces to souls; so let every soul have access to it (570).

Let the rays of grace enter your soul; they bring with them light, warmth, and life (1486).

Knowledge/Love

The more I come to know Him, the more ardently, the more fiercely I love Him (231).

Each time the Lord draws close to me and my knowledge of Him grows deeper, a more perfect love grows within my soul (231).

Oh, how I rejoice at Your greatness, O Lord! The more I come to know You, the more ardently I yearn for You and sigh after You! (273).

Why do so few people know You? (278).

O Lord … grant me the grace of knowing You; for the better I know You, the more I desire You, and the more my love for You grows (605).

Eternal Truth, give me a ray of Your light that I may come to know You, O Lord, and worthily glorify Your infinite mercy. And at the same time, grant me to know myself, the whole abyss of misery that I am (727).

I very much desire to know God more deeply and to love Him more ardently, for I have understood that the greater the knowledge, the stronger the love (974).

O my Jesus, give me wisdom, give me a mind great and enlightened by Your light, and this only, that I may know You better, O Lord. For the better I get to know You, the more ardently will I love You (1030).

I often ask the Lord Jesus for an intellect enlightened by faith. I express this to the Lord in these words: "Jesus, give me an intellect, a great intellect, for this only, that I may understand You better; because the better I get to know You, the more ardently will I love You. Jesus, I ask You for a powerful intellect, that I may understand divine and lofty matters. Jesus, give me a keen intellect with which I will get to know Your Divine Essence and

Your indwelling, Triune life. Give my intellect these capacities and aptitudes by means of Your special grace (1474).

Loneliness/Longing

Jesus, Friend of a lonely heart, You are my haven, You are my peace. ... You are everything to a lonely soul. You understand the soul even though it remains silent (247).

Even when I am dealing with very important matters which require attention, I do not lose the presence of God in my soul, and I am closely united with Him. With Him I go to work, with Him I go for recreation, with Him I suffer, with Him I rejoice; I live in Him and He in me. I am never alone, because He is my constant companion (318).

I have only one trusted friend in whom I confide everything, and that is Jesus — the Eucharist, and His representative — my confessor (504).

O my Jesus ... I expect no help from people; all my hope is in You (650).

I have understood that at certain and most difficult moments I shall be alone, deserted by everyone, and that I must face all the storms and fight with all the strength of my soul, even with those from whom I expected to get help.

But I am not alone, because Jesus is with me, and with Him I fear nothing. I am well aware of everything, and I know what God is demanding of me. Suffering, contempt, ridicule, persecution, and humiliation will be my constant lot. I know no other way. For sincere love — ingratitude; this is my path, marked out by the footprints of Jesus (746).

Know that My eyes follow every move of your heart with great attention. I am bringing you into seclusion so that I Myself may form your heart according to My future plans (797).

An extraordinary yearning fills my soul. I am surprised that it does not separate the soul from the body. I desire God; I want to become immersed in Him. I understand that I am in a terrible exile; my soul aspires for God with all its might. O you inhabitants of my fatherland, be mindful of this exile! When will the veils be lifted for me as well? Although I see and feel to a certain extent how very thin is the veil separating me from the Lord, I long to see Him face to face; but let everything be done according to Your will (807).

Today I felt bad that a week had gone by and no one had come to visit me. When I complained to the Lord, He answered, **Isn't it enough for you that I visit you every day?** I apologized to the Lord and the hurt vanished. O God, my strength, You are sufficient for me (827).

I marvel at how many humiliations and sufferings [Fr. Sopocko] accepts in this whole matter. ... The Lord has few such souls. ... Such souls do not have friends; they are solitary. And in this solitude, they gain strength; they draw their strength from God alone. With humility, but also with courage, they stand firmly in the face of all the storms that beat upon them. Like high-towering oaks, they are unmoved. And in this there is just this one secret: that it's from God that they draw this strength, and everything whatsoever they have need of, they have for themselves and for others. They not only carry their own burden, but also know how to take on, and are capable of taking on, the burdens of others. They are pillars of light along God's ways; they live in light themselves and shed light upon others. They themselves live on the heights, and know how to show the way to lesser ones and help them attain those heights (838).

Oh, what infinite longing envelops my soul! Jesus, how can You still leave me in this exile? I am dying of longing for You. Every touch of my soul by You wounds me immensely. Love and suffering go together; yet I would not exchange this pain caused by You for any treasure, because it is the pain of incomprehensible delights, and these wounds of the soul are inflicted by a loving hand (843).

During the morning meditation, I felt an aversion and a repugnance for all created things. Everything pales before my eyes; my spirit is detached from all things. I desire only God Himself, and yet I must live. This is a martyrdom beyond description. God imparts Himself to the soul in a loving way and draws it into the infinite depths of His divinity, but at the same time He leaves it here on earth for the sole purpose that it might suffer and die of longing for Him. And this strong love is so pure that God Himself finds pleasure in it; and self-love has no access to its deeds, for here everything is totally saturated with bitterness, and thus is totally pure. Life is a continuous dying, painful and terrible, and at the same time it is the depth of true life and of inconceivable happiness and the strength of the soul; and because of this, [the soul] is capable of great deeds for the sake of God (856).

My heart is steeped in continual bitterness, because I want to go to You, Lord, into the fullness of life. O Jesus, what a dreadful wilderness this life seems to me! There is on this earth no nourishment for either my heart or my soul. I suffer because of my longing for You, O Lord. You have left me the Sacred Host, O Lord, but it enkindles in my soul an even greater longing for You, O my Creator and Eternal God! Jesus, I yearn to become united with You. Deign to hear the sighs of Your dearly beloved. Oh, how I suffer because I am still unable to be united with You. But let it be done according to Your wishes (867).

O Jesus concealed in the Host, my sweet Master and faithful Friend, how happy my soul is to have such a Friend who always keeps me company. I do not feel lonely even though I am in isolation. Jesus-Host, we know each other — that is enough for me (877).

Although the earth is so filled with people, I feel all alone, and the earth is a terrible desert to me. O Jesus, Jesus, You know and understand the fervors of my heart; You, O Lord, alone can fill me (918).

I do not fear at all being abandoned by creatures because, even if all abandoned me, I would not be alone, for the Lord is with me (1022).

There is no greater happiness than when God gives me to know interiorly that every beat of my heart is pleasing to Him, and when He shows me that He loves me in a special way (1121).

Oh, how much I feel I am in exile! I see that no one understands my interior life. You alone understand me, You who are hidden in my heart and yet are eternally alive (1141).

I would have liked to hide and rest for a while in solitude, in a word, to be alone. At such moments, no creature is capable of giving me comfort, and even if I had wanted to say something about myself, I would have experienced new anguish. Therefore, I have kept silent at such moments and submitted myself, in silence, to the will of God — and that has given me relief. I demand nothing from creatures and communicate with them only in so far as is necessary. I will not take them into my confidence unless this is for the greater glory of God (1200).

During this conversation, I came to know [Fr. Sopocko's] anguished soul. This crucified soul resembles the Savior. Where he expects, with good reason, to find consolation, he finds the cross. He lives among many friends, but has no one but Jesus. This is how God strips the soul He especially loves (1259).

With great longing, I gaze upon you, my homeland,
When will this, my exile, come to an end?
O Jesus, such is the call of Your bride
Who suffers agony in her thirst for You (1304).

In the greatest torments of soul I am always alone, but no — not alone, for I am with You, Jesus; but here I am speaking about [other] people. None of them understands my heart, but this does not surprise me anymore (1445).

I realize how painful it is not to be understood, and especially by those whom one loves and with whom one has been very open. ... Learn from this that no one will understand a soul entirely — that is beyond human ability. Therefore, I have remained on earth to comfort your aching heart and to fortify your soul, so that you will not falter on the way (1487).

My child, make the resolution never to rely on people. Entrust yourself completely to My will (1487).

When the chaplain brought me Holy Communion, I had to control myself by sheer effort of will to keep from crying out at the top of my voice, "Welcome, my true and only Friend!" (1509).

Even among the sisters you will feel lonely. Know then that I want you to unite yourself more closely to Me. I am concerned about every beat of your heart. Every stirring of your love is reflected in My Heart. I thirst for your love (1542).

Although loneliness and darkness and sufferings of all kinds beat against my heart, the mysterious power of God supports and strengthens me (1580).

Although the times of loneliness are terrible, You make them sweet for me (1655).

When boredom and discouragement beat against your heart, run away from yourself and hide in My Heart (1760).

The Lord's Promises*

Call upon My mercy on behalf of sinners; I desire their salvation. When you say this prayer, with a contrite heart and with faith on behalf of some sinner, I will give him the grace of conversion. This is the prayer:

O Blood and Water, which gushed forth from the Heart of Jesus as a fount of mercy for us, I trust in You (186).

God has promised a great grace especially to you and to all those ... **who will proclaim My great mercy. I shall protect them Myself at the hour of death, as My own glory** (378).

With souls that have recourse to My mercy and with those that glorify and proclaim My great mercy to others, I will deal according to My infinite mercy at the hour of their death (379).

By this novena [to Divine Mercy], **I will grant every possible grace to souls** (796).

The Lord is faithful; what He once ordains — He fulfills (935).

Souls who spread the honor of My mercy I shield through their entire lives as a tender mother her infant, and at the hour of death I will not be a Judge for them, but the Merciful Savior. At that last hour, a soul has nothing with which to defend itself except My mercy. Happy is the soul that during its lifetime immersed itself in the Fountain of Mercy, because justice will have no hold on it (1075).

On each day [of the Divine Mercy Novena] **you will bring to My Heart a different group of souls, and you will immerse them in this ocean of My mercy, and I will bring all these souls into the house of My Father. You will do this in this**

---

* See also the Lord's other promises scattered throughout this appendix, especially found under the topics "Chaplet of Divine Mercy," "Divine Mercy," "Divine Mercy — for Sinners," "Divine Mercy Sunday," "Image of Divine Mercy," and "Trust."

life and in the next. I will deny nothing to any soul whom you will bring to the fount of My mercy (1209).

All those souls who will glorify My mercy and spread its worship, encouraging others to trust in My mercy, will not experience terror at the hour of death. My mercy will shield them in that final battle (1540).

Mortification

I don't demand mortification from you, but obedience. By obedience you give great glory to Me and gain merit for yourself (28).

I have granted the grace you asked for on behalf of that soul, but not because of the mortification you chose for yourself. Rather, it was because of your act of complete obedience to My representative that I granted this grace to that soul for whom you interceded and begged mercy. Know that when you mortify your own self-will, then Mine reigns within you (365).

There is more merit to one hour of meditation on My sorrowful Passion than there is to a whole year of flagellation that draws blood; the contemplation of My painful wounds is of great profit to you, and it brings Me great joy (369).

God will refuse me nothing when I entreat Him with the voice of His Son. My sacrifice is nothing in itself, but when I join it to the sacrifice of Jesus Christ, it becomes all-powerful (482).

At the beginning of Lent, I asked my confessor for some mortification for this time of fast. I was told not to cut down on my food but, while eating, to meditate on how the Lord Jesus, on the Cross, accepted vinegar and gall. This would be my mortification. I did not know that this would be so beneficial to my soul. The benefit is that I am meditating constantly on His sorrowful Passion and so, while I am eating,

I am not preoccupied with what I am eating, but am reflecting on my Lord's death (618).

Faithful submission to the will of God, always and everywhere, in all events and circumstances of life, gives great glory to God. Such submission to the will of God carries more weight with Him than long fasts, mortifications and the most severe penances. Oh, how great is the reward for one act of loving submission to the will of God! (724).

My daughter, you give Me most glory by patiently submitting to My will, and you win for yourself greater merit than that which any fast or mortification could ever gain for you (904).

Today, I received some oranges. When the sister had left, I thought to myself, "Should I eat the oranges instead of doing penance and mortifying myself during Holy Lent? After all, I am feeling a bit better." Then I heard a voice in my soul: **My daughter, you please Me more by eating the oranges out of obedience and love of Me than by fasting and mortifying yourself of your own will. A soul that loves Me very much must, ought to live by My will. I know your heart, and I know that it will not be satisfied by anything but My love alone (1023).**

[Mary:] *My daughter, I strongly recommend that you faithfully fulfill all God's wishes, for that is most pleasing in His holy eyes. I very much desire that you distinguish yourself in this faithfulness in accomplishing God's will. Put the will of God before all sacrifices and holocausts (1244).*

I want the eyes of your soul to be always fixed on My holy will, since it is in this way that you will please Me most. No sacrifices can be compared to this (1327).

It occurred to me to take my medicine, not by the spoonful, but just a little at a time, because it was expensive. Instantly, I heard a voice, **My daughter, I do not like such conduct. Accept with gratitude everything I give you through the superiors, and in this way you will please Me more** (1381).

Because you are a child, you shall remain close to My Heart. Your simplicity is more pleasing to Me than your mortifications (1617).

Do nothing beyond what I demand of you, and accept everything that My hand gives you (1779).

Novena to Divine Mercy

Novena to The Divine Mercy which Jesus instructed me to write down and make before the Feast of Mercy. It begins on Good Friday.

I desire that during these nine days you bring souls to the fountain of My mercy, that they may draw therefrom strength and refreshment and whatever grace they need in the hardships of life, and especially, at the hour of death.

On each day you will bring to My Heart a different group of souls, and you will immerse them in this ocean of My mercy, and I will bring all these souls into the house of My Father. You will do this in this life and in the next. I will deny nothing to any soul whom you will bring to the fount of My mercy. On each day you will beg My Father, on the strength of My bitter Passion, for graces for these souls (1209).

FIRST DAY. **Today, bring to Me all mankind, especially all sinners, and immerse them in the ocean of My mercy. In this way you will console Me in the bitter grief into which the loss of souls plunges Me.**

Most Merciful Jesus, whose very nature it is to have compassion on us and to forgive us, do not look upon our sins, but upon the trust which we place in Your infinite goodness. Receive us all into the abode of Your Most Compassionate Heart, and never let us escape from It. We beg this of You by

Your love which unites You to the Father and the Holy Spirit.

Eternal Father, turn Your merciful gaze upon all mankind and especially upon poor sinners, all enfolded in the Most Compassionate Heart of Jesus. For the sake of His sorrowful Passion, show us Your mercy, that we may praise the omnipotence of Your mercy forever and ever. Amen (1210-1211).

SECOND DAY. **Today bring to Me the souls of priests and religious, and immerse them in My unfathomable mercy. It was they who gave Me the strength to endure My bitter Passion. Through them, as through channels, My mercy flows out upon mankind.**

Most Merciful Jesus, from whom comes all that is good, increase Your grace in men and women consecrated to Your service,* that we may perform worthy works of mercy, and that all who see us may glorify the Father of Mercy who is in heaven.

Eternal Father, turn Your merciful gaze upon the company [of chosen ones] in Your vineyard — upon the souls of priests and religious; and endow them with the strength of Your blessing. For the love of the Heart of Your Son, in which they are enfolded, impart to them Your power and light, that they may be able to guide others in the way of salvation, and with one voice sing praise to Your boundless mercy for ages without end. Amen (1212-1213).

THIRD DAY. **Today bring to Me all devout and faithful souls, and immerse them in the ocean of My mercy. These souls brought Me consolation on the Way of the Cross. They were that drop of consolation in the midst of an ocean of bitterness.**

Most Merciful Jesus, from the treasury of Your mercy, You impart Your graces in great abundance to each and all. Receive us into the abode of Your Most Compassionate Heart and never let us escape from It. We beg this of You by that most wondrous love for the heavenly Father with which Your Heart burns so fiercely.

---

* In the original text, St. Faustina uses the pronoun "us" since she was offering this prayer as a consecrated religious sister. The wording adapted here is intended to make the prayer suitable for universal use.

Eternal Father, turn Your merciful gaze upon faithful souls, as upon the inheritance of Your Son. For the sake of His sorrowful Passion, grant them Your blessing and surround them with Your constant protection. Thus may they never fail in love or lose the treasure of the holy faith, but rather, with all the hosts of Angels and Saints, may they glorify Your boundless mercy for endless ages. Amen (1214-1215).

FOURTH DAY. **Today bring to Me those who do not believe in God* and those who do not yet know Me. I was thinking also of them during My bitter Passion, and their future zeal comforted My Heart. Immerse them in the ocean of My mercy.**

Most Compassionate Jesus, You are the Light of the whole world. Receive into the abode of Your Most Compassionate Heart the souls of those who do not believe in God and those who as yet do not know You. Let the rays of Your grace enlighten them that they, too, together with us, may extol Your wonderful mercy; and do not let them escape from the abode which is Your Most Compassionate Heart.

Eternal Father, turn Your merciful gaze upon the souls of those who do not believe in God and those who as yet do not know You, but who are enclosed in the Most Compassionate Heart of Jesus. Draw them to the light of the Gospel. These souls do not know what great happiness it is to love You. Grant that they, too, may extol the generosity of Your mercy for endless ages. Amen (1216-1217).

FIFTH DAY. **Today bring to Me the souls of those who have separated themselves from My Church,† and immerse them**

---

* Our Lord's original words here were "the pagans." Since the pontificate of Pope John XXIII, the Church has seen fit to replace this term with clearer and more appropriate terminology.

† Our Lord's original words here were "heretics and schismatics," since he spoke to St. Faustina within the context of her times. As of the Second Vatican Council, Church authorities have seen fit not to use those designations in accordance with the explanation given in the Council's Decree on Ecumenism (3). Every pope since the Council has reaffirmed that usage. Saint Faustina herself, her heart always in harmony with the mind of the Church, most certainly would have agreed. When at one time, because of the decisions of her superiors and father confessor, she was not

in the ocean of My mercy. During My bitter Passion they tore at My Body and Heart; that is, My Church. As they return to unity with the Church, My wounds heal, and in this way they alleviate My Passion.

Most Merciful Jesus, Goodness Itself, You do not refuse light to those who seek it of You. Receive into the abode of Your Most Compassionate Heart the souls of those who have separated themselves from Your Church. Draw them by Your light into the unity of the Church, and do not let them escape from the abode of Your Most Compassionate Heart; but bring it about that they, too, come to extol the generosity of Your mercy.

Eternal Father, turn Your merciful gaze upon the souls of those who have separated themselves from Your Church, who have squandered Your blessings and misused Your graces by obstinately persisting in their errors. Do not look upon their errors, but upon the love of Your own Son and upon His bitter Passion, which He underwent for their sake, since they, too, are enclosed in the Most Compassionate Heart of Jesus. Bring it about that they also may glorify Your great mercy for endless ages. Amen (1218-1219).

SIXTH DAY. **Today bring to Me the meek and humble souls and the souls of little children, and immerse them in My mercy. These souls most closely resemble My Heart. They strengthened Me during My bitter agony. I saw them as earthly Angels, who would keep vigil at My altars. I pour out upon them whole torrents of grace. Only the humble soul is able to receive My grace. I favor humble souls with My confidence.**

Most Merciful Jesus, You Yourself have said, "Learn from Me for I am meek and humble of heart." Receive into the abode of Your Most Compassionate Heart all meek and humble souls and the souls of little children. These souls send all

---

able to execute Our Lord's inspirations and orders, she declared: "I will follow Your will insofar as You will permit me to do so through Your representative. O my Jesus, I give priority to the voice of the Church over the voice with which You speak to me" (*Diary*, 497). The Lord confirmed her action and praised her for it.

heaven into ecstasy, and they are the heavenly Father's favorites. They are a sweet-smelling bouquet before the throne of God; God Himself takes delight in their fragrance. These souls have a permanent abode in Your Most Compassionate Heart, O Jesus, and they unceasingly sing out a hymn of love and mercy.

Eternal Father, turn Your merciful gaze upon meek and humble souls, and upon the souls of little children, who are enfolded in the abode which is the Most Compassionate Heart of Jesus. These souls bear the closest resemblance to Your Son. Their fragrance rises from the earth and reaches Your very throne. Father of mercy and of all goodness, I beg You by the love You bear these souls and by the delight You take in them: Bless the whole world, that all souls together may sing out the praises of Your mercy for endless ages. Amen (1220-1221; 1223).

SEVENTH DAY. **Today bring to Me the souls who especially venerate and glorify My mercy,* and immerse them in My mercy. These souls sorrowed most over My Passion and entered most deeply into My Spirit. They are living images of My Compassionate Heart. These souls will shine with a special brightness in the next life. Not one of them will go into the fire of hell. I shall particularly defend each one of them at the hour of death.**

Most Merciful Jesus, whose Heart is Love Itself, receive into the abode of Your Most Compassionate Heart the souls of those who particularly extol and venerate the greatness of Your mercy. These souls are mighty with the very power of God Himself. In the midst of all afflictions and adversities they go forward, confident of Your mercy. These souls are united to Jesus and carry all mankind on their shoulders. These souls will

---

* The text leads one to conclude that in the first prayer directed to Jesus, who is the Redeemer, it is "victim" souls and contemplatives that are being prayed for; those persons, that is, that voluntarily offered themselves to God for the salvation of their neighbor (see Col 1:24; 2 Cor 4:12). This explains their close union with the Savior and the extraordinary efficacy that their invisible activity has for others. In the second prayer, directed to the Father from whom comes "every worthwhile gift and every genuine benefit," we recommend the "active" souls, who promote devotion to Divine Mercy and exercise with it all the other works that lend themselves to the spiritual and material uplifting of their brethren.

not be judged severely, but Your mercy will embrace them as they depart from this life.

Eternal Father, turn Your merciful gaze upon the souls who glorify and venerate Your greatest attribute, that of Your fathomless mercy, and who are enclosed in the Most Compassionate Heart of Jesus. These souls are a living Gospel; their hands are full of deeds of mercy, and their spirit, overflowing with joy, sings a canticle of mercy to You, O Most High! I beg You, O God: Show them Your mercy according to the hope and trust they have placed in You. Let there be accomplished in them the promise of Jesus, who said to them, **I Myself will defend as My own glory, during their lifetime, and especially at the hour of their death, those souls who will venerate My fathomless mercy** (1224-1225).

EIGHTH DAY. **Today bring to Me the souls who are in the prison of Purgatory, and immerse them in the abyss of My mercy. Let the torrents of My Blood cool down their scorching flames. All these souls are greatly loved by Me. They are making retribution to My justice. It is in your power to bring them relief. Draw all the indulgences from the treasury of My Church and offer them on their behalf. Oh, if you only knew the torments they suffer, you would continually offer for them the alms of the spirit and pay off their debt to My justice.**

Most Merciful Jesus, You Yourself have said that You desire mercy; so I bring into the abode of Your Most Compassionate Heart the souls in Purgatory, souls who are very dear to You, and yet, who must make retribution to Your justice. May the streams of Blood and Water which gushed forth from Your Heart put out the flames of the purifying fire, that in that place, too, the power of Your mercy may be praised.

Eternal Father, turn Your merciful gaze upon the souls suffering in Purgatory, who are enfolded in the Most Compassionate Heart of Jesus. I beg You, by the sorrowful Passion of Jesus Your Son, and by all the bitterness with which

His most sacred Soul was flooded, manifest Your mercy to the souls who are under Your just scrutiny. Look upon them in no other way than through the Wounds of Jesus, Your dearly beloved Son; for we firmly believe that there is no limit to Your goodness and compassion (1226-1227).

NINTH DAY. **Today bring to Me souls who have become lukewarm,* and immerse them in the abyss of My mercy. These souls wound My Heart most painfully. My soul suffered the most dreadful loathing in the Garden of Olives because of lukewarm souls. They were the reason I cried out: "Father, take this cup away from Me, if it be Your will." For them, the last hope of salvation is to flee to My mercy.**

Most Compassionate Jesus, You are Compassion Itself. I bring lukewarm souls into the abode of Your Most Compassionate Heart. In this fire of Your pure love let these tepid souls, who, like corpses, filled You with such deep loathing, be once again set aflame. O Most Compassionate Jesus, exercise the omnipotence of Your mercy and draw them into the very ardor of Your love; and bestow upon them the gift of holy love, for nothing is beyond Your power.

Eternal Father, turn Your merciful gaze upon lukewarm souls, who are nonetheless enfolded in the Most Compassionate Heart of Jesus. Father of Mercy, I beg You by the bitter Passion of Your Son and by His three-hour agony on the Cross: Let them, too, glorify the abyss of Your mercy (1228-1229).

Offering to Merciful Love

I desire that priests proclaim this great mercy of Mine towards souls of sinners. Let the sinner not be afraid to

---

* To understand who are the souls designated for this day, and who in the *Diary* are called "lukewarm," but are also compared to ice and to corpses, we would do well to take note of the definition that the Savior Himself gave them when speaking to St. Faustina about them on one occasion: **There are souls who thwart My efforts** (1682). **Souls without love or devotion, souls full of egoism and selfishness, proud and arrogant souls full of deceit and hypocrisy, lukewarm souls who have just enough warmth to keep themselves alive: My Heart cannot bear this. All the graces I pour out upon them flow off them as off the face of a rock. I cannot stand them because they are neither good nor bad** (1702).

approach Me. The flames of mercy are burning Me — clamoring to be spent; I want to pour them out upon these souls (50).

O Most Holy Trinity! As many times as I breathe, as many times as my heart beats, as many times as my blood pulsates through my body, so many thousand times do I want to glorify Your mercy (163).

I desire to bestow My graces upon souls, but they do not want to accept them. You, at least, come to Me as often as possible and take these graces they do not want to accept. In this way you will console My Heart. Oh, how indifferent are souls to so much goodness, to so many proofs of love! My Heart drinks only of the ingratitude and forgetfulness of souls living in the world. They have time for everything, but they have no time to come to Me for graces (367).

My daughter, take the graces that others spurn; take as many as you can carry (454).

I want to give myself to souls and to fill them with My love, but few there are who want to accept all the graces My love has intended for them. My grace is not lost; if the soul for whom it was intended does not accept it, another soul takes it (1017).

The flames of mercy are burning Me. I desire to pour them out upon human souls. Oh, what pain they cause Me when they do not want to accept them! (1074).

The Lord has given me to know that when a soul does not accept the graces intended for it, another soul receives them immediately. O my Jesus, make me worthy of accepting Your graces because, of myself, I can do nothing. Without Your help, I cannot even utter Your Name worthily (1294).

After Holy Mass, I went out to the garden to make my meditation, since there were not yet any patients in the garden at this time, and so I felt at ease. As I was meditating on the blessings of God, my heart was burning with a love so strong that it seemed my breast would burst. Suddenly Jesus stood before me and said, **What are you doing here so early?** I answered, "I am thinking of You, of Your mercy and Your goodness toward us. And You, Jesus, what are You doing here?" **I have come out to meet you, to lavish new graces on you. I am looking for souls who would like to receive My grace** (1705).

Passion of the Lord

I desire that you know more profoundly the love that burns in My Heart for souls, and you will understand this when you meditate on My Passion (186).

During the last days of the carnival, when I was making a Holy Hour, I saw how the Lord Jesus suffered as He was being scourged. Oh, such an inconceivable agony! How terribly Jesus suffered during the scourging! O poor sinners, on the day of judgment how will you face the Jesus whom you are now torturing so cruelly? His blood flowed to the ground, and in some places His flesh started to fall off. I saw a few bare bones on His back. The meek Jesus moaned softly and sighed (188).

I please Him best by meditating on His sorrowful Passion (267).

O my Jesus, my only hope, thank You for the book which You have opened before my soul's eyes. That book is Your Passion which You underwent for love of me. It is from this book that I have learned how to love God and souls. In this book there are found for us inexhaustible treasures. O Jesus, how few souls understand You in Your martyrdom of love! Oh, how great is the fire of purest love which burns in Your Most Sacred Heart! Happy the soul that has come to understand the love of the Heart of Jesus! (304).

When I become immersed in the Lord's Passion, I often see the Lord Jesus, during adoration, in this manner: after the scourging, the torturers took the Lord and stripped Him of

His own garment, which had already adhered to the wounds; as they took it off, His wounds reopened; then they threw a dirty and tattered scarlet cloak over the fresh wounds of the Lord. The cloak, in some places, barely reached His knees. They made Him sit on a piece of beam. And then they wove a crown of thorns, which they put on His sacred head. They put a reed in His hand and made fun of Him, bowing to Him as to a king. Some spat in His face, while others took the reed and struck Him on the head with it. Others caused Him pain by slapping Him; still others covered His face and struck Him with their fists. Jesus bore all this with meekness. Who can comprehend Him — comprehend His suffering? Jesus' eyes were downcast. I sensed what was happening in the most sweet Heart of Jesus at that time. Let every soul reflect on what Jesus was suffering at that moment. They tried to outdo each other in insulting the Lord. I reflected: Where does such malice in man come from? It is caused by sin. Love and sin have met (408).

When I came for adoration, an inner recollection took hold of me immediately, and I saw the Lord Jesus tied to a pillar, stripped of His clothes, and the scourging began immediately. I saw four men who took turns at striking the Lord with scourges. My heart almost stopped at the sight of these tortures. The Lord said to me, **I suffer even greater pain than that which you see.** And Jesus gave me to know for what sins He subjected himself to the scourging: these are sins of impurity. Oh, how dreadful was Jesus' moral suffering during the scourging! Then Jesus said to me, **Look and see the human race in its present condition.** In an instant, I saw horrible things: the executioners left Jesus, and other people started scourging Him; they seized the scourges and struck the Lord mercilessly. These were priests, religious men and women; and high dignitaries of the Church, which surprised me greatly. There were lay people of all ages and walks of life. All vented their malice on the innocent Jesus. Seeing this, my heart fell as if into a mortal agony. And while the executioners had been scourging Him, Jesus had been silent and looking into the distance; but when those other souls I mentioned scourged Him, Jesus closed His eyes, and a soft, but most painful moan escaped from His Heart. And Jesus gave me to know in detail the gravity of the malice of these ungrateful souls: **You see, this is a torture greater than My death.** Then my lips too fell silent, and I began to experience the agony of death, and I felt that no one would comfort me or snatch me from that state but the One who had put me into it. Then the Lord said to me, **I see the sincere pain of your heart which brought great solace to My Heart. See and take comfort** (445).

Palm Sunday. This Sunday, I experienced in a special way the sentiments of the most sweet Heart of Jesus. My spirit was there where Jesus was. I saw Jesus riding on a donkey's foal, and the disciples and a great multitude with branches in their hands joyfully accompanying the Lord Jesus. Some strewed them before His feet where He was riding, while others raised their branches in the air, leaping and jumping before the Lord and not knowing what to do for joy. And I saw another crowd which came out to meet Jesus, likewise with joyful faces and with branches in their hands, and they were crying out unceasingly with joy. There were little children there also. But Jesus was very grave, and the Lord gave me to know how much He was suffering at the time. And at that moment, I saw nothing but only Jesus, whose Heart was saturated with ingratitude (642).

It is in My Passion that you must seek light and strength. After the confession, I meditated on Jesus' terrible Passion, and I understood that what I was suffering was nothing compared to the Savior's Passion, and that even the smallest imperfection was the cause of this terrible suffering (654).

Jesus allowed me to enter the Cenacle, and I was a witness to what happened there. However, I was most deeply moved when, before the Consecration, Jesus raised His eyes to heaven and entered into a mysterious conversation with His Father. It is only in eternity that we shall really understand that moment. His eyes were like two flames; His face was radiant, white as snow; His whole personage full of majesty, His soul full of longing. At the moment of Consecration, love rested satiated — the sacrifice fully consummated. Now only the external ceremony of death will be carried out — external destruction; the essence [of it] is in the Cenacle. Never in my whole life had I understood this mystery so profoundly as during that hour of adoration. Oh, how ardently I desire that the whole world would come to know this unfathomable mystery! (684).

This evening, I saw the Lord Jesus just as He was during His Passion. His eyes were raised up to His Father, and He was praying for us (736).

There are few souls who contemplate My Passion with true feeling; I give great graces to souls who meditate devoutly on My Passion (737).

Today, during the Passion Service, I saw Jesus being tortured and crowned with thorns and holding a reed in His hand. Jesus was silent as the soldiers were bustling about, vying with each other in torturing Him. Jesus said nothing, but just looked at me, and in that gaze I felt His pain, so terrible that we have not the faintest idea of how much He suffered for us before He was crucified. ... When I see Jesus tormented, my heart is torn to pieces, and I think: what will become of sinners if they do not take advantage of the Passion of Jesus: In His Passion, I see a whole sea of mercy (948).

And when it seems to you that your suffering exceeds your strength, contemplate My wounds, and you will rise above human scorn and judgment. Meditation on My Passion will help you rise above all things (1184).

I saw the suffering Savior. What struck me was that Jesus was so peaceful amidst His great sufferings. I understood that this was a lesson for me on what my outward behavior should be in the midst of my various sufferings (1467).

My daughter, meditate frequently on the sufferings which I have undergone for your sake, and then nothing of what you suffer for Me will seem great to you. You please Me most when you meditate on My Sorrowful Passion. Join your little sufferings to My Sorrowful Passion, so that they may have infinite value before My Majesty (1512).

Palm Sunday. During Mass, Jesus gave me to know the pain of His soul, and I could clearly feel how the hymns of *Hosanna* reverberated as a painful echo in His Sacred Heart. My soul, too, was inundated by a sea of bitterness, and each *Hosanna* pierced my own heart to its depths. My whole soul was drawn close to Jesus. I heard Jesus' voice: **My daughter, your compassion for Me refreshes Me. By meditating on My Passion, your soul acquires a distinct beauty** (1657).

Look into My Heart and see there the love and mercy which I have for humankind, and especially for sinners. Look, and enter into My Passion (1663).

My daughter, today consider My Sorrowful Passion in all its immensity. Consider it as if it had been undertaken for your sake alone (1761).

Prayer

Every single grace comes to the soul through prayer (146).

I often wait with great graces until towards the end of prayer (268).

I understood how much God loves us, how simple He is, though incomprehensible, and how easy it is to commune with Him, despite His great majesty. With no one do I feel as free and as much at ease as with Him (603).

On the eve of the retreat, I started to pray that the Lord Jesus might give me just a little health so that I could take part in the retreat, because I was feeling so ill that I thought perhaps it might be my last. However, as soon as I had started praying I felt a strange dissatisfaction. I interrupted the prayer of supplication and began to thank the Lord for everything He sends me, submitting myself completely to His holy will. Then I felt profound peace of soul (724).

There are times in life when the soul finds comfort only in profound prayer. Would that souls knew how to persevere in prayer at such times. This is very important (860).

Jesus gave me to understand how a soul should be faithful to prayer despite torments, dryness and temptations; because oftentimes the realization of God's great plans depends mainly on such prayer. If we do not persevere in such prayer, we frustrate what the Lord wanted to do through us or within us. Let every soul remember these words: "And being in anguish, He prayed longer." I always prolong such prayer as much as is in my power and in conformity with my duty (872).

Although I know that there is a capability through grace which the Church gives me, there is still a treasure of graces which You give us, O Lord, when we ask You for them (1474).

When we pray, we ought not force the Lord God to give us what we want, but we should rather submit to His holy will (1525).

Prayer — Bold/Powerful

God will refuse me nothing when I entreat Him with the voice of His Son. My sacrifice is nothing in itself, but when I join it to the sacrifice of Jesus Christ, it becomes all powerful (482).

God grants everything that we ask of Him with trust (609).

On this particular day, when I was feeling so bad and still went to work, every now and then I would feel sick. It was so very hot that, even without working, a person felt terrible, not to mention what it was like when one had to work while suffering. So, before noon, I straightened up from my work, looked up to the sky with great trust and said to the Lord, "Jesus, cover the sun, for I cannot stand this heat any longer." And, O wonder, at that very moment a white cloud covered the sun and, from then on, the heat became less intense. When a little while later I began to reproach myself that I did not bear the heat, but begged for relief, Jesus Himself put me at ease (701).

"Jesus, I beg You, by the inconceivable power of Your mercy, that all the souls who will die today escape the fire of hell, even if they have been the greatest sinners. Today is Friday, the memorial of Your bitter agony on the Cross; because Your mercy is inconceivable, the Angels will not be surprised at this." Jesus pressed me to His Heart and said, **My beloved daughter, you have come to know well the depths of My mercy. I will do what you ask, but unite yourself continually with My agonizing Heart and make reparation to My justice. Know that you have asked Me for a great thing, but I see that this was dictated by your pure love for Me; that is why I am complying with your requests** (873).

This morning after completing my spiritual exercises, I began at once to crochet. I sensed a stillness in my heart; I sensed that Jesus was resting in it. That deep and sweet consciousness of God's presence prompted me to say to the Lord, "O Most Holy Trinity dwelling in my heart, I beg You: grant the grace of conversion to as many souls as the [number of] stitches that I will make today with this crochet hook." Then I heard these words in my soul: **My daughter, too great are your demands.** "Jesus, You know that for You it is easier to grant much rather than a little." **That is so, it is less difficult for Me to grant a soul much rather than a little, but every conversion of a sinful soul demands sacrifice.** "Well, Jesus, I offer You this whole-hearted work of mine; this offering does not seem to me to be too small for such a large number of souls; You know, Jesus, that for thirty years You were saving souls by just this kind of work. And since holy obedience forbids me to perform great penances and mortifications, therefore I ask You, Lord: accept these mere nothings stamped with the seal of obedience as great things." Then I heard a voice in my soul: **My dear daughter, I comply with your request** (961).

I thirst. I thirst for the salvation of souls. Help Me, My daughter, to save souls. Join your sufferings to My Passion and offer them to the heavenly Father for sinners (1032).

Join your little sufferings to My Sorrowful Passion, so that they may have infinite value before My Majesty (1512).

I recommend that you unite, in a special way, even your smallest deeds to My merits, and then My Father will look upon them with love as if they were My own (1543).

When I immersed myself in prayer and united myself with all the Masses that were being celebrated all over the world at that time, I implored God, for the sake of all these Holy Masses, to have mercy on the world and especially on poor sinners who were dying at that moment. At the same instant, I received an interior answer from God that a thousand souls had received grace through the prayerful mediation I had offered to God. We do not know the number of souls that is ours to save through our prayers and sacrifices; therefore, let us always pray for sinners (1783).

Prayer — Conversation with the Lord

When I feel that the suffering is more than I can bear, I take refuge in the Lord in the Blessed Sacrament, and I speak to Him with profound silence (73).

I spoke much with the Lord, without uttering a single word (137).

Jesus, living Host, You are my Mother, You are my all! It is with simplicity and love, with faith and trust that I will always come to You, O Jesus! I will share everything with You, as a child with its loving mother, my joys and sorrows — in a word, everything (230).

At that moment Jesus asked me, **My child, how is your retreat going?** I answered, "But Jesus, You know how it is going." **Yes, I know, but I want to hear it from your own lips and from your heart** (295).

I sense His divine gaze; I have long talks with Him without saying a word (411).

Jesus gave me to know that I should ask Him more questions and seek His advice (560).

I will tell you most when you converse with Me in the depths of your heart (581).

When you reflect upon what I tell you in the depths of your heart, you profit more than if you had read many books. Oh, if souls would only want to listen to My voice when I am speaking in the depths of their hearts, they would reach the peak of holiness in a short time (584).

With no one else is it so easy to talk as with You, O God (670).

I spend every free moment at the feet of the hidden God. He is my Master; I ask Him about everything; I speak to Him about everything. Here I obtain strength and light; here I learn everything; here I am given light on how to act toward my neighbor (704).

I am very pleased that you confide your fears to Me, My daughter: Speak to Me about everything in a completely simple and human way; by this you will give Me great joy. I understand you because I am God-Man. This simple

language of your heart is more pleasing to Me than the hymns composed in My honor. Know, My daughter, that the simpler your speech is, the more you attract Me to yourself. And now, be at peace close to My Heart (797).

My Jesus, You see that I do not know how to write well and, on top of that, I don't even have a good pen. And often it scratches so badly that I must put sentences together, letter by letter. And that is not all. I also have the difficulty of keeping secret from the sisters the things I write down, and so I often have to shut my notebook every few minutes and listen patiently to someone's story, and then the time set aside for writing is gone. And when I shut the notebook suddenly, the ink smears (839).

My daughter, I am told that there is much simplicity in you, so why do you not tell Me about everything that concerns you, even the smallest details? Tell Me about everything, and know that this will give Me great joy. I answered, "But You know about everything, Lord." And Jesus replied to me, Yes, I do know; but you should not excuse yourself with the fact that I know, but with childlike simplicity talk to Me about everything, for My ears and Heart are inclined towards you, and your words are dear to Me (921).

You will give Me much pleasure if, each evening, you will speak to Me especially about this task [of being assigned to gate duty] (1267).

Tell me all, My child, hide nothing from Me, because My loving Heart, the Heart of your Best Friend, is listening to you (1486).

Poor soul, I see that you suffer much and that you do not have even the strength to converse with Me. So I will speak to you. Even though your sufferings were very great, do not lose heart or give in to despondency (1487).

But tell Me, My child, who has dared to wound your heart? Tell Me about everything, be sincere in dealing with Me, reveal all the wounds of your heart. I will heal them, and your suffering will become a source of your sanctification (1487).

Talk to Me simply, as a friend to a friend (1487).

Speak, My beloved child, for I am always listening. I wait for you. What do you desire to say? (1489).

In silence I tell You everything, Lord, because the language of love is without words (1489).

Let us talk confidentially and frankly, as two hearts that love one another do (1489).

In the evening, I went in for a long talk with the Lord Jesus. … I poured out my whole heart before Him, all my troubles, fears and apprehensions. Jesus lovingly listened to me and then said, Be at peace, My child, I am with you (1674).

My Lord and Creator, Your goodness encourages me to converse with You. Your mercy abolishes the chasm which separates the Creator from the creature. To converse with You, O Lord, is the delight of my heart (1692).

The moments which are most pleasant to me are those when I converse with the Lord within the center of my being. I try my very best not to leave Him alone. He likes to be always with us (1793).

Prayer — Gaze of the Lord

[Regarding Fr. Sopocko:] By day and by night My gaze is fixed upon him (86).

[Regarding Fr. Sopocko:] My gaze is on him day and night (90).

We understand each other mutually with one look (201).

I sense His divine gaze; I have long talks with Him without saying a word (411).

Truly, how sweet is the look of my Lord; His eyes penetrate my soul to its most secret depths. My spirit communicates with God without any word being spoken (560).

I know that the gaze of the Mighty One rests upon me (708).

Under His loving gaze, my soul gains strength and power and an awareness that it loves and is especially loved. It knows that the Mighty One protects it. Such prayer, though short, benefits the soul greatly, and whole hours of ordinary prayer do not give the soul that light which is given by a brief moment of this higher form of prayer (815).

During supper in the refectory today, I felt God's gaze in the depths of my heart. Such a vivid presence pervaded my soul that, for a while, I had no idea where I was. The sweet presence of God kept filling my soul and, at times, I could not understand what the sisters were saying to me (1391).

Prayer — Intercession

O Jesus, eternal Truth, our Life, I call upon You and I beg Your mercy for poor sinners. O sweetest Heart of my Lord, full of pity and unfathomable mercy, I plead with You for poor sinners. O Most Sacred Heart, Fount of Mercy from which gush forth rays of inconceivable graces upon the entire human race, I beg of You light for poor sinners. O Jesus, be mindful of Your own bitter Passion and do not permit the loss of souls redeemed at so dear a price of Your most precious Blood (72).

Gather all sinners from the entire world and immerse them in the abyss of My mercy. ... On the day of My feast, the Feast of Mercy, you will go through the whole world and

bring fainting souls to the spring of My mercy. I shall heal and strengthen them (206).

God does not always accept our petitions for the souls [in purgatory] we have in mind, but directs these to other souls. Hence, although we do not relieve the souls we intended to relieve in their purgatorial suffering, still our prayer is not lost (621).

I pray most of all for souls that are experiencing inner sufferings (694).

My daughter, don't be exerting yourself so much with words. Those whom you love in a special way, I too love in a special way, and for your sake, I shower My graces upon them. I am pleased when you tell Me about them, but don't be doing so with such excessive effort (739).

How terribly souls suffer [in hell]! Consequently, I pray even more fervently for the conversion of sinners (741).

With my heart I encompass the whole world, especially countries which are uncivilized or where there is persecution. I am praying for mercy upon them (742).

Oh, how much we should pray for the dying! Let us take advantage of mercy while there is still time for mercy (1035).

The loss of each soul plunges Me into mortal sadness. You always console Me when you pray for sinners. The prayer most pleasing to Me is prayer for the conversion of sinners. Know, My daughter, that this prayer is always heard and answered (1397).

I steeped myself in profound prayer and asked the Lord for graces for [those who are dear to me] as a group and then for each one individually. Jesus gave me to know how much this pleased Him, and my soul was filled with even greater joy to see that God loves in a special way those whom we love (1438).

All the treasures of My Heart are open to you. Take from this Heart all that you need for yourself and for the whole world (1489).

Pray as much as you can for the dying. By your entreaties, obtain for them trust in My mercy, because they have most need of trust, and have it the least. Be assured that the grace of eternal salvation for certain souls in their final moment depends on your prayer. You know the whole abyss of My mercy, so draw upon it for yourself and especially for poor sinners. Sooner would heaven and earth turn into nothingness than would My mercy not embrace a trusting soul (1777).

Prayer — Recollection/Silence

I will not allow myself to be so absorbed in the whirlwind of work as to forget about God (82).

Great are the faults committed by the tongue. The soul will not attain sanctity if it does not keep watch over its tongue (92).

In order to hear the voice of God, one has to have silence in one's soul and to keep silence; not a gloomy silence, but an interior silence; that is to say, recollection in God. One can speak a great deal without breaking silence and, on the contrary, one can speak little and be constantly breaking silence. ... God does not give Himself to a chattering soul which, like a drone in a beehive, buzzes around but gathers no honey. A talkative soul is empty inside (118).

I spoke much with the Lord, without uttering a single word (137).

The soul that reflects receives much light. A distracted soul runs the risk of a fall. ... But for the Spirit of God to act in the soul, peace and recollection are needed (145).

I prayed as I do at certain times, without saying a word (154).

Even when I am dealing with very important matters which require attention, I do not lose the presence of God in my soul, and I am closely united with Him. With Him I go to work, with Him I go for recreation, with Him I suffer, with Him I rejoice; I live in Him and He in me. I am never alone, because He is my constant companion (318).

I sense His divine gaze; I have long talks with Him without saying a word (411).

If only souls would become recollected, God would speak to them at once, for dissipation drowns out the word of the Lord (452).

Silence is a sword in the spiritual struggle. A talkative soul will never attain sanctity. The sword of silence will cut off everything that would like to cling to the soul. We are sensitive to words and quickly want to answer back, without taking any regard as to whether it is God's will that we should speak. A silent soul is strong; no adversities will harm it if it perseveres in silence. The silent soul is capable of attaining the closest union with God. It lives almost always under the inspiration of the Holy Spirit. God works in a silent soul without hindrance (477).

I try to keep You company throughout the day, I do not leave You alone for even a moment. Although I am in the company of other people or with our wards, my heart is always united to Him. When I am asleep I offer Him every beat of my heart; when I awaken I immerse myself in Him without saying a word. When I awaken I adore the Holy Trinity for a short while and thank God for having deigned to give me yet another day, that the mystery of the incarnation of His Son may once more be repeated in me, and that once again His sorrowful Passion may unfold before my eyes. I then try to make it easier for Jesus to pass through me to other souls. I go everywhere with Jesus; His presence accompanies me everywhere (486).

I will safeguard my interior and exterior silence so that Jesus can rest in my heart (504).

The Holy Spirit does not speak to a soul that is distracted and garrulous. He speaks by His quiet inspirations to a soul that is recollected, to a soul that knows how to keep silence. If silence were strictly observed, there would not be any grumbling, bitterness, slandering, or gossip, and charity would not be tarnished. In a word, many wrongs would not be done. Silent lips are pure gold and bear witness to holiness within (552).

Keeping silent when one ought to speak is an imperfection and sometimes even a sin (553).

The Mother of God told me to do what She had done, that, even when joyful, I should always keep my eyes fixed on the cross (561).

[Mary:] *My daughter, strive after silence and humility, so that Jesus, who dwells in your heart continuously, may be able to rest. Adore Him in your heart; do not go out from your inmost being. My daughter, I shall obtain for you the grace of an interior life which will be such that, without ever leaving that interior life, you will be able to carry out all your external duties with even greater care. Dwell with Him continuously in your own heart. He will be your strength. Communicate with creatures only in so far as is necessary and is required by your duties. You are a dwelling place pleasing to the living God, in you He dwells continuously with love and delight* (785).

My room is next to the men's ward. I didn't know that men were such chatterboxes. From morning till late at night, there is talk about various subjects. The women's ward is much quieter. It is women who are always blamed for this; but I have had occasion to be convinced that the opposite is true. It is very difficult for me to concentrate on my prayer in the midst of these jokes and this laughter. They do not disturb me when the grace of God takes complete possession of me, because then I do not know what is going on around me.

My Jesus, how little these people talk about You. They talk about everything but You, Jesus. And if they talk so little [about You], it is quite probable that they do not think about You at all. The whole world interests them; but about You, their Creator, there is silence. Jesus, I am sad to see this great indifference and ingratitude of creatures. O my Jesus, I want to love You for them and to make atonement to You, by my love (803-804).

Silence is so powerful a language that it reaches the throne of the living God. Silence is His language, though secret, yet living and powerful (888).

The Lord gave me to know how displeased He is with a talkative soul. **I find no rest in such a soul. The constant din tires Me, and in the midst of it the soul cannot discern My voice** (1008).

I want to be a quiet little dwelling place for Jesus to rest in (1021).

In silence I tell You everything, Lord, because the language of love is without words (1489).

O my Jesus, I know that, in order to be useful to souls, one has to strive for the closest possible union with You, who are Eternal Love. One word from a soul united to God effects more good in souls than eloquent discussions and sermons from an imperfect soul (1595).

Strive for a life of recollection so that you can hear My voice, which is so soft that only recollected souls can hear it (1779).

I am trying my best for interior silence in order to be able to hear His voice (1828).

Priests

I have offered this day for priests. I have suffered more today than ever before, both interiorly and exteriorly (823).

O my Jesus, I beg You on behalf of the whole Church: Grant it love and the light of Your Spirit, and give power to the words of priests so that hardened hearts might be brought to repentance and return to You, O Lord. Lord, give us holy priests; You Yourself maintain them in holiness. O Divine and Great High Priest, may the power of Your mercy accompany them everywhere and protect them from the devil's traps and snares which are continually being set for the souls of priests. May the power of Your mercy, O Lord, shatter and bring to naught all that might tarnish the sanctity of priests, for You can do all things (1052).

The Lord Jesus greatly protects His representatives on earth. How closely He is united with them; and He orders me to give priority to their opinion over His. I have come to know the great intimacy which exists between Jesus and the priest. Jesus defends whatever the priest says, and often complies with his wishes, and sometimes makes His own relationship with a soul depend on the priest's advice. O Jesus, through a special grace, I have come to know very clearly to what extent You have shared Your power and mystery with them, more so than with the Angels. I rejoice in this, for it is all for my good (1240).

[Fr. Sopocko] **is a priest after My own Heart; his efforts are pleasing to Me. You see, My daughter, that My will must be done and that which I had promised you, I shall do. Through him I spread comfort to suffering and careworn souls. Through him it pleased Me to proclaim the worship of My mercy. And through this work of mercy more souls will come close to Me than otherwise would have, even if he had kept giving absolution day and night for the rest of his life, because by so doing, he would have labored only for as long as he lived; whereas, thanks to** this work of mercy, he will be laboring till the end of the world (1256).

Tell My priests that hardened sinners will repent on hearing their words when they speak about My unfathomable mercy, about the compassion I have for them in My Heart. To priests who proclaim and extol My mercy, I will give wondrous power; I will anoint their words and touch the hearts of those to whom they will speak (1521).

My daughter, do not pay so much attention to the vessel of grace as to the grace itself which I give you, because you are not always pleased with the vessel, and then the graces, too, become deficient. I want to guard you from that, and I want you never to pay attention to the vessel in which I send you My grace. Let all the attention of your soul be concentrated on responding to My grace as faithfully as possible (1599).

[To be read in light of 1052:] During Holy Mass, I came to know that a certain priest does not effect much in souls because he thinks about himself and so is alone. God's grace takes flight; he relies on trifling external things, which have no importance in the eyes of God; and, being proud, he fritters away his time, wearing himself out to no purpose (1719).

O most compassionate Jesus, I have not always known how to profit from these priceless gifts, because I have paid too little attention to the gift itself and too much to the vessel in which You were giving me Your gifts. My most sweet Master, it will be different from now on. I will put Your gifts to the best use of which my soul is capable. Living faith will support me. Whatever the form might be, under which You send me Your grace, I will accept it as coming directly from You, without considering the vessel in which You send it. If it will not always be within my power to accept it with joy, I will always accept it with submission to Your holy will (1759).

Purity of Intention

One thing is needed to please God: to do even the smallest things out of great love (140).

The soul must divert the stream of its love, but not into the mud or into a vacuum, but into God (373).

I always consider what is more pleasing to Jesus (380).

On a certain occasion, I understood how very displeased God is with an act, however commendable, that does not bear the stamp of a pure intention. Such deeds incite God to punishment rather than to reward. May such deeds be as few as possible in our lives; indeed, in religious life, there should be none at all (484).

I was told to do everything with the pure intention of reparation for poor sinners. This keeps me in continual union with God, and this intention perfects my actions, because everything I do is done for immortal souls. All hardships and fatigue are as nothing when I think that they reconcile sinful souls with God (619).

The greatest works are worthless in My eyes if they are done out of self-will, and often they are not in accord with My will and merit punishment rather than reward (639).

If one does not know what is better, one must reflect, consider and seek advice, because one must not act with an uncertain conscience. When uncertain, say to yourself: "Whatever I do will be good. I have the intention of doing good." The Lord God accepts what we consider good, and the Lord God also accepts and considers it as good. One should not worry if, after some time, one sees that these things are not good. God looks at the intention with which we begin, and will reward us accordingly. This is a principle which we ought to follow (800).

Even if I did not accomplish any of the things the Lord is demanding of me, I know that I shall be rewarded as if I had fulfilled everything, because He sees the intention with which I begin (822).

O my Jesus, give me strength to endure suffering so that I may not make a wry face when I drink the cup of bitterness. Help me Yourself to make my sacrifice pleasing to You. May it not be tainted by my self-love, even though it extend over many years. May purity of intention make it pleasing to You, fresh and full of life. This life of mine is a ceaseless struggle, a constant effort to do Your holy will; but may everything that is in me, both my misery and my strength, give praise to You, O Lord (1740).

Put your self-love in the last place, so that it does not taint your deeds (1760).

Sanctity According to the Little Way

[St. Thérèse to Sr. Faustina:] "Yes, you will be a saint just as I am, but you must trust in the Lord Jesus" (150).

O my Master, shape my soul according to Your will and Your eternal designs! (195).

My Heart was moved by great mercy towards you, My dearest child, when I saw you torn to shreds because of the great pain you suffered in repenting for your sins. I see your love, so pure and true that I give you first place among the virgins. You are the honor and glory of My Passion. I see every abasement of your soul, and nothing escapes my attention. I lift up the humble even to my very throne, because I want it so (282).

O God, one in the Holy Trinity, I want to love You as no human soul has ever loved You before; and although I am utterly miserable and small, I have, nevertheless, cast the anchor of my trust deep down into the abyss of Your mercy … . In spite of my great misery I fear nothing, but hope to sing You a hymn of glory forever. Let no soul, even the most miserable, fall prey to doubt; for, as long as one is alive, each one can become a great saint, so great is the power of God's grace. It remains only for us not to oppose God's action (283).

O my Jesus, how very easy it is to become holy; all that is needed is a bit of good will. If Jesus sees this little bit of good will in the soul, He hurries to give Himself to the soul, and nothing can stop Him, neither shortcomings nor falls — absolutely nothing. Jesus is anxious to help that soul, and if it is faithful to this grace from God, it can very soon attain the highest holiness possible for a creature here on earth. God is very generous and does not deny His grace to anyone. Indeed He gives more than what we ask of Him. Faithfulness to the inspirations of the Holy Spirit — that is the shortest route (291).

With no other soul do I unite Myself as closely and in such a way as I do with you, and this is because of the deep humility and ardent love which you have for Me (587).

O eternal God, how ardently I desire to glorify this greatest of Your attributes; namely, Your unfathomable mercy. I see all my littleness, and cannot compare myself to the heavenly beings who praise the Lord's mercy with holy admiration. But I, too, have found a way to give perfect glory to the incomprehensible mercy of God.

O most sweet Jesus, who have deigned to allow miserable me to gain a knowledge of Your unfathomable mercy; O most sweet Jesus, who have graciously demanded that I tell the whole world of Your incomprehensible mercy, this day I take into my hands the two rays that spring from Your merciful Heart; that is, the Blood and the Water; and I scatter them all over the globe so that each soul may receive Your mercy and, having received it, may glorify it for endless ages. O most sweet Jesus who, in Your incomprehensible kindness, have deigned to unite my wretched heart to Your most merciful Heart, it is with

Your own Heart that I glorify God, our Father, as no soul has ever glorified Him before (835-836).

You see, I can give you everything in one moment. I am not constrained by any law (1153).

Jesus, You Yourself have deigned to lay the foundations of my sanctity, as my cooperation has not amounted to much (1331).

I want to come out of this retreat a saint, and this, in spite of everything; that is to say, in spite of my wretchedness, I want to become a saint, and I trust that God's mercy can make a saint even out of such misery as I am (1333).

This firm resolution to become a saint is extremely pleasing to Me. I bless your efforts and will give you opportunities to sanctify yourself. Be watchful that you lose no opportunity that My providence offers you for sanctification. If you do not succeed in taking advantage of an opportunity, do not lose your peace, but humble yourself profoundly before Me and, with great trust, immerse yourself completely in My mercy. In this way, you gain more than you have lost, because more favor is granted to a humble soul than the soul itself asks for (1361).

I have come to a knowledge of my destiny; that is, an inward certainty that I will attain sanctity. This deep conviction has filled my soul with gratitude to God, and I have given back all the glory to God, because I know very well what I am of myself (1362).

Tell souls not to place within their own hearts obstacles to My mercy, which so greatly wants to act within them. My mercy works in all those hearts which open their doors to it. Both the sinner and the righteous person have need of My mercy. Conversion, as well as perseverance, is a grace of My mercy.

Let souls who are striving for perfection particularly adore My mercy, because the abundance of graces which I grant them flows from My mercy. I desire that these souls distinguish themselves by boundless trust in My mercy. I myself will attend to the sanctification of such souls. I will provide them with everything they will need to attain sanctity. The graces of My mercy are drawn by means of one vessel only, and that is — trust. The more a soul trusts, the more it will receive. Souls that trust boundlessly are a great comfort to Me, because I pour all the treasures of My graces into them. I rejoice that they ask for much, because it is My desire to give much, very much. On the other hand, I am sad when souls ask for little, when they narrow their hearts (1577-1578).

If souls would put themselves completely in My care, I Myself would undertake the task of sanctifying them, and I would lavish even greater graces on them (1682).

Despite my misery, with Your help, I can become a saint (1718).

My dearest secretary, write that I want to pour out My divine life into human souls and sanctify them, if only they were willing to accept My grace. The greatest sinners would achieve great sanctity, if only they would trust in My mercy. The very inner depths of My being are filled to overflowing with mercy, and it is being poured out upon all I have created. My delight is to act in a human soul and to fill it with My mercy and to justify it. My kingdom on earth is My life in the human soul. Write, My secretary, that I Myself am the spiritual guide of souls — and I guide them indirectly through the priest, and lead each one to sanctity by a road known to Me alone (1784).

In order for God to act in a soul, it must give up acting on its own; otherwise, God will not carry out His will in it (1790).

Suffering

Suffering is a great grace; through suffering the soul becomes like the Savior; in suffering love becomes crystallized; the greater the suffering, the purer the love (57).

You are not living for yourself but for souls, and other souls will profit from your sufferings. Your prolonged suffering will give them the light and strength to accept My will (67).

When I feel that the suffering is more than I can bear, I take refuge in the Lord in the Blessed Sacrament, and I speak to Him with profound silence (73).

I see that God never tries us beyond what we are able to suffer. Oh, I fear nothing; if God sends such great suffering to a soul. He upholds it with an even greater grace, although we are not aware of it. One act of trust at such moments gives greater glory to God than whole hours passed in prayer filled with consolations (78).

It is not for the success of a work, but for the suffering that I give reward (90).

Once during an adoration, the Lord demanded that I give myself up to Him as an offering, by bearing a certain suffering in atonement, not only for the sins of the world in general, but specifically for transgressions committed in this house. Immediately I said, "Very good; I am ready." But Jesus gave me to see what I was going to suffer, and in one moment the whole passion unfolded itself before my eyes. Firstly, my intentions will not be recognized; there will be all kinds of suspicion and distrust as well as various kinds of humiliations and adversities. I will not mention everything here. All these things stood before my soul's eye like a dark storm from which lightning was ready to strike at any moment, waiting only for my consent. For a moment, my nature was frightened. Then suddenly the dinner bell rang. I left the chapel, trembling and undecided. But the sacrifice was ever present before me, for I had neither decided to accept it, nor had I refused the Lord. I wanted to place myself completely in His will. If the Lord Jesus Himself were to impose it on me, I was ready. But Jesus gave me to know that I myself was to give my free consent and accept it with full consciousness, or else it would be meaningless. Its whole power was contained in my free act before God. But at the same time, Jesus gave me to understand that the decision was completely within my power. I could do it or not do it. And so I then answered immediately, "Jesus, I accept everything that You wish to send me; I trust in Your goodness." At that moment, I felt that by this act I glorified God greatly. But I armed myself with patience. As soon as I left the chapel, I had an encounter with reality. I do not want to describe the details, but there was as much of it as I was able to bear. I would not have been able to bear even one drop more (190).

In suffering, I must be patient and quiet, knowing that everything passes in time (253).

True works of God always meet opposition and are marked by suffering (270).

Great love can change small things into great ones, and it is only love which lends value to our actions. And the purer our love becomes, the less there will be within us for the flames of suffering to feed upon, and the suffering will cease to be a suffering for us; it will become a delight! By the grace of God, I have received such a disposition of heart that I am never so happy as when I suffer for Jesus, whom I love with every beat of my heart (303).

Once when I was suffering greatly, I left my work and escaped to Jesus and asked Him to give me His strength. After a very short prayer I returned to my work filled with enthusiasm and joy. Then, one of the sisters said to me, "You must have many consolations today, Sister; you look so radiant. Surely, God is giving you no suffering, but only consolations." "You are greatly mistaken, Sister," I answered, "for it is precisely when

I suffer much that my joy is greater; and when I suffer less, my joy also is less." However, that soul was letting me recognize that she does not understand what I was saying. I tried to explain to her that when we suffer much we have a great chance to show God that we love Him; but when we suffer little we have less occasion to show God our love; and when we do not suffer at all, our love is then neither great nor pure. By the grace of God, we can attain a point where suffering will become a delight to us, for love can work such things in pure souls (303).

Once, the Mother of God came to visit me. She was sad. Her eyes were cast down. She made it clear that She wanted to say something, and yet, on the other hand, it was as if She did not want to speak to me about it. When I understood this, I began to beg the Mother of God to tell me and to look at me. Just then Mary looked at me with a warm smile and said, *You are going to experience certain sufferings because of an illness and the doctors; you will also suffer much because of the image, but do not be afraid of anything* (316).

There is but one price at which souls are bought, and that is suffering united to My suffering on the Cross (324).

Suffering is the greatest treasure on earth; it purifies the soul. In suffering we learn who is our true friend (342).

True love is measured by the thermometer of suffering. Jesus, I thank You for the little daily crosses, for opposition to my endeavors, for the hardships of communal life, for the misinterpretation of my intentions, for humiliations at the hands of others, for the harsh way in which we are treated, for false suspicions, for poor health and loss of strength, for self-denial, for dying to myself, for lack of recognition in everything, for the upsetting of all my plans.

Thank You, Jesus, for interior sufferings, for dryness of spirit, for terrors, fears and incertitudes, for the darkness and the deep interior night, for temptations and various ordeals, for torments too difficult to describe, especially for those which no one will understand, for the hour of death with its fierce struggle and all its bitterness (343).

Then I saw the Lord Jesus nailed to the Cross. When He had hung on it for a while, I saw a multitude of souls crucified like Him. Then I saw a second multitude of souls, and a third. The second multitude were not nailed to [their] crosses, but were holding them firmly in their hands. The third were neither nailed to [their] crosses nor holding them firmly in their hands, but were dragging [their] crosses behind them and were discontent. Jesus then said to me, **Do you see these souls? Those who are like Me in the pain and contempt they suffer will be like Me also in glory. And those who resemble Me less in pain and contempt will also bear less resemblance to Me in glory** (446).

In the midst of all sufferings, both physical and spiritual, as well as in darkness and desolation, I will remain silent, like a dove, and not complain (504).

And the Lord also gave me to understand what unimaginable glory awaits the person who resembles the suffering Jesus here on earth. That person will resemble Jesus in His glory. The Heavenly Father will recognize and glorify our soul to the extent that He sees in us a resemblance to His Son. I understood that this assimilation into Jesus is granted to us while we are here on earth. ...

O Holy Trinity, Eternal God, I thank You for allowing me to know the greatness and the various degrees of glory to which souls attain. Oh, what a great difference of depth in the knowledge of God there is between one degree and another! Oh, if people could only know this! O my God, if I were thereby able to attain one more degree, I would gladly suffer all the torments of the martyrs put together. Truly, all those torments seem as nothing to me compared with the glory that is awaiting us for all eternity (604-605).

[Mary:] *Fear nothing. Be faithful to the end. I sympathize with you* (635).

My daughter, suffering will be a sign to you that I am with you (669).

Amid the greatest torments, I fix the gaze of my soul upon Jesus Crucified; I do not expect help from people, but place my trust in God. In His unfathomable mercy lies all my hope (681).

[A particularly intense time of suffering] was an occasion for me to unite myself with Jesus, suffering on the Cross. Beyond that, I was unable to pray (696).

Suffering is the thermometer which measures the love of God in a soul (774).

[Mary] pressed me to Her heart and said, *"I feel constant compassion for you."* (805).

Set a guard over my lips, so that the fragrance of my sufferings may be known and pleasing to You alone (831).

[O Lord,] seal my lips against all murmuring and complaint. When I am silent, I know I shall be victorious (896).

In difficult moments, I will fix my gaze upon the silent Heart of Jesus, stretched upon the Cross, and from the exploding flames of His merciful Heart, will flow down upon me power and strength to keep fighting (906).

My child, rest on My Heart; I see that you have worked hard in My vineyard (945).

Oh, if only the suffering soul knew how it is loved by God, it would die of joy and excess of happiness! Some day, we will know the value of suffering, but then we will no longer be able to suffer. The present moment is ours (963).

Set a guard upon my lips that they may address no word of complaint to creatures (1065).

O Jesus, in these days of suffering, I am not capable of any kind of prayer. The oppression of my body and soul has increased. O my Jesus, You do see that Your child is on the decline. I am not forcing myself further, but simply submitting my will to the will of Jesus (1204).

I have come to see that if the will of the Heavenly Father was fulfilled in this way in His well-beloved Son, it will be fulfilled in us in exactly the same way: by suffering, persecution, abuse, disgrace. It is through all this that my soul becomes like unto Jesus. And the greater the sufferings, the more I see that I am becoming like Jesus. This is the surest way. If some other way were better, Jesus would have shown it to me. Sufferings in no way take away my peace. On the other hand, although I enjoy profound peace, that peace does not lessen my experience of suffering. Although my face is often bowed to the ground, and my tears flow profusely, at the same time my soul is filled with profound peace and happiness (1394).

God, in his unfathomable decrees, often allows it to be that those who have expended most effort in accomplishing some work do not enjoy its fruits here on earth; God reserves all their joy for eternity. But for all that, God sometimes lets them know how much their efforts please Him. And such moments strengthen them for further struggles and ordeals. These are the souls that bear closest resemblance to the Savior who, in the work which He founded here on earth, tasted nothing but bitterness (1402).

I do not ask, Lord, that You take me down from the cross, but I implore You to give me the strength to remain steadfast upon it (1484).

I am giving you a share in [My] sufferings because of My special love for you and in view of the high degree of holiness I am intending for you in heaven. A suffering soul is closest to My Heart (1487).

Jesus, do not leave me alone in suffering. You know, Lord, how weak I am. I am an abyss of wretchedness, I am nothingness itself; so what will be so strange if You leave me alone and I fall? I am an infant, Lord, so I cannot get along by myself. However, beyond all abandonment I trust, and in spite of my own feeling I trust, and I am being completely transformed into trust — often in spite of what I feel. Do not lessen any of my sufferings, only give me strength to bear them. Do with me as You please, Lord, only give me the grace to be able to love You in every event and circumstance. Lord, do not lessen my cup of bitterness, only give me strength that I may be able to drink it all (1489).

O my Jesus, how good it is to be on the cross, but with You! (1609).

I am uniting myself with Jesus through suffering. When I meditate on His Painful Passion, my physical sufferings are lessened (1625).

Once again, I am feeling worse today. A high fever is beginning to consume me, and I cannot take any food. I would like to have something refreshing to drink, but there is not even any water in my pitcher. All this, O Jesus, to obtain mercy for souls (1647).

Accept, most merciful Jesus, this, my inadequate sacrifice, which I offer to You today before heaven and earth. May Your Most Sacred Heart, so full of mercy, complete what is lacking in my offering, and offer it to Your Father for the conversion of sinners. I thirst after souls, O Christ (1680).

My daughter, know that if I allow you to feel and have a more profound knowledge of My sufferings, that is a grace from Me. But when your mind is dimmed and your sufferings are great, it is then that you take an active part in My Passion, and I am conforming you more fully to Myself. It is your task to submit yourself to My will at such times, more than at others (1697).

O my Jesus, give me strength to endure suffering so that I may not make a wry face when I drink the cup of bitterness. Help me Yourself to make my sacrifice pleasing to You. May it not be tainted by my self-love, even though it extend over many years. May purity of intention make it pleasing to You, fresh and full of life. This life of mine is a ceaseless struggle, a constant effort to do Your holy will; but may everything that is in me, both my misery and my strength, give praise to You, O Lord (1740).

In order to gain merit for my suffering, I will unite myself more closely, in suffering, to the Passion of the Lord Jesus, asking of Him grace for dying souls, so that the mercy of God may embrace them in this grave moment (1762).

You will save more souls through prayer and suffering than will a missionary through his teachings and sermons alone (1767).

When, in heaven, you see these present days [of suffering], **you will rejoice and will want to see as many of them as possible** (1787).

My God, although my sufferings are great and protracted, I accept them from Your hands as magnificent gifts. I accept them all, even the ones that other souls have refused to accept. You can come to me with everything, my Jesus; I will refuse You nothing. I ask You for only one thing: give me the strength to endure them and grant that they may be meritorious. Here is my whole being; do with me as You please (1795).

May Your grace, which flows down upon me from Your Compassionate Heart, strengthen me for the struggle and sufferings, that I may remain faithful to You. And, although I am such misery, I do not fear You, because I know Your mercy well. Nothing will frighten me away from You, O God, because everything is so much less than what I know [Your mercy to be] — I see that clearly (1803).

If the angels were capable of envy, they would envy us for two things: one is the receiving of Holy Communion, and the other is suffering (1804).

Three O'clock Hour

[The "Three O'clock Hour Prayer":] You expired, Jesus, but the source of life gushed forth for souls, and the ocean of mercy opened up for the whole world. O Fount of Life, unfathomable Divine Mercy, envelop the whole world and empty Yourself out upon us (1319).

At three o'clock, implore My mercy, especially for sinners; and, if only for a brief moment, immerse yourself in My Passion, particularly in My abandonment at the moment of agony. This is the hour of great mercy for the whole world. I will allow you to enter into My mortal sorrow. In this hour, I will refuse nothing to the soul that makes a request of Me in virtue of My Passion (1320).

I remind you, My daughter, that as often as you hear the clock strike the third hour, immerse yourself completely in My mercy, adoring and glorifying it; invoke its omnipotence for the whole world, and particularly for poor sinners; for at that moment mercy was opened wide for every soul. In this hour you can obtain everything for yourself and for others for the asking; it was the hour of grace for the whole world — mercy triumphed over justice.

My daughter, try your best to make the Stations of the Cross in this hour, provided that your duties permit it; and if you are not able to make the Stations of the Cross, then at least step into the chapel for a moment and adore, in the Blessed Sacrament, My Heart, which is full of mercy; and should you be unable to step into the chapel, immerse yourself in prayer there where you happen to be, if only for a very brief instant (1572).

Trust

Why do souls avoid You, Jesus? — I don't understand that (57).

Although it seems to me that you do not hear me, I put my trust in the ocean of Your mercy, and I know that my hope will not be deceived (69).

O Lord, though I cannot comprehend You and do not understand Your ways, I nonetheless trust in Your mercy (73).

Even if you kill me, still will I trust in You! [cf. Job 13:15] (77).

Do what You will with me, O Jesus; I will adore You in everything. May Your will be done in me, O my Lord and my God, and I will praise Your infinite mercy (78).

One act of trust at such moments [of suffering] gives greater glory to God than whole hours passed in prayer filled with consolations (78).

O Blood and Water, which gushed forth from the Heart of Jesus as a fount of mercy for us, I trust in You! (84, 187).

Oh, how good it is to abandon oneself totally to God and to give Him full freedom to act in one's soul! (134).

The flames of mercy are burning Me — clamoring to be spent; I want to keep pouring them out upon souls; souls just don't want to believe in My goodness (177).

Jesus, I accept everything that You wish to send me; I trust in Your goodness (190).

My daughter, your confidence and love restrain My justice, and I cannot inflict punishment because you hinder Me from doing so. Oh, how great is the power of a soul filled with confidence! (198).

Once, when I was deeply moved by the thought of eternity and its mysteries, my soul became fearful; and when I pondered about these a little longer, I started to be troubled by various doubts. Then Jesus said to me, **My child, do not be afraid of the house of your Father. Leave these vain inquiries to the wise of this world. I want to see you always as a little child** (290).

Encourage the souls with whom you come in contact to trust in My infinite mercy. Oh, how I love those souls who have complete confidence in Me — I will do everything for them (294).

Mankind will not have peace until it turns with trust to My mercy (300).

I hope against all hope in the ocean of Your mercy (309).

O my God, my only hope, I have placed all my trust in You, and I know I shall not be disappointed (317).

Most Holy Trinity, I trust in Your infinite mercy. God is my Father and so I, His child, have every claim to His divine Heart; and the greater the darkness, the more complete our trust should be (357).

I do not understand how it is possible not to trust in Him who can do all things. With Him, everything; without Him, nothing. He is Lord. He will not allow those who have placed all their trust in Him to be put to shame (358).

I understand souls who are suffering against hope, for I have gone through that fire myself. But God will not give [us anything] beyond our strength. Often have I lived hoping against hope, and have advanced my hope to complete trust in God (386).

Do not fear; I Myself will make up for everything that is lacking in you (435).

Why are you fearful and why do you tremble when you are united to Me? I am displeased when a soul yields to vain terror. Who will dare to touch you when you are with Me? Most dear to Me is the soul that strongly believes in My goodness and has complete trust in Me. I heap My confidence upon it and give it all it asks (453).

Many souls striving for perfection ... are not aware of this great goodness of God (458).

All my nothingness is drowned in the sea of Your mercy. With the confidence of a child, I throw myself into Your arms, O Father of Mercy, to make up for the unbelief of so many souls who are afraid to trust in You. Oh, how very few souls really know You! (505).

Why are you afraid? Do you think that I will not have enough omnipotence to support you? (527).

Even if I were to hear the most terrifying things about God's justice, I would not fear Him at all, because I have come to know Him well. God is love, and His Spirit is peace. I see now that my deeds which have flowed from love are more perfect than those which I have done out of fear. I have placed my trust in God and fear nothing. I have given myself over to His holy will; let Him do with me as He wishes, and I will still love Him (589).

I then pleaded with Jesus for a certain soul [Father Sopocko], asking the Lord to grant him the grace to fight, and to take this trial from him. As you ask, so shall it be, but his merit will not be lessened. Joy reigned in my soul that God is so good and merciful; God grants everything that we ask of Him with trust (609).

I desire that the whole world know My infinite mercy. I desire to grant unimaginable graces to those souls who trust in My mercy (687).

On the initial day of the retreat, I was visited by one of the sisters who had come to make her perpetual vows. She confided to me that she had no trust in God and became discouraged at every little thing. I answered her, "It is well that you have told me this, Sister; I will pray for you." And I spoke a few words to her about how much distrust hurts the Lord Jesus, especially distrust on the part of a chosen soul. She told me that, beginning with her perpetual vows, she would practice trust. Now I know that even [some] souls that are chosen and well advanced in the religious life or the spiritual life do not have the courage to entrust themselves completely to God. And this is so because few souls know the unfathomable mercy of God and His great goodness (731).

My Jesus, my strength and my only hope, in You alone is all my hope. My trust will not be frustrated (746).

I know that I am under Your special gaze, O Lord. I do not examine with fear Your plans regarding me; my task is to accept everything from Your hand. I do not fear anything, although the storm is raging, and frightful bolts strike all around me, and I then feel quite alone. Yet, my heart senses You, and my trust grows, and I see all Your omnipotence which upholds me. With You, Jesus, I go through life, amid storms and rainbows, with a cry of joy, singing the song of Your mercy (761).

At [the hour of my death] more than at any other time, I trust in the abyss of Your mercy and am reminding You, O merciful Jesus, sweet Savior, of all the promises You have made to me (825).

Have confidence in God, for He is good and inconceivable. His mercy surpasses our understanding (880).

O my Creator and Father of great mercy, I trust in You, for You are Goodness Itself. Souls, do not be afraid of God, but trust in Him, for He is good, and His mercy is everlasting (908).

When I began this big novena for three intentions, I saw a tiny insect on the ground and thought: how did it get here in the middle of winter? Then I heard the following words in my soul: **You see, I am thinking of it and sustaining it, and what is it compared to you? Why was your soul fearful for a moment?** I apologized to the Lord for that moment. Jesus wants me to always be a child and to leave all care to Him, and to submit blindly to His holy will. He took everything upon Himself (922).

The soul gives the greatest glory to its Creator when it turns with trust to The Divine Mercy (930).

Love has overtaken my whole heart, and even if I were to be told of God's justice and of how even the pure spirits tremble and cover their faces before Him, saying endlessly, "Holy," which would seem to suggest that my familiarity with God would be to the detriment of His honor and majesty, [I would reply,] "O no, no, and once again, no!" (947).

Eternal God, in whom mercy is endless and the treasury of compassion inexhaustible, look kindly upon us and increase Your mercy in us, that in difficult moments we might not despair nor become despondent, but with great confidence submit ourselves to Your holy will, which is Love and Mercy itself (950).

Your most merciful Heart is all my hope. I have nothing for my defense but only Your mercy; in it lies all my trust (1065).

I am Love and Mercy itself. When a soul approaches Me with trust, I fill it with such an abundance of graces that it cannot contain them within itself, but radiates them to other souls (1074).

O Eternal Trinity, yet ever-gracious God,
Your compassion is without measure.
And so I trust in the sea of Your mercy (1298).

Hail, open Wound of the Most Sacred Heart,
From which the rays of mercy issued forth
And from which it was given us to draw life
With the vessel of trust alone (1321).

Jesus, hide me in Your mercy and shield me against everything that might terrify my soul. Do not let my trust in Your mercy be disappointed. Shield me with the omnipotence of Your mercy, and judge me leniently as well (1480).

My child, do you fear the God of mercy? My holiness does not prevent Me from being merciful. Behold, for you I have established a throne of mercy on earth — the tabernacle — and from this throne I desire to enter into your heart. I am not surrounded by a retinue or guards. You can come to me at any moment, at any time; I want to speak to you and desire to grant you grace (1485).

My child, know that the greatest obstacles to holiness are discouragement and an exaggerated anxiety (1488).

The soul desirous of more of God's mercy should approach God with greater trust; and if her trust in God is unlimited, then the mercy of God toward it will be likewise limitless (1489).

O Lord, sometimes You lift me up to the brightness of visions, and then again You plunge me into the darkness of night and the abyss of my nothingness, and my soul feels as if it were alone in the wilderness. Yet, above all things, I trust in You, Jesus, for You are unchangeable. My moods change, but You are always the same, full of mercy (1489).

I entrust myself to You as a little child does to its mother's love. Even if all things were to conspire against me, and even if the ground were to give way under my feet, I would be at peace close to Your Heart. You are always a most tender mother to me, and You surpass all mothers. I will sing of my pain to You by my silence, and You will understand me beyond any utterance (1490).

I am always with you, even if you don't feel My presence at the time of battle (1499).

Whoever places his trust in My mercy will be filled with My divine peace at the hour of death (1520).

I firmly trust and commit myself entirely to Your holy will, which is mercy itself (1574).

You should not worry too much about adversities. The world is not as powerful as it seems to be (1643).

I am ready for [my death], not only today, but ever since the moment when I placed my complete trust in the Divine Mercy, resigning myself totally to His most holy will, full of mercy and compassion. I know what I am of myself (1679).

Christ and Lord, You are leading me over such precipices that, when I look at them, I am filled with fright, but at the same time I am at peace as I nestle close to Your Heart. Close to Your Heart, I fear nothing. In these dangerous moments, I act like a little child, carried in its mother's arms; when it sees something which menaces it, it clasps its mother's neck more firmly and feels secure (1726).

I fly to Your mercy, Compassionate God, who alone are good. Although my misery is great, and my offenses are many, I trust in Your mercy, because You are the God of mercy; and, from time immemorial, it has never been heard of, nor do heaven or earth remember, that a soul trusting in Your mercy has been disappointed (1730).

Sooner would heaven and earth turn into nothingness than would My mercy not embrace a trusting soul (1777).

My child, you should know how to master yourself amid the greatest difficulties, and let nothing drive you away from Me, not even your falls (1823).

REFERENCES
AND NOTES

References and Notes

Page 15: "By the way, if the idea seems strange to you ..." Jesus is alive and speaks to us today. Of course, he — and also the Holy Spirit — speaks to us whenever we hear or read his Word, that is, Sacred Scripture. Yet he can also speak to us in many other ways such as through people, events, and through the peace and joy he puts in our hearts. Some of the people through whom God speaks to us are the prophets. Of course, we've all heard of prophets in the Old Testament, people such as Jeremiah, Isaiah, and Ezekiel. Yet we may be surprised to learn that there have been prophets throughout the Church's history, even up to our own day. (The surprise often comes despite the fact that St. Paul writes in his letters about the charism of prophecy in the life of the Church: See Eph 2:20; 4:11-12; 1 Cor 14:1-5, 22-25, 29-32.) In fact, even though they aren't frequently thought of as prophets, well-known saints such as Francis of Assisi, Ignatius of Loyola, Thérèse of Liseiux, Faustina Kowalska, and Blessed Mother Teresa of Calcutta truly had prophetic missions. In other words, they (and many other saintly people) had powerful experiences of God that they were then called to share at a given time for the strengthening of other people's faith, hope, and love. Sometimes their experiences of God came through extraordinary mystical experiences, such as in the case of St. Faustina. At other times, their experiences came through the silent, hidden action of the Holy Spirit, such as in the case of St. Thérèse. Whatever the nature of his experience of God, if a prophet is authentic — of which only the Church has the authority to make a final, definitive determination — then his experience becomes a gift for the people of his time.

By the way, St. Faustina's *Diary* is a major source for this retreat because her testimony is a powerful prophetic witness for our day. Pope John Paul II makes this point in the following excerpt from his homily on the occasion of the dedication of the Shrine of Divine Mercy in Krakow Lagiewniki on August 17, 2002:

> Today, therefore, in this Shine, I wish *solemnly to entrust the world to Divine Mercy.* I do so with the burning desire that the message of God's merciful love, proclaimed here through Saint Faustina, *may be made known to all the peoples of the earth* and fill their hearts with hope. May this message radiate from this place to our beloved homeland and throughout the world. May the binding promise of the Lord Jesus be fulfilled: from here there must go forth "the spark which will prepare the world for his final coming" (cf. *Diary*, 1732). This spark needs to be lighted by the grace of God. This fire of mercy needs to be passed on to the world. *In the mercy of God the world will find peace and mankind will find happiness!* (emphasis in original; 5).

Having said that the charism of prophecy has been alive and active in the life of the Church through the ages, I'd now like to make an important point: The words of post-Biblical prophets do not carry the same weight as Divine Revelation, which is communicated to us through Sacred Scripture and Sacred Tradition. Thus, we should always consider the words of prophetic saints in light of Divine Revelation and keep in mind that their words do not contain the same fullness of authority as, for instance, the words of Jesus in the Gospels or the teachings of the Magisterium of the Church. Still, the Church may decide that the prophetic testimony of a saint (or group of saints) contributes to and comprises a part of Sacred Tradition (for instance, when a saint is made a Doctor of the Church). The testimony of such a saint would then have greater weight. On this topic, it may be helpful to meditate on words from the Dogmatic Constitution on Divine Revelation, *Dei Verbum* (8) as it teaches about the role of believers in the development of Sacred Tradition:

> This Tradition which comes from the apostles develops in the Church with the help of the Holy Spirit. For there is a growth in the understanding of the realities and the words which have been handed down. *This happens through the contemplation and study made by believers, who treasure these things in their hearts* (cf. Lk 2:19, 51), *through a penetrating understanding of the realities which they experience,* and through the preaching of those who have received through Episcopal succession the sure gift of truth. For as the centuries succeed one another, the Church constantly moves forward toward the fullness of divine truth until the words of God reach their complete fulfillment in her (emphasis added; cited from *The Sixteen Documents of Vatican II* ed. Marianne Lorraine Trouvè. Boston: Pauline Books and Media, 1999).

For an excellent and thorough study of prophecy and its role in the life of the Church, see Niels Christian Hvidt's *Christian Prophecy: The Post Biblical Tradition* (Oxford/New York: Oxford University Press, 2007).

INTRODUCTION

Page 17: "Few things help one to grow in holiness more quickly than the *Spiritual Exercises* ..." I base this assertion on the following logic. When people want to grow in holiness in a short period of time, they make a retreat, and the best form of retreat, according to the Church, is the *Spiritual Exercises of St. Ignatius.* I say that because Ignatius's retreat has received more than 600 statements of high praise from pope after pope. (Source: J. Ignacio Tellechea Idígoras, *Ignatius of Loyola: The Pilgrim Saint,* trans. Cornelius Michael Buckley, SJ [Chicago: Loyola University Press, 1994], p. 504.) One example of such high praise is Pope Pius XI's entire encyclical letter *Mens Nostra: On the Promotion of the Spiritual Exercises.* No other form of retreat even comes close to the *Exercises* in terms of the amount of papal approbation received.

Page 17: "... but who's got 30 days?" Knowing that 30 full days is too long for most people to make a retreat, St. Ignatius allowed for an adapted version of his *Exercises* that could be made during one's everyday life. Yet this version of his retreat (called "the 19th Annotation of the *Spiritual Exercises*") is also somewhat difficult to make. For instance, it requires the retreatant to be faithful to an hour and a half of prayer every day over the course of three to five months. It also requires regular meetings with a retreat director. While this can be a fruitful way of making the *Spiritual Exercises*, it asks a lot of the average person (perhaps too much).

Page 19: "... even someone like him could become a saint." The reader may notice that although Fr. Lanteri has been declared "Venerable" by the Church, he has not yet been beatified or canonized. This doesn't mean he's not a saint. It simply means the Church hasn't declared him to be one. She may do so in the future. Yet, even if she never does, it still doesn't mean he's not a saint. People can be saints without officially being declared so by the Church. By "saint," I mean someone whose faith, hope, and love is heroic and whose life bears tremendous spiritual fruit — whether the saint (or others) see it or not. Surely, there are many hidden saints about whom the world knows nothing.

Page 20: "De Montfort predicted a couple of interesting things about his book." Regarding the first thing, that his book would be hidden away, see *True Devotion to Mary*, trans. Frederick W. Faber (Charlotte, NC: TAN Books, 1941), p. 69: "I clearly see that raging beasts shall come in fury to tear with their diabolical teeth this little writing ... or at least to smother it in the darkness and silence of a coffer, that it may not appear." Regarding the second thing, that the manuscript of his book would be discovered and that its spirituality would form some of the greatest saints in the history of the Church, see the rest of the citation from p. 69: "This very foresight encourages me, and makes me hope for great success, that is to say, for a great squadron of brave and valiant soldiers of Jesus and Mary, of both sexes, to combat the world, the devil and corrupted nature, in those more than ever perilous times which are about to come." Also, see the following: "I have said that this would come to pass ... because the Most High with His holy Mother has to form for Himself great saints who shall surpass most of the other saints in sanctity as much as the cedars of Lebanon outgrow little shrubs" (p. 26).

Page 21: "... the kind of great saints de Montfort foresaw." That de Montfort understood the great saints he foresaw to be very little souls is clear from the following passage:

> But the power of Mary over all the devils will especially shine forth in the latter times, when Satan will lay his snares against her heel: that is to say, her humble slaves and her poor children, whom she will raise up to make war against him. They shall be little and poor in the world's esteem, and abased before all like the heel, trodden underfoot and persecuted as the heel is by the other members of the body. But in return for

this they shall be rich in the grace of God, which Mary shall distribute to them abundantly. They shall be great and exalted before God in sanctity, superior to all other creatures by their lively zeal, and so well sustained with God's assistance that, with the humility of their heel, in union with Mary, they shall crush the head of the devil and cause Jesus Christ to triumph" (*True Devotion*, pp. 32-33; see also p. 100).

In the next citation, de Montfort speaks directly to these little souls:

Poor children of Mary, your weakness is extreme, your inconstancy is great, your inward nature is very much corrupted. You are drawn (I grant it) from the same corrupt mass as all the children of Adam and Eve. Yet do not be discouraged because of that. Console yourselves and exult in having the secret which I will teach you — a secret unknown to almost all Christians, even the most devout (p. 113).

In light of the idea that the great saints foreseen by de Montfort will be little Marian souls, it's interesting to read what Mary herself said to the Vietnamese mystic, Marcel Van:

Van, listen to me. As Jesus has already told you, at the beginning of the struggle, *my Apostles will appear to be so weak*, that you might think that they would not be able to stand against Hell. This will teach my Apostles to be more humble. However, just as at one time Hell appeared victorious, so now this time, it will be disgraced, because it will be *my children*, not I, who will crush the head of Satan. Satan will be disgraced when he sees that I use the feet of my weak children to crush him (emphasis in original; Marie Michel, *Love Cannot Die: A Life of Marcel Van* [Paris: Les Amis de Van, 1996], p. 216).

Page 22: "… our time truly can be called a 'time of mercy' …" To St. Faustina, Jesus sometimes spoke of our time as a "time of mercy" (*Diary of St. Maria Faustina Kowalska: Divine Mercy in My Soul.* [Stockbridge, MA: Marian Press, 1987.] 1160, 1261). As if to emphasize this point, he said to her:

In the Old Covenant I sent prophets wielding thunderbolts to My people. Today I am sending you with My mercy to the people of the whole world. I do not want to punish aching mankind, but I desire to heal it, pressing it to My Merciful Heart. … Before the Day of Justice I am sending the Day of Mercy (Ibid., 1588).

Pope John Paul II echoed this idea that ours is a time of mercy during a homily he gave in his native Poland (Blonie, Kraków) on August 18, 2002 for the occasion of the beatification of four of his countrymen. He said:

> From the beginning of her existence the Church, pointing to the mystery of the Cross and the Resurrection, has preached the mercy of God, a pledge of hope and a source of salvation for man. Nonetheless, it would appear that *we today have been particularly called* to proclaim this message before the world. We cannot neglect this mission, if God himself has called us to it through the testimony of Saint Faustina.
>
> God has chosen our own times for this purpose. Perhaps because the twentieth century, despite indisputable achievements in many areas, was marked in a particular way by the "*mystery of iniquity*." With this heritage both of good and of evil, we have entered the new millennium. New prospects of development are opening up before mankind, together with hitherto unheard of dangers. Frequently man lives as if God did not exist, and even puts himself in God's place. He claims for himself the Creator's right to interfere in the mystery of human life. He wishes to determine human life through genetic manipulation and to establish the limit of death. Rejecting divine law and moral principles, he openly attacks the family. In a variety of ways he attempts to silence the voice of God in human hearts; he wishes to make God the "great absence" in the culture and the conscience of peoples. The "mystery of iniquity" continues to mark the reality of the world.
>
> In experiencing this mystery, man lives in fear of the future, of emptiness, of suffering, of annihilation. Perhaps for this very reason, it is as if Christ, using the testimony of a lowly Sister, entered our time in order to indicate clearly the source of relief and hope found in the eternal mercy of God.
>
> *The message of merciful love needs to resound forcefully anew*. The world needs this love. The hour has come to bring Christ's message to everyone: to rulers and the oppressed, to those whose humanity and dignity seem lost in the *mysterium iniquitatis*. The hour has come when the message of Divine Mercy is able to fill hearts with hope and to become the spark of a new civilization: the civilization of love (emphasis in original; 3).

Page 22: "I will not profit from ..." Jean C.J. d'Elbée, *I Believe in Love: A Personal Retreat Based on the Teaching of St. Thérèse of Lisieux*, trans.

Marilyn Teichert and Madeleine Stebbins (Manchester, NH: Sophia Institute Press, 2001), p. 278.

PART ONE

Page 30: "... weighty voice of a Doctor of the Church." The Catholic Church recognizes certain extraordinarily wise, canonized saints with the distinction, "Doctor of the Church." It declares that the members of this elite group (there are only 33 of them) teach with a special authority. In other words, their writings carry a greater weight than those of most other saints. Saint Thérèse of Lisieux was declared a Doctor of the Church in 1997 by Pope John Paul II.

Page 30: "Alas! I have always noticed ..." *Story of a Soul: The Autobiography of St. Thérèse of Lisieux*, trans. John Clarke, OCD (Washington, DC: The Institute of Carmelite Studies, 1996), p. 207.

Page 31: "... she searches out a 'totally new' way to holiness ..." Of course, Thérèse's Little Way isn't "totally new" in the sense that one can't find it in Sacred Scripture. Her Little Way is in Scripture, and in this sense it's not new at all. However, it is new in the sense that her writings reveal new insights and undiscovered treasures in the Word of God. In his apostolic letter, *Divini Amoris Scientia* (1997), written for the occasion of St. Thérèse being made a Doctor of the Church, Pope John Paul II makes this same point, "During her life Thérèse discovered 'new lights'" that she expressed with a "particular originality" (1). Later, in the same letter, he goes on to write that she "discovered hidden treasures" (9) in Sacred Scripture, treasures that make her Little Way "something unique" (10).

Page 31: "We are living now ..." *Story of a Soul*, pp. 207-208.

Page 33: "**Be not afraid of your Savior** ..." *Diary*, 1485.

Page 33: "His Sacred Heart will do everything ..." Cited in *I Believe in Love*, p. 85.

Page 34: "Man is created to praise ..." Saint Ignatius of Loyola, *The Spiritual Exercises of St. Ignatius*, trans. Louis J. Puhl, SJ (Chicago: Loyola Press, 1951), 23. Hereafter in citations, the book *Spiritual Exercises* is abbreviated *SpirEx*.

Page 36: "... to know the Lord more intimately ..." *SpirEx*, 104.

Page 37: "... a clarity that grips us ..." Jerome Nadal, SJ, cited by Gilles Cusson, SJ, *Biblical Theology and the Spiritual Exercises*, trans. Mary Angela Roduit, RC, and George E. Ganss, SJ (Saint Louis: The Institute of Jesuit Sources, 1994), p. 99.

Page 38: "... 'the primacy of contemplation' ..." Cusson uses this term in *Biblical Theology and the Spiritual Exercises*, p. 170.

Page 42: "There it is, that Heart ..." Jesus' words to St. Margaret Mary, cited by Timothy O'Donnell, STD, *Heart of the Redeemer: An Apologia for the Contemporary and Perennial Value of the Devotion to the Sacred Heart of Jesus* (San Francisco: Ignatius Press, 1989), p. 135.

Page 42: "Jesus Christ, my kind Master ..." Jesus' words to St. Margaret Mary, cited by O'Donnell, Ibid., p. 131.

Page 43: "... this can be the principle and foundation of our lives." To make the sorrow of the Sacred Heart of Jesus one's principle and foundation does not depart from the Ignatian ideal. I say that because devotion to the Sacred Heart and Ignatian Spirituality go together. In fact, the devotion to the Sacred Heart, which received it's impetus from St. Margaret Mary, was taken up by the Jesuits and incorporated by them into their spirituality. Thus, one of the great experts on Ignatian Spirituality, Joseph de Guibert, SJ, writes in *The Jesuits: Their Spiritual Doctrine and Practice*, trans. William Young, SJ (St. Louis: Institute of Jesuit Sources, 1964):

> [A]nother element which holds a highly important place in the spiritual life of modern Jesuits, [is] the devotion to the Sacred Heart. ... This did not entail the introduction of any element which was foreign or without real attachments to the whole spirituality which it had come to crown. Far from it. In fact, numerous Jesuits were found among the precursors of the movement of Paray[-le-Monial]; and more important still, everything in the *Exercises* themselves orientated the Jesuits to enter fully into this movement. But even so this remains true: For the generations which came after Paray, the devotion contained a new and powerful factor of spiritual life (543).

Page 43: "... the source and summit of the Christian life." *Lumen Gentium*, 11.
Page 43: "... contains all the mysteries of the faith in summary ..." See Pius XI, *Miserentissimus Redemptor*, 3 and Pius XII, *Haurietis Aquas* 15, 86.
Page 43: "... mandatory for all Catholics." For example, see Pius XI, *Miserentissimus Redemptor*, in which he states the purpose of the encyclical:

> Since some Christians, perhaps, are ignorant of, and others are indifferent to, the sorrows which the most loving Jesus revealed to St. Margaret Mary Alacoque in His apparitions to her, as well as His wishes and desires which He manifested to mankind, all of which in the last analysis work to man's advantage, it is Our pleasure, Venerable Brothers, to write you at some length of *the obligation which rests upon all* to make those amends which we owe to the Most Sacred Heart of Jesus (emphasis added; 1).

The pope goes on to call honor given to the Sacred Heart of Jesus "the highest expression of Christian piety" (106). Also, Pius XII in *Haurietis Aquas* writes, "There is no question here of some ordinary form of piety which anyone at his own whim may treat as of little consequence or set aside as inferior to others" (109).
Page 43: "... the Sacred Heart and the Eucharist are one ..." For

example, Pius XII, *Haurietis Aquas*, 122: "... not the least part of the revelation of that [Sacred] Heart is the Eucharist, which He gave to us out of the great charity of His own Heart." See also Pope John Paul II's meditation at the Basilica of the Sacred Heart in Montmartre, June 1, 1980:

> We are at Montmartre, in the Basilica of the Sacred Heart, consecrated to the contemplation of Christ's love present in the Blessed Sacrament. ... [The mystery of Christ's love] is the mystery of the Holy Eucharist, the center of our faith, the center of our worship of Christ's merciful love manifested in his Sacred Heart.

Finally, we have the testimony of a mystic, Mother Louise Margaret Claret de la Touche, who writes in *The Sacred Heart and the Priesthood*, trans. Patrick O'Connell (Rockford, IL: TAN Books, 1979), pp. 184-185: "The Sacred Heart, the Blessed Eucharist, love are one and the same thing! ... [T]he love of Jesus is the love of His Heart: it is His Heart, to sum up all in one word. Thus, the Blessed Eucharist is explained only by the Sacred Heart."

Page 48: "Give me one who loves ..." Pius XI, *Miserentissimus Redemptor*, 13.

Page 48: "... the idea that we can give Jesus 'retroactive consolation.'" I first came across the term "retroactive consolation" while reading Robert Stackpole's book *Jesus, Mercy Incarnate: St. Faustina and Devotion to Jesus Christ* (Stockbridge, MA: John Paul II Institute of Divine Mercy/Marian Press, 2000), 60. Dr. Stackpole is an expert on the theology that underlies Consoling spirituality. (He wrote his doctoral thesis in theology at the Angelicum in Rome on this topic.) His thorough research on this topic has been helpful to me in coming to a better theological understanding of how we can console Jesus. I will be citing various footnotes from his book in several of the notes that follow.

Page 48: "Now if, because of our sins ..." Pius XI, *Miserentissimus Redemptor*, 13.

Page 49: "... the teaching that Jesus Christ ... was able to know ("foresee") ..." Some contemporary theologians have called into question the idea that Jesus possessed a special knowledge that would have enabled him to see future generations. Stackpole responds to their arguments in the following footnote from his book, *Jesus, Mercy Incarnate* (n. 16, pp. 91-92):

> That Jesus possessed universal knowledge in His human soul, even prior to His Resurrection, was the nearly unanimous teaching of the ancient Fathers of the Church, including St. Augustine, St. Gregory the Great, and St. John Chrysostom, each of whom held it to be a test of orthodoxy; see William Most, *The Consciousness of Christ* (Front Royal, VA: Christendom, 1980), 118-119, 123-126. The Fathers

generally did not hold this view because they were bound by an *a priori* Greek ideal of intellectual "perfection" which Jesus had to fulfill. Rather, their most common argument was drawn from the doctrine of the Trinity: if Jesus was the divine Word incarnate, then even in His human soul, the divine Word and Wisdom could not be ignorant of anything. This teaching was defended and developed later by several "Doctors" of the Church, including St. Thomas Aquinas and St. Robert Bellarmine, who divided the forms of Christ's human knowledge into "beatific," "infused," and "acquired" knowledge. In the 20th century, Pope Benedict XV taught that it is unsafe to contradict the traditional teaching on Christ's universal human knowledge, and Pius XII explicitly endorsed this teaching as well in *Haurietis Aquas* (1956), but especially in *Mystici Corporis* (1943). The *Catechism* also seems to preserve this teaching, if entries 473 and 478 are read, as they should be, in the light of the explanatory reference notes to the text.

The main arguments against the traditional teaching are (a) that the natural reading of Scripture seems to show that Jesus grew in knowledge as a youth, and even as an adult was ignorant of various empirical facts, e.g. Lk. 2:52, Mk. 5:9, 6:38, 9:20, and ignorant of the date and time of the End of the World, see Mk. 13:32; and (b) that if the mind of Jesus on earth was continually flooded with the light of supernatural knowledge, then He could not have suffered a true agony and dereliction for us on the Cross. In response to the latter point, however, it seems to be a common teaching of the saints that even while abiding in a state of mystical union with God, a human being can experience the most terrible bodily and emotional suffering; see St. Francis De Sales, *Treatise on the Love of God* (Westminster, MD: Newman, 1945), 9.3 and 9.12, p. 371-372, 395-397. This would seem to be the closest analogy we possess to the spiritual condition of Jesus on the Cross; cf. St. Catherine of Siena, *The Dialogue* (New York: Paulist Press, 1980), no. 78, p. 146, and Pope John Paul II, *Jesus: Son and Savior, A Catechesis on the Creed,* (Boston: Pauline Books and Media, 1996), 472. Besides, if Jesus possessed the light of universal foreknowledge in His human soul at the time of His Passion, then much of what He would have foreseen — all the sins, mistrust, and ingratitude of future generations — surely would have increased rather than mitigated His sorrows; see St. John Eudes, *The Sacred Heart* (New York: P.J. Kennedy and Sons, 1946), 105. As for the witness of Scripture, it may be possible to reconcile it with the traditional teaching if we bear in mind the distinction between what Jesus had present before His conscious mind, and all the infused knowledge that He held subconsciously, an habitual knowledge to which He had access only as the needs of His mission and His Father's will permitted; on this see Karl Adam, *The Christ of Faith* (New York: Pantheon, 1955), 291-312. On the whole modern theological controversy regarding the scope of the human knowledge of the earthly Jesus, see Most, Consciousness, 148-173, and Betrand De Margerie, S.J., *The Human Knowledge of Christ* (Boston: Daughters of St. Paul, 1980).

Page 49: "Jesus knew and loved us ..." *Catechism of the Catholic Church*, 478.

Page 49: "Just as [Jesus] allowed himself ..." O'Donnell, *Heart of the Redeemer*, p. 179. O'Donnell is not alone in echoing Pope Pius XI's words from *Miserentissimus Redemptor*, 13. Many prominent theologians do the same. In *Jesus, Mercy Incarnate* (n. 42, pp. 95-96), Stackpole cites two of them. The first of them, Reginald Garrigou Lagrange, OP, in his essay "Consolare il Cuore di Gesù?" in *Vita Cristiana*, no. 16, 1947, states:

> During his earthly life, and particularly while in Gethsemane, Jesus suffered from all future acts of profanation and ingratitude. He knew them in detail with a superior intuition that *governed all times*, He could see them much better than the saints, who sometimes can read the secret plagues of the human heart. Thus, his suffering encompassed the present instant and extended to future centuries. "This drop of my blood, I shed it for you." So, in the Garden of Olives, Jesus suffered for all, and for each of us in particular, because he foresaw our ingratitude; but in that painful hour he was also consoled by the sight of those souls, who would take part with Him, for Him, and in Him in the work of redemption. He was *consoled* by the sight of such as St. Francis of Assisi, St. Benedict Joseph Labré, St. Catherine of Siena, and St. Gemma Galgani (emphasis in orginal; p. 30).

Stackpole then cites Louis Vereheylezoon, SJ, from his book *Devotion to the Sacred Heart* (Rockford, IL: TAN Books, 1978):

> The fruit of this reparation is not lost for Jesus. Our making amends consoled and rejoiced His Heart during His mortal life. That we were able to do so, before we existed, is owing to His prescience, His foreknowledge of the future. Theologians hold for certain that by the infused prescience with which God invested His soul, Jesus knew all that was in any way connected with the work of Redemption. He foresaw, then, all the good and evil which would occur in the

course of time, and hence also whatever would be done for or against Him. He knew then, in particular, how men would repay His love. One may even say that this prevision was one of the causes of His deathly sorrow at Gethsemane. But at the same time He foresaw the tokens of love which He would receive from His faithful followers, and particularly the reparation they would make to Him for the ingratitude of others. ... [T]his prospect consoled, encouraged, and fortified Him, and helped Him to give Himself up to suffering and death in spite of His prevision of the ingratitude of so many. Whenever, then, we pay to Jesus some homage of reparation, we may cherish the gratifying conviction that, especially during His agony in the Garden, He saw us in the far off distance of time, that He gratefully looked upon us, and that our reparation really soothed His sorrow to some extent, and comforted and strengthened Him in His agony (p. 88).

For a full treatise on the theology of giving consolation to the Heart of Jesus, see Algelico Koller, SCJ, *Reparation to the Sacred Heart: Theology of Consolation* (Hales Corners, Wisconsin: Priests of the Sacred Heart, 1971). For the full history of this theology and the spirituality that flows from it, which includes a response to Karl Rahner's critique of Consoling spirituality, see Stackpole's doctoral thesis for the Angelicum in Rome, *Consoling the Heart of Jesus: A History of its Notion and Practice, especially as found in the Ascetical and Mystical Tradition of the Church* (2001).
Page 50: "... we can still console him (according to the idea of "retroactive consolation") ..." Another angle from which one might consider retroactive consolation is to think of it in light of the *Catechism's* teaching on the Paschal mystery of Christ in its section on the liturgy:

His Paschal mystery is a real event that occurred in our history, but it is unique: all other historical events happened once, and then they pass away, swallowed up in the past. The Paschal mystery of Christ, by contrast, cannot remain only in the past, because by his death he destroyed death, and all that Christ is — all that he did and suffered for all men — participates in the divine eternity, and so transcends all times while being made present in them all. The event of the Cross and Resurrection *abides* and draws everything toward life (emphasis in orginal; 1085).

Deacon James McCormack, MIC, a friend of mine who understands Consoling spirituality well, offers the following thoughts that help explain retroactive consolation from the perspective of the above citation from the *Catechism*:

The historical events of Jesus' life, including and especially his Passion and death, are "God-events" because of
the subject. Being God-events, they do not exist only in
time, but also outside of time since God acts in the "eternal
now." Thus, these events exist, in a sense, before the eyes of
God in the "eternal now." It seems that the Jews saw
Passover and other events in salvation history in this light.
Therefore, a key feature of their liturgies was calling to
mind (remembering or *anamnesis*) these God-events with
the understanding that, by doing so, they "entered into"
these "now-events" in heaven. According to my
Liturgiology class, we can speak of the Eucharistic Prayer in
the Mass with the same understanding.

Thus, I think Jesus' sufferings can be understood in this
light. It may sound almost identical to the retroactive suffering, but I think there's a nuance, which is this: I understand
retroactive suffering (and consolation) to be saying that Jesus
in the past can see me in the future, perhaps through his
prophetic knowledge, and so my praying now brings him consolation. I understand my alternative thought to be saying that
those events are "now" in heaven (the "eternal now"), and so,
through prayer (especially the liturgy), I can be present to
Jesus in those events, taken up into those events, not merely
as historical events but as "now-events." Thus, I can see this
as being yet another sense in which Jesus is suffering in heaven
"now" in that the historical events are still present now.

This may get complicated, but if what I've said so far
holds, then perhaps we can apply this to all the "God-
events," for example, the nativity, the Passion/death, the
Resurrection and the Ascension/exaltation. If that's so,
then it would seem that we can, in one moment, be present
to Jesus suffering in the Passion and death ... and a moment
later be present to him not yet suffering (much) in the
nativity, or no longer suffering in the Resurrection and
Ascension/exaltation.

Deacon James's alternative thought on retroactive consolation
made me think of the "eternal now" as being like a special "place" where
we actually meet with Jesus as he lives all the mysteries of his life. Because
Jesus lived (lives) every moment of his life in the eternal now, he's always
present to us and, in a sense, waits for us to meet him there. We meet
Jesus there, we become present to him, through our prayer. So, for
instance, when we pray the Rosary and meditate on the mysteries of
Christ's life, it's not just a mental exercise. For, if our hearts have faith and
love, then by these supernatural virtues we truly enter into the mysteries
themselves. As Pope John Paul II writes in his apostolic letter *Rosarium
Virginis Mariae*, 15: "The Rosary mystically transports us to Mary's side

as she is busy watching over the human growth of Christ in the home of Nazareth. This enables her to train us and to mold us with the same care." It's an amazing thought: Through prayer we become "mystically transported" to Christ, who is always present to us (and to Mary, who lived her life in the eternal now with Jesus). We join him in the "meeting place" of the eternal now and truly connect with him. Moreover, as Deacon James alluded to, the primary place where this meeting occurs is through Liturgical prayer, especially the Mass. For the Mass is the place where the Paschal Mystery is truly made present to us as the eternal hour of Christ's Passion and Glorification. (See *Catechism*, 1362-1367.)

Page 50: "Indeed, for centuries, popular and beloved books of Christian piety ..." In *Jesus, Mercy Incarnate* (n. 24, p. 93), Stackpole states: "The sufferings of Jesus during His Agony in the Garden from His prevision of all the ingratitude of future generations is also an important theme in the devotional literature of the Sacred Heart; see John Croiset, SJ, *The Devotion to the Sacred Heart of Jesus* (Rockford, IL: TAN Books, 1988), 273-279."

Page 51: "[Second Day] **Today bring to me** ..." *Diary*, 1209-1229.

Page 52: "... [W]hen persecutions are stirred up against the Church ..." Pius XI, *Miserentissimus Redemptor*, 14.

Page 53: "... is no longer subject to ..." Pius XII, *Haurietis Aquas*, 62.

Page 53: "When I say that the risen Christ 'suffers' ..." Thomas Weinandy, OFM, Cap., *Does God Suffer?* (Notre Dame: University of Notre Dame Press, 2000), p. 252.

Page 54: "In the Garden of Olives ..." John Paul II, Apostolic Letter *Novo Millenio Inuente*, 35-36.

Page 55: "My Saviour grieves even now ..." Origen, *In Lev. Hom.* 7,2, cited by Josef Ratzinger in *Eschatology: Death and Eternal Life*, trans. Michael Waldstein, ed. Aidan Nichols, OP (Washington, DC: The Catholic University of America Press, 1988), p. 185-186.

Page 56: "Love cannot, then, close itself ..." Ratzinger, Ibid., p. 188.

Page 57: "During the night, the Mother of God ..." *Diary*, 25.

Page 57: "... God ... doesn't need us ..." God doesn't need us, and yet two passages from the *Diary* of St. Faustina are worth pondering. First, she writes:

> It seems to me as though Jesus could not be happy without me, nor could I, without Him. Although I understand that, being God, He is happy in Himself and has absolutely no need of any creature, still, His goodness compels Him to give Himself to the creature, and with a generosity which is beyond understanding (244).

Second, she relates, "I do not know how to live without God, but I also feel that God, absolutely self-sufficient though He is, cannot be happy without me" (1120).

Page 58: "... he allows himself to be in need of mercy from us." See John Paul II, *Dives in Misericordia*:

The events of Good Friday and, even before that, in prayer in Gethsemane, introduce a fundamental change into the whole course of the revelation of love and mercy in the messianic mission of Christ. The one who "went about doing good and healing" and "curing every sickness and disease" now Himself seems to merit the greatest mercy and to *appeal for mercy*, when He is arrested, abused, condemned, scourged, crowned with thorns, when He is nailed to the cross and dies amidst agonizing torments. It is then that He particularly deserves mercy from the people to whom He has done good, and He does not receive it ...

[T]he cross will remain the point of reference for other words too of the Revelation of John: "Behold, I stand at the door and knock; if anyone hears my voice and opens the door, I will come in and eat with him and he with me." In a special way, God also reveals His mercy when He invites man to have "mercy" on His only Son, the crucified one.

... Christ, precisely as the crucified one, is the Word that does not pass away, and He is the one who stands at the door and knocks at the heart of every man, without restricting his freedom, but instead seeking to draw from this very freedom love, which is not only an act of solidarity with the suffering Son of man, but also a kind of "mercy" shown by each one of us to the Son of the eternal Father. In the whole of this messianic program of Christ, in the whole revelation of mercy through the cross, could man's dignity be more highly respected and ennobled, for, in obtaining mercy, He is in a sense the one who at the same time "shows mercy"? (emphasis in original; 7-8).

Page 58: "After many experiences and a lot of thinking ..." Karol Wojtyla, cited by George Weigel in *Witness to Hope: The Biography of Pope John Paul II* (New York, NY: HarperCollins Publishers, Inc., 1999), p. 102.

Page 58: "Now, as Aristotle pointed out ..." *Nicomachean Ethics*, Book VIII, 5, 8.

PART TWO

First Obstacle: *Fear of Suffering*

Page 65: "The first [consideration] is ..." *SpirEx*, 230-231.

Page 65: "This is to ask for ..." Ibid, 233.

Page 66: "... God *will* speak." God speaks to us all the time through Sacred Scripture, liturgy, people, circumstances, events, and in other ways. Sometimes we have difficulty hearing the Lord's voice due to the noise of the world. The *Spiritual Exercises* are a privileged time for us to hear the Lord speak because so much of the world's noise gets blocked out. In a prolonged, quiet, prayerful atmosphere such as a 30-day Ignatian retreat, God does indeed speak, and it's easier to hear him. Of course, he may not speak directly, that is, through audible words — though rare, it's possible — but he truly does speak. (For more on this topic, see Appendix One under the sub-section "Listen.")

Page 67: "All I want is for you to be my friend ..." After reading an early draft of this retreat, a friend of mine, Sr. Bernadette Marie Allain-Dupré, FM, pointed out to me that Jesus spoke in a similar way to the French mystic "Fiola." The following is Sr. Bernadette's translation (from the original French) of the conversation between Fiola and Jesus from the book *Chemin de Luminère* by Fr. Jean Dominique (Paris: Tequi, 1975), p. 48:

Fiola:	My Jesus, I would like to ask you what most pleases You in Your brides?
Jesus:	O My daughter, simplicity!
Fiola:	My Jesus, is that all?
Jesus:	Yes, My daughter.
Fiola:	My Jesus, tell me what true simplicity means.
Jesus:	Childlike trust in Me.
Fiola:	Is that all?
Jesus:	Yes, My daughter.
Fiola:	My Jesus, you don't ask for much!
Jesus:	Daughter of My Heart, this is all: all is there.

Page 68: "... we might even begin to find in suffering a source of joy ..." For example, St. Faustina gives the following testimony on how God changed her suffering into a source of joy: "... [T]he purer our love becomes, the less there will be within us for the flames of suffering to feed upon, and the suffering will cease to be a suffering for us; it will become a delight! By the grace of God, I have received such a disposition of heart that I am never so happy as when I suffer for Jesus, whom I love with every beat of my heart" (303). But, again, let's not get ahead of ourselves.

Page 70: "... he became amazed at just how much Jesus was suffering." See Appendix Two under the section, "Passion of the Lord."

Page 72: "Jesus taught St. Faustina ... the Chaplet of Divine Mercy." See *Diary*, 476. The Chaplet of Divine Mercy can be prayed on ordinary Rosary beads. One begins by praying an Our Father, a Hail Mary, and the Apostle's Creed. On the large bead before each decade, the following prayer is said, "Eternal Father, I offer You the Body and Blood, Soul and Divinity of Your dearly beloved Son, Our Lord Jesus Christ, in atonement for our sins and those of the whole world." On each bead of the decade, one prays, "For the sake of His sorrowful Passion, have mercy on us and on the whole world." The concluding prayer is, "Holy God, Holy Mighty One, Holy Immortal One, have mercy on us and on the whole world." To learn about the amazing power of the chaplet and the promises that the

Lord attached to praying it, see Appendix Two under the section, "Chaplet of Divine Mercy."

Page 72: **"For your sake I will withhold ..."** *Diary*, 431. For other examples of how just one soul can make a world of difference, see Appendix Two under the section, "For Your Sake ..."

Page 72: "... souls are bought only at the price of suffering." See *Diary*, 324.

Page 74: "*Redemptive Suffering.*" On the topic of redemptive suffering, I highly recommend Pope John Paul II's apostolic letter *Salvifici Doloris: On the Christian Meaning of Human Suffering*.

Page 74: "I rejoice in my sufferings ..." An important point to grasp in coming to understand better St. Paul's theology of redemptive suffering is the truth that believers are members of Christ's Body. At the moment of our baptism, it becomes a metaphysical reality: We truly *become* Christ's Body. Now, if we truly are Christ's Body, then the principle "Christ's suffering is redemptive" applies to us as well. That is, when we suffer as members of Christ's Body, then our suffering has redemptive power. That being said, as I'll soon explain in the text, the nature of this redemptive power differs from that of Christ, the Head of the Mystical Body, in a crucially important respect.

Page 74: "Think, for instance, of Our Lady of Fatima ..." Message of Our Lady of Fatima, August 13, 1917. (Source: *Fatima in Lucia's Own Words*, ed. Louis Kondor, SVD [Fatima: Postulation Center, 1989], p. 75.)

Page 75: **"Be assured that the grace of eternal salvation ..."** *Diary*, 1777.

Second Obstacle: *Our Weaknesses, Sinfulness, and Attachments*

Page 79: "... Jesus comes down, lifts us up, and eventually carries us to the heights." On this topic, it's worth pondering some of St. Thérèse's words cited by Conrad de Meester, OCD, in his book *With Empty Hands: The Message of St. Thérèse of Lisieux*, trans. Mary Seymour (Washington, DC: ICS Publications, 2002):

> Agree to be that little child. Through the practice of all the virtues, raise your little foot to scale the stairway of holiness. You won't succeed in reaching the first step, but God requires you only to demonstrate your good will. Soon, conquered by your futile efforts, he will descend himself, gather you up in his arms, and carry you off to his kingdom for ever (pp. 112-113).

Page 82: "Dear Sister, ... How can you ask me ..." Letter 197 to Sr. Marie of the Sacred Heart, September 17, 1896. *Letters of St. Thérèse of Lisieux*, vol. II, 1890-1897, trans. John Clarke, OCD (Washington, DC: ICS Publications, 1982), p. 998. The French mystic, Mother Louise Margaret Claret de la Touche, in *The Love and Service of God, Infinite Love*, trans. Patrick O'Connell (Rockford, IL: TAN Books, 1987), wrote similar words that are worth pondering: "It is not because I am good, it is not because I am humble, it is not because I am mortified, or faithful, or patient, or fervent, that Our Lord has granted me so many graces. ... If God has favored me so much, it is solely because I have believed in His Love" (p. 41).

Page 83: "The 'greatest saint of modern times' ... " Words of Pope St. Pius X as cited in *I Believe in Love*, p. 68.

Page 84: "O Jesus! why can't I tell ..." *Story of a Soul*, p. 200. Also on the topic of little souls being placed on the heights of holiness right beside Thérèse herself, we read the following from her autobiography: "O my Jesus, it is perhaps an illusion but it seems to me that You cannot fill a soul with more love than the love with which You have filled mine; it is for this reason that I dare to ask You *'to love those whom you have given me with the love with which you loved me'* (Jn 17:23)" (emphasis in original, p. 256).

Page 84: "I once heard a story, attributed to St. Thérèse ..." I have not yet been able to locate this story in Thérèse's writings. Still, even if it were never written down, we can easily imagine her saying it. I asked an expert on Thérèse's writings, Fr. Marc Foley, OCD, if he had ever heard this story. He said it definitely sounds like Thérèse, but he also wasn't able to locate it. Nonetheless, he did find in print a similar story told by her. In that story, a king is pursuing a rabbit. When the rabbit senses that the king's dogs are about to pounce on it, it jumps up into the king's arms. As a result of the rabbit's confidence, the king cherishes the rabbit. Thérèse concludes, "This is how God will treat us if when hunted down by the claims of Divine Justice represented by the little dogs in the story, we run for refuge into the very arms of our Judge." This story can be found in the book by Thérèse's sister, Sr. Genevieve of the Holy Face (Céline Martin), *My Sister St. Thérèse*, trans. Carmelite Sisters of New York of Conseils et Souvenirs (Rockford, IL: TAN Books, 1997), p. 59.

Page 85: "Even though I had on my conscience ..." Ibid., p. 259.

Page 86: "**The flames of mercy** ..." *Diary*, 1074.

Page 86: "It rests Me to forgive." Our Lord's words to Josefa Menendez, cited by Fr. Vincent Martin Lucia in *Come to Me in the Blessed Sacrament* (Mt. Clemens, MI: Apostolate for Perpetual Adoration, 1993), p. 153.

Page 86: "When you give me yours sins ..." These words of the Lord come from a pamphlet published by the Missionary of Charity Fathers entitled, "I Thirst." (See www.mcpriests.com/15legacy/ingles.htm.)

Page 86: "I am Love!" *Come to Me in the Blessed Sacrament*, p. 151.

Page 87: "Like fire that transforms ..." Ibid., p. 205.

Page 87: "... From our evil it can bring out not only good ..." See *Catechism*, 312, 412 and *Dives in Misericordia*, 6.

Page 88: "O Jesus, I feel like I've ruined everything ..." Prayer composed by author.

Page 91: "If the dog won't drop the ball, try getting down there with it." I recommend this only if you know the dog well, and if it's not the kind of dog that bites people.

Third Obstacle: *Fear of Suffering, Again*

Page 93: "He told her that what hurts him most ... " See *Diary*, 50, 300, 1076.

Page 96: "Jesus does not demand great actions ... " *Story of a Soul*, p. 188. Saint Faustina writes something similar: "I want to live in the spirit of faith. I accept everything that comes my way as given me by the loving will of God, who sincerely desires my happiness. And so I will accept with submission and gratitude everything that God sends me" (1549).

Page 96: "... the focus isn't on actively choosing ..." The key word here is *focus*. Of course, we can still (and, perhaps, sometimes should) choose appropriate mortifications and penances. Before we do, I suggest we first read Appendix Two under the section "Mortification."

Page 98: "Before she was to begin her annual retreat ..." Sophia Michalenko, CMGT, *The Life of Faustina Kowalska: The Authorized Biography* (Ann Arbor: Servant Publications, 1999), p. 89. The Lord's words cited in this passage are from the *Diary of St. Faustina*, 369.

Page 99: "... especially in his abandonment on the Cross." *Diary*, 1320.

Page 101: "Listen and put it into your heart ..." These are Our Lady of Guadalupe's words to Blessed Juan Diego when she appeared to him near present-day Mexico City in 1531.

Page 103: "I wish I could suffer even more." These words remind us of what Jesus said to St. Margaret Mary in the revelation we read in Part One, "Even a little love from them in return — and I should regard all that I have done for them as next to nothing, and look for a way of doing still more."

Page 104: "**You see what you are of yourself** ..." *Diary*, 718. On this same topic, St. Faustina wrote the following about herself, "There is no soul more wretched than I am, as I truly know myself, and I am astounded that divine Majesty stoops so low" (440). See also Appendix Two under the section, "Divine Mercy — And Misery."

Page 105: "For then he can act with his full power ..." On this point, it's helpful to consider the words of St. Faustina, "Oh, how good it is to abandon oneself totally to God and to give Him full freedom to act in one's soul!" (*Diary*, 134). Also, on this topic, Jesus said to St. Faustina, "... [N]**ot every soul receives Me with the same living faith as you do, My daughter, and therefore I cannot act in their souls as I do in yours**" (1407).

Page 105: "... a 'mist' before the eyes of Jesus ..." See *Diary*, 284.

Page 107: "Some are astonished ..." *I Believe in Love*, p. 176. A related idea is expressed in the following passage from St. Faustina's *Diary*: "I am consumed with sorrow at the sight of those who are cold and ungrateful; and I then try to have such a love for God that it will make amends for those who do not love Him, those who feed their Savior with ingratitude at its worst" (481).

Page 108: "You, worry only about loving me ..." The original words are in Italian, "Tu pensa solo ad amarmi, lo penserò a tutto il resto, fino ai minimi particolari." They can be found in the book by Fr. Lorenzo Sales, *II Cuore di Gesù al Mundo* (Vatican City: Liberia Editrice Vaticana, 1999), p. 172. Jesus said something similar to St. Margaret Mary, "Take care of my interests and I shall take care of yours" (cited in *I Believe in Love*, p. 103).

Page 108: "If we stay fixed on our goal, he'll take care of ... all those who are dear to us ..." When we focus on consoling the Heart of Jesus, the Lord takes care of those whom we love. Thus, even if we were to spend all our time of prayer consoling Jesus, we'd be wrong to think that we'd thereby be neglecting our family and friends and those for whom we've promised to support with our prayers. St. Thérèse beautifully explains this in the following passage of *Story of a Soul*:

> Since I have two brothers and my little Sisters, the novices, if I wanted to ask for each soul what each one needed and go into detail about it, the days would not be long enough and I fear I would forget something important. For simple souls there must be no complicated ways; as I am of their number, one morning during my thanksgiving, Jesus gave me a simple means of accomplishing my mission.
>
> He made me understand these words of the Canticle of Canticles: "*DRAW ME, WE SHALL RUN after you in the odor of your ointments* (1:3). O Jesus, it is not even necessary to say: "*When drawing me, draw the souls whom I love!*" This simple statement: "Draw me" suffices; I understand, Lord, that when a soul allows herself to be captivated by the odor of your ointments, she cannot run alone, all the souls whom she loves follow in her train; this is done without constraint, without effort, it is a natural consequence of her attraction for You. Just as a torrent, throwing itself with impetuosity into the ocean, drags after it everything it encounters in its passage, in the same way, O Jesus, the soul who plunges into the shore-less ocean of Your Love, draws with her all the treasures she possesses. Lord, You know it, I have no other treasures than the souls it has pleased You to unite to mine; it is You who entrusted these treasures to me (emphasis in original; 254).

Fourth Obstacle: *The Sensitivity of the Lord's Heart*

Page 110: "... 'the surest, easiest, shortest ..." *True Devotion*, pp. 33, 96-107.

Page 112: "... the already unfathomably deep bond ..." Saint Louis de Montfort understood the bond between the Holy Spirit and Mary to be a moral one. Saint Maximilian Kolbe, on the other hand, through his reflections on Mary's words to St. Catherine Laboré at Rue du Bac

(1830) and to St. Bernadette Soubirous at Lourdes (1858), came to a deeper understanding of the bond between the Holy Spirit and Mary. Kolbe's deeper understanding can be found in a book on his Marian spirituality, *Immaculate Conception and the Holy Spirit*, by H.M. Manteau-Bonamy, OP, trans. Richard Arnandez, FSC (Kenosha: Franciscan Marytown Press, 1977). In the following passage from this book, the author compares the teaching of de Montfort and Kolbe on the bond between the Holy Spirit and Mary:

> Father Kolbe ... knew that de Montfort, who never heard of the apparitions of the Rue du Bac or of Lourdes, had remained limited to the consideration of a moral bond between Mary and the Holy Spirit. But since it is perfectly possible to understand the union which St. de Montfort writes about, in the meaning acquired at Lourdes, Father Kolbe does not hesitate to interpret it so (101).

What is the union between Mary and the Holy Spirit according to St. Kolbe? He holds that it's something deeper than the bond of marriage and that it occurred well before the Annunciation, at the first moment of Mary's conception, causing her Immaculate Conception:

> Among creatures made in God's image, the union brought about by married love is the most intimate of all. In a much more precise, more interior manner, the Holy Spirit lives in the soul of the Immaculata, in the depths of her very being. He makes her fruitful from the very first instant of her existence, all during her life, and for all eternity. This eternal "Immaculate Conception" (which is the Holy Spirit) produces, in an immaculate manner, divine life itself in the womb (or depths) of Mary's soul, making her the Immaculate Conception. The virginal womb of Mary's body is kept sacred for him; there he conceives in time — because everything that is material happens in time — the human life of the man-God (57).

Page 112: "So, it's Mary's great God-given task ..." Mary's specially appointed task in the work of salvation does not in any way detract from Christ as the one who perfectly completes this work in himself. That Christ shares this work with Mary (and all of us) shows forth its greatness. Thus, the *Catechism* (citing the Second Vatican Council document, *Lumen Gentium* 60, 62) states:

> Mary's function as mother of men in no way obscures or diminishes [the] unique mediation of Christ, but rather shows its power. But the Blessed Virgin's salutary influence on men ... flows forth from the superabundance of the merits of Christ, rests on his mediation, depends entirely on

it, and draws all its power from it.

... No creature could ever be counted along with the Incarnate Word and Redeemer; but just as the priesthood of Christ is shared in various ways both by his ministers and the faithful, and as the one goodness of God is radiated in different ways among his creatures, so also the unique mediation of the Redeemer does not exclude but rather gives rise to a manifold cooperation which is but a sharing in this one source (970).

Page 112: "... to unite everyone to the Body of Christ." Because of Mary's role in uniting us to the Body of Christ, since the Middle Ages, she's been called, "The Neck of the Mystical Body of Christ."

Page 113-114: "She makes the lessons of the Cross into something sweet ..." *True Devotion*, pp. 142-143.

Page 114: "... Mary's faith makes up for what we lack." See Ibid., pp. 137-138.

Page 115: "It is as if a peasant ..." Ibid., p. 93.

Page 116: "... '[H]er whole life revolved around it.'" Christopher O'Mahoney, ed. and trans., *St. Thérèse of Lisieux by Those Who Knew Her* (Dublin: Veritas Publications, 1995), p. 46.

Page 116: "... 'greatest saint of modern times'?" Words of Pope St. Pius X as cited in *I Believe in Love*, p. 68.

Page 116: "Amazingly, the Lord accepted such deals." One of the most striking examples of the Lord accepting such a deal comes from the French Revolution when a whole convent of nuns, the Carmelite sisters of Compiègne, offered themselves as a sacrifice to "appease the anger of God" that, they believed, had been unleashed on their country during the Revolution. About two years later, on July 17, 1794, all 16 sisters were martyred at the guillotine. Only 10 days after consuming them, the Reign of Terror, that most horrible and murderous period of the French Revolution, came to an abrupt end. According to the Catholic historian, Warren Carroll, there is no more striking example in all of Church history of the power of the Cross to overcome evil. (See *The Revolution Against Christendom: A History of Christendom, Vol. 5*. [Front Royal, VA: Christendom College Press, 2005], pp. 275-279.) Saint Thérèse, a Carmelite sister herself, surely would have heard of the Carmelite sisters of Compiègne, for they died in her native France just 80 years before her birth, and their sacrifice was well known.

Page 117: "I was thinking about the souls who offer ..." *Story of a Soul*, p. 180.

Page 117: "O my God!" Ibid., pp. 180-181.

Page 118: "Thérèse specifically declares in the text of her offering ..." The text of Thérèse's offering is as follows:

O My God! Most Blessed Trinity, I desire to *Love* You and make You *Loved*, to work for the glory of Holy Church by saving souls on earth and liberating those suffering in purgatory. I desire to accomplish Your will perfectly and to reach the degree of glory You have prepared for me in Your Kingdom. I desire, in a word, to be a saint, but I feel my helplessness and I beg You, O my God! to be Yourself my *Sanctity!*

Since You loved me so much as to give me Your only Son as my Savior and my Spouse, the infinite treasures of His merits are mine. I offer them to You with gladness, begging You to look upon me only in the Face of Jesus and in His heart burning with *Love.*

I offer You, too, all the merits of the saints (in heaven and on earth), their acts of Love, and those of the holy angels. Finally, I offer You, *O Blessed Trinity!* the Love and merits of the *Blessed Virgin, my dear Mother.* It is to her I abandon my offering, begging her to present it to You. Her Divine Son, my *Beloved* Spouse, told us in the days of His mortal life: "*Whatsoever you ask the Father in my name he will give it to you!*" I am certain, then, that You will grant my desires; I know, O my God! that *the more You want to give, the more You make us desire.* I feel in my heart immense desires and it is with confidence I ask You to come and take possession of my soul. Ah! I cannot receive Holy Communion as often as I desire, but, Lord, are You not *all-powerful?* Remain in me as in a tabernacle and never separate Yourself from Your little victim.

I want to console You for the ingratitude of the wicked, and I beg of You to take away my freedom to displease You. If through weakness I sometimes fall, may Your *Divine Glance* cleanse my soul immediately, consuming all my imperfections like the fire that transforms everything into itself.

I thank You, O my God! for all the graces You have granted me, especially the grace of making me pass through the crucible of suffering. It is with joy I shall contemplate You on the Last Day carrying the scepter of Your Cross. Since You deigned to give me a share in this very precious Cross, I hope in heaven to resemble You and to see shining in my glorified body the sacred stigmata of Your Passion.

After earth's Exile, I hope to go and enjoy You in the Fatherland, but I do not want to lay up merits for heaven. I want to work for Your *Love alone* with the one purpose of pleasing You, consoling Your Sacred Heart, and saving souls who will love You eternally.

In the evening of this life, I shall appear before You with empty hands, for I do not ask You, Lord, to count my works. All our justice is stained in Your eyes. I wish, then, to be clothed in Your own *Justice* and to receive from Your *Love* the eternal possession of *Yourself*. I want no other *Throne*, no other *Crown* but You, my *Beloved!*

Time is nothing in Your eyes, and a single day is like a thousand years. You can, then, in one instant prepare me to appear before You.

In order to live in one single act of perfect Love, I OFFER MYSELF AS A VICTIM OF HOLOCAUST TO YOUR MERCIFUL LOVE, asking You to consume me incessantly, allowing the waves of *infinite tenderness* shut up within You to overflow into my soul, and that thus I may become a *martyr* of Your *Love*, O my God!

May this martyrdom, after having prepared me to appear before You, finally cause me to die and may my soul take its flight without any delay into the eternal embrace of *Your Merciful Love*.

I want, O my *Beloved*, at each beat of my heart to renew this offering to You an infinite number of times, until the shadows having disappeared I may be able to tell You of my *Love* in an *Eternal Face to Face!* (emphasis in orginal; *Story of a Soul*, p. 276-277).

Page 118: "**My Heart overflows** ..." *Diary*, 367. For further citations from the *Diary* related to the Offering to Merciful Love, see Appendix Two under the section, "Offering to Merciful Love."

Page 119: "This kind of heartache isn't so intimidating." It may not be so intimidating, but it can become rather intense. One of St. Thérèse's sisters in religious life, Sr. Mary Magdalene of the Blessed Sacrament, related the following incident: "One day when I was in [Thérèse's] room she said to me in a tone of voice that I cannot reproduce: 'God is not loved enough! And yet he is so good and kind. ... Oh, I wish I could die!' And she began to sob. Not understanding what it was to love God so vehemently, I looked on in amazement ..." (O'Mahoney, 261). On one occasion, St. Faustina tells Jesus about her own experience of the kind of heartache that comes from having offered oneself to merciful love:

> "Jesus, I have so much to tell You." And the Lord said to me with great love, **Speak, My daughter**. And I started to enumerate the pains of my heart; that is, how greatly concerned I am for all mankind, that "they all do not know You, and those who do know You do not love You as You deserve to be loved. I also see how terribly sinners offend You; and then again, I see how severely the faithful, especially Your servants, are oppressed and persecuted. And then, too, I see many souls rushing headlong into the terrible abyss of hell. You see, Jesus, this is the pain that gnaws at my heart and bones. And, although You show me special love and inundate my heart

with streams of Your joys, nevertheless, this does not appease the sufferings I have just mentioned, but rather they penetrate my poor heart all the more acutely. Oh, how ardently I desire that all mankind turn with trust to Your mercy. Then, seeing the glory of Your name, my heart will be comforted" (929).

Page 119: "God seems to have taken him up on that deal, ..." Lest one begin to think of God the Father as a blood-thirsty, vindictive judge, it's important to understand that the theology of salvation (soteriology) provides more than one explanation of how we are saved. Although the heavily juridical salvation theories of some theologians — such as St. Anselm in his *Cur Deus Homo* — might give the impression of God as a vindictive judge, theirs aren't the only theories to choose from. (Still, such theories were part of the theological atmosphere of St. Thérèse's convent, and they provide part of the context for her explanation of her "Offering to Merciful Love.") I think St. Thomas Aquinas offers one of the best theories to explain how we are saved. (For an article-length treatment of his theory, see Rik Van Nieuwenhove, "Bearing the Marks of Christ's Passion" in *The Theology of Thomas Aquinas*, ed. Rik Van Nieuwenhove and Joseph Wawrykow [Notre Dame: University of Notre Dame Press, 2005], 277-302.) Aquinas's soteriology doesn't teach that Jesus' suffering and death appeases the wrath of some angry God, but rather that it's a kind of medicine meant to heal and transform us. In other words, being fallen, wounded creatures distrustful of God, we need a dramatic revelation of God's love to convince us of it and help us to accept it. We find such a dramatic revelation especially in Jesus' Passion and death on the Cross, for there is truly no greater love than when someone lays down his life for others (see Jn 15:13). In the following excerpt from his book, *The Godly Image: Christ and Salvation in Catholic Thought from Anselm to Aquinas* (Petersham, MA: St. Bede Publications, 1990), Fr. Romanus Cessario, OP, writes more about the part of Aquinas soteriology I've just explained:

> God does not accept anything in exchange or relent on account of something which Christ does. If Christ substitutes for sinful man in the experience of his passion, he does so only to enable men and women themselves to experience again the compassion of God. It is not that God then resumes being compassionate; rather, the human person is then free to accept God's love. All in all, satisfaction changes us, not God (165).

Page 119: "... making her a 'victim of mercy.'" Of course, Jesus also experienced an unfathomably deep heart suffering during his Passion. His Heart obviously burned with love and compassion for sinners, "Behold this Heart which loves so much ..."
Page 120: "You permitted me, dear Mother ..." *Story of a Soul*, p. 181.
Page 120: "... the Offering to Merciful Love is a sweet deal, indeed!" It's an even a sweeter deal for *families* when they make what I call a "Family

Offering to Merciful Love." Such an offering is basically where a family makes a "mercy deal" with Jesus. In other words, they ask Jesus to pour out on them the rejected mercy other families refuse, and for their part, they strive to accept this rejected mercy and share it with others. In our time, when the family is so much under attack, when, sadly, so many families refuse God's mercy, Jesus' Heart is especially wounded. A Family Offering to Merciful Love is meant to give Jesus the consolation of a family that chooses to receive his rejected merciful love. This doesn't mean the family has to be perfect. In fact, the more imperfect they are, the more Jesus longs to pour out his mercy on them. They simply need to be open to receiving and sharing his merciful love. I suggest the following formula for making a Family Offering to Merciful Love, which begins with Jesus' words to St. Faustina:

> Jesus, you said to St. Faustina: **The flames of mercy are burning me. I desire to pour them out upon human souls. Oh, what pain they cause Me when they do not want to accept them!** (1074). **You, at least, come to Me as often as possible and take these graces they do not want to accept. In this way you will console My Heart. Oh, how indifferent are souls to so much goodness, to so many proofs of love! My Heart drinks only of the ingratitude and forgetfulness of souls living in the world. They have time for everything, but they have no time to come to Me for graces** (367). **My daughter, take the graces that others spurn; take as many as you can carry** (454). **I want to give myself to souls and to fill them with My love, but few there are who want to accept all the graces My love has intended for them. My grace is not lost; if the soul for whom it was intended does not accept it, another soul takes it** (1017).
>
> Lord Jesus, if you want to pour your mercy out on souls, how much more must you desire to pour it out on whole families, especially in our time when so many families reject you. Therefore, we the _____

Family offer ourselves to your merciful love and ask for the graces and mercy that other families refuse. We ask this in order to console your Heart and because we need your mercy. Fill us with your mercy, Lord. Please forgive us our sins, and give us the grace to be merciful to one another in our deeds, words, and prayers. May the rays of mercy that go forth from your Heart reign in our home and in our hearts. Please make our home a place where your mercy can rest and where we, too, can find rest in your mercy. Bless us with your mercy when we leave our home and bless us again when we return. Bless everyone we meet with the mercy you pour into our hearts. Especially bless those who visit our home — may they experience your mercy here.

Mary, Mother of Mercy, help us to faithfully live our Offering to God's Merciful Love. We give ourselves to you and ask you to share with us your Immaculate Heart. Help us to accept your Son's mercy with your own openness of heart at the Annunciation. Help us to be grateful for God's mercy with your own joyful heart at the Visitation. Help us to trust in God's mercy, especially during times of darkness, with your own steadfast faith at Calvary. Finally, Mary, protect and preserve our family in love, so that one day we may rejoice together with you and all the saints in the communion of the eternal Family of Love, Father, Son, and Holy Spirit. Amen.

St. Joseph, pray for us.

St. Faustina, pray for us.

St. Thérèse, pray for us.

I recommend that a family make such an offering on one of their favorite Marian Feasts, on St. Joseph's Feast (March 19), or on one of the "Mercy Feasts" such as the memorial of St. Thérèse of Lisieux (Oct. 1) or St. Faustina (Oct. 5), Divine Mercy Sunday (the second Sunday of Easter) or Trinity Sunday, which is the day St. Thérèse first made her Offering to Merciful Love. I further recommend that the Family Offering be accompanied by a Divine Mercy Enthronement, meaning that the family put up in their home an Image of Divine Mercy (if there isn't one already) and ask Jesus to reign there. An appropriate prayer for such an enthronement is as follows:

Jesus, you said to St. Faustina: **"I am offering people a vessel with which they are to keep coming for graces to the fountain of mercy. That vessel is this image with the signature: 'Jesus, I trust in You' (327). By means of this image I shall be granting many graces to souls"** (570).

Lord Jesus, through this image of your mercy, please grant us your grace. Whenever we look at it, help us to remember your love and mercy and fill our hearts with trust. Just as your mercy is depicted in this image as going forth from your pierced Heart, surround our home with the rays of your mercy. May the blood and water that flows forth from your Heart always be upon us! Jesus, we trust in you.

I recommend concluding such a prayer by praying a Divine Mercy Chaplet. Also, it might be a good idea to invite a priest to bless your home and your Image of Divine Mercy.

Page 120: "According to ... St. Thomas Aquinas ..." See *Summa Theologiae*, III, q. 80, a. 2, s.c. and ad. 3, that is, Part 3 of the *Summa Theologiae*, question 80, article 2, both the main reply and the reply to objection 3:

I answer that ... . In another way one may eat Christ spiritually, as He is under the sacramental species, inasmuch as a man believes in Christ, while desiring to receive this sacrament; and this is not merely to eat Christ spiritually, but likewise to eat this sacrament; which does not fall to the lot of the angels. And therefore although the angels feed on Christ spiritually, yet it does not belong to them to eat this sacrament spiritually.

   Reply to Objection 3: Christ dwells in men through faith ... .

Fifth Obstacle: *The Insensitivity of Our Hearts*

Page 127: "... this pope's teaching on God's mercy is an authoritative mandate ..." To learn more about Pope John Paul II's teaching on Divine Mercy, see George Kosicki, CSB, *John Paul II: The Great Mercy Pope* (Stockbridge, MA: Marian Press, 2001). Also, to learn how Pope Benedict XVI takes up and develops the Divine Mercy teachings of Pope John Paul II, see *Pope Benedict's Divine Mercy Mandate* (Stockbridge, MA: Marian Press, 2009), by David Came.

Page 128: "A hard heart is the opposite of mercy." My translation from the Italian of the opening address, "Relazione di apertura al primo congress mondiale sulla Divina Misericordia," to the First World Apostolic Congress on Mercy in Rome, delivered by Cardinal Christoph Schönborn on April 2, 2008.

Page 133: "My daughter, your compassion ..." *Diary*, 1657.

Page 134: "... the more deeply he brings us into the mystery of his Passion." Regarding the mystery of the Lord's suffering, it may be helpful for Consolers to prayfully reflect on what Jesus said to a Mexican mystic, Venerable Concepcion Cabrera de Armida ("Conchita"), on November 4, 1899:

The Apostolate of the Cross is the work which continues and completes that of My Heart and which was revealed to Margaret Mary. I tell you that this does not mean only My external Cross is a divine instrument of Redemption. This Cross is presented to the world to bring souls toward My Heart, pierced on that Cross. The essence of this work consists in making known the Interior Sufferings of My Heart which are ignored, and which constitute for me a more painful Passion than that which My Body underwent on Calvary, on account of its intensity and its duration, mystically perpetuated in the Eucharist. I tell you, up to this day, the world has known of the love of My Heart manifested to Margaret Mary, but it was reserved for present times to make known its suffering, the symbols of which I had shown simply and in an external way. I say again, there must

be a penetration into the Interior of this boundless ocean of
bitterness and an extension of knowledge of it throughout
the world for bringing about the union of the suffering of the
faithful with the immensity of the sufferings of My Heart, for
their suffering is mostly wasted. I wish them to profit from it
by way of the Apostolate of the Cross for the benefit of souls
and for the consolation of My Heart ... (Cited in Marie
Michael Philipon, OP, *Conchita*, trans. Aloysius J. Owen, SJ
(New York: Alba House, 1978), p. 33).

Page 135: "I give great graces ..." *Diary*, 737.

Page 135: "... perhaps more than any other ..." The practice of
contemplating the Lord's Passion may be the best way to soften our
hearts, especially when it is done after receiving Christ's sacrificial love
for us in the Eucharist and when we ourselves suffer with Christ.

Page 136-137: "Envy is more directly destructive ..." The *Catechism*
defines envy as follows: "Envy is a capital sin. It refers to the sadness at
the sight of another's goods and the immoderate desire to acquire them
for oneself, even unjustly" (2539). Although the very nature of envy is a
sadness at the sight of another's goods, it leads to and results in joy at
another's misfortune because, as St. Thomas Aquinas says, "Grief over
our neighbor's good which is envy, gives rise to joy in his evil" (*Summa
Theologiae*, II-II, q. 36, a. 4, ad. 3).

Page 139: "... interpret insofar as possible ..." *Catechism*, 2478.

Page 140: "Or do I give in to anger ..." The *Catechism* teaches: "Anger
is a desire for revenge. 'To desire vengeance in order to do evil to someone who should be punished is illicit,' but it is praiseworthy to impose
restitution 'to correct vices and maintain justice'" (2302).

Page 140: "We resemble God most when ..." *Diary*, 1148.

Page 142: "**I am giving you three ways** ..." Ibid., 742.

Page 142: "The first: the act of mercy ..." Ibid., 163.

Page 142-143: "When I hesitate on how to act ..." Ibid., 1354.

Page 143: "Second suggestion: Reflect on the three degrees of mercy."
As a further aid to growing in prudent compassion, I recommend reflecting on the section under Appendix Two, "Divine Mercy — Way of Life."

Page 143: "There are infinite ways of doing deeds of mercy." On this
point, consider St. Faustina's words: "I understand that mercy is manifold; one can do good always and everywhere and at all times. An ardent
love of God sees all around itself constant opportunities to share itself
through deed, word, and prayer" (Ibid., 1313).

Page 143: "Yet reflecting on 14 points is still a lot ..." The traditional list
of the *corporal* works of mercy is as follows:

1. Feed the hungry.	5. Visit the sick.
2. Give drink to the thirsty.	6. Ransom the captive.
3. Clothe the naked.	7. Bury the dead.
4. Give shelter to the homeless.	

Here is the traditional list of the seven *spiritual* works of mercy:

1. Instruct the ignorant.
2. Counsel the doubtful.
3. Admonish sinners.
4. Bear wrongs patiently.
5. Forgive offenses willingly.
6. Comfort the afflicted.
7. Pray for the living and the dead.

The *Catechism* offers a slightly different version of the corporal and spiritual works of mercy:

> The works of mercy are charitable actions by which we come to the aid of our neighbor in his spiritual and bodily necessities. Instructing, advising, consoling, comforting are spiritual works of mercy as are forgiving and bearing wrongs patently. The corporal works of mercy consist especially in feeding the hungry, sheltering the homeless, clothing the naked, visiting the sick and imprisoned, and burying the dead. Among all these, giving alms to the poor is one of the chief witnesses to fraternal charity: it is also a work of justice pleasing to God (2447).

Page 144: "We must also continually purify all our actions ..." *Dives in Misericordia*, 14.
Page 146: "You made us for Yourself ..." Saint Augustine, *Confessions*, I, I, I: PL 32, 659-661.
Page 146: "Pascal came up with an insightful theory ..." Blaise Pascal, *Pensées*, 139.
Page 146: "... the worst torture for modern man ..." Ibid.
Page 149: "... to know him more fully so as to love ..." See Appendix Two under the section, "Knowledge/Love."
Page 150: "It's just more of a challenge ..." In *this* sense someone could speak of finding Christ "hidden" in other people without falling into the over-spiritualized outlook.
Page 151: "You are great." According to young people who knew him well, Karol Wojtyla (later Pope John Paul II) had the ability to look at people in a way that convinced them of their call to greatness. (See *Witness to Hope*, p. 108.)
Page 156: "Before closing this long but important section ..." Because this section on the merciful outlook was so long and important, I thought it might be helpful to offer a summary of the main points of what the merciful outlook is.

The merciful outlook is ...

... truly merciful, because it recognizes that mercy is a

bilateral reality such that as we give we also receive — thus, it isn't the patronizing outlook;

... evangelization, proclaiming the good news of Christ's love through an authentic love for the other person — thus, it's not the proselytizing outlook;

... a response to existential loneliness that gives a cup of love to help quench our neighbor's thirst as well as our own;

... the gaze of God: It sees the good in others and brings it to light, draws it out — thus, it's not the judgmental outlook, which focuses on and draws out evil;

... wonderful, because of the sense of awe and wonder we feel at seeing the other as an unrepeatable manifestation of Christ's own beauty;

... a terribly loving gaze that says, "You are great," because it sees the true greatness as well as the potential for greatness in the other;

... deep-sea diving: knowing there is buried treasure in the other, a facet of the face of Christ not found in any other, and swimming through murky waters to find it;

... something that takes courage and perseverance because it sometimes meets with misunderstanding, coldness, and rejection;

... to truly delight in each and every person we meet, because we see in each one the unique member of the Body of Christ he is — thus, it's not the over-spiritualized outlook;

... loving others with the Heart of Christ, because each of us is a member of his body and thus shares the same Heart with him.

Page 156: "That's a big question ..." The full answer to questions concerning our proper attachment to others requires an investigation into the nature of human love. My favorite author on this topic is Dietrich von Hildebrand. Blessed with the rare combination of a brilliant intellect, remarkably deep affectivity, and unshakable faith, von Hildebrand marvelously maps out much of love's uncharted territory and leads the way for those who seek to order their love according to the truth of Christ. His most thorough treatment of love is *The Nature of Love* (St. Augustine's Press, 2009), a book that's written at a particularly high level and that may pose an extreme challenge to those without a background in philosophy. A more accessible yet still challenging book is *The Heart: An Analysis of Divine and Human Affectivity* (St. Augustine's Press, 2007). See especially von Hildebrand's masterful treatment of human love on pages 115-126, which span the chapters, "The Heart of the True Christian" and "*Amare in Deo.*"

Page 159: "According to St. Faustina ..." *Diary*, 163.

Page 160: "Because of this connection between the chaplet and the Mass ..." In the following passage, St. Faustina helps us understand better the power that comes from uniting our prayers with the Sacrifice of the Mass:

> When I immersed myself in prayer and united myself with all the Masses that were being celebrated all over the world at that time, I implored God, for the sake of all these Holy Masses, to have mercy on the world and especially on poor sinners who were dying at that moment. At the same instant, I received an interior answer from God that a thousand souls had received grace through the prayerful mediation I had offered to God. We do not know the number of souls that is ours to save through our prayers and sacrifices; therefore, let us always pray for sinners (Ibid., 1783).

Page 160: "Today I was awakened by a great storm. ..." Ibid., 1731.
Page 161: "Suddenly, I found myself in a strange cottage ..." Ibid., 1797-1798.
Page 161: "**My daughter, encourage souls to say the chaplet ...**" Ibid., 1541.
Page 161: "... which, by the way, is part of what it means to be consecrated to her ..." See *True Devotion*, pp. 78-79.
Page 163: "... nobody is more in need of trust ..." Regarding prayer for sinners, Jesus said to Faustina: "**Do not grow weary of praying for sinners. You know what a burden their souls are to My Heart. Relieve My deathly sorrow; dispense My mercy**" (*Diary*, 975). Also, he told her: "**The loss of each soul plunges Me into mortal sadness. You always console Me when you pray for sinners. The prayer most pleasing to Me is prayer for the conversion of sinners. Know, My daughter, that this prayer is always heard and answered**" (1397). Regarding prayer for the dying, Jesus said: "**Pray as much as you can for the dying. By your entreaties, obtain for them trust in My mercy, because they have most need of trust, and have it the least. Be assured that the grace of eternal salvation for certain souls in their final moment depends on your prayer. You know the whole abyss of My mercy, so draw upon it for yourself and especially for poor sinners**" (1777).
Page 163: "... great battles are waged for despairing souls at the hour of death." After reading this, some might wonder if it's worthwhile to pray for people who have committed suicide. Perhaps they think there's no hope for such souls because suicide is a sign of great despair. Well, I say this: Pray for them! There's hope. But don't just take my word for it. The *Catechism* teaches:

> Grave psychological disturbances, anguish, or grave fear of hardship, suffering, or torture can diminish the responsibility of the one committing suicide.
>
> We should not despair of the eternal salvation of persons who have taken their own lives. By ways known to

him alone, God can provide the opportunity for salutary repentance. The Church prays for persons who have taken their own lives (2282-2283).

In his book, *The Cross at Ground Zero* (Huntington: Our Sunday Visitor, 2001), Fr. Benedict Groeschel, CFR, drawing from St. Faustina's writings, writes about how God reaches out to people who commit suicide, giving them a chance to accept his mercy:

> We Catholics have been very impressed in recent years by the revelations and mystical experiences of a humble Polish nun, St. Faustina Kowalska, a simple peasant woman who spoke and wrote a great deal about the divine mercy. She tells us that Jesus revealed to her that in His divine mercy He calls out to every soul in that millionth of a millionth of a second between life and death. He doesn't rely on us clergy. He doesn't rely on the Christians. He Himself calls every soul because He does not will the death of the sinner but wills that the person be saved. He has said: "As I live, says the Lord God, I have no pleasure in the death of the wicked [that is, the sinner], but that the wicked turn from his way and live; turn back, turn back from your evil ways" (Ezekiel 33:11). I take St. Faustina's revelations very seriously, and I have much hope. In Appendix Three of this book there is a passage from her diary in which she records a conversation revealed to her of Christ speaking to a despairing soul (42-43).

For the conversation of Christ speaking to a despairing soul that Fr. Groeschel mentions above, see Appendix Two under the section, "Conversation with a Despairing Soul." Two other passages from the *Diary of St. Faustina* seem to apply particularly well to cases of suicide:

> I often communicate with persons who are dying and obtain the divine mercy for them. Oh, how great is the goodness of God, greater than we can understand. There are moments and there are mysteries of the divine mercy over which the heavens are astounded. Let our judgment of souls cease, for God's mercy upon them is extraordinary (1684).

> I often attend upon the dying and through entreaties obtain for them trust in God's mercy, and I implore God for an abundance of divine grace, which is always victorious. God's mercy sometimes touches the sinner at the last moment in a wondrous and mysterious way. Outwardly, it seems as if everything were lost, but it is not so. The soul, illumined by a ray of God's powerful final grace, turns to God in the last moment with such a power of love that, in an instant, it

receives from God forgiveness of sin and punishment, while outwardly it shows no sign either of repentance or of contrition, because souls [at that stage] no longer react to external things. Oh, how beyond comprehension is God's mercy! But — horror! — there are also souls who voluntarily and consciously reject and scorn this grace! Although a person is at the point of death, the merciful God gives the soul that interior vivid moment, so that if the soul is willing, it has the possibility of returning to God. But sometimes, the obduracy in souls is so great that consciously they choose hell; they [thus] make useless all the prayers that other souls offer to God for them and even the efforts of God Himself ... (1698).

Page 163: "**Call upon My mercy on behalf of sinners** ..." Ibid., 186.
Page 164: "We can read example after example ..." For examples, see Appendix Two under the section "Prayer — Bold/Powerful."
Page 164: "... To Faustina, he even emphasized ..." Ibid., 1273, 1605.
Page 164: "Moreover, he also emphasized ..." See, for example, Ibid., 1578.

CONCLUSION

Page 169: "... their principle and foundation (which happens to be the same as ours)." Blessed Mother Teresa of Calcutta wrote an amazingly moving letter to the members of the congregation she founded, the Missionaries of Charity, about their principle and foundation. Because their principle and foundation is essentially the same as ours, I highly recommend meditating on the following excerpt from her letter:

Jesus wants me to tell you again ... how much love He has for each one of you — beyond all you can imagine. I worry some of you still have not really met Jesus — one to one — you and Jesus alone. We may spend time in chapel — but have you seen with the eyes of your soul how He looks at you with love? Do you really know the living Jesus — not from books but from being with Him in your heart? Have you heard the loving words He speaks to you? Ask for the grace, He is longing to give it. Until you can hear Jesus in the silence of your own heart, you will not be able to hear Him saying "I thirst" in the hearts of the poor. Never give up this daily intimate contact with Jesus as the real living person — not just the idea. How can we last even one day without hearing Jesus say "I love you" — impossible. Our soul needs that as much as the body needs to breathe the air. If not, prayer is dead — meditation only thinking. Jesus wants you each to hear Him — speaking in the silence of your heart.

Be careful of all that can block that personal contact with the living Jesus. The Devil may try to use the hurts of life, and sometimes our own mistakes — to make you feel it is impossible that Jesus really loves you, is really cleaving to you. This is a danger for all of us. And so sad, because it is completely opposite of what Jesus is really wanting, waiting to tell you. Not only that He loves you, but even more — He longs for you. He misses you when you don't come close. He thirsts for you. He loves you always, even when you don't feel worthy. When not accepted by others, even by yourself sometimes — He is the one who always accepts you. My children, you don't have to be different for Jesus to love you. Only believe — you are precious to Him. Bring all you are suffering to His feet — only open your heart to be loved by Him as you are. He will do the rest.

You all know in your mind that Jesus loves you — but in this letter Mother wants to touch your heart instead. Jesus wants to stir up our hearts, so not to lose our early love, specially in the future after Mother leaves you. That is why I ask you to read this letter before the Blessed Sacrament, the same place it was written, so Jesus Himself can speak to you each one.

… His words on the wall of every MC chapel ["I Thirst"], they are not from the past only, but alive here and now, spoken to you. Do you believe it? If so, you will hear, you will feel His presence. Let it become as intimate for each of you, just as for Mother — this is the greatest joy you could give me. Mother will try to help you understand — but Jesus Himself must be the one to say to you "I Thirst." Hear your own name. Not just once. Every day. If you listen with your heart, you will hear, you will understand.

Why does Jesus say "I Thirst"? What does it mean? Something so hard to explain in words — if you remember anything from Mother's letter, remember this — "I thirst" is something much deeper than Jesus just saying "I love you." Until you know deep inside that Jesus thirsts for you — you can't begin to know who He wants to be for you. Or who He wants you to be for Him.

… [Our Lady] was the first person to hear Jesus' cry "I Thirst" with St. John, and I am sure Mary Magdalen. Because Our Lady was there on Calvary, she knows how real, how deep is His longing for you and for the poor. Do we know? Do we feel as she? Ask her to teach … . Her role is to bring you face to face, as John and Magdalen, with the love in the Heart of Jesus crucified. Before it was Our Lady pleading with Mother, now it is Mother in her name pleading with you — "listen to Jesus' thirst." Let it be for each … a Word of Life.

How do you approach the thirst of Jesus? Only one secret — the closer you come to Jesus, the better you will know His thirst. "Repent and believe," Jesus tells us. What are we to repent? Our indifference, our hardness of heart. What are we to believe? Jesus thirsts even now, in your heart and in the poor — He knows your weakness, He wants only your love, wants only the chance to love you. He is not bound by time. Whenever we come close to Him — we become partners of Our Lady, St. John, Magdalen. Hear Him. Hear your own name. Make my joy and yours complete (source: www.mcpriests.com/legacy/varanasi.htm).

Page 171: "O Jesus, I surrender this to you ..." This prayer is attributed to St. Padre Pio's spiritual director, Dom Dolindo Ruotolo. It is said that to this priest Jesus promised that whoever would surrender his worries, difficulties, and problems to Jesus with the words of this prayer, Jesus would take special, even miraculous care of what is surrendered to him.

Page 171: **"You will give me pleasure ..."** *Diary*, 1485.

Page 175: **"At three o'clock, implore my mercy ..."** Ibid., 1320.

Page 175: **"I remind you, My daughter ..."** Ibid., 1572.

Page 176: "You expired, Jesus, but the source of life ..." Ibid., 186, 1319.

Page 176: "The following 'map,' ..." I'm grateful to Deacon James McCormack, MIC, for making this map for me and allowing me to use it here.

Page 178: "... is based on the one taught by St. Ignatius ..." See *SpirEx*, 43.

Page 178: "... without having to spend long hours of prayer in the chapel." It's interesting to note that St. Ignatius discouraged his Jesuits from spending long hours of prayer in the chapel. He knew from his own experience that reaching the heights of prayer doesn't require so much time of formal prayer. He was convinced that one could become a contemplative-in-action by striving to find God in all things. In *Ignatius of Loyola: The Pilgrim Saint*, Ignacio Idígoras summarizes Ignatius's teaching on prayer:

> [Ignatius] never obliged by rule more than one hour of prayer a day, and even this hour was to be distributed over the whole day, and it included his famous examinations of conscience. He wanted his students to study and the others to work. They could make their work a prayer, and they should spend special effort in finding God outside of their formal prayer, in their daily occupations, and in the people they dealt with. Ignatius himself was a living example of such effort (p. 475; see also p. 543).

In *The Jesuits*, Joseph de Guibert also summarizes Ignatius's teaching on prayer. He does so by citing the saint's own words. For instance, he gives Ignatius's response to a superior who had asked for directives for training new Jesuits: "As to prayer and meditation ... [I approve] rather the effort to find God in all that one does, rather than the giving of much time to such prayer" (p. 88). And again, de Guibert cites a letter in which Ignatius writes to another superior of new Jesuits:

> [T]hey can exercise themselves in seeking the presence of our Lord in all things, such as their conversations, their walks, in all that they see, taste, hear, and understand, and in all their actions, since it is true that His Divine Majesty is in all things by his presence, power, and essence. This manner of meditating which finds God our Lord in all things is easier than raising ourselves to the consideration of divine things which more abstract, and to which we can make ourselves present only with effort. This good exercise, by exciting good dispositions in us, will bring great visitations from the Lord, even though they occur in a short prayer" (ibid.; see also pp. 86-87, 89, 564).

Page 179: "The examination ... should be made sometime toward the end of the day." This examen, which is made at the end of the day, is called by St. Ignatius the "general examination of conscience" (*SpirEx*, 32). Ignatius also teaches another kind of examen, what he calls the "particular examination of conscience" (ibid., 24). This latter form of the examen has as its focus the correction of a particular sin or defect.

The particular examen is a spiritual exercise for three times during the day, the first of which isn't actually the examen, but rather a mental preparation for it: (1) *in the morning*, one calls to mind, immediately on rising, the sin or defect that one intends to correct and then resolves to guard against it; (2) then, *before or after lunch*, one asks God for the grace to make the examen well, reflects on one's conduct during the morning regarding the sin or defect, repents of any falls, and resolves to guard oneself against the particular sin or defect for the remainder of the day; (3) finally, *before or after dinner*, one again asks God for the grace to make the examen well, reflects on one's conduct throughout the afternoon regarding the sin or defect, and then repents of any falls. For Ignatius's full treatment of the particular examination of conscience, see *SpirEx*, 24-31.

Three further points concerning the particular examen are worth considering: First, some people find it helpful to combine the third time of the particular examen with one's general examen. Related to this idea, I find it helpful to use my time for the midday examen not only to focus on the particular fault I may be seeking to correct but also as an occasion to recognize the blessings of the morning and to praise and thank God for them (the "B" of our general examen, *B-A-K-E-R*, as we'll soon learn). Second, on St. Ignatius's recommendation, some people find it helpful to keep a written list of their victories and defeats regarding the particular sin or defect they intend to overcome. For example, see St. Faustina's lists in her *Diary* (162, 1352-1355). Third, the particular examen need not be restricted to correcting sins or defects. It can also be used to cultivate particular virtues. For example, Faustina often used the particular examen to build the virtue of interior recollection to the merciful Christ (see *Diary*, 162, 1352). Also, Ignatius is said to have made a particular examen not just three times a day but *every hour*. He did so for the purpose of cultivating the virtue of purity of intention. Thus, every hour he would ask himself, "Have I consciously undertaken my works and activities of the last hour solely for the glory of God?" (Consolers might put it a bit differently: "Have I consciously undertaken my works and activities of the last hour for the purpose of consoling Jesus?")

Page 179: "... an examination of *consciousness*." See George Ashenbrenner, SJ, "Consciousness Examen" in *Review for Religious*. vol. 31, no. 1, 1972, pp. 14-21.

Page 179: "... it provides a record of one's spiritual life, which can then easily be reviewed ..." I find it helpful to write out my examination of conscience (in small writing) on 3x5 index cards.

Page 179: "Actually, we also have to remember ..." As you get in the habit of making the examen, you may find that, with time, you won't need to rely on as structured a method as the one I'm about to present in the text. Still, in the beginning, you'll probably find that structure is necessary. It's kind of like learning to dance. At first, one needs to follow dance steps. Then, after some practice, one begins to move more freely to the music and has to think less and less about the steps. Eventually, after a lot of practice, one begins to improvise on the steps to suit one's own dance style. So it is with the examen: The dance steps are the points, the music is the inspiration of the Holy Spirit, and one's own dance style is the personalized manner of making the examen that seems best to the one who makes it.

Page 179: "... the most important of the five points." Fr. Timothy Gallagher, OMV, in his work, *The Examen Prayer* (New York: The Crossroad Publishing Company, 2006), has a chapter entitled "First Step: Gratitude." He cites a letter of Ignatius to Simon Rodrigues of March 18, 1542. It can be found in *San Ignacio de Loyola: Obras Completas*, edited by Ignacio Iparraguire, SJ, and Candido de Dalmases, SJ (Madrid: Biblioteca de Autores Cristianos, 1982), p. 679. Saint Ignatius says:

> It seems to me, in the light of the divine Goodness, though others may think differently, that ingratitude is one of the things most worthy of detestation before our Creator and Lord, and before all creatures capable of his divine and everlasting glory, out of all the evils and sins which can be imagined. For it is a failure to recognize the good things, the graces, and the gifts received. As such, it is the cause, beginning, and origin of all evils and sins. On the contrary, recognition and gratitude for the good things and gifts received is greatly loved and esteemed both in heaven and on earth.

Fr. Gallagher responds to this:

> It would be difficult to express more strongly a sense of the
> incomparable value of gratitude. If you and I were asked to
> name the most unbearable of all evils and sins in this world,
> what might we choose? If you and I were asked to identify
> "the cause, beginning, and origin of all evils and sins in our
> world," how might we reply? For Ignatius, who has become
> so conscious of God as constantly pouring out gifts of love
> upon our world and upon each one of us, the answer to both
> questions is utterly clear: it is the simple failure to recognize
> (*des-conocimiento*) 'the good things, the graces, and the gifts
> received from God" (*Examen Prayer*, p. 59).

According to Fr. Gallagher, this idea of Ignatius flows from his
experience of God, who is always giving gifts of love greater than we can
imagine. As he told a laywoman, Ines Pascual, "We will much sooner tire
of receiving his gifts than He of giving them" (*Obras Completas*, 613).
The only just and reasonable attitude toward this constant activity of God
is profound and constant gratitude. Fr. Gallager states:

> For Ignatius then, the consciously chosen remembrance of
> God's gifts is not just a moment in a spiritual day or simply a
> devout practice considered generally advisable and helpful. It
> is the heart itself of the way he understands God and relates
> to God. The only God he ever knew from the first moment
> of his conversion was this God who constantly bestows gifts
> of grace upon us, revealing through these gifts the infinite
> love with which we are loved. When Ignatius tells us that the
> examen begins with gratitude for God's concrete gifts during
> the day, he is opening a window into the deepest reality of
> our spiritual loves: God's unbounded love for us and desire
> for our response, in love, to the love revealed in this giving
> (*Examen Prayer*, pp. 58-59).

Page 180: "... he'll send us more and more." On this point, consider
Jesus' words to St. Faustina, **"Be grateful for the smallest of My graces,
because your gratitude compels Me to grant you new graces"** (*Diary*,
1701).
Page 182: "So, the examen is a great way to live our principle and foun-
dation ..." For more information on how to pray the examen, see Fr.
Gallagher's book mentioned in the previous note.
Page 183: "(Matrimony, Anointing of the Sick, Holy Orders)." The
Sacrament of Holy Orders can be received three different times in the fol-
lowing sequence: Deaconal, Priestly, and Episcopal Ordination. For those
who receive Holy Orders twice (that is, when they're ordained a priest),
I'm sure they're happy to receive the Sacrament of Holy Orders "more

than once" — especially after the many years of seminary training.

Page 184: "'Such contrition,' says the *Catechism* ..." *Catechism*, 1452. On the topic of perfect contrition, these words of St. Faustina are worth pondering, "Heartfelt repentance immediately transforms the soul" (*Diary*, 388).

Page 184: "To learn more about mortal sin ..." The *Catechism's* treatment of mortal sin falls under the heading, "The Gravity of Sin: Mortal and Venial Sin," and can be found in paragraph numbers 1854-1864. Here is an excerpt from the first two paragraphs:

> Sins are rightly evaluated according to their gravity. The distinction between mortal and venial sin, already evident in Scripture, became part of the tradition of the Church. It is corroborated by human experience.
>
> *Mortal sin* destroys charity in the heart of man by a grave violation of God's law; it turns man away from God, who is his ultimate end and his beatitude, by preferring an inferior good to him. ... *Venial sin* allows charity to subsist, even though it offends and wounds it (emphasis in original; 1854-1855).

The *Catechism* goes on to speak about the three conditions for committing a mortal sin:

> For a sin to be *mortal*, three conditions must together be met: "Mortal sin is sin whose object is grave matter and which is also committed with full knowledge and deliberate consent" (emphasis in original; 1857).

The first condition, grave matter, is specified by the Ten Commandments. I recommend reading the *Catechism's* treatment of the Ten Commandments (2052-2557) to get a clear idea of what specific sins are meant as "grave." (Reading this treatment is also a great way to form one's conscience.) Regarding the second and third conditions, full knowledge and deliberate consent, we read the following:

> Mortal sin requires *full knowledge* and *complete consent*. It presupposes knowledge of the sinful character of the act, of its opposition to God's law. It also implies a consent sufficiently deliberate to be personal choice. Feigned ignorance and hardness of heart do not diminish, but rather increase, the voluntary character of sin.
>
> *Unintentional ignorance* can diminish or even remove the imputability of a grave offence. But no one is deemed to be ignorant of the principles of the moral law, which are written in the conscience of every man. The promptings of feelings and passions can also diminish the voluntary and

free character of the offense, as can external pressures or pathological disorders (emphasis in original; 1859-1860).

The *Catechism* provides a more concrete explanation of how the "voluntary and free character of the offence" may be diminished when it treats the sin of masturbation, that is, "the deliberate stimulation of the genital organs in order to derive sexual pleasure." Masturbatory acts, it says, are "intrinsically and gravely disordered" (2352). Having said that, the *Catechism* then goes on to teach the following:

> To form an equitable judgment about the subjects' moral responsibility and to guide pastoral action, one must take into account the affective immaturity, force of acquired habit, conditions of anxiety, or other psychological or social factors that can lessen, if not even reduce to a minimum, moral culpability.

Page 184: "Jesus waits for us in the Sacrament of Love, ..." Pope John Paul II, Apostolic Letter *Dominicae Cenae*, 3 (also cited in the *Catechism*, 1380).

Page 184: "... a time slot of adoration." Parishes with perpetual adoration have sign-up sheets for those who want to commit themselves to a specific hour of adoration weekly or several times a week. Signing up is important for keeping perpetual adoration going, because when Jesus is placed in a monstrance for adoration, there must always be someone present with him. Thus, without adorers (consolers), a parish can't have perpetual adoration.

Page 185: "One of the best ways to develop a deeper life of prayer ..." Saint Teresa of Avila is an expert on teaching people how to visit Jesus in the tabernacle of one's heart, what she calls the prayer of "recollection." Because this form of prayer is so important for Consolers, I'm now going to summarize Teresa's teaching on it. The citations from her writings that follow come from *The Collected Works of St. Teresa of Avila* (3 Vols.), trans. Kieran Kavanaugh, OCD, and Otilio Rodriguez, OCD (Washington: Institute of Carmelite Studies, 1976-1987).

Saint Teresa gives several definitions of the prayer of recollection. I'll now summarize them according to the following three-part definition: Recollection is (1) a particularly effective form of prayer that always lies within our power to practice (2) by which we keep the Lord interiorly present (3) by gazing on him or speaking with him there.

1. A particularly effective form of prayer that always lies within our power to practice. Over and over, when writing about the prayer of recollection, St. Teresa uses phrases like, "you can ...", "if you try ...", "I strove ... ." The importance she gives to personal effort is evident in statements such as, "Keeping Christ present is *what we ourselves can do*" (emphasis added; *The Book of Her Life*, 12, 4); and, "You must understand that this recollection is not something supernatural, but that it is something *we can desire and achieve ourselves* with the help of God ..." (emphasis added; *The*

Way of Perfection, 29, 4); and again, "I conclude in saying that whoever wishes to acquire [the prayer of recollection] — since, as I say, *it lies within our power* — should not tire of getting used to what has been explained [about recollecting oneself]" (emphasis added; Ibid., 29, 7). Moreover, even though this recollection is something one should practice at the beginning stage of prayer (*Life*, 12, 2-4), Teresa also says that it's "beneficial in all stages" (Ibid., 12, 3). In fact, it's so beneficial that she writes: "This is an excellent way of making progress, and in a very short time. I consider that soul advanced who strives to remain in [recollection]" (Ibid., 12, 2). According to Teresa, no other method of prayer draws the divine master "more quickly" to give the beginner the prayer of quiet (*Way*, 28, 4). Thus, the prayer of recollection is particularly effective not only because it takes one to the goal but because it does so quickly.

   2. By which we keep the Lord interiorly present. The second part of my three-part definition says that recollection is a form of prayer "by which we keep the Lord interiorly present." In other words, Teresa's prayer of recollection is not simply a practice of the presence of God generally speaking — as Br. Lawrence teaches in his classic work on the subject, *The Practice of the Presence of God*, for example — rather, what she means by recollection has a specific direction, namely, inward. She says, "This prayer is called 'recollection' because the soul collects its faculties together and enters *within itself* to be with its God" (emphasis added; *Way*, 28, 4).

   The interior presence of God within the soul is the foundation of Teresa's whole spiritual edifice (hence, the title of her most important work on prayer, *The Interior Castle*). Thus, she strongly emphasizes the importance of practicing the prayer of recollection and, while recognizing that God can be found everywhere (and *should* be found everywhere — remember the examen!), she thinks that it's even better to find him within:

> [We should] consider the Lord as very deep within [our] souls; such a thought is much more alluring and fruitful than thinking of Him as outside oneself. ... Within oneself, very clearly, is the best place to look; and it's not necessary to go to heaven, nor any further than our own selves; for to do so is to tire the spirit and distract the soul, without gaining as much fruit (*Life*, 4, 6).

   3. By gazing on him or speaking with him there. So, recollection has to do with turning inward to the Lord, who dwells in our souls. The third part of my three-part definition comes when we ask, "But how are we to do this? How do we turn inward to God dwelling in our souls?" Teresa gives two tips for doing this. First, simply look at him. Second, simply talk with him. Regarding the first she writes: "[W]e should occupy ourselves in looking at Christ who is looking at us ... (Ibid., 14, 22). I'm not asking you to do anything more than look at Him ... even if you do so just for a moment (*Way*, 26, 3)." Regarding the second, she advises:

[The soul] can keep Him ever present and speak with Him, asking for its needs and complaining of its labors, being glad with Him in its enjoyments and not forgetting Him because of them, trying to speak to Him, not through written prayers but with words that conform to its desires and needs (*Life*, 12, 2).

For more information on the prayer of recollection, see Appendix Two under the sections, "Prayer — Conversation with the Lord," "Prayer — Gaze of the Lord," and "Prayer — Recollection/Silence." I also highly recommend one of Blessed Mother Teresa of Calcutta's favorite books, *One with Jesus: The Life of Identification with Christ* by Fr. Paul de Jaegher, SJ. This book treats the prayer of recollection from the perspective of the Ignatian tradition of spirituality.

Note: The Ignatian spiritual tradition differs from the Carmelite tradition in that it is both contemplative and *active*. (The Carmelite tradition is strictly contemplative.) Ignatius would agree with St. Theresa that interior recollection is a foundation of the spiritual life, but he also emphasizes a radical mysticism of the exterior, a "finding God in all things."

Page 188: "St. Teresa of Avila wrote that she couldn't ..." *Life*, 4, 9.

Page 190: "... the prayer of the Psalms as the great school ..." *Catechism*, 304.

Page 190: "... it's a compilation of various citations from the *Diary* ..." If you end up finding Appendix Two spiritually fruitful, perhaps you'd be interested in dipping into the treasures of the *Diary of St. Faustina* every day. I recommend two daily devotionals arranged by Fr. George W. Kosicki, CSB: (1) *Mercy Minutes: Daily Gems of St. Faustina to Transform Your Prayer Life* (Stockbridge, MA: Marian Press, 2006) and (2) *Mercy Minutes with Jesus: Praying Daily on Jesus' Words from the Diary of St. Faustina* (Stockbridge, MA: Marian Press, 2008).

Page 191: "... it's worth reading because of the deep spiritual riches it contains ..." Saint Maximilian Kolbe's writings also provide a powerful teaching on Marian consecration.

Page 191: "The reading of [de Montfort's book] ..." De Montfort, *True Devotion*, Introductory pages. While many popes have strongly encouraged the faithful to consecrate themselves to Jesus through Mary, John Paul's endorsement of Marian consecration (or, as he calls it, Marian "entrustment") is the most impressive. Above all, it comes through his personal example. It is said that he daily renewed his total consecration to Jesus through Mary according to the long form of de Montfort's formula of consecration. In fact, his consecration was so central to his spirituality that he adopted as his papal motto a phrase that comes from de Montfort, "*totus tuus*" ("totally yours"), which is an abbreviation of a more complete form of entrustment to the Mother of God. (See John Paul's book, *Gift and Mystery* [New York: Doubleday, 1996], pp. 29-30, where he explains this.) By totally entrusting himself to Mary's motherly care, John Paul was simply imitating his Lord and Savior who did the same thing in Nazareth some 2000 years earlier.

CONSOLER CHEAT SHEET

Those who intend to follow the spirituality contained in this retreat (Consolers) may want to photocopy or download this cheat sheet as an aid to remembering its main prayers and resolutions.

"Behold this Heart which loves so much yet is so little loved."

Consoler Principle and Foundation

I_____, on this day _____ , choose as my principle and foundation to console the Heart of Jesus.

Dear Jesus, relying on your grace and the prayers of Mary and of all the angels and saints, I will strive to keep before my eyes the deep sorrow of your Heart and respond, with Mary, by consoling you in the following two ways:

First, I will give you my trust. Jesus, I trust in you. I will try not to be afraid of going to you as I am (*ecce*), even when my sins and weaknesses weigh heavily upon me. With an open heart, I choose to accept your mercy (*fiat*), even all that mercy other souls reject. Finally, I will do my best to praise and thank you in all things (*magnificat*), even when you give me the privilege of sharing in your Cross.

Second, I will strive to show mercy to my neighbor through my deeds, words, and prayers, remembering that by consoling others, I am also consoling you.

Heavenly Father, for the sake of the sorrowful Passion of your Son, I beg you: Send forth your Holy Spirit to help me fulfill this choice.

A Consoler's Three Promises

1. I will live my principle and foundation of consoling Jesus, with Mary, by giving him my trust (see "A Summary of Trust" below) and by doing acts of mercy according to the following three degrees:
    (a) Deed — especially the merciful outlook
    (b) Word — especially the merciful question
    (c) Prayer — especially the Chaplet of Divine Mercy and "breathing prayer."

2. I will keep to a simple schedule of daily prayer:
    (a) Morning Offering (see below)
    (b) Three O'clock Hour (see next page)
    (c) Examination of Conscience: B-A-K-E-R (see next page)

3. I will frequent the Sacraments and take time for spiritual reading.
    I will frequent the Sacraments by going to Mass every Sunday and maybe even during the week. I will go to confession at least once a year and maybe even once or twice a month. I will consider visiting Jesus in the Blessed Sacrament more regularly, and I will strive to visit him frequently in the tabernacle of my heart.

A Summary of Trust: *Ecce, Fiat, Magnificat*

1. *Ecce* = "Behold." Behold, Lord, here I am, weaknesses, sinfulness and all.
2. *Fiat* = "Let it be done to me." Lord Jesus, pour out the ocean of your mercy into the abyss of my misery. I choose to accept your mercy, even the mercy that others refuse.
3. *Magnificat* = "My soul proclaims the greatness of the Lord!" I praise and thank you, Lord Jesus, for the great gift of your mercy and for all your gifts, including my small sharing in your Cross.

Morning Offering

Dear Jesus, I know that your Sacred Heart is sorrowful because so many people neither love you nor trust in you. Behold, Lord, here I am. Though weak and sinful, I love you and I trust in you. I intend that all my actions this day be for the purpose of consoling you.

Text continues on the next page.

Heavenly Father, in union with all the Masses being offered today, I give you praise and thanks for the many gifts you will send me, including the gift of my small sharing in the Cross. May this my prayer glorify you and console your Son. With the help of your grace, I resolve to remain all day in this prayerful spirit of praise and thanks and, further, to console Jesus by being merciful to my neighbor through my deeds, words, and prayers.

Mary, my mother, come with your spouse the Spirit. Make my sacrifice of praise, thanks, and mercy a most pleasing consolation to your Son. Behold, I present to you all I am and have. Take my offering so it may pass through your Immaculate Heart, to Jesus' Sacred Heart, and on to the Father, for his greater glory. Amen.

Three Ways to Keep the Three O'clock Hour

1. We can *immerse ourselves in the Lord's Passion, especially in his abandonment on the Cross.* We can do this briefly (even "for an instant") or for a longer period of time. For example, we can simply look at a crucifix, think of Jesus in his Passion, or pray the Three O'clock Hour Prayer:

> You expired, Jesus, but the source of life gushed forth for souls, and the ocean of mercy opened up for the whole world. O Fount of Life, unfathomable Divine Mercy, envelop the whole world and empty Yourself out upon us. ... O Blood and Water, which gushed forth from the Heart of Jesus as a fount of mercy for us, I trust in You.

If we have more time, we can pray the sorrowful mysteries of the Rosary or make the Stations of the Cross. Here, again, is the map for busy people who want to make the stations over the course of two weeks:

Sunday	Monday	Tuesday	Wednesday	Thursday	Friday	Saturday
I. Jesus is condemned to death.	II. Jesus takes up his Cross.	III. Jesus falls the first time.	IV. Jesus meets his blessed mother.	V. Simon of Cyrene helps Jesus to carry the Cross.	VI. Veronica wipes the face of Jesus.	VII. Jesus falls a second time.

Sunday	Monday	Tuesday	Wednesday	Thursday	Friday	Saturday
VIII. Jesus consoles the women of Jerusalem.	IX. Jesus falls the third time.	X. Jesus is stripped of his garments.	XI. Jesus is nailed to the Cross.	XII. Jesus dies on the Cross.	XIII. Jesus is laid in the arms of his blessed mother.	XIV. Jesus is laid in the tomb.

2. We can *present our petitions to the Father by virtue of his Son's Passion.* Our petitions should be made with bold confidence because of the indescribable power of Jesus' Passion and the great promises attached to the Hour of Great Mercy. I recommend presenting one's petitions in the context of praying the Divine Mercy Chaplet. (Don't forget to pray for unrepentant sinners and the dying, especially for unrepentant sinners who are dying.)

3. The three o'clock hour is a great time to *visit Jesus, truly present in the Blessed Sacrament.*

Examination of Conscience: B-A-K-E-R

    (Begin by putting yourself in the presence of God.)

B = Blessings. Spend the most time here, praising and thanking God for the blessings of the day.

A = Ask. Ask the Holy Spirit to enlighten you, so you can recognize your sins.

K = Kill. It was our sins that killed and crucified Jesus. Search for commissions and omissions.

E = Embrace. Be sorry for sin and allow Jesus to embrace you with the rays of his mercy.

R = Resolution. Look ahead to the next day, anticipating potential pitfalls and opportunities.

We invite you to continue your experience with
Consoling the Heart of Jesus at our web address:

thedivinemercy.org/chj

- Download the Consoler Cheat Sheet and other prayers related to the retreat.

- Read recommendations and spiritual reflections from the author.

- Purchase additional copies of *Consoling the Heart of Jesus* for family and friends.

- Join the *Confraternity of Consolers*, a spiritual benefit society.

- Find a Divine Mercy Cenacle in your area or start one at your parish.

  (A Divine Mercy Cenacle is a group of people who, as a small Christian community, meet regularly for prayer and discussion on Scripture, the *Catechism*, and the writings of St. Faustina. They perform works of mercy in their local communities.)

If you don't have internet access and would like to purchase additional copies of *Consoling the Heart of Jesus*, please call 1-800-462-7426. Also, for Marian Press's complete line of DVDs, books, and more, visit marian.org/giftshop or call the number above to have the latest catalog sent to you. (See the Marian Press advertisement on the next two pages.)

PROMOTING DIVINE MERCY SINCE 1941

Marian Press, the publishing apostolate of the Marian Fathers of the Immaculate Conception of the B.V.M., has published and distributed millions of religious books, magazines, and pamphlets that teach, encourage, and edify Catholics around the world. Our publications promote and support the ministry and spirituality of the Marians worldwide. Loyal to the Holy Father and to the teachings of the Catholic Church, the Marians fulfill their special mission by:

- Fostering devotion to Mary, the Immaculate Conception.

- Promoting The Divine Mercy message and devotion.

- Offering assistance to the dying and the deceased, especially the victims of war and disease.

- Promoting Christian knowledge, administering parishes, shrines, and conducting missions.

Based in Stockbridge, Mass., Marian Press is known as the publisher of the *Diary of Saint Maria Faustina Kowalska,* and the Marians are the leading authorities on The Divine Mercy message and devotion.

Stockbridge is also the home of the National Shrine of The Divine Mercy, the Association of Marian Helpers, and a destination for thousands of pilgrims each year.

Globally, the Marians' ministries also include missions in developing countries where the spiritual and material needs are enormous.

To learn more about the Marians, their spirituality, publications or ministries, visit **marian.org** or **thedivinemercy.org**, the Marians' website that is devoted exclusively to Divine Mercy.

Below is a view of the National Shrine of The Divine Mercy and its Residence in Stockbridge, Mass. The Shrine, which was built in the 1950s, was declared a National Shrine by the National Conference of Catholic Bishops on March 20, 1996.

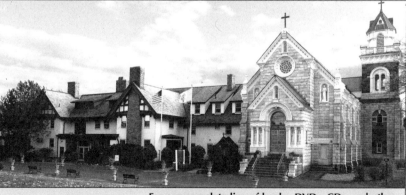

© MARIE ROMAGNANO